LE MANS
'THE FERRARI YEARS'
1958-1965

Compiled
by
R.M.Clarke
with an introduction and annual race summaries
by
Anders Ditlev Clausager

ISBN 1 85520 3723

BROOKLANDS BOOKS LTD.
P.O. BOX 146, COBHAM,
SURREY, KT11 1LG. UK
sales@brooklands-books.com

Printed in Hong Kong

MOTORING
B.B. ROAD TEST SERIES
Abarth Gold Portfolio 1950-1971
AC Ace & Aceca 1953-1983
Alfa Romeo Giulietta Gold Portfolio 1954-1965
Alfa Romeo Giulia Coupés 1963-1976
Alfa Romeo Giulia Coupés Gold Port. 1963-1976
Alfa Romeo Spider 1966-1990
Alfa Romeo Spider Gold Portfolio 1966-1991
Alfa Romeo Alfasud 1972-1984
Alfa Romeo Alfetta Gold Portfolio 1972-1987
Alfa Romeo Alfetta GTV6 1980-1986
Allard Gold Portfolio 1937-1959
Alvis Gold Portfolio 1919-1967
AMX & Javelin Muscle Portfolio 1968-1974
Armstrong Siddeley Gold Portfolio 1945-1960
Aston Martin Gold Portfolio 1948-1971
Aston Martin Gold Portfolio 1972-1985
Aston Martin Gold Portfolio 1985-1995
Audi Quattro Gold Portfolio 1980-1991
Audi Quattro Takes On The Competition
Austin A30 & A35 1951-1962
Austin-Healey 100 & 100/6 Gold Port. 1952-1959
Austin-Healey 3000 Ultimate Portfolio 1959-1967
Austin-Healey Sprite Gold Portfolio 1958-1971
Berkeley Sportscars Limited Edition
BMW 6 & 8 Cyl. Cars Limited Edition 1935-1960
BMW 1600 Collection No. 1 1966-1981
BMW 2002 Gold Portfolio 1968-1976
BMW 6 Cylinder Coupés & Saloons Gold P. 1969-1976
BMW 316, 318, 320 (4 cyl.) Gold Port. 1975-1990
BMW 320, 323, 325 (6 cyl.) Gold Port. 1977-1990
BMW 3 Series Gold Portfolio 1991-1997
BMW 5 Series Gold Portfolio 1981-1987
BMW 5 Series Gold Portfolio 1988-1995
BMW 6 Series Gold Portfolio 1976-1989
BMW 7 Series Performance Portfolio 1977-1986
BMW Alpina Performance Portfolio 1967-1987
BMW Alpina Performance Portfolio 1988-1998
BMW M Series Gold Portfolio 1976-1997
BMW Z3 & Z3M Limited Edition
Borgward Isabella Limited Edition
Bricklin Gold Portfolio 1974-1975
Bristol Cars Gold Portfolio 1946-1992
Buick Muscle Cars 1965-1970
Cadillac Allanté 1986-1993
Cadillac Automobiles 1949-1959
Cadillac Automobiles 1960-1969
Checker Limited Edition
Chevrolet 1955-1957
Impala & SS Muscle Portfolio 1958-1972
Corvair Performance Portfolio 1959-1969
El Camino & SS Muscle Portfolio 1959-1987
Chevy II & Nova SS Muscle Portfolio 1962-1974
Chevelle & SS Muscle Portfolio 1964-1972
Caprice Limited Edition 1965-1976
Chevrolet Muscle Cars 1966-1971
Chevy Blazer 1969-1981
Camaro Muscle Portfolio 1967-1973
Chevrolet Camaro & Z-28 1973-1981
High Performance Camaros 1982-1988
Chevrolet Corvette Gold Portfolio 1953-1962
Chevrolet Corvette Sting Ray Gold Port. 1963-1967
Chevrolet Corvette 1968-1977
High Performance Corvettes 1983-1989
Chrysler 300 Gold Portfolio 1955-1970
Imperial Limited Edition 1955-1970
Valiant 1960-1962
Citroen Traction Avant Gold Portfolio 1934-1957
Citroen 2CV Ultimate Portfolio 1948-1990
Citroen DS & ID 1955-1975
Citroen DS & ID Gold Portfolio 1955-1975
Citroen SM 1970-1975
Shelby Cobra Gold Portfolio 1962-1969
Cobras & Cobra Replicas Gold Portfolio 1962-1989
Crosley & Crosley Specials Limited Edition
Cunningham Automobiles 1951-1955
Datsun Roadsters 1962-1971
Datsun 240Z & 260Z Gold Portfolio 1970-1978
Datsun 280Z & ZX 1975-1983
DeLorean Gold Portfolio 1977-1995
De Soto Limited Edition 1952-1960
Charger Muscle Portfolio 1966-1974
Dodge Viper Performance Portfolio 1990-1998
ERA Gold Portfolio 1934-1994
Excalibur Collection No.1 1952-1981
Facel Vega 1954-1964
Ferrari Limited Edition 1947-1957
Ferrari Limited Edition 1958-1963
Ferrari Dino 1965-1974
Ferrari Dino 308 & Mondial Gold Portfolio 1974-1985
Ferrari 328 348 Mondial Ultimate Portfolio 1986-94
Fiat 500 Gold Portfolio 1936-1972
Fiat 600 & 850 Gold Portfolio 1955-1972
Fiat Pininfarina 124 & 2000 Spider 1968-1985
Fiat X1/9 Gold Portfolio 1973-1989
Fiat Abarth Performance Portfolio 1972-1987
Ford Consul, Zephyr, Zodiac Mk. I & II 1950-1962
Ford Zephyr, Zodiac, Executive Mk. III & IV 1962-1971
Ford Cortina 1600E & GT 1967-1970
High Performance Capris Gold Portfolio 1969-1987
Capri Muscle Portfolio 1974-1987
High Performance Fiestas 1979-1991
Ford Escort RS & Mexico Limited Edition 1970-1979
High Performance Escorts Mk. I 1968-1974
High Performance Escorts Mk. II 1975-1980
High Performance Escorts 1980-1985
High Performance Escorts 1985-1990
High Perf. Sierras & Merkurs Gold Port. 1983-1990
Ford Automobiles 1949-1959
Ford Fairlane Performance Portfolio 1955-1970
Ford Ranchero Muscle Portfolio 1957-1979
Edsel Limited Edition 1957-1960
Falcon Performance Portfolio 1960-1970
Ford Galaxie & LTD Limited Edition 1960-1973
Ford GT40 Gold Portfolio 1964-1987
Ford Torino Limited Edition 1968-1974
Ford Bronco 4x4 Performance Portfolio 1966-1977
Ford Bronco 1978-1988
Goggomobil Limited Edition
Holden 1948-1962
Honda S500 • S600 • S800 Limited Edition 1962-1970
Honda CRX 1983-1987
International Scout Gold Portfolio 1961-1980
Isetta Gold Portfolio 1953-1964
ISO & Bizzarrini Gold Portfolio 1962-1974
Jaguar and SS Gold Portfolio 1931-1951
Jaguar XK120, 140, 150 Gold Portfolio 1948-1960
Jaguar Mk. VII, VIII, IX, X, 420 Gold Port. 1950-1970
Jaguar Mk. 1 & Mk. 2 Gold Portfolio 1959-1969
Jaguar E-Type Gold Portfolio 1961-1971
Jaguar E-Type V-12 1971-1975

Jaguar S-Type & 420 Limited Edition 1963-1968
Jaguar XJ12, XJ5.3, V12 Gold Portfolio 1972-1990
Jaguar XJ6 Series I & II Gold Portfolio 1968-1979
Jaguar XJ6 Series III Perf. Portfolio 1979-1986
Jaguar XJ6 Gold Portfolio 1986-1994
Jaguar XJS Gold Portfolio 1975-1988
Jaguar XJ-S V12 Ultimate Portfolio 1988-1996
Jaguar XK8 Limited Edition
Jeep CJ-5 & CJ-6 1960-1976
Jeep CJ-5 & CJ-7 4x4 Perf. Portfolio 1976-1986
Jeep Wagoneer Performance Portfolio 1963-1991
Jeep J-Series Pickups 1970-1982
Jeepster & Commando Limited Edition 1967-1973
Jeep Cherokee & Comanche Pickups
        Performance Portfolio 1984-1991
Jeep Wrangler 4x4 Performance Portfolio 1987-1999
Jeep Cherokee & Grand Cherokee 4x4
        Performance Portfolio 1992-1998
Jensen Interceptor Gold Portfolio 1966-1986
Jensen - Healey Limited Edition 1972-1976
Kaiser - Frazer Limited Edition 1946-1955
Lagonda Gold Portfolio 1919-1964
Lancia Aurelia & Flaminia Gold Portfolio 1950-1970
Lancia Fulvia Gold Portfolio 1963-1976
Lancia Beta Gold Portfolio 1972-1984
Lancia Delta Gold Portfolio 1979-1994
Lancia Stratos 1972-1985
Land Rover Series I 1948-1958
Land Rover Series II & IIa 1958-1971
Land Rover Series III 4x4 Perf. Portfolio 1971-1985
Land Rover 90 110 Defender Gold Portfolio 1983-1994
Land Rover Discovery 1989-1994
Land Rover Story Part One 1948-1971
Fifty Years of Selling Land Rover
Lincoln Gold Portfolio 1949-1960
Lincoln Continental Performance Portfolio 1961-1969
Lincoln Continental 1969-1976
Lotus Sports Racers Gold Portfolio 1953-1965
Lotus Seven Gold Portfolio 1957-1973
Lotus Caterham Seven Gold Portfolio 1974-1995
Lotus Elan Gold Portfolio 1962-1974
Lotus Elan & SE 1989-1992
Lotus Europa Gold Portfolio 1966-1975
Lotus Elite & Eclat 1974-1982
Lotus Elise Limited Edition
Marcos Coupés & Spyders Gold Portfolio 1960-1997
Matra Limited Edition 1965-1983
Mazda Miata MX-5 Performance Portfolio 1989-1997
Mazda Miata MX-5 Takes On The Competition
Mazda RX-7 Gold Portfolio 1978-1991
McLaren F1 Sportscar Limited Edition
Mercedes 190 & 300 SL 1954-1963
Mercedes G-Wagen 1981-1994
Mercedes S & 600 1965-1972
Mercedes S Class 1972-1979
Mercedes 230 • 250 • 280SL Gold Portfolio 1963-1971
Mercedes SLs & SLCs Gold Portfolio 1971-1989
Mercedes SLs Performance Portfolio 1989-1994
Mercury Limited Edition 1947-1959
Mercury Comet & Cyclone Limited Edition 1960-1970
Cougar Limited Edition 1967-1973
Messerschmitt Gold Portfolio 1954-1964
MG Gold Portfolio 1929-1939
MG TA & TC Gold Portfolio 1936-1949
MG TD & TF Gold Portfolio 1949-1955
MGA & Twin Cam Gold Portfolio 1955-1962
MG Midget Gold Portfolio 1961-1979
MGB Roadsters 1962-1980
MGB MGC & V8 Gold Portfolio 1962-1980
MGB GT 1965-1980
MGC & MGB GT V8 Limited Edition
MG Y-Type & Magnette ZA/ZB Limited Edition
MGF Limited Edition
Mini Gold Portfolio 1959-1969
Mini Gold Portfolio 1969-1980
Mini Gold Portfolio 1981-1997
High Performance Minis Gold Portfolio 1960-1973
Mini Cooper Gold Portfolio 1961-1971
Mini Moke Gold Portfolio 1964-1994
Morgan Three-Wheeler Gold Portfolio 1910-1952
Morgan Plus 4 & Four 4 Gold Portfolio 1936-1967
Morris Minor Collection No. 1 1948-1980
Shelby Mustang Muscle Portfolio 1965-1970
High Performance Mustang IIs 1974-1978
Mustang 5.0L Muscle Portfolio 1982-1993
Nash & Nash-Healey Limited Edition 1949-1957
Nash-Austin Metropolitan Gold Portfolio 1954-1962
NSU Ro80 Limited Edition
NSX Performance Portfolio 1989-1999
Oldsmobile Automobiles 1955-1963
Oldsmobile Muscle Portfolio 1964-1971
Cutlass & 4-4-2 Muscle Portfolio 1964-1974
Oldsmobile Toronado 1966-1978
Opel GT Gold Portfolio 1968-1973
Opel Manta Limited Edition 1970-1975
Packard Gold Portfolio 1946-1958
Pantera Gold Portfolio 1970-1989
Panther Gold Portfolio 1972-1990
Barracuda Muscle Portfolio 1964-1974
Pontiac Limited Edition 1949-1960
Pontiac Tempest & GTO 1961-1965
GTO Muscle Portfolio 1964-1974
Firebird & Trans-Am Muscle Portfolio 1967-1972
Firebird & Trans-Am Muscle Portfolio 1973-1981
High Performance Firebirds 1982-1988
Pontiac Fiero 1984-1988
Porsche 356 Gold Portfolio 1953-1965
Porsche 912 Limited Edition
Porsche 911 1965-1969
Porsche 911 1970-1972
Porsche 911 1973-1977
Porsche 911 SC & Turbo Gold Portfolio 1978-1983
Porsche 911 Carrera & Turbo Gold Port. 1984-1989
Porsche 911 Gold Portfolio 1990-1997
Porsche 914 Ultimate Portploio
Porsche 924 Gold Portfolio 1975-1988
Porsche 928 Performance Portfolio 1977-1994
Porsche 928 Takes On The Competition
Porsche 944 Gold Portfolio 1981-1991
Porsche 968 Limited Edition
Porsche Boxster Limited Edition
Railton & Brough Superior Gold Portfolio 1933-1950
Range Rover Gold Portfolio 1970-1985
Range Rover Gold Portfolio 1986-1995
Range Rover Takes on the Competition

Reliant Scimitar 1964-1986
Renault Alpine Gold Portfolio 1958-1994
Riley Gold Portfolio 1924-1939
R. R. Silver Cloud & Bentley 'S' Series Gold P. 1955-65
Rolls Royce Silver Shadow Ultimate Portfolio 1965-80
Rolls Royce & Bentley Gold Portfolio 1980-1989
Rolls Royce & Bentley Limited Edition 1990-1997
Rover P4 1949-1959
Rover 3 & 3.5 Litre Gold Portfolio 1958-1973
Rover 2000 & 2200 1963-1977
Rover 3500 & Vitesse 1976-1986
Saab Sonett Collection No.1 1966-1974
Saab Turbo 1976-1983
Studebaker Gold Portfolio 1947-1966
Studebaker Hawks & Larks 1956-1963
Avanti 1962-1990
Suzuki SJ Gold Portfolio 1971-1997
Vitara, Sidekick & Geo Tracker Perf. Port. 1988-1997
Sunbeam Tiger & Alpine Gold Portfolio 1959-1967
Toyota Land Cruiser Gold Portfolio 1956-1987
Toyota Land Cruiser 1988-1997
Toyota MR2 Gold Portfolio 1984-1997
Toyota MR2 Takes On The Competition
Triumph TR2 & TR3 Gold Portfolio 1952-1961
Triumph TR4, TR5, TR250 1961-1968
Triumph TR6 Gold Portfolio 1969-1976
Triumph TR7 & TR8 Gold Portfolio 1975-1982
Triumph Herald 1959-1971
Triumph Vitesse 1962-1971
Triumph Spitfire Gold Portfolio 1962-1980
Triumph 2000, 2.5, 2500 1963-1977
Triumph GT6 Gold Portfolio 1966-1974
Triumph Stag Gold Portfolio 1970-1977
Triumph Dolomite Sprint Limited Edition
TVR Gold Portfolio 1959-1986
TVR Performance Portfolio 1986-1994
VW Beetle Gold Portfolio 1935-1967
VW Beetle Gold Portfolio 1968-1991
VW Beetle Collection No.1 1970-1982
VW Karmann Ghia 1955-1982
VW Bus, Camper, Van 1954-1967
VW Bus, Camper, Van Perf. Portfolio 1968-1979
VW Bus, Camper, Van 1979-1989
VW Scirocco 1974-1981
Volvo PV444 & PV544 1945-1965
Volvo 120 Amazon Ultimate Portfolio
Volvo 1800 Gold Portfolio 1960-1973
Volvo 140 & 160 Series Gold Portfolio 1966-1975
Forty Years of Selling Volvo
Westfield Limited Edition

B.B. ROAD & TRACK SERIES
Road & Track on Alfa Romeo 1964-1970
Road & Track on Alfa Romeo 1971-1976
Road & Track on Aston Martin 1962-1990
R & T on Auburn Cord and Duesenburg 1952-84
Road & Track on Audi & Auto Union 1952-1980
Road & Track on Audi & Auto Union 1980-1986
Road & Track on Austin Healey 1953-1970
Road & Track on BMW Cars 1966-1974
Road & Track on BMW Cars 1975-1978
Road & Track on BMW Cars 1979-1983
R & T on Cobra, Shelby & Ford GT40 1962-1992
Road & Track on Corvette 1953-1967
Road & Track on Corvette 1968-1982
Road & Track on Corvette 1982-1986
Road & Track on Corvette 1986-1990
Road & Track on Ferrari 1975-1981
Road & Track on Ferrari 1981-1984
Road & Track on Ferrari 1984-1988
Road & Track on Fiat Sports Cars 1968-1987
Road & Track on Jaguar 1950-1960
Road & Track on Jaguar 1961-1968
Road & Track on Jaguar 1968-1974
Road & Track on Jaguar 1974-1982
Road & Track on Jaguar 1983-1989
Road & Track on Lamborghini 1964-1985
Road & Track on Lotus 1972-1983
R & T on Mazda RX-7 & MX-5 Miata 1986-1991
Road & Track on Mercedes 1952-1962
Road & Track on Mercedes 1963-1970
Road & Track on Mercedes 1971-1979
Road & Track on Mercedes 1980-1987
Road & Track on MG Sports Cars 1949-1961
Road & Track on MG Sports Cars 1962-1980
R & T on Nissan 300-ZX & Turbo 1984-1989
Road & Track on Pontiac 1960-1983
Road & Track on Porsche 1951-1967
Road & Track on Porsche 1968-1971
Road & Track on Porsche 1972-1975
Road & Track on Porsche 1975-1978
Road & Track on Porsche 1979-1982
Road & Track on Porsche 1985-1988
R & T on Rolls Royce & Bentley 1950-1965
R & T on Rolls Royce & Bentley 1966-1984
Road & Track on Saab 1972-1992
R & T on Toyota Sports & GT Cars 1966-1984
R & T on Triumph Sports Cars 1953-1967
R & T on Triumph Sports Cars 1967-1974
R & T on Triumph Sports Cars 1974-1982
Road & Track on Volkswagen 1951-1968
Road & Track on Volkswagen 1968-1978
Road & Track on Volkswagen 1978-1985
Road & Track on Volvo 1957-1974
Road & Track on Volvo 1977-1994
Road & Track - Henry Manney at Large & Abroad
Road & Track - Peter Egan "At Large"
Road & Track - Best of PS

B.B. CAR AND DRIVER SERIES
Car and Driver on BMW 1955-1977
Car and Driver on Corvette 1978-1982
Car and Driver on Corvette 1983-1988
C and D on Datsun Z 1600 & 2000 1966-1984
Car and Driver on Ferrari 1955-1962
Car and Driver on Ferrari 1963-1975
Car and Driver on Ferrari 1976-1983
Car and Driver on Mopar 1956-1967
Car and Driver on Mustang 1964-1972
Car and Driver on Pontiac 1961-1975
Car and Driver on Porsche 1955-1962
Car and Driver on Porsche 1963-1970
Car and Driver on Porsche 1970-1976
Car and Driver on Porsche 1977-1981
Car and Driver on Porsche 1982-1986
Car and Driver on Volvo 1955-1986

RACING & THE LAND SPEED RECORD
The Land Speed Record 1898-1919
The Land Speed Record 1920-1929
The Land Speed Record 1930-1939
The Land Speed Record 1940-1962
The Land Speed Record 1963-1999
The Carrera Panamericana Mexico - 1950-1954
Le Mans - The Bentley & Alfa Years - 1923-1939
Le Mans - The Jaguar Years - 1949-1957
Le Mans - The Ferrari Years - 1958-1965
Le Mans - The Ford & Matra Years - 1966-1974
Le Mans - The Porsche Years - 1975-1982
Le Mans - The Porsche & Jaguar Years - 1983-91
Le Mans - The Porsche & Peugeot Years - 1992-99
Mille Miglia - The Alfa & Ferrari Years - 1927-1951
Mille Miglia - The Ferrari & Mercedes Years - 1952-57
Targa Florio - The Post War Years - 1948-1973
Targa Florio - The Porsche & Ferrari Years - 1955-1964
Targa Florio - The Porsche Years - 1965-1973

B.B. PRACTICAL CLASSICS SERIES
PC on Austin A40 Restoration
PC on Land Rover Restoration
PC on Midget/Sprite Restoration
PC on MGB Restoration
PC on Sunbeam Rapier Restoration
PC on Triumph Herald/Vitesse

B.B. HOT ROD 'ENGINE' SERIES
Chevy 265 & 283
Chevy 302 & 327
Chevy 348 & 409
Chevy 350 & 400
Chevy 396 & 427
Chevy 454 thru 512
Chrysler Hemi
Chrysler 273, 318, 340 & 360
Chrysler 361, 383, 400, 413, 426 & 440
Ford 289, 302, Boss 302 & 351W
Ford 351C & Boss 351
Ford Big Block

B.B. RESTORATION & GUIDE SERIES
Auto Restoration Tips & Techniques
Basic Bodywork Tips & Techniques
BMW 2002 - A Comprehensive Guide
BMW '02 Restoration Guide
Classic Camaro Restoration
Chevrolet High Performance Tips & Techniques
Chevy Engine Swapping Tips & Techniques
Chevy-GMC Pickup Repair
Chrysler Engine Swapping Tips & Techniques
Engine Swapping Tips & Techniques
Land Rover Restoration Tips & Techniques
MG 'T' Series Restoration Guide
MGA Restoration Guide
Mustang Restoration Tips & Techniques

MOTORCYCLING
B.B. ROAD TEST SERIES
AJS & Matchless Gold Portfolio 1945-1966
BMW Motorcycles Gold Portfolio 1950-1971
BMW Motorcycles Gold Portfolio 1971-1976
BSA Singles Gold Portfolio 1945-1963
BSA Singles Gold Portfolio 1964-1974
BSA Twins A7 & A10 Gold Portfolio 1946-1962
BSA Twins A50 & A65 Gold Portfolio 1962-1973
BSA & Triumph Triples Gold Portfolio 1968-1976
Ducati Gold Portfolio 1960-1973
Ducati Gold Portfolio 1974-1978
Ducati Gold Portfolio 1978-1982
Harley-Davidson Sportsters Pref. Port. 1965-1976
Harley-Davidson Super Glide Perf. Port. 1971-1981
Harley-Davidson FXR Series Perf. Port. 1982-1992
Honda CB750 Gold Portfolio 1969-1978
Honda CB500 & 550 Fours Perf. Port. 1971-1977
Honda CB350 & 400 Fours Perf. Port. 1972-1978
Honda Gold Wing Gold Portfolio 1975-1995
Honda CBX 1000 Gold Portfolio 1978-1982
Honda RC30 Performance Portfolio 1988-1992
Kawasaki Z1 900 Performance Portfolio 1972-1977
Laverda Gold Portfolio 1967-1977
Laverda Performance Portfolio 1978-1988
Laverda Jota Performance Portfolio 1976-1985
Moto Guzzi Gold Portfolio 1949-1973
Moto Guzzi Le Mans Performance Portfoio 1976-89
Norton Commando Gold Portfolio 1968-1977
Suzuki GT 750 Performance Portfolio 1971-1977
Suzuki GS1000 Performance Portfolio 1978-1981
Triumph Bonneville Gold Portfolio 1959-1983
Vincent Gold Portfolio 1945-1980
Yamaha RD350/400 Performance Portfolio 1972-79

B.B. CYCLE WORLD SERIES
Cycle World on BMW 1974-1980
Cycle World on BMW 1981-1986
Cycle World on Ducati 1982-1991
Cycle World on Harley-Davidson 1962-1968
Cycle World on Harley-Davidson 1978-1983
Cycle World on Harley-Davidson 1983-1987
Cycle World on Harley-Davidson 1987-1990
Cycle World on Harley-Davidson 1990-1992
Cycle World on Honda 1962-1967
Cycle World on Honda 1968-1971
Cycle World on Honda 1971-1974
Cycle World on Husqvarna 1966-1976
Cycle World on Husqvarna 1977-1984
Cycle World on Kawasaki 1966-1971
Cycle World on Kawasaki Off-Road Bikes 1972-1979
Cycle World on Kawasaki Street Bikes 1972-1976
Cycle World on Norton 1962-1971
Cycle World on Suzuki 1962-1970
Cycle World on Suzuki Off-Road Bikes 1971-1976
Cycle World on Suzuki Street Bikes 1971-1976
Cycle World on Triumph 1967-1972
Cycle World on Yamaha 1962-1969
Cycle World on Yamaha Off-Road Bikes 1970-1974
Cycle World on Yamaha Street Bikes 1970-1974

MILITARY
B.B. MILITARY VEHICLES SERIES
Complete WW2 Military Jeep Manual
Dodge Military Vehicles No. 1 1940-1945
Hail To The Jeep
Military & Civilian Amphibians 1940-1990
Off Road Jeeps: Civilian & Military 1944-1971
US Military Vehicles 1941-1945
US Army Military Vehicles WW2-TM9-2800
VW Kubelwagen Military Portfolio 1940-1990
WW2 Jeep Military Portfolio 1941-1945

CONTENTS

ACKNOWLEDGEMENTS

Our Le Mans series would not have been possible without the goodwill and support of the worlds leading motoring journals. We are indebted to the publishers of *Autocar, Autosport, Car and Driver, Modern Motor, Motor, Motor Trend, Road & Track, Sporting Motorist* and *Wheels* for allowing us to reissue their invaluable copyright reports. Our thanks also go to Anders Clausager, who allowed us to freely quote from his informative 1983 book *Le Mans* now sadly out of print.

We are also grateful to Nick Watts for allowing us to reproduce on our front cover his splendid painting - "Le Mans - 1958" which depicts the winning Ferrari 250TR driven by Phil Hill and Oliver Gendebien (see notice on inside back cover). Finally we would like to thank Bill Boddy for so succinctly putting Le Mans into perspective for us in the paragraphs below.

R.M. Clarke

FOREWORD

This book is about one of the greatest races in the International fixture-list. Indeed the Le Mans 24-hour race continues to attract large numbers of supporters, many of them British, and to intrigue historians. The "at-the-time" reports will bring back many memories and answer countless questions.

All credit to the famous French motor journalist Charles Feroux, who picked-up a suggestion by Emile Coquille and his 100,000 francs, and organised the marathon contest he had thought of, at the same time as Coquille, and ran it for the Automobile Club de L'Ouest for many years. At a time when most of the events were for racing cars, the plan for a sports-car contest was especially apt. Motoring was getting almost fully into its 1920's stride and such a race would improve the kind of cars people bought to use on the public roads and might well publicise the better ones and increase demand for them especially if they were French. Le Mans represented a very stern test of such cars and the idea of running it through the hours of darkness was clever, because although almost all cars were by now electrically-lit, their lighting and starting sets were not entirely effective, or even reliable. A 24-hour race should improve these also.

In fact, the scheme was even more of a durability affair, allied to speed, than was sometimes realised, for the outright Le Mans winner would be found only after the third consecutive race, the first two being but qualifiers, so 72 racing hours in all. Further rules, such as starting hoods erect, having to re-start engines with the starter-motors after pit-pauses, and the specifications of the competing cars having to be very closely related to the cars in catalogues and showrooms, made this very much, in the beginning, a production-car show. That was eventually to change, to broaden out, but for several years the foregoing applied.

This led to racing of great interest, if not exactly to the chap who somehow had to use the Clapham omnibus, certainly to those about to invest in a fastish touring or sports car. When tough John Duff won in 1924 with a two-wheel-braked 3-litre Bentley it was a British bonus, although the English pilgrimage was yet to begin. I believe that even W.O. Bentley went to see his car win at the last moment, and by train. But after the dramatic victory of a Bentley in 1927, although damaged in the "famous" White House accident, and the 1, 2, 3, 4 finish by the big green Bentleys in 1929, the newspapers not only of Europe but in this country, were avid for the news (the 3.4-litre Lorraines had their 1, 2, 3 in 1926).

A 6-and a half-litre Speed Six Bentley won again in 1930 and although the Bentley Company then gave up motor racing, the victory by our Earl Howe and Sir Henry Birkin, Bt. with a 2.3 Alfa Romeo the following year kept the English invasion of Le Mans going.

The whole evocative story unfolds in the following pages. In later times the rules let in prototype cars and speeds rose dramatically. Le Mans had the excitement of a Grand Prix, and lasted so much longer! It was, naturally, tiring to watch. I recall the year we went there in a chartered Airspeed Consul, not booking an hotel, as we thought to snatch a little sleep in the comfort of the aeroplane. But there being no Customs at the Sarthe circuit its keys were requisitioned. The long if exciting dark hours were spent in the Press stand, sustained with red wine and an elongated French loaf. Returning, the Consul made a sudden nose dive when over the Channel - the aged pilot, who had seen the race with us, had dropped off.

Bill Boddy, MBE
Founder Editor: Motor Sport

The C.S.I. decreed a limit of three-litres capacity for the sports car championship in 1958 and the Le Mans race followed suit. There were 55 starters; Ferrari again numerically dominant with 11 cars, of which ten were three-litre 250 TRs - works cars and privately entered - the odd man out being a two-litre car entered privately by the Rodriguez brothers from Mexico. As Ricardo Rodriguez was refused entry - being of tender years - his but slightly older brother Pedro was partnered by Jose Behra in the race. By contrast Maserati seemed to have lost interest as there were only two privately entered cars of this make - one three-litre and one two-litre model. Again there were five Jaguar D-types entered by various teams, including two from Ecurie Ecosse, while Duncan Hamilton and Ivor Bueb shared a third. They all used the new short stroke versions of the XK engine, with carburettors rather than fuel injection. Similar engines were found in a pair of Lister-Jaguars, the first Le Mans appearance of this make. The final important contender in the three-litre class was Aston Martin with three works entered DBR ls and a single DB.3 S driven by the Whitehead brothers, Peter and Graham.

Lotus this year entered six cars, led by their first ever entry in the two-litre class, a Climax engined model XV which had proved very fast in practice. Otherwise, they had one 1½ litre car and two each in the 1,100 cc and 750 cc classes. Having found Le Mans to their liking, AC came back with two two-litre cars, and also in this class was a very sturdy touring Peerless GT; the only Le Mans race for this Triumph TR based fibreglass bodied 2+2 which later changed its identity to become the Warwick. Porsche fielded five entries including two cars with 1.6 litre engines which therefore had to compete in the two-litre class; the remaining three were 1½ litres. Alfa Romeo made their second post-war comeback, more modestly than in 1953, with a pair of Zagato bodied Giulietta coupes which ran in the 1½ litre class. Apart from the two Lotuses, the only other 1,100cc car was a Climax-engined Tojeiro (another British newcomer to Le Mans); and again apart from the two Lotus entries, the 750cc class was given over to the usual bunch of French and Italian cars, including four DBs and four Monopoles (all Panhard based), three Stanguellinis, two Oscars and a VP-Renault.

As in 1954, the 1958 race was largely decided by the weather; a number of thunderstorms causing numerous accidents and retirements. However, there were also other factors contributing such as the too weak fuel mixture which burned pistons on both the Ecurie Ecosse Jaguars soon after the start. The two-litre Lotus was another early retirement. Stirling Moss (whose co-driver was Jack Brabham) had taken the lead from the start in one of the works Aston Martins, but in less than three hours a con rod broke, ending another unlucky Le Mans race for Moss. Soon after one of the Lister-Jaguars and another works Aston Martin dropped out of the race. These setbacks inevitably reduced the chance of a British win; meanwhile the works Ferrari of Oliver Gendebien and Phil Hill took the lead, pursued by other Ferraris while the Brooks/Trintignant Aston Martin and the Hamilton/Bueb Jaguar were still in the running. Mike Hawthorn, who shared a works Ferrari with Peter Collins, put in the fastest lap at 121.416 mph before retiring with a worn out clutch; but he failed to break his own 1957 record. This was Hawthorn's last Le Mans; within a few months he had been killed in a road accident. Ironically, Peter Collins was also killed soon after the 1958 Le Mans race.

At half time the Gendebien/Hill Ferrari was still in the lead, followed by the Brooks/Trintignant Aston Martin; but now one of the 1.6 litre Porsches had moved into fourth place, while the Aston Martin DB.3 S was fifth. There were only two other Ferraris left in the race, and no other Aston Martins or Jaguars; a French entered Jaguar had overturned on the Tertre Rouge section, and its driver 'Mary' (whose real name was Brousselet) was killed. Early Sunday morning saw the retirement of the Brooks/Trintignant Aston Martin, and when Duncan Hamilton went off the road at Arnage at noon the Ferrari was left with a comfortable lead over the following cars. Phil Hill and Oliver Gendebien drove to victory at an average of 106.2 mph for a total distance of 2,548.813 miles - rather less than the 1957 record figures. They were followed home by the Whitehead brothers in the privately entered Aston Martin DB.3 S, and Porsche filled third, fourth and fifth places. The two other surviving Ferraris were sixth and seventh, and an AC eighth, another Porsche ninth, and tenth place went to a 750 cc Osca which also won on Index. It was co-driven by Colin Davis - son of Sammy Davis, the 1927 winner- and the Argentinean Allessandro de Tomaso, car manufacturer to be. A total of 20 cars finished, but three failed to qualify on the minimum distance for their respective classes; these included the other AC, and the Peerless. The double triumph for Italian entries completely reversed the 1957 results.

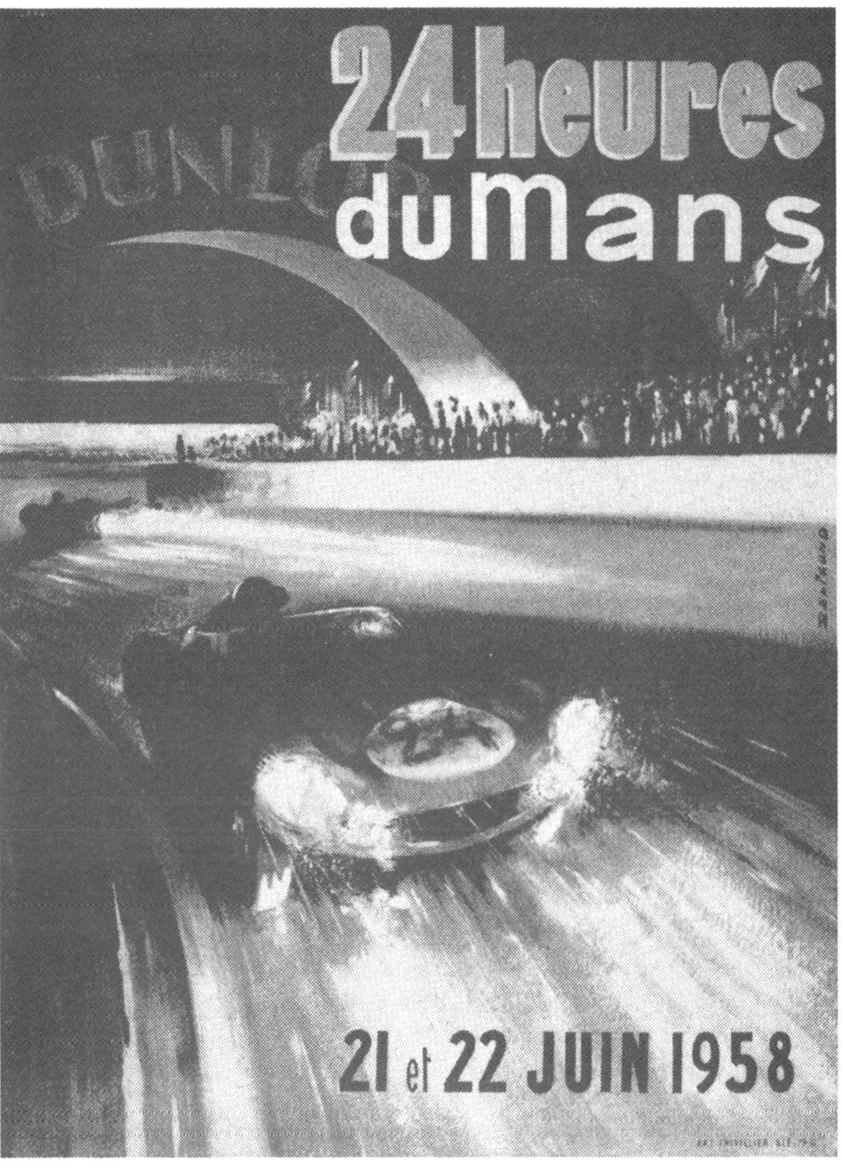

Le Mans Again . . .

ONCE again there will be a large British invasion for Le Mans, this country being represented by Aston Martin, Jaguar, Lotus, Peerless, Lister-Jaguar and A.C. Obviously the chief obstacle to another "green cover" victory is Scuderia Ferrari, with its powerful team comprising Collins/Musso, Hawthorn/Hill and Gendebien/von Trips, backed up by several privately entered machines. The 3-litre Ferrari is undoubtedly very quick, but there are indications that brakes and clutches may not be quite up to the sustained flogging which cars receive in a 24 hours race. However,

there is little doubt that the Maranello technicians will be on their toes.

Chief adversary as regards speed must be the David Brown Aston Martins, with such fine drivers as Moss/Brabham, Brooks/Lewis-Evans, Salvadori/Shelby and Trintignant as stand-by. There is also the Whitehead brothers' privately entered machine. As was proved at Nürburgring, the 3-litre Astons are extremely rapid and, for the first time at Le Mans, do not have to give away cubic capacity. Victory at Sarthe has, so far, eluded the men of Feltham, but 1958 may prove to be their year of rejoicing. They have one advantage over Scuderia Ferrari, and that is being able to concentrate entirely on the development and preparation of sports-racing machines, instead of having to run a team of single-seaters as well.

Next come the two Ecurie Ecosse Jaguars, with a marque that has practically dominated Le Mans since the war. Although the D-types must be about three years old, the superb preparation of "Wilkie" Wilkinson and his men, and the careful race-strategy of David Murray, has ensured victory the past two years. None of the Le Mans entrants will make the mistake of underrating the capabilities of "Ecurie Scotch". There are, in addition, three more D-types, one of which is entered by past-winner Duncan Hamilton.

There are also the two Lister-Jaguars, making their first appearance at Sarthe, one of which is in the hands of the successful Belgian équipe: the other is entered by Bruce Halford, with Brian Naylor as "co-pilote". The bigger cars are completed by a couple of privately entered Maseratis, of which the Bonnier/Godia machine will have a certain amount of works backing.

The 2-litre Lotus "Fifteen" must not be overlooked: it will be fast, very fast, and in view of the surprise packet last year in the shape of the experimental

PROTAGONISTS: Amongst the many marques contesting the Grand Prix d'Endurance will be the Jaguars of Ecurie Ecosse and the Porsches. In the last round of the Championship, the Nürburgring 1,000 km. race, Jack Fairman (Jaguar) is seen leading Edgar Barth in one of the new, finned works Porsches.

"750", the marque cannot be written off as unlikely winners. This car has been built to try for an outright win, and its speed should also make it a formidable challenger for the "Index". Lotus are making a great effort in four categories, having machines of 2-litre, 1,500 c.c., 1,100 c.c. and 750 c.c. Their chief worry in the 1,500 c.c. section will be Porsche, the new version of which is astonishingly speedy. Naturally, there will be an all-out assault in the smaller classes by the blue French cars, but Chapman's chief concern will be Osca.

The 2-litre Peerless G.T. machines are entered in the hope of proving their

FERRARI will be strongly represented with four of their latest 3-litre V-12 Testa Rossas, their drivers including Peter Collins (left).

ASTON MARTIN have three of their DBR1/300s which have proved to be as fast as anything the Continent can field at the moment. Stirling Moss (below) leads the team and doubtless hopes for his Nürburgring victory to be repeated at Sarthe.

LOTUS have entered cars of almost every capacity, from 750 c.c. to 2 litres. Last year a 750 c.c. Lotus captured the Index of Performance from the traditional French hands. The latest Lotus Fifteen (below, left) is still further developed from last year's model.

reliability, rather than their chances of picking up even a class win. This year there is plenty of competition in the once poorly-supported 2-litre class, including the new A.C.-Bristol. A newcomer to Le Mans is the Tojeiro to be driven by Bridger/Blond: it is powered by the popular Climax unit.

It will be interesting to see whether or not the 3-litre cars will surpass the lap speeds achieved by the bigger-engined cars. However, there has been a full year of development, and it is anticipated that the speeds will tend to rise slightly—particularly during that opening "Grand Prix" which helps to fill the dead car park, and considerably reduces the field before the race is

quarter-completed. It would not be real motor-racing if the top-line pilots were disciplined to hold back: in any case, who would risk a rival building up a huge lead in the early stages?

Le Mans is Le Mans: 24 hours race or not, the faster cars are driven almost flat-out from the start. It is a sort of survival of the fittest, and, who knows, the gamble might come off! G.

LE MANS-type start for sports car races has entered into the language and become an ever-popular spectacle at almost every circuit. Here is the start of the Nürburgring 1,000 km. race, as the drivers dash to their cars. In the foreground are Hawthorn, Moss, von Trips, Brooks and Behra.

REAR SUSPENSION of the new Le Mans A.C. is independent by helical springs and double wishbones with diagonal pivots. Brakes are inboard discs. Note the huge tail tank and spare wheel mounting. A space-frame chassis has been adopted for the first time.

FULLY exposed by virtue of the one-piece front body section, the Bristol 2-litre engine with its three Solex carburetters is easy to reach, as is the front suspension—also by helical springs and double tubular wishbones. The little square tank holds an emergency half gallon of oil.

A.C.
★
New for Le Mans
★

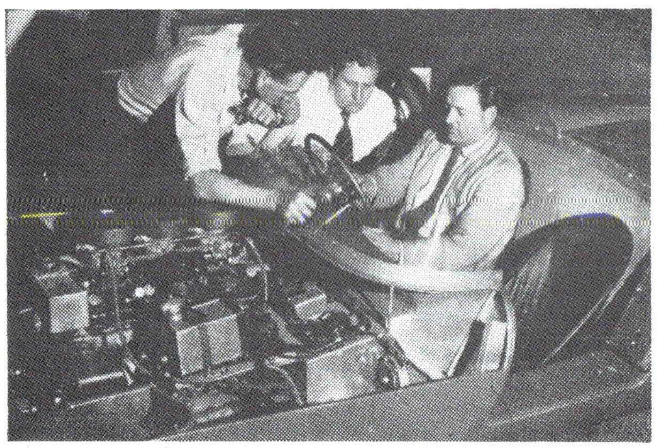

A BRAND NEW A.C.-Bristol has been entered for Le Mans. With chassis designed by John Tojeiro and body by Cavendish Morton (as also in the case of the Tojeiro below), it is in full sports-racing trim. Striking in appearance and beautifully finished, the new car will be in the capable hands of Dick Stoop (trying it for size, left) and Peter Bolton.

TOJEIRO

JOHN TOJEIRO'S Le Mans car from his own stable is this 1,100 c.c. Climax-powered machine. Rear suspension is de Dion and the gearbox-cum-final drive is based on a VW unit (above). Note the single inboard disc brake.

THE RAIN is still falling hard and relentlessly, but our tired backs have received so much water during the past 24 hours that we no longer pay any attention to our soaked clothes. This is a moving moment. The *Star-Spangled Banner* is playing over hundreds of loud speakers, and facing a crowded grandstand on a podium, looking tired but beaming with joy, two young men seem to be on top of the world. One is the Belgian Olivier Gendebien and the other one is the popular Santa Monica hero, Phil Hill. They have just scored a most impressive win with their Ferrari in the toughest Le Mans race in history.

This is indeed a great moment and Americans can be justly proud of Hill, first American sportsman to win this great 24-hour classic. Hill and Gendebien can also be proud of winning this 26th 24 Hours of Le Mans, which was run under such terrible conditions that only 20 cars out of 55 starters were able to complete the race, and actually only 17 could be classified as having covered the official distance.

The winners average was 106.2 miles per hour, only 7.4 mph slower than last year's victory by the bigger Jaguar, running with ideal weather conditions. Great honor must also go to that little 750-cc Osca, driven by de Tomaso and Davis, for winning the Index of Performance in spite of the late and aggressive attacks of the favorite DB-Panhard. Osca and Ferrari—two Italian makes, two victories—made the Italians forget their defeat of last year.

Let us now go back a few days earlier. On Wednesday and Thursday nights before race day (Saturday, June 21st), practice was on and the latest and best sports cars of the world were noisily animating the 8.3 miles of this beautifully made circuit. The crowds were already gathering to watch the finest of sports cars. All the factory teams we can think of were there, with the exception of the greatly missed and colorful teams of Mercedes and Maserati.

It was the same for all three factory Ferraris which, except for minor details, were the same. At the last moment Ferrari wisely decided not to enter his two prototypes, the 3-liter V-6 and the V-12, 4–overhead cam, judging that his well proven 3-liter 12-cylinder Testa Rossa was just the car for Le Mans, and he was so right! The teams were Hawthorn/Collins, Hill/Gendebien and von Trips/Seidel. A fourth team was planned but Munaron had an accident and Musso had not recovered from his Spa incident. The Ferrari factory was certainly well supported with no less than six other Testa Rossas privately entered. Three of those were driven by Americans: one by Gurney/Kessler, one by Hugus/Erickson and the other by Martin and the Frenchman Tavano. The big-car list was completed by the 3-liter Maserati of Godia/Bonnier.

In the 2-liter class we had a French Maserati and a 2-liter Ferrari of the 18-year-old Pedro Rodriguez, co-driving with Behra's brother Jose. Rodriguez' 16-year-old brother Ricardo was turned down by the organizers as being too young. Porsche had entered a 1600 Spyder driven by Behra/Herrmann. In direct competition with the Porsche was the 2-liter Lotus of Allison and Hill. This class was completed by a Peerless (a plastic-bodied GT coupe using a Triumph engine) and two AC-Bristols, one being a sleek-looking prototype reminding us of the earlier Lotus-Bristols.

In the 1500 class Porsche had two factory cars, plus two privately owned ones to compete with the sole 1500 Lotus of Chamberlain/Lovely. Factory Porsches were driven by Barth/Frere and Frankenberg/Storez. The others were driven by de Beaufort/Linge and Colas/Kerguen. Frankenberg's and Barth's were the latest type fin-tailed cars while the others were normal Spyders. The 1500 class also included two new Alfa Romeo Giulietta coupes with bodies by Zagato. Needless to say, they were not there to

Although Jaguar was not quite there officially, it was still very much present in the form of the twice-winning Ecurie Ecosse. This time the successful Scotsmen had two cars, 3-liter D-types driven by Fairman/Gregory and Lawrence/Sanderson. The Jaguar forces were completed by the factory-supported car of Hamilton, driving with Bueb, the two Lister-Jaguars of Halford/Naylor and Dubois/Roussell (Belgian) and the French Jaguar of Mary/Guelfi. Later on, when a car dropped out of practice, the Jaguar of Charles/Young joined forces, making an impressive total of Coventry products.

Aston Martin had three cars of the factory DBR-1 type plus the two-year-old DB-1-S of the Whitehead brothers. The teams for Aston Martin were Moss/Brabham, Brooks/Trintignant and Salvadori/Shelby. There was nothing new about these cars that we had just seen at the Nurburg Ring.

beat the Porsches but to give a good demonstration of their possibilities.

Three cars were entered in the 1100-cc class: two Lotuses and one Tojeiro, a new sports car using a Coventry-Climax engine with a Volkswagen 4-speed gearbox. The Tojeiro had only one rear brake, that being a single disc mounted on the car's differential.

The 750-cc class was of course mainly French, with four DB-Panhards, four factory Panhards and two Renault VP's. Facing the French cars were three Stanguellinis, two Lotuses and two Oscas. One of the Oscas was the factory entry of de Tomaso/Davis and the other was a French-owned car to be driven by La Roche/Radix. That car had a new streamlined body which reminded us very much of its adversary, the Lotus. From the outside the Lotus looked like all other Lotuses, but this time the engine they were

Hill and Gendebien, triumphant and tired, are surrounded by the crowd and many photographers after their win. Hamilton's D-Jag passes the remains of Mary's D-Jag on the hill just before the esses and below is the streamlined 750 Osca of Laroche/Radix.

using was not a sleeved-down 1100-cc Coventry-Climax, but a 4-cylinder marine engine also made by Coventry-Climax with its original displacement of 650 cc raised to 750 cc.

The DB and Panhard firms have really worked hard during these past months to present new cars and engines. Two in each team were Spyders and the other two were coupes. Better streamlining had been achieved in both instances and weight was at last cut down to 945-990 pounds. The DB had a new twin-ignition head giving 60 hp, and Panhard had a new twin–overhead cam head giving them 66 hp at 7500 rpm, a gain of 12 hp over previous engines. As we can see by this list, there were actually very few *nouveautés* presented this year at Le Mans, where we have been used to seeing so many interesting prototypes. It seems that with the new regulations and with the competition getting keener all the time, manufacturers are not inclined to run untried prototypes at Le Mans—this is unfortunate. Perhaps a special prize should be given to manufacturers entering new cars in the race in order to encourage them.

The inspection of the cars was handled in a familiar atmosphere and was marked by an amusing incident. As we said earlier, Ferrari was minus a car because of injury to two of his pilots, Musso and Munaron. When we arrived from Paris with Peter Collins and Mike Hawthorn, we decided to play a joke on Ferrari's racing director, Tavoni. Peter, helped by Mike, arrived at the inspection grounds with his arm tucked under his jacket and in a sling. He said to Tavoni, "Well, I guess this is it. No Le Mans for me this year!" The emotional Tavoni almost fainted, and it took a long time and many laughs before he recuperated. Back in the inspection lines, in the big-car class Jaguar weighed the most along with, surprisingly, the Ferraris. They were both around 2200 lb, while the Aston Martins were a good 220 lb less.

According to Le Mans tradition practice was held in the evenings, which allowed only short daylight training for the cars. There were no spectacular battles between makes this year as everyone was careful and reasonable, thinking of the long day of racing ahead. It was wise of them, but of course it killed the interest in the trials a bit. Although there was a big crowd (nearly 50,000 who came to see just a few cars practicing in the dark!), the atmosphere was not as warm as in other years.

Most of the trials were run on dry pavement and the best time was achieved by Stirling Moss who pushed his Aston Martin to 121.7 mph or 4 minutes 7 seconds. Brooks's Aston Martin took the second-best time and the majority of other Aston Martin drivers were quicker than the other cars. The fastest Jaguar, driven by Fairman, did 4 min 13 sec, while the same time was done by Hawthorn in the Ferrari. The others from Ferrari were around 4 min 20 sec.

Sensation of the trials was the time done by Allison's 2-liter Lotus. The sleek English car did 4 min 13 sec for an

RY AND PHOTOS BY BERNARD CAHIER

Hill, left, in the winning Ferrari and at the right is the Index of Performance winner, the Osca of de Tomaso/Davis. The newest AC-Bristol finished eighth in the hands of Bolton and Stoop. Laureau's DB-Panhard, second on Index, passes a wrecked Panhard coupe.

average speed of 117.45 mph, a lot faster than Behra's Porsche which did 4 min 29 sec. Barth was the fastest of the 1500's with 4 min 31 sec, while the Lotus was the best in the 1100 class with 5 min 10 sec. De Tomaso's Osca was the best in the 750's with 5 min 19 sec, a time which shook everyone, especially the French 750's whose best was about 6 sec slower. The general opinion of those trials was marking Aston Martin as favorite, with Jaguar and Ferrari behind them with equal chances. In the 2-liter class the Lotus was not expected to hold out for 24 hours against the Porsche, which was also favored in the 1500 class. In the 750-cc as well as in the Index the Osca was favored over the French cars and the Lotus (last year's Index winner) which had been disappointing in practice, their Coventry-Climax marine engine being not yet perfected.

Encouraged by what looked like fine weather, a very large crowd (which was to total 150,000 by racing time) invaded the circuit in the morning, early enough to have a picnic on the spot and to have a good look close up at the cars before the 4:00 start. At Le Mans the cars are required to line up in front of the pits several hours before the start, which is a good thing for public interest and which adds a great deal to the pre-race atmosphere. A large majority of the drivers are also around their cars giving a last-minute check to their seat positions and checking every detail with their mechanics and team managers.

With 30 minutes to go a solid line of blue-uniformed gendarmes began clearing the track of all unauthorized people, leaving only the drivers, mechanics and a few officials on the track. With 5 minutes to go the drivers took their positions across the track from their cars. The tension gradually increased and the crowd shouted their enthusiasm and their disapproval of the photographers who were gathered on the banking along the track partly blocking their vision.

The loudspeaker then asked for silence in the tradition of the Le Mans start, and the amazing thing is that when the Race Director raises his flag marking 30 seconds to go, complete silence reigns in front of the stands. From then on the emotions take over and things start happening so fast that time no longer counts. You can hear the cavalcade of 55 pairs of feet running quickly across the track, then a short dead period before the first engine roars to life, immediately followed by the thunder of dozens of others. The first car sparking to life was the green car, No. 2. Almost simultaneously the car was shooting toward the bridge, so spectacularly fast that by the time it went under the other cars had barely started to move. The driver of the green Aston Martin was Stirling Moss, who was renewing his exploit of the Nurburg Ring by taking a 200-yard lead on the next man. This time it was Tony Brooks, who was pressed by a horde of Jaguars and Ferraris.

With the road full of multi-colored cars and the stands *(continued on page 12)*

LE MANS

packed to capacity, it made a very beautiful sight. The crowd talked excitedly about the really indescribable spectacle they had just seen, while the engine noises were disappearing far away through the esses of Tertre Rouge and down the long 4-mile straight. Four minutes and 30 seconds after his standing but flying start, Moss shot past the pits with a long quarter of a mile lead on Hawthorn, Brooks, von Trips and Gendebien. Then leading the big pack came Salvadori's Aston Martin. The show was on and right from the beginning you could feel the struggle of the first hours, or as I call it, the Grand Prix of Le Mans.

Today was no different from other years and we were witnessing that always spirited duel between Moss and Hawthorn. Last year Mike won this short fight, but this year it was Moss's turn. After 5 laps Stirling was 13 seconds ahead and was gaining on every lap, in spite of the fact that Mike was pushing harder all the time. It was finally Hawthorn who set the lap record with the remarkable time of 4 min 8 sec or 124.4 mph, a slower time than last year's but let us not forget that the cars had an engine displacement 25% smaller.

After an hour of faultless driving Moss was leading the field (meaning Hawthorn) by 26 sec. Then came von Trips, Brooks, Gendebien and the first Jaguar driven by Hamilton. The pace had been so great, over 116 mph, that all the competitors with the exception of the first three leaders had been lapped at least once. Behra was leading in the 2-liter class and Storez in the 1500 class, clearly emphasizing the potentialities of the Porsche. In the 750-cc class de Tomaso was running away from everyone and leading the Index as well. Disaster had already struck the Jaguar clan with both Ecurie Ecosse cars retiring with piston trouble, just as they did at Sebring. The fabulously fast 2-liter Lotus of Allison, which went as high as eighth overall in the early stages of the race, was also out with overheating problems.

The following hour saw Moss increasing his lead over Hawthorn to 1 min 35 sec, lapping regularly at a speed close to the lap record of the day (121 mph). Hawthorn, in order to stay with Moss, had perhaps asked too much from his car which now seemed to be suffering from a slipping clutch. Von Trips and Brooks were rapidly closing in on him some 15 sec ahead of Gendebien, who was easily leading Hamilton's Jaguar. Dan Gurney was seventh, driving very well indeed for his first time out at Le Mans. Shortly after the two-hour mark Moss was suddenly missing and the news came soon that his crankshaft had broken. At just about the same moment an enormous storm fell on the circuit flooding the track and nearly drowning the spectators. Visibility was nil, the drivers had to turn on their headlights and it was under these conditions that the first change of drivers was made—with many cars overshooting their pits. Rapidly the whole aspect of the race changed with the new drivers having to get the feel of the track under such hazardous conditions.

With the night falling and the rain pouring harder than ever things became worse on the track and a terrible series of accidents began, a series which was to end only with the checkered flag. Between 6:30 in the evening and 10:00 at night no less than 12 cars were involved in bad crashes.

Several people were injured and one unfortunately lost his life when his Jaguar went out of control just beyond the Dunlop bridge. The driver of the car was Mary who finished third last year in the same Jaguar. Also involved in this terrible accident was Bruce Kessler who ran into the remains of the Jaguar at high speed just a few seconds after the crash. Luckily, Kessler was thrown out of his car and received only serious bruises and broken ribs. His car, however, was completely demolished and burned. Another American, Jay Chamberlain, crashed his Lotus and was lucky to be picked up off the track before Picard's Ferrari crashed into the totally destroyed car. Jay and Picard were both fortunate in receiving only minor injuries. Among the other casualties were Lewis-Evans (who had replaced Shelby as co-driver with Salvadori) in his Aston Martin, Hebert whose Giulietta burned to nothing and Charles, whose Jaguar crashed at high speed into a Lotus, sending another pilot to the hospital. All this had been a dark series and it is surprising in a way that we did not have more serious injuries or consequences. The race had been so full of excitement so far that neither the cold, the rain nor the mud seemed to have discouraged the spectators, who were still watching the grind in great numbers.

At 10:00 P.M. we found the Hill/Gendebien Ferrari leading the race by over a minute in front of von Trips/Seidel. Then, closing up rapidly, was the Hamilton/Bueb Jaguar which had just passed the last Works Aston Martin of Brooks/Trintignant. High-speed driving coupled to unthinkable weather conditions had really taken their toll among the entries, and after only six hours of racing no less than 21 cars were already eliminated. The Hawthorn/Collins Ferrari had fallen back to 11th place while the Behra/Herrmann Porsche had moved up into fifth. The next hour saw the Jaguar driver Bueb driving magnificently, quite at ease in the wet.

After a remarkable progression the Jaguar was passing the leading Ferrari (then driven by Gendebien) shortly after 11:00. The two cars, the red and the green, were now traveling together and the pair was soon joined by von Trips, splendidly driving the other Ferrari. The hour was exciting and everyone felt that the final winner of those 24 hours would be the car coming out victoriously from this three-way battle. A few minutes before midnight Hill took over Gendebien's Ferrari and it was not long before Hamilton did the same on the Jaguar and Seidel on the second Ferrari. This brings us to the most crucial moment of the race. It was this moment, full of tension, that Hill chose to give us the best demonstration of his talents and to establish himself as one of the world's finest sports car drivers on a wet surface. In roughly two hours and a half this California driver not only regained first place, but managed to put his car over a lap ahead of Hamilton's Jaguar. It is known in motor racing circles that Hamilton is one of the best you can find in the wet, and especially at Le Mans. Well, it was this man who was beaten there by Hill and everyone could only cheer in praise of this performance.

The halfway mark found only 26 cars left in the running. The hour was now 4:00 A.M. The weather was by no means improving, and it was on a sort of desolate battlefield that a sad glare announced to us the light of a new day. In the near-empty pits the weary mechanics and team managers were doing their best to keep up their spirits against the elements, but you could now count the number of spectators left.

Still in the lead was the Hill/Gendebien Ferrari, beautifully holding its hard-fought place. In second, still trying hard, was the Jaguar, a lap behind the Ferrari. Von Trips' Ferrari had disappeared from the scene after Seidel crashed it quite badly. In third place, some 5 laps behind the leader, was Brooks/Trintignant's Aston Martin which was still going strong. In fourth was the very fast Porsche 1600 of Behra/Herrmann, in fifth the Whitehead brothers' Aston Martin, in sixth the well driven Lister-Jaguar of Halford/Taylor, and in seventh place overall, the undisputed leader of the 1500 class, Barth/Frere's Porsche. The only 100% American team left was Hugus/Erickson, doing very well in ninth position. The battle for the Index of Performance was truly terrific with the lead changing several times during the night between de Tomaso's Osca and Laureau's Deutsch-Bonnet. Because the cars were in the same 750-cc class, it greatly increased the interest in this competition.

As we have said earlier, the turning point of the race was during the night hours when Phil Hill firmly secured first place. Hill's co-driver, Gendebien, lapping with perfect regularity, was definitely more at ease in the daylight. He beautifully completed Hill's job by keeping the stubborn Jaguars away.

The morning hours, along with more storms, had naturally taken more casualties, and the conditions were most miserable for all. Hawthorn/Collins' Ferrari had retired, Brooks/Trintignant's Aston Martin was out with gearbox trouble, and we had not a single car left in the 1100-cc class. The Lister-Jaguar had had difficulties but was able to rejoin the race after a 35-minute pit stop during which a broken camshaft was changed. The Behra/Herrmann Porsche had been in and out of its pit with brake difficulties, after leading the Whitehead Aston Martin for many hours. The well driven Aston had taken third place away from the Porsche, but their terrific duel was by no means finished and was to last until the checkered flag fell.

With only a few hours left in the running it seemed that nothing could now alter the final issue of this well fought race. At one time the Jaguar gained on the Ferrari, but soon the red car put on more steam and its lead was increased rapidly to just under two laps. This display of superior speed did not seem to impress Hamilton who seemed to be driving faster all the time. This fine showing was not going to pay off for the fighting Hamilton, however. Before noon, just as a new storm fell heavily on the circuit, Hamilton left the road and was sent to the hospital with only slight injuries. With him disappeared the last Jaguar, making it a tough day for the Coventry firm.

It was under a menacing black sky that a triumphant Phil Hill crossed the finish line, ending one of the wettest and most difficult 24 Hours of Le Mans in history. It had been a most interesting race, but what a calvary for the drivers, spectators and photographers (whose cameras had a splendid test of reliability)! Second car home was the valiant Aston Martin, and third was the

Behra/Herrmann Porsche. Their 1600-cc car was followed just a lap later by Barth/Frere who certainly finished strongly in this race. The performances of these two Porsches were truly remarkable and were admirably complimented by the fifth place overall de Beaufort/Linge Porsche which had gone splendidly for an older-type car. Sixth place was taken by the Belgian Ferrari of de Changy/Beurlys, beating the American team of Hugus/Erickson whose performance was commendable. Behind Hugus was the AC-Bristol prototype which had given a first-class performance for its first racing appearance. It was driven by Bolton/Stoop. The Index of Performance winner was the de Tomaso/Davis Osca which accomplished the feat of finishing 11th overall, just a lap in front of its direct adversary, the DB of Laureau/Cornet. Those two cars had given us a wonderful show during all of the 24 hours, and although the brilliant Osca victory was truly merited, the defeat of the DB was more than honorable. The little French car, derived from a production machine, had the consolation of taking second place in the Index and the whole official DB team of three cars managed to finish the race.

The 1958 24 Hours of Le Mans was a real triumph for the Italians, and a sweet revenge for their defeat there last year. Ferrari had also secured his title of Champion of the World's Constructors, and Osca confirmed their Sebring Index of Performance victory which places them now on the top of the world's best smaller cars. Germany had a good day once again with the Porsche which placed four cars in the first 10. It had been a very bad day for England whose sports car honor was fortunately saved by the privately entered Aston Martin. All of the Jaguars had retired, as did the factory Aston Martins and all the Lotuses except one— the 750-cc which finished in last place. It was a good thing that the two AC-Bristols finished up in the list, while for its first time out, the Peerless was able to compete without trouble through the long hard test. It was the third time that Ferrari has won Le Mans, and it was in the wet against Hamilton that they did it the last time in 1954 when Gonzalez/Trintignant won at the wheel of the 5-liter. The Osca had truly given us a sensational demonstration of the possibilities of their 750-cc car. Two Oscas were entered and two were at the finish. One was first in Index and the other one fourth, a reliability display which should give a boost to Osca's sales.

The winning 3-liter Testa Rossa Ferrari can now be rated as one of the most successful sports cars made by Ferrari, with four wins out of five starts in this year's season. The Ferrari victory and the Jaguar defeat might speed up another significant event. It was rumored here that the Coventry firm will return to competition next year. Jaguar officials did not confirm this, but it would be wonderful to see Jaguar and Ferrari resume their terrific competition here.

The Le Mans organization was tops, as usual, with excellent press and photographer facilities. The only thing that was not up to their usual high standard was the slowness of emergency crews in getting to the scene of an accident.

When we left the track, more rain was falling. We were wet and tired, but we were happy to have seen this great race. We hope next year's weather will be better. ◉

In a howling, confused pack, the field streams away from the start towards the Esses at the commencement of this year's 24-hour test of speed and endurance, which was to see the retirement of so many, hours before the final flag fell. Moss, first away, is out of the picture.

ITALIAN COME-BACK IN

Ferrari Wins 24-hour Grand Prix d'Endurance from Privately-entered Aston Martin. OSCA Best on Index of Performance. Twenty out of Fifty-five Stay the Course at Le Mans.

VICTORY in this year's Le Mans 24-hour Race, the world's sports car classic run last week-end, eluded the British and awarded the laurels to the Belgian driver Olivier Gendebien and the American Phil Hill driving a works-entered V-12 3 litre Testa Rossa Ferrari at 106 m.p.h. after a 4 p.m. to 4 p.m. race punctuated by storms of rain which turned the 8.35 mile-circuit into a skating rink.

Stirling Moss (Aston Martin DBR1/300) shot into the lead and began to run away with the race pursued by Ferraris of which the Hawthorn/Collins car worked past its team-mates to tail the Aston Martin. The Ecurie Ecosse Jaguars went out together with piston failure thought to be due to trouble with the fuel before the race had really begun, followed by the 2-litre Lotus. Then the Aston Martin team fell out, Moss with engine trouble, Trintignant with trouble unspecified and Lewis-Evans after a crash.

The first rainstorm lashed the circuit before dark during which many cars crashed, one with fatal results. Except for the winning car, the works Ferraris all disappeared after Hawthorn had made the fastest lap, and after midnight the order became static—the winning Ferrari leading Hamilton-Bueb on the D-Type Jaguar which came up during the rain, only to spin off the road in a thunderstorm four hours from the finish. Into second place sailed the private Aston Martin of the brothers Whitehead, too far back to challenge the Ferrari but safely ahead of the 1,600 c.c. Porsche driven by Behra and the German Herrmann which, slowed by brake troubles, could not close with them although faster on the circuit. Porsches came in 3rd, 4th and 5th and Ferraris 1st, 6th and 7th, the last American-driven.

In the handicap division where each car is allotted a minimum speed to be exceeded as much as possible the prize went to de Tomaso and the young Englishman Colin Davis with a 750 c.c. OSCA, a French D.B. second, another D.B. third.

This year the ultra-light Lotus cars were eliminated one by one but the 750 c.c. machine, having been dug out of a sand bank was repaired and put back into the race to finish and the Halford Lister-Jaguar also rejoined the race after serious gearbox trouble.

The Triumph-engined Peerless in its first race ran the whole 24 hours without trouble and both A.C.-Bristols finished the race with complete reliability.

This year the event, France's contribution to the Sports Car Championship, was limited to cars under 3-litres, the winner averaging 106.12 m.p.h. In contrast, the 3.8-litre Ecurie Ecosse Jaguar which won in 1957 (Flockhart-Bueb) averaged 113.85 m.p.h., while Hawthorn's 4.1 Ferrari put in a record lap at 125.6 m.p.h. This year the fastest lap was 121.32 m.p.h.

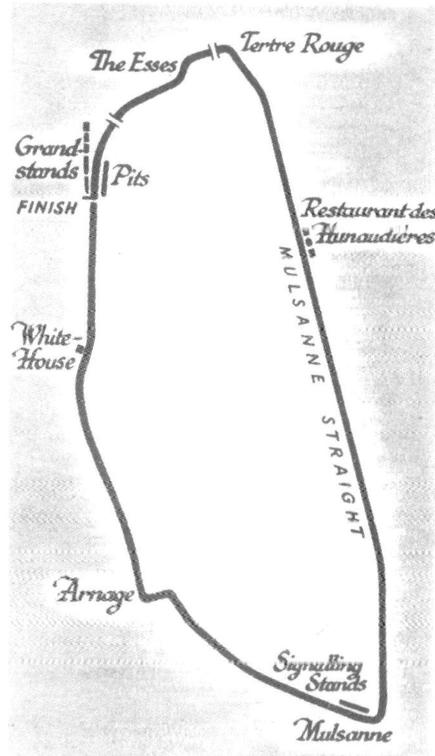

STORM-SWEPT RACE

HERE, again, in the unique atmosphere of the Le Mans 24 Hours, a crowd of some 200,000 assembled to watch the long-drawn-out battle between the leading manufacturers of the world's sports cars.

The afternoon was sultry and overcast with a promise of rain, but the circuit was dry as the competitors took their places on the opposite side of the track, the cars lined up with their tails to the pit counters in the traditional manner that Le Mans has founded.

This year no one could forecast a winner—the Jaguars which have won here five times, but with 3-litre engines in

MAIN PROVISIONAL RESULTS
General Category

1. O. Gendebien-P. Hill (Ferrari), 2,547.76 miles, 106.12 m.p.h.
2. P. N. Whitehead-A. G. Whitehead (Aston Martin), 2,447.8 miles, 101.9 m.p.h.
3. Jean Behra-H. Herrmann (Porsche), 2,428.3 miles, 101.2 m.p.h.
4. E. Barth-P. Frère (Porsche), 2,420.0 miles, 100.8 m.p.h.
5. G. de Beaufort-H. Linge (Porsche), 2,403.3 miles, 100.1 m.p.h.
6. Beurlys-A. de Changy (Ferrari), 2,325.8 miles, 96.9 m.p.h.
7. J. Hugus-Erikson (Ferrari), 2,318.6 miles, 96.6 m.p.h.
8. P. Bolton-R. Stoop (A. C.-Bristol), 2,142.8 miles, 89.3 m.p.h.
9. H. Pathey-G. Berger (A.C.-Bristol), 2,128.3 miles, 88.7 m.p.h.
10. J. Colas-Kerguen (Porsche), 2,121.24 miles, 88.4 m.p.h.

Dominating the race in the early stages, Stirling Moss established nearly a minute's lead with the Aston Martin before the car was forced to retire with mechanical trouble. As this photograph, showing the Aston Martin in a steep angle of drift at Tertre Rouge, suggests, Moss was saving every fraction of a second by superb cornering.

LE MANS
1 9 5 8

A fine performance was put up by the Jopp/Crabb Peerless saloon, making its first appearance in an international classic. It kept going throughout and is seen here being slip-streamed by the DB of Adda/Bonnet as they chase a group of cars down into Tertre Rouge during the early stages of the race.

second and third, five seconds apart. The 3-litre Maserati was not in this race at all. The 2-litre Maserati was in the pits, and, after an hour of racing, the Lotus, which had been Britain's hope for the 2-litre class, was pushed away with a blown gasket.

Positions in General Classification at 1 hour
1. Moss-Brabham (Aston Martin), 14 laps: 118.68 m.p.h.
2. Hawthorn-Collins (Ferrari), 14 laps:
3. Von Trips-Seidel (Ferrari), 14 laps.
4. Brooks-Trintignant (Aston Martin), 14 laps.
5. Gendebien-Hill (Ferrari), 14 laps.
6. Hamilton-Bueb (Jaguar), 14 laps.

Retirements During Period
Martin-Dagorne (Maserati) (transmission); Lawrence-Sanderson (Jaguar) (piston); Fairman-Gregory (Jaguar) (piston); Cotton-Beaulieu (Panhard-Monopole) (fuel supply).

The lap time was rapidly coming down. Stirling, drawing away by three or four seconds a lap, did 4 min. 13.9 sec. (well outside the record, but these were three-litre cars), then 4 min. 12 sec. (119.8 m.p.h.), then 4 min. 9.4 sec. (120.74 m.p.h.).

At the other end of the field, Dumazer's 750 c.c. V.P. ran into trouble and proceeded slowly, before abandoning the chase. At 5.15 p.m. also, the French-entered Lotus of Masson and Hechard—running with the new Coventry Climax engine, whereas the works car had changed back to the old type after breakage in practice—started a series of pit stops which ended two hours later in the dead car park with lack of water after a crash.

Pace or strategy began to tell. Moss' time stayed fairly constant around 4 min. 9 sec. for the lap, but his lead rose quickly to over a minute at the end of 20 laps, while Brooks with the second Aston

chassis at least three years old; the Aston Martins, winners of the 3-litre class for the past three years, and now with an even chance by reason of the 3-litre limit for sports cars in the championship races; or Ferrari, with the V-12 engine in the light Testa Rossa chassis.

As the flag dropped in a hush from the dense crowds, Moss was into his Aston Martin and away, Brooks (Aston Martin) behind him, Hawthorn's Ferrari next. At the end of the first lap, Moss led, Hawthorn second, 5 sec. away—their average about 108 m.p.h.—Brooks third, and the leading Jaguar in 10th place. Dubois' Lister-Jaguar came into the pits.

On the second lap von Trips (Ferrari) was in second place, Mike having evidently overdone a corner, Moss still in the lead and drawing away, Brooks (Aston Martin) third, Mike now fourth.

On Lap 3, Moss led by 12 sec. from von Trips, and Sanderson's Jaguar was at the pits with a recurrence of the piston trouble they had had in practice. Martin's 2-litre Maserati with him, to retire. At the same time, in came Allison with the 2-litre Lotus, the bonnet went up and mechanics peered anxiously beneath.

On Lap 5, after 40 miles of the 24-hour race, Moss led Trips, Brooks and Hawthorn, closing in viciously, Gendebien (Ferrari) and Salvadori (Aston Martin). Now Chamberlain's 1½-litre Lotus came into the pits with fuel starvation troubles. A lap later Hawthorn (who had said he was not going to join in any 10-lap Grand Prix) was back in second place, 13 sec. behind Moss, von Trips third, Brooks fourth, Gendebien fifth, and Bueb in

Hamilton's private Jaguar was lying sixth.

Then Fairman was at rest with the second of the Ecurie Ecosse Jaguars (winners last year) and retired, just as Chamberlain restarted with the Lotus. Moss, Hawthorn and von Trips were already out in front on their own.

By 11 laps Moss' Aston Martin was still more firmly in the lead, 15 sec. ahead of Hawthorn's Ferrari, and 2½ minutes ahead of the 1,600 c.c. Porsche driven by Jean Behra. At 12 laps, the Moss car was 18 sec. in front, Hawthorn and von Trips

Early casualty was the Martin/Dagorne Maserati, which went out with transmission trouble when the race was but three laps old. Moss in the Aston Martin is seen here passing the abandoned car.

crept up on the two Ferraris which lay second and third. At a quarter to six, four laps later, Brooks passed von Trips, but now ominous spots of rain appeared. Hawthorn, undaunted, made the fastest lap to date, 4 min. 8.0 sec. (121.32 m.p.h.). Moss was running to orders (more or less) a shade faster than last year's winning average. Von Trips woke up and No. 16 Ferrari suddenly hurtled past both Brooks and Hawthorn to be second for a short space—and then Stirling spun on a patch of wet road coming out of Tertre Rouge, but stayed near enough to the road to get going with only 11 seconds lost—order still Moss, von Trips, Hawthorn, Brooks.

One more lap and the leaders would be due in for fuel after their minimum 31 laps.

Then the loudspeakers burbled with excitement. Moss had stopped at Mulsanne, after coasting half a mile with an engine that had begun to seize in full cry down the straight. Again Moss, the Le Mans pace-maker, was out.

Hawthorn took up the lead, but only for as long as it took him to reach the pits and come in for a quick stop to refuel and hand over to Peter Collins. The pit crews leapt out for action, and promptly joined the drivers beneath a sudden, overwhelming rainsquall which clamped on the whole circuit, blotting out visibility.

A minute before, the cars had been racing in broad daylight, and now yellow headlamps glowed dimly through the blinding spray. The track became terribly dangerous, with mud washing across the road where drivers braked for the fast corner under the Dunlop bridge. The

Having used his disc brakes to go deep into Mulsanne corner before slowing, Halford here accelerates his Lister-Jaguar past the Martin/Tavano Ferrari on the apex of the corner itself.

And down came the rain, after brilliant weather for the first few laps. The Ubezzi/Catalle Alfa Romeo Giulietta halts at the pits in a torrential down-pour while the Brooks/Trintignant Aston Martin and the Jopp/Crabb Peerless roar past the almost deserted terraces into the early dusk.

Stacey/Dickson Lotus made the best of a bad job, taking to the grass and then the escape road, but restarted. Gomez Mena and Bianchi spun their respective Ferraris at Mulsanne. Charles (Jaguar), Hechard (Lotus), and Poch (Panhard) had a multiple collision at the approach to the pits, Charles being slightly hurt, but Poch able to continue.

The rest of the leaders came in for their refuelling stops in due order, von Trips (Ferrari) followed by Brooks (Aston Martin) so that the two cars departed in frightful conditions still only a few seconds apart, driven by Seidel and Trintignant. Hawthorn's stop took longer, and Seidel now led the race, followed by Hill on the Ferrari taken over from Gendebien, Trintignant, not liking the wet at all in the big Aston Martin, Collins, Lewis-Evans with the third works Aston, Kessler (Ferrari) and Duncan Hamilton settling down to a nice, wet drive in his own private Jaguar just handed over by Ivor Bueb.

For a few minutes the race took on a freakish appearance. Even when the rain stopped the road remained soaking, and lap speeds came down with a bump. Collins, after starting gingerly, settled at about 4 min. 35. sec., whereas neither Trintignant nor Lewis-Evans could get within 10 seconds of him. Phil Hill sprang into the limelight as a master of this kind of driving, lapping at 111 m.p.h. in spite of it all, while Hamilton crept—almost rushed—up the scoreboard. At 7.30 p.m. Hill was out in front, chased by Seidel, Trintignant, Hamilton and then Collins, whose Ferrari had an ailing clutch. Five minutes later, Collins swept into his pit as another rainstorm swept over the entire scene, and it was a clear 20 minutes before he was back in the fray.

Once more the road was flooded. Trintignant nearly lost his third place prematurely as the Aston swerved under braking—and thereafter he joined those who changed down for the 100 m.p.h. corner after the pits. Lewis-Evans was less lucky. His car began a pair of slow

LE MANS
1 9 5 8

spins as it passed under the bridge, then touched the bank and whipped round twice more. He finished the lap, but the Aston was minus a headlight and was forced by the regulations to retire. Now there were no Ecosse Jaguars and only one works Aston Martin left; the Belgian Lister was pushed away as well. Hawthorn stormed past a subdued Trintignant under the bridge, and Hamilton's old Jaguar was third. Thus it was Ferrari, Ferrari, Jaguar, Aston Martin, Ferrari (Kessler-Gurney)—and the Behra/Herrmann Porsche of only 1.6 litres going like a train in sixth place, apparently more stable in the wet than the dry.

Only two mechanics apart from the refueller may work on a car at a pit stop: a scene at the Ferrari pit with the Hawthorn/Collins car the subject of attention. The two drivers can be seen exchanging brief comment while standing on the pit counter.

Wayside repairs were carried out by Stacey on the 750 c.c. Lotus— a magnificent job of work which got the car back into the race again. Here, the Mary/Guelfi Jaguar, which subsequently crashed, and the Dubois/Rousselle Lister-Jaguar are photographed passing the scene of activity.

Bearing No. 1, but nowhere near the lead, the Godia/Bonnier 3-litre Maserati hotly chased round Mulsanne by the Barth/Frère Porsche, which finished fourth, and the privately entered Ferrari of Gomez Mena and Drogo.

Positions in General Classification at 4 hours
1 Gendebien-Hill (Ferrari), 52 laps: 3 hr. 54 min. 31 sec., 111.54 m.p.h.
2 Von Trips-Seidel (Ferrari), 52 laps: 3.55.34.
3 Hamilton-Bueb (Jaguar), 52 laps: 3.58.11.
4 Brooks-Trintignant (Aston Martin), 52 laps: 3.59.24.
5 Gurney-Kessler (Ferrari), 52 laps: 3.59.28.
6 Behra-Herrmann (Porsche), 51 laps: 3.59.59.

Positions of Index of Performance
1 Tomaso-Davis (OSCA), 1.360.
2 Laroche-Radix (OSCA), 1.348.
3 Behra-Hermann (Porsche), 1.335.

Retirements During Period
Dumazer-Dutoit (V.P.) (gearbox); Allison-Hill (Lotus) (gasket); Moss-Brabham (Aston Martin) (engine); Masson-Héchard (Lotus) (accident); Bianchi-Mairesse (Ferrari) (accident); Rousselle-Dubois (Lister) (lost oil); Salvadori-Lewis-Evans (Aston Martin) (accident).

With ten-tenths cloud, headlamps were needed by 9 p.m. and, with rain falling steadily but no longer violently, Duncan Hamilton continued to show great skill on the partly flooded course. With the exception of Brooks' and Whitehead's Aston Martins, the British champions were all out of the race. The machines from Maranello were masters of the situation when the whole field was slowed by disaster to Mary's Jaguar. Although running nearly last (18 laps behind the leader) the car swept far too fast under the Dunlop bridge, got out of control and turned over. A yellow warning light was flashed, but not, unfortunately, before Kessler driving the Testa Rossa Ferrari, then lying 5th, hit the wreckage. Mary was killed outright, and the Ferrari caught fire; a grievous end to a fine American effort, for despite this being their maiden appearance the Kessler-Gurney team were only a lap behind the leader. Kessler was injured, but later reported to be "satisfactory."

The Ferraris seemed rather steadier in the wet than the Aston Martins, and the Porsches, converted by the conditions, not only to water cooling but also perhaps to under-steering, the most stable of all. By contrast the Godia/Bonnier 3-litre Maserati, the 2-litre Ferrari of Rodriguez and the lesser known Jose Behra, and one of the 750 Stanguellinis spun together at Mulsanne and then went on with the loss only of time and dignity.

At 10 p.m., with a quarter of the race run, the two leading Ferraris were reaping the reward of the largest piston area by a lap lead over the Jaguar, which in turn lay a lap ahead of the Brooks/Trintignant Aston Martin, sole survivor of a team which had started with every hope of victory. A mere ten minutes later came another example of the weak bringing down the strong. Chamberlain, lying last on the twin-cam 1½-litre Lotus which had only intermittently fired on all four cylinders and had averaged only a modest 50 m.p.h., spun before the Dunlop bridge, and, striking the bank, cast a wheel on the course. Picard, driving a Testa Rossa in tenth place, went straight into the damaged Lotus, enabling the opportunist Hamilton to profit by the ensuing excitement (in which there was no serious hurt) to get past the von Trips/Seidel Ferrari and

With headlights blazing into the streaming dusk the A.C. Ace of Pathey/ Berger chases its own reflections around White House corner.

snatch second place with an admirable sang-froid.

Meantime the clutch of the Hawthorn-Collins Ferrari yielded to adjustment and their car was going really well, although 9 laps behind in tenth place at 10.30 p.m. The Aston Martin was still fourth and the very latest Porsche, with widely spaced Webers and lightweight frame, going strong in fifth position, half a lap ahead of the privately entered DB3S Aston Martin of the Whiteheads.

By now, 20 cars no longer troubled the scoreboard attendants. Of this unhappy band, no fewer than nine had found the road too narrow, the 11th hour being too much for Hébert who inverted his Giulietta (without injury) and forfeited his 27th place. It is well known that Bueb hates being second, and at 11.20 p.m. he was only 4 seconds behind Gendebien's Ferrari. Having won back 10 seconds a lap, he took the lead at 11.25 p.m. on the 92nd lap. Normality was thereby restored, but only momentarily, as Hill led again on the 99th lap, and on the 100th it was Bueb, the margin between them after 8 hours of racing being mere seconds, and the general classification:

Positions in General Classification at 8 hours
1 Hamilton-Bueb (Jaguar), 101 laps: 7 hr. 58 min. 51 sec., 105.8 m.p.h.
2 Gendebien-Hill (Ferrari), 100 laps: 7.55.39.
3 Seidel-von Trips (Ferrari), 100 laps: 7.59.57.
4 Brooks-Trintignant (Aston Martin), 98 laps: 7.56.13.
5 Behra-Herrmann (Porsche), 96 laps: 7.57.19.
6 Whitehead-Whitehead (Aston Martin), 95 laps: 7.55.53.

Positions of Index of Performance
1 Tomaso-Davis (OSCA), 1.278.
2 Laureau-Cornet (D.B.), 1.255.
3 Laroche-Radix (OSCA), 1.212.

Retirements During Period
Mary-Guelfi (Jaguar) (accident); von Trips-Seidel (Ferrari) (accident); Gurney-Kessler (Ferrari) (accident); Picard-Juhan (Ferrari) (accident); Frankenberg-Storez (Porsche) (accident); Chamberlain-Lovely (Lotus) (accident); Ubezzi-Catulle (Alfa Romeo) (fuel supply); Sigrand-Revillon (Stanguellini) (accident).

At 12.10, Bueb handed the Jaguar over to Hamilton without losing his lead, but with a full tank the Jaguar needed care on the slippery course and the Ferrari went past after Hill had stopped and handed back to Gendebien. Nevertheless, the fortunes of Coventry seemed likely to be consolidated, as Hamilton is good in the dark. In fact, however, he began to fall back, but Seidel, after having been in the first three since Moss suffered his bulging crankcase, goaded No. 16 Ferrari into the Arnage ditch at half past midnight. Having no chance of removing it, he let the Aston Martin into third place behind the Ferrari-Jaguar struggle, in which Italy was leading by some 90 seconds. Against this, the Whiteheads had worked up to fourth place, slightly ahead of the Porsche. The Hawthorn/Collins car was in the ninth place, with the Halford/Naylor Lister sixth.

From the beginning of the race, the Maserati brothers had kept their fingers firmly in the Index money by virtue of the splendid performance of the 750 c.c. OSCA which had rushed steadily round at 82.5 m.p.h. in the hands of Tomaso and, showing hereditary skill, Colin Davis (whose father won outright at 61.35 m.p.h. on a 3-litre Bentley in 1927).

By 2 a.m. the rain had stopped and, with the road drying, Hamilton's art could not offset the superior power of Gendebien's Ferrari, which drew slowly away. At this stage, 29 runners remained (less than half of the starters), and amongst them, the A.C. Bristols were placed 12th and 13th; a 1,100 c.c. Lotus 16th; the Peerless 19th; and a 750 c.c. Lotus 24th. The Tojeiro, which lay 20th at midnight, had retired soon after.

After 10 hours, we had a Jaguar steadily second; Aston Martins third and fourth; the Lister sixth; so the slightest slip by Gendebien or Hill, or a weakening of the Ferrari drum brakes, or simply a short stop for some minor adjustment and some British car could be well set for yet another win in a race that has been yielded to "a foreigner" only twice in the past seven years. Collins had to leave his Ferrari on the circuit when he had covered 112 laps,

Urgent signals from the pit area warn drivers of an accident after Dunlop Bridge, a little distance up the road.

and at 131 laps Gendebien stopped briefly at his pit without jeopardizing the lead. Porsche, incidentally, led the 2-litre class with Behra and Herrmann, and the 1½-litre class with Barth and Frère, while Lotus had some consolation for a string of troubles in that Ireland and Taylor's 1100 was the sole car still motoring in this category.

Just before 3 a.m., fuel and Bueb were put into the No. 8 Jaguar in 70 seconds, and with 11 hours gone, the Laureau-Cornet DB temporarily had the lead on Index at 1.251 compared with the OSCA'S 1.247; the positions of the leaders on distance remained the same. Half an hour later, the drivers of Panhard 48 (Bruwaen-Lefourel) left the road at Tertre Rouge.

During the last hours of darkness, a great battle for the lead in the Index was being fought between the OSCA and the DB. The latter's lead lasted only a little while during a refuelling stop on the part of the OSCA.

Positions in General Classification at 12 hours
1. Gendebien-Hill (Ferrari), 153 laps. 11 hr. 59 min. 54 sec., 106.58 m.p.h.
2. Hamilton-Bueb (Jaguar), 152 laps: 11.59.37.
3. Brooks-Trintignant (Aston Martin), 149 laps: 11.59.53.7.
4. Behra-Herrmann (Porsche), 145 laps: 11.59.44.3.
5. Whitehead-Whitehead (Aston Martin), 144 laps: 11.55.42.9.
6. Halford-Naylor (Lister-Jaguar), 143 laps: 11.56.30.1.

Positions of Index of Performance
1. Tomaso-Davis (OSCA), 1.255.
2. Laureau-Cornet (D.B.), 1.253.
3. Laroche-Radix (OSCA), 1.205.

Retirements
Bridger-Blond (Tojeiro) (rear axle); Hawthorn-Collins (Ferrari) (mechanical trouble); Bruwaen-Lefourel (Panhard) (accident); Rodriguez-Jose Behra (Ferrari) (radiator).

As the race entered its 13th hour, the sky began to lighten swiftly in the east and the cars once again assumed their individual shapes instead of being merely dark forms singing through the night behind their own headlamp beams. Rain

had not fallen for some time past and the track was slowly drying.

The loudspeakers, which for hours had confined themselves to terse announcements about the race in the usual Lo-Fi French, unleashed a burst of female song on the reawakening world which ceased abruptly in mid-note. All around the circuit, in small and sodden tents, in the backs of cars and in pits, rough-looking characters feeling even rougher than they looked, straightened cramped limbs and returned to a semblance of life as the cold ate into their bones and the growing light penetrated their bleary eyes. This is the hour when the Vingt-Quatre Heures du Mans lies stripped of all its glamour.

The race was still most interesting. The Jaguar and the leading Ferrari were now a lap apart, but the Jaguar was again closing steadily and by 5 a.m. was back on the same lap as the leader. Behind the leading trio, Jean Behra and Herrmann had brought the Porsche right up to fourth place, to the great delight of the French, for Jean Behra is idolized as the champion of France among the aces.

Just after 5.15 a.m., Bueb brought the Jaguar in to refuel and Duncan Hamilton took over, but the stop put the Jaguar once more a lap behind the leader plus about 1 min. 21.8 sec. Soon afterwards, both the Aston Martins came in to refuel, Brooks handing over to Trintignant and Graham Whitehead to brother Peter.

At 5.30 a.m. there was some slight drama when the 3-litre Maserati carrying

the race number 1 suffered considerable internal confusion in its engine just after passing the pits; it coasted to rest trailing blue smoke and a stream of oil. There was a momentary flicker of flame from underneath as driver Godia switched off, but it died and went out. After coasting the big car backwards downhill out of the way—and thoughtfully doing it on the verge so as not to trail oil on the circuit—Godia set off on foot to tell his pit all about it.

The truly heartbreaking news came at 6 a.m. when the speakers suddenly announced that the sole survivor of the Aston Martin works team had coasted to a standstill at Mulsanne with trouble in engine or gearbox, which the pit crew could not diagnose on the spot as Trintignant promptly disappeared from the pursuit of questioners. Once again the high hopes with which Aston Martin came to Le Mans had been disappointed and the sympathy of all the British spectators went out to the company which has made such great Le Mans history in the past and has so often seemed to be on the point of doing so again only to suffer cruel mischance.

The ever reliable Aston Martin DB3S of the Whitehead brothers, which went so well in the 1000 Kilometres Race at the Nurburgring, was once again running well in fourth place and in due course overtook the Behra-Herrmann Porsche to gain third position, thereafter increasing its lead over the German car by a few yards at a time in a hard fought duel. However, the Aston

Signals from the pit are transmitted by telephone to a special signalling station shortly after Mulsanne Corner, where drivers are going relatively slowly and have their information in plenty of time. Here are the Halford/Naylor Lister-Jaguar, Bruwaen/Lefourel Panhard, Guyot/Ros Stanguellini, following a DB saloon through this area.

A valiant effort to keep Jaguar in the picture after the early retirement of the Ecurie Ecosse cars was made by Duncan Hamilton's privately entered D-type, seen here being cornered by co-driver Ivor Bueb. Impressively steady driving brought them up to 2nd place, when at midday on Sunday Hamilton spun off the wet road at Arnage and retired.

Winner on Index was the extremely fast OSCA driven by Alessandro de Tomaso and Colin Davis. Here Tomaso leads Ubezzi and Catulle's Giulietta through Arnage.

Just before the race completed its 16th hour, the bright promise of the early morning sun which had kindly dispersed the stray wisps of mist (which so often form a drivers' nightmare at dawn on this circuit) gave place to the usual torrential rain, and Duncan Hamilton came in and handed over the Jaguar to Bueb to go motor boating in after it had been refuelled.

Positions in General Classification at 16 hours
1 Gendebien-Hill (Ferrari), 206 laps: 15 hr. 56 min. 11 sec., 108.4 m.p.h.
2 Hamilton-Bueb (Jaguar), 205 laps: 15.56.57.
3 Behra-Herrmann (Porsche), 196 laps: 15.56.49.
4 Whitehead-Whitehead (Aston Martin), 196 laps: 15.58.37.
5 Barth-Frère (Porsche), 194 laps: 15.58.32.
6 de Beaufort-Linge (Porsche), 192 laps: 15.59.01.

Positions of Index of Performance
1 Tomaso-Davis (OSCA), 1.270.
2 Laureau-Cornet (D.B.), 1.262.
3 Laroche-Radix (OSCA), 1.233.

Retirements During Period
Brooks - Trintignant (Aston Martin) (mechanical trouble); Godia-Bonnier (Maserati) (engine); Ireland-Taylor (Lotus) (mechanical trouble); Lailler-Bartholoni (D.B.) (seized piston).

At 8.15 a.m. the Behra-Herrmann Porsche came in to refuel and, at the same time, the opportunity was taken to reline the brakes which, on the latest Porsche, is a simple, swift and apparently necessary operation. During this stage, the Whitehead Aston Martin went by in third place once more, but, when Behra restarted, he set off to such effect, in spite of the wet road which produced twin plumes of spray from the silver Porsche, that he whittled away the Aston's lead by nine seconds a lap until he was in front once again. Hardly had he regained his third place, however, when a further pit stop became necessary to adjust the relined brakes, and the drama was repeated as the Aston Martin repassed, was chased and was recaught, only for the Porsche to stop yet again for an intensive examination of the left front brake, in which the drum was replaced in 4 min. 45 sec.

The rain ceased, a watery sun struggled somewhat ineffectually to dry out the soggy, muddy ground across which the spectators, returning to the circuit after some comfortable sleep in real beds, squelched their miserable way.

By 10 a.m. the circuit, at any rate, was drying rapidly, and the leading Ferrari was lapping at around 4 min. 38 sec., un-

never managed to shake off the Porsche and eventually the Porsche closed right up and repassed, then went on to build up an ever-increasing distance between its tail and the nose of the British car.

By 7 a.m., after the race had been in progress for 15 hours, only 20 of the 55 starters were still running, but among the going concerns were a respectable number of British cars, including, still, the two A.C.s (present and future models), the Peerless and the dark green Lister-Jaguar driven by Halford/Naylor, which was now lying 7th after a prolonged pit stop during the night, during the course of which no less a component than a camshaft had been replaced.

The leading Ferrari came into refuel and changed drivers at 7.15 a.m., and restarted without losing its lead to the Jaguar which, to the gloom of British spectators, had been steadily losing a few seconds a lap to the Ferrari for the past hour or so. However, after the Ferrari pit stop, the Jaguar was now a lap and 52 seconds behind instead of a lap and about 2 min. 30 sec., and Hamilton at the wheel of the Jaguar began steadily to reduce the gap—on some laps by as much as six seconds—until the difference was down to one lap and 44 seconds. But maybe Gendebien, who had taken over the leading Ferrari from Phil Hill, was just playing himself in carefully and not risking being voted by all Italians the most unpopular man of 1958, which fate would assuredly befall him if he ran the still surviving works Ferrari out of road. After some cautious opening laps, he increased speed and began to draw away from the Jaguar once more.

The Lotus story continued on its dramatic way for, just as the 750 c.c. car reappeared at the pits filled to the brim with sand from Tertre Rouge where Tom Dickson had been digging steadily to extricate it for the past 2½ hours, the Lotus driven by Ireland/Taylor disappeared out on the circuit around Mulsanne, where Taylor indulged in some intensive work on the timing.

LE MANS
1 9 5 8

The winning Ferrari, Hill at the wheel, comes through Mulsanne in the closing stages, streaming spray from its wheels.

hurried and at ease, as well it might with a lead of nearly two laps at this stage of the race over the Jaguar. There was still a further six hours of racing—some 600 high-speed miles to be covered—and the race was in its holding stage. Later might come the attack. Right now, the struggle for the Index was going fiercely, first and second cars separated by no more than a half of one per cent.

The situation in the 750 c.c. class, which this year contained so many of the technical novelties of the race, was very interesting. The OSCAs were reproducing their Sebring form, lying first and third in the class and the Index. The French were making a fighting come-back after their defeat by the Lotus last year, and the Laureau-Cornet D.B. (with the latest engine fitted with the new D.B. cylinder head with wide angle valves) was an ever-present threat in second place, although by now it was two laps behind the leading car. The new Panhard engine with twin overhead camshafts did not prove so successful, the two cars fitted with this unit having retired early in the race on the 10th and 44th laps.

Nor, this year, did the 750 c.c. Lotus repeat its 1957 triumph, for the new engine in the works car blew up during the practising period and was replaced by the 1957 engine, whilst the French-entered 750 Lotus with a similar new "square" 750 c.c. engine had been eliminated by a collision on the 19th lap.

Soon after 10.30 a.m. the Jaguar came in for a routine fuelling stop and it left the pits with Duncan Hamilton at the wheel, just ahead of the leading Ferrari which thereafter maintained station astern of the Jaguar for a number of laps.

At 11.10 the fastest Porsche (Behra and Herrmann) once more was lifted at the front so that the Zuffenhausen mechanics could keep in practice at brake adjustment; perhaps from now on the disc

brake will be more sympathetically considered in this area than it has been in the past. In any event this car was now a defender and no longer an attacker. As Hill and Whitehead had settled in their stride, Hamilton was the only man in the race with reason to hurry, but he could not pull away from the leader, who sat resolutely 100 yards behind, 1.999 laps in

front of him. Whether the American kept his headlamps on by accident or with the intention of promoting a *crise des nerfs* was an interesting speculation; in any case they were switched off by 11.30 a.m.

At 11.30 thunder heralded heavy rain, to the discomfort of most with the exception of the Peerless conductors, snug in their plastic box, which at the 19th hour

Peter Whitehead, lying second, sets the road twinkling with spray from the wheels of the DB3S Aston as he approaches the second leg of Arnage.

LE MANS
1 9 5 8

The Porsches of Behra-Herrmann and Barth-Frère dive into the "pond" at Arnage, on their way to individual class victories and 3rd and 4th overall.

averaged 88 m.p.h. and stood 16th in the field of 22. Just before noon the weather conditions were of really unprecedented nastiness, and to flashes of lightning and peals of thunder the Ferrari came past the pits slowly—and alone! Whatever had happened to Duncan must have been seen by Hill. What had happened was a slide off the road when leaving Arnage, which slightly injured the driver's leg, but placed the car beyond recall. At noon the overall positions were:

Positions in General Classification at 20 hours
1. Gendebien-von Trips (Ferrari), 257 laps: 19 hr. 58 min. 36·8 sec., 107.6 m.p.h.
2. Whitehead-Whitehead (Aston Martin), 244 laps: 19.55.05·4.
3. Behra-Herrmann (Porsche), 242 laps: 19.57.13·1.
4. Barth-Frère (Porsche), 240 laps: 19.58.39·7.
5. de Beaufort-Linge (Porsche), 228 laps: 19.58.43·6.
6. Beurlys-de Changy (Ferrari), 215 laps: 19.58.07·0.

Positions of Index of Performance
1. de Tomaso-Davis (OSCA), 1.267.
2. Laureau-Cornet (D.B.), 1.263.
3. Laroche-Radix (OSCA), 1.226.

Retirements During Period
Hamilton-Bueb (Jaguar) (accident).

The Gentlemen were now following on 13 laps behind the Players, but there were still 400 odd miles to go for the score of cars continuing on the course. Of these, the Sigrand-Revillon 750 c.c. Stanguellini was barely going, with certainly no more than half a litre effective. Porsche was however the only marque who could peer into the future with some sense of security, as the 1.6-litre car led the 2-litre class and was placed 4th, and the privately-owned 1½-litre was second in its class and 5th overall.

Running like trains, the two A.C. Ace-Bristols finished 8th and 9th, the new car seen here being but 14½ miles ahead of its older namesake at the finish.

Sole survivor of a strong Lotus attack, and smallest of them all, the battered 750 c.c. car driven by Stacey and Dickson motors through the Sunday afternoon rain.

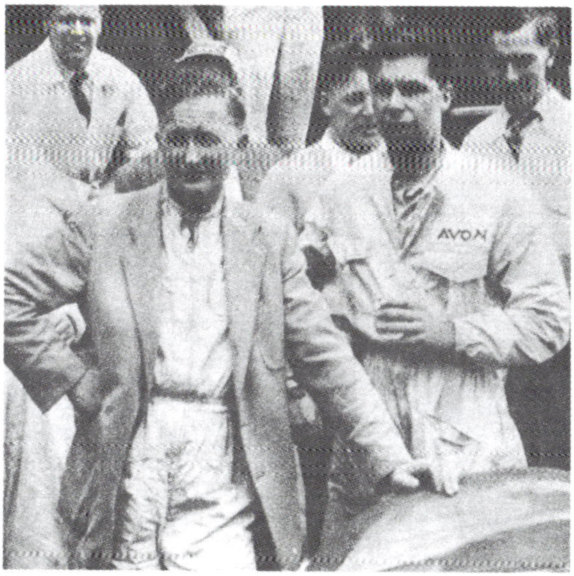

(*Below*) Peter Whitehead (on left) and half-brother Graham brought their private DB3S into a well-earned second place, saving British cars from complete eclipse among the race finishers.

(*Right*) Clinching the Sports-car Championship for Ferrari, Phil Hill (on left), from America, and Oliver Gendebien averaged over 106 m.p.h. in appalling conditions. One or other of them has been in each of Ferrari's winning cars in the Championship this year.

At 12.30 Gendebien came in for Hill, still with a 110-mile lead which must be a comforting margin to anyone. In any case the Belgian was now cruising round at 100 m.p.h., compared with a Whitehead speed of 104 m.p.h. The Lister suffered a great delay due this time to gearbox bother, but it was brought home by the driver for further attention at one end of the pits, while the Laroche-Radix OSCA (now 3rd on Index) was in trouble, with the bonnet open, at the other. Meantime the 1.6-litre and 1.5-litre Porsches were running in station, on the same lap, barely 20 yards apart and nicely fixed in 3rd and 4th places with a lap speed of about 105 m.p.h.

The Whiteheads physically challenged the leader just as the Lister rejoined the struggle, but now entirely out of the competitive picture, if indeed such a thing existed at this stage. Even the Porsche couplet was disrupted when Barth came in to hand over to Frère and Peter Whitehead reduced his arrears to a baker's dozen by overtaking Gendebien just before. With only three more hours the other British contributors amounted to the A.C.s in 8th and 9th places; the Lister 13th; Peerless 16th (but below its required Index speed); and the 750 Lotus 20th and last. Not, let us face it, a pleasing prospect, but one need not begrudge the Italians and the Germans the solid satisfaction to which they were entitled.

The final hour . . . the race in the bag for the Ferrari—and very well deserved at that. Only 20 cars left in this race which began 23 hours ago. The order seemed impregnable: Gendebien and Hill (Ferrari) 13 laps in the lead at 3 p.m., the Whiteheads (Aston Martin DB3S), 2nd, the Behra-Herrmann Porsche 3rd, three laps behind that, Barth and Frère (1,500 Porsche) 4th on the same lap, Holland's de Beaufort and Linge (1,500 Porsche) 5th, and Beurlys and de Changy (2.9 Ferrari) 6th, not far ahead of the Americans Hugus and Erikson (2.9 Ferrari).

It was about an hour before this that it was bruited around that the leading Ferrari was running with its tanks unsealed, a breach of regulations. Whether this was so or not was not confirmed at this stage, but the Whiteheads, who would have been winners if the gallant Ferrari was disqualified on such a technical error, refused to take any action, which is what we expected. The matter therefore became a discussion behind the official door.

The Final Climax

As the hands of the clock moved over from 3 p.m. towards the final 4 p.m., the leaders on handicap were still Colin Davis—son of Sammy Davis, winner here with the Bentley after the White House pile-up of 30-odd years ago, with de Tomaso on the excellent little 750 c.c. OSCA—and once again the 750 c.c. class dominating this division of the race which carries a prize equal with that for the Endurance Grand Prix.

As always at Le Mans, the tension began to mount as the watches clicked into the last half hour. The Ferrari was running, as they say, like a train, 13 laps or about 114 miles in the lead. In the Ferrari pit there was tranquillity, as tired workers, their tasks completed, snored loudly in their chairs. No one was racing anyone any more. The 20 survivors of the 56 who had started were now motoring at moderate speed to finish the long and exhausting race.

The pits, in the two storeys plus the gallery at the top, were crammed with people. The afternoon had turned sunny, with a stiff breeze, rain clouds floating about the horizon, but blue sky over the circuit. A rain squall soon after 3 p.m. had cleared off and the circuit was dry again. The bars and buvettes emptied as the crowds pressed to the rails to see the end of this sports-car marathon. Officials massed on the finishing line, helicopters fluttered overhead, the police began to assemble in great strength along the line of pits. All eyes were fixed on the final straight up from White House. The three Porsches were all in an impressive line ahead although separated by many laps on the chart. The Peerless, after a good demonstration of reliability, was just outside the minimum qualifying speed, together with the Lister-Jaguar, which had been at rest so many hours with its gearbox trouble and the earlier change of camshaft, but was back on the course.

Five minutes to go . . . and the surviving Aston Martin of the Whiteheads was slowing with a gearbox which had stiffened up. The Swiss-entered A.C. Bristol was just on its minimum speed, running a handicap index of 1.0—exactly what it had been set to do.

Four minutes . . . three . . . two . . . one . . . and down went the flag and the great classic was over once more. Finish: Ferrari—Aston Martin—Porsche. . . .

LE MANS 24-HOUR RACE

HOUR-BY-HOUR POSITIONS

DRIVERS	CARS	1	2	3	4	5	6	7	8	9	10	11	12	13	14	15	16	17	18	19	20	21	22	23	24
Godia—Bonnier	Maserati	12	12	16	12	12	13	12	12	10	11	13	15	17	17	—									
Moss—Brabham	Aston Martin	1	1	—																					
Brooks—Trintignant	Aston Martin	4	4	3	4	5	4	4	4	3	3	3	3	3	—										
Salvadori—Lewis-Evans	Aston Martin	7	7	7	8	—																			
Whitehead—Whitehead	Aston Martin	15	15	10	7	7	6	6	6	4	4	4	5	5	5	4	4	3	3	3	2	2	2	2	2
Fairman—Gregory	Jaguar	51	—																						
Lawrence—Sanderson	Jaguar	54	—																						
Hamilton—Bueb	Jaguar	6	6	5	3	3	3	2	1	2	2	2	2	2	2	2	2	2	2	2	2	—			
Rousselle—Dubois	Lister	25	20	15	—																				
Halford—Naylor	Lister	16	16	11	9	8	7	7	7	6	6	6	6	6	8	7	7	7	7	9	9	13	13	13	15
Mary—Guelfi	Jaguar	18	49	44	39	34	37	—																	
Hawthorn—Collins	Ferrari	2	3	4	16	14	11	10	10	9	9	—													
Gendebien—Hill	Ferrari	5	5	1	1	1	1	1	2	1	1	1	1	1	1	1	1	1	1	1	1	1	1	1	1
Von Trips—Seidel	Ferrari	3	2	2	2	2	2	3	3	—															
Gomez-Mena—Drogo	Ferrari	24	26	41	42	39	39	35	—																
Gurney—Kessler	Ferrari	8	8	6	5	4	17	—																	
Martin—Tavano	Maserati	20	19	18	15	15	14	13	—																
Picard—Juhan	Ferrari	13	13	14	13	10	10	—																	
Beurlys—De Changy	Ferrari	10	11	9	18	19	22	19	15	14	13	10	10	10	21	9	9	9	9	7	6	6	6	6	6
Hugus—Erikson	Ferrari	14	14	13	11	11	12	11	11	11	10	9	9	9	9	8	8	8	8	8	7	7	7	7	7
Martin—Dagorne	Maserati	23	50	—																					
Jopp—Crabb	Peerless	41	38	31	28	26	25	22	16	21	20	19	18	19	19	17	17	16	16	16	15	16	16	16	16
Rodriguez—Behra	Ferrari	27	24	21	20	18	16	14	16	15	16	14	—												
Allison—Hill	Lotus	53	—																						
Pathey—Berger	A.C.	34	30	25	23	21	19	16	13	13	14	12	12	12	12	11	11	11	11	11	10	9	9	9	9
Bolton—Stoop	A.C.	30	28	24	22	20	18	15	14	12	12	11	11	11	11	10	10	10	10	10	8	8	8	8	8
Behra—Herrmann	Porsche	11	10	8	6	6	5	5	5	5	5	5	4	4	4	3	3	4	5	4	3	3	3	3	3
von Frankenberg—Storez	Porsche	17	18	12	10	17	32	34	32	—															
Barth—Frère	Porsche	22	22	17	14	9	8	8	9	7	7	7	7	7	6	5	5	5	4	5	4	4	4	4	4
De Beaufort—Linge	Porsche	21	21	19	17	13	9	9	8	8	8	8	8	8	7	6	6	6	6	6	5	5	5	5	5
Colas—Kerguen	Porsche	26	23	20	19	16	15	21	23	21	19	18	17	16	16	14	12	12	13	12	11	10	10	10	10
Chamberlain—Lovely	Lotus	52	48	46	43	41	40	37	—																
Ubezzi-Catulle	Alfa Romeo	31	46	42	41	40	41	38	—																
Lauga—Hébert	Alfa Romeo	50	44	33	29	27	28	33	—																
Ireland—Taylor	Lotus	29	27	22	21	22	21	18	19	16	15	15	13	13	13	12	15	18	18	21	—				
Frost—Hicks	Lotus	28	25	—																					
Bridger—Blond	Tojeiro	33	29	26	26	25	24	23	20	—															
Laroche—Radix	OSCA	35	32	30	27	28	26	24	22	20	21	20	19	18	18	16	16	15	15	15	14	14	15	15	14
De Tomaso—Davis	OSCA	32	31	27	24	23	20	17	17	18	18	16	14	14	14	13	13	13	12	13	12	11	11	11	11
Dumazer—Dutoit	V.P.	55	—																						
Laureau—Cornet	D.B.	37	34	28	25	24	23	20	18	17	17	17	16	15	15	15	14	14	14	14	13	12	12	12	12
Adda—Bonnet	D.B.	45	40	37	34	36	35	31	30	29	29	27	24	24	22	21	21	21	21	20	19	19	19	18	18
Armagnac—Vidilles	D.B.	39	36	40	30	29	27	25	24	22	22	21	20	20	20	18	18	17	17	17	16	15	14	14	13
Lailler—Bartholoni	D.B.	47	42	36	31	30	31	28	26	25	24	23	22	22	—										
Bruwaen—Lefourel	Panhard	48	43	38	36	33	30	26	25	23	26	25	—												
Cotton—Beaulieu	Panhard	40	—																						
Consten—Vinatier	Panhard	36	33	29	40	38	38	36	33	—															
Poth—Dunand-Saultier	Panhard	46	41	39	35	31	29	27	27	26	25	24	25	26	23	20	20	20	20	18	17	17	17	17	17
Guyot—Ros	Stanguellini	44	39	32	33	—																			
Sigrand—Revillon	Stanguellini	49	45	43	38	35	34	30	29	27	27	26	23	23	19	19	19	19	19	19	18	18	18	19	19
Faure—Nicol	Stanguellini	43	37	34	32	32	36	32	31	28	28	28	26	25	—										
Stacey—Dickson	Lotus	42	35	35	37	37	33	29	28	24	23	22	21	21	21	22	22	22	22	22	20	20	20	20	20
Masson—Héchard	Lotus	38	47	45	—																				
Charles—Young	Jaguar	19	17	—																					
Bianchi—Mairesse	Ferrari	9	9	23	—																				

This table is compiled from official figures. The fact that some cars are shown as holding a position when, in fact, they were out of the race is because they may not have been declared retired by the entrant.

While the three-litre limitation on prototypes was still in force, a new idea was to divide the entries into two categories - Sports Prototypes and Grand Tourisme cars - picking a winner from each; the Biennial Cup was revived after having missed out two years, while another innovation was the introduction of an Index of Thermal Efficiency in addition to the Index of Performance. The new Index took not only speed but also fuel consumption and the car's weight into account. Of the 53 starting cars, 31 were classified as sports prototypes and 22 as GT cars. Ferrari again fielded the largest number of entries; in the prototype class, six 250 Testa Rossa models with three-litre V12 engines, and a single 'Dino' V6 model in the twolitre class; complemented by four 250 GT coupes in the GT class. A single Jaguar D-type, two Lister-Jaguars and a Tojeiro-Jaguar were all in the prototype class; Aston Martin had four DBR I prototypes, and a Swiss entered DB,4 coupe in the GT class. As Maserati was absent for the 1959 race, these completed the entries over two litres.

Cooper had a two-litre 'Monaco' in the prototype class; Lotus also had a two Litre prototype as well as two prototypes in the 750 cc class, and three Elite coupes (with 1,216 cc engines) in the GT class. Remaining British entries were all in the GT class, and included an AC Ace and a Frazer-Nash (both still with the venerable Bristol two litre engine), three Triumph TRS Models with the dohc Sabrina engines, and an MGA Twin-Cam which was sponsored by the MG Car Club. Of the six Porsche prototypes, four were in the 1½ litre class and two in the two-litre class; seven DB-Panhards were split between the prototype and GT classes, one car in each class had an 850 cc engine, the remainder were all 750 ccs. Two Oscas and three Stanguellinis were all in the 750 cc prototype class. All the way from Trollhattan in Sweden came two very innocent looking SAAB 93 saloons; they started in the 750 cc GT class, and had three-cylinder two-stroke engines driving the front wheels.

For the first time, a practice day was held in April and the results of this seemed to favour the Ferrari V12 prototypes yet again; the Testa Rossa models were now fitted with disc brakes, six years after these brakes had first appeared at Le Mans. However, in the race itself, it was the Aston Martin DBR 1 of Stirling Moss and Jack Fairman which first took the lead, probably deliberately baiting the Ferraris, on the instructions of Aston Martin team manager Reg Parnell - himself a seasoned Le Mans driver. Sure enough, the Ferraris of Gendebien/Hill and Behra/Gurney followed Moss in second and third places in the initial stages of the race; a third Ferrari was fourth and the D-type Jaguar was fifth. None of these cars were to finish the race.

First to retire of the leading cars was the Ferrari of Allison and da Silva Ramos; but then the Moss/Fairman Aston went out with engine trouble. The D-type Jaguar broke a con rod while lying second, and the Behra/Gurney Ferrari which had taken the lead from Moss dropped to fourth place before being put out with transmission failure. The Aston Martin of Roy Salvadori and Carroll Shelby had taken the lead by now but was constantly challenged by the Gendebien/Hill Ferrari. The two cars changed places several times, and were followed by the Aston Martin DBR 1 of Trintignant/Frere which occupied third place for most of the race. With the depletion of the Ferrari ranks - at half time only one of the prototypes, the Gendebien/Hill car, was still in the race - the next four cars were amazingly enough all 1.6 and 1.5 litre Porsches, and they were followed by the four Ferrari 250 GTs, in eighth to eleventh places.

However, none of the small Porsches lasted for very long; the Hugus/Ericksson car had crept into fourth place by midday on Sunday when its engine finally gave up, about the same time a sister car retired with clutch failure - and all the Porsches were out of the race. The next drama came when the Gendebien/Hill Ferrari overheated, stopped at the pit, re-started and completed two very slow laps before being withdrawn. It was then that a Le Mans victory came within Aston Martin's grasp, after 30 years of dogged persistence the result was a 1-2 victory, the Salvadori/Shelby car (average 112.569 mph, distance 2,701.654 miles) leading Trintignant/Frere; both had a comfortable margin over the four Ferrari GTs which had gradually moved up as the Porsches dropped out, and which defended Maranello's honour by finishing third, fourth, fifth and sixth; the leading car also winning the GT class.

The Biennial Cup was won by the DB-Panhard of Cornet/Cotton; they also won the Index of Performance, while the new Index of Thermal Efficiency went to another DB-Panhard, the Consten/ Armagnac car; it is perhaps of interest to note that at an average speed of 86.4 mph this car returned better than 25 mpg. By contrast the winning Aston Martin's fuel consumption was a shade worse than 10 mpg. The fastest lap was recorded by Jean Behra in one of the Ferrari prototypes at 124.995 mph but Hawthorn's absolute record from 1957 was still untouched. Only 13 cars of 53 starters finished this race, and one of the SAABs was twelfth.

Perhaps the closest parallel to the 1959 result was that of the 1935 race: in both cases the winner was a British car favoured by luck, though admittedly there was less of the fluke about Aston Martin's 1959 victory than there had been about the 1935 Lagonda win. For Aston Martin, it was a reward for persistent dedication since their first Le Mans race in 1928, and participation in every race since 1931. But it was also the last time before 1975 that a purely British car won the Le Mans 24-hour race - although Britain is not placed badly on the overall scoreboard of 50 Le Mans races, with a total of 13 victories - the same as Italy, and more than either France, Germany or the USA has achieved.

AND NOW — LE MANS

Next Week-end Sees the 27th Grand Prix d'Endurance—the Greatest Sports Car Race in the World. British Cars once again Dominate the Entry, but there is a Strong Challenge from both Italy and Germany

THE ENTRIES

(With Starting Numbers)

Lister-Jaguar (2,996 c.c.) entered by Brian Lister: (1) Bruce Halford—Ivor Bueb; (2) Walter Hansgen—Ed Crawford. 2,986 c.c. entered by Ecurie Nationale Belge: (9) L. Bianchi—J. Croisier. **Tojeiro Jaguar** (2,986 c.c.) entered by Ecurie Ecosse; (8) Ron Flockhart—Masten Gregory; **Jaguar** modified D-type (2,994 c.c.) entered by Ecurie Ecosse; (3) John Lawrence—Innes Ireland. **Aston Martin** (2,992 c.c.) entered by David Brown: (4) Roy Salvadori—Carroll Shelby; (5) Stirling Moss—Jack Fairman; (6) Paul Frere—Maurice Trintignant. Spare driver: Henry Taylor. Entered by Graham Whitehead: (7) Whitehead—J. B. Naylor. DB3S (2,922 c.c.) entered by Ecurie Trois Chevrons: (22) Hubert Patthey—J. Calderari. **Lotus** (2,494 c.c.) entered by Lotus Ltd.: (23) Graham Hill—Peter Loveley.

Ferrari (2,953 c.c.) entered by Ferrari: (12) Jean Behra—Cliff Allison; (14) Phil Hill—Olivier Gendebien; (15) Dan Gurney—H. da Silva Ramos. Entered by Ecurie Nationale Belge: (10) Ransom—Beurlys; (11) A. de Changy—A. Milhoux. Entered by F. Tavano: (16) Tavano—Grossman. Entered by North Atlantic Racing Team (Luigi Chinetti): (17) Carveth—Gaiter; (18) Lance Reventlow—Lovelyn. Entered by J. Hugus: (19) Hugus—R. Erickson. Entered by E. Martin: (20) E. D. Martin—B. Kimberley. Entered by Lino Fayen: (21) Fayen—R. Ottolina.

2-litre Class

Ferrari (2,000 c.c.) entered by Ferrari: (24) G. Cabianca—Giorgio Scarlatti. **Cooper** (2,000 c.c.) entered by Cooper Cars: (25) Jim Russell—Bruce McLaren. **Triumph** (1,984 c.c.) entered by Standard Ltd.: (26) Ninian Sanderson—J. R. Stoop; (27) Peter Bolton—M. Rothschild; (28) Peter Jopp—Claud Dubois. **A.C.** (1,971 c.c.) entered by A.C. Cars: (29) A. Blary—Andre Pilette. Entered by Rudd Racing Ltd.. (30) Whiteaway—J. Turner. **Lotus** (1,960 c.c.) entered by Lotus Ltd.: (31) Alan Stacey—Innes Ireland. **Porsche** (1,587 c.c.) entered by Porsche Ltd.: (32) drivers not nominated; (33) drivers not nominated. **M.G.** (1,588 c.c.) entered by N.W. Centre, M.G. Car Club: (34) Ted Lund—C. G. Escott.

1,500 c.c. Class

Porsche (1,498 c.c.) entered by Porsche Ltd.: (35) drivers not nominated. Entered by J. Kerguen: (36) Kerguen—J. Dewez. Entered by Godin de Beaufort: (37) de Beaufort—H. Linge. **Cooper** (1,490 c.c.) entered by Los Amigos: (38) J. C. Vidilles—J. F. Malle. **Alfa Romeo** (1,290 c.c.) entered by V. Conrero: (39) drivers not nominated; (40) drivers not nominated. **Lotus** (1,220 c.c. Elite) entered by Car Exchange Ltd.: (41) B. Frost—J. Lawry. Entered by Border Reivers: (42) J. Clark—T. Dickson.

1,100 c.c. Class

No entries.

750 c.c. Class

Saab (748 c.c.) entered by S. A. Hurrell: (43) Hurrell—R. M. North. Entered by the drivers: (44) B. Jonsson—S. Nottorp. **Fiat** (748 c.c.) entered by Pagani (45) P. Alfranco—M. Poltronieri. **D.B.** (747 c.c.) entered by Automobiles D.B.: (46) Consten—Armagnac; (47) René Cotton—"X"; (48) Chancel—Laureau; (49) Bartholoni—Jeager. Entered by R. Masson: (50) Masson—M. Vinatier. **Osca** (745 c.c.) entered by A. de Tomaso: (51) de Tomaso—"X." Entered by Osca factory: (52) Rodriguez brothers; (53) Laroche—"X." **Lotus** (742 c.c.) entered by Lotus Ltd.: (54) Michael Taylor—J. Steff. **Stanguellini** (740 c.c.) entered by Stanguellini factory: (55) drivers not nominated; (56) drivers not nominated.

Reserves in Order of Precedence

57, **Lotus** 742 c.c. entered by Lotus Ltd. 58, **D.B.** 745 c.c. entered by Hechard. 59, **Lotus** 1,220 c.c. entered by J. R. Stoop. 60, **D.B.** 745 c.c. entered by C. Faucher. 61, **Frazer-Nash** 1,911 c.c. entered by Dashwood. 62, **Stanguellini** 741 c.c. entered by the factory. 63, **E.F.A.C.** 741 c.c. entered by the factory.

No drivers nominated for the reserve entries.

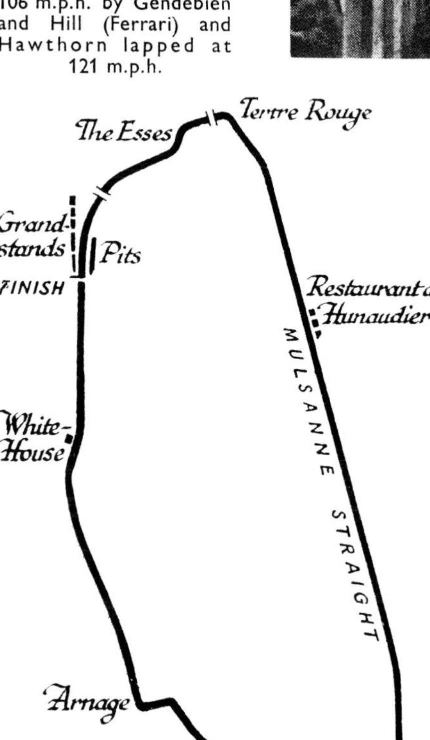

Shoulder to shoulder in enclosures and pits balconies the crowd watch the cars as they line up for the fast right-hand curve under the Dunlop Bridge. (Below) the 8.36-mile Circuit of the Sarthe where last year's race was won at 106 m.p.h. by Gendebien and Hill (Ferrari) and Hawthorn lapped at 121 m.p.h.

Next Saturday, June 20, at four o'clock in the afternoon, the tricolour of France will fall to unleash the greatest sports car race in the world. At the same hour on Sunday, after a race as long as a dozen Grands Prix in a row, the Le Mans 24-Hour Grand Prix of Endurance will finish and the survivors of the 55 cars which set out will come streaming over the line to the cheers of the packed grandstands.

The limelight of world publicity blazes upon this annual marathon of speed contested by the cream of Europe's fastest cars competing in the third round of the World Championship for Manufacturers of Sports Cars, which has so profound an effect on sales throughout the world, not only of the models entered for the race but of production cars bearing the same radiator badges.

This country once again dominates the scene with 23 cars out of the field of 55, 10 of them there to reverse the victory of Ferrari last year. Since the war British cars have won this exhausting race five times—each time a triumph for the house of Jaguar, and once again the Jaguar entry is in private hands, the factory having withdrawn from racing for the time being. Other factories which have not entered are Alfa Romeo, Lancia, Mercedes, Maserati and the nationalized French Renault.

In the 3-litre class, which is the upper engine-size limit for World Championship sports car races and in which we may expect to see the outright winner, Britain is represented by the Ecurie Ecosse Jaguar and Tojeiro Jaguar, Lister-Jaguar, Lotus and Aston Martin—three of which are factory entries. Against them is a phalanx of no fewer than 11 Ferraris, including the factory team of three. These are the V-12 models of the type which won at Sebring in March. The 2-litre class holds Cooper Monaco. Triumph (a works trio), A.C. with Bristol engine, Lotus and a very special works-prepared twin-camshaft M.G. A entered by the M.G. Car Club, challenging works Porsche and an official Ferrari. The 1,500 c.c. group holds Cooper, Alfa Romeo, Porsche and Lotus Elite. This year there are no entries in the 1,100 c.c. class. France figures only in the 750 c.c. category — five D.B. with Panhard engines; Sweden sends two Saab, Italy three Osca (made by the Maserati brothers), two of Stanguellini's neat cars and, for the first time for many years, a Fiat. The lone British entry is the Lotus of the type which won the handicap section of the race in 1957.

Many Grand Prix drivers figure in the list. Following the success of the Aston Martin at the German 1,000 Kilometres Stirling Moss has been invited by the Aston Martin team as "guest driver" with Jack Fairman, Roy Salvadori, the American Carroll Shelby, Frenchman Maurice Trintignant and the Belgian journalist-driver, Paul Frere. Henry Taylor stands by as spare man. Bruce Halford and Ivor Bueb share a Lister-Jaguar; two Americans have another. Ecurie Ecosse, winners in 1956 and 1957, will again have Ron Flockhart, who drove the winning car in both those races. The Ferrari team has Jean Behra, Cliff Allison, last year's winners and victors at Sebring in March, Hill and Gendebien, the American newcomer Dan Gurney and Brazil's da Silva Ramos. Lance Revent-

low, whose Scarab is over 3-litres and ineligible, will drive a Ferrari. Graham Hill has a Lotus with the American Peter Lovely. Other well-known Grand Prix men are Jim Russell and Bruce McLaren (New Zealand Champion) with a Cooper Monaco.

Amateur Graham Whitehead, who farms in Berkshire, shares his Aston Martin DBR1/300 with J. B. Naylor. The brothers Rodriguez, from Mexico, who are 18 and 19 respectively, drive a 750 c.c. Osca. Partner with Flockhart two years ago, Ninian Sanderson is in the Triumph team of TR3S cars—the new model destined for production as a competition machine, with twin-camshaft engine. The Jaguar engines, prepared with factory co-operation, are the latest 3-litre type with " square " dimensions of 86 by 86 mm. The cars weigh about 17 cwt.

Last year, when a storm of wind and rain lashed the circuit for several hours, the winning Ferrari averaged 106 m.p.h., covering 2,548 miles, driven in turn by Phil Hill and Olivier Gendebien. In second place were the privateers Graham and Peter Whitehead (Aston Martin), 100 miles behind, third, the 1,600 c.c. Porsche of Jean Behra and Hans Herrmann, 20 miles farther back, and a 1,500 c.c. Porsche only eight miles behind them. The fastest lap was made by Mike Hawthorn (3-litre Ferrari) at 121.3 m.p.h. The handicap division was won by de Tomaso and Colin Davis (Osca 750).

There are really four competitions going on at the same time. First there is the 22nd annual Distance Cup for the outright winner, irrespective of class, with a cash prize of just under £5,000. Secondly, and regarded in France, at least, as of equal importance, the handicap Index of Performance Cup, based on the exact size of each engine, which likewise carries a cash award of £5,000 to the winner. Thirdly, there is the Final round of the 25th Biennial Cup, open to those manufacturers whose cars finished the race last year and are competing again, with the result decided on the Index of Performance formula. Those who finish this year will qualify to compete in the Biennial Cup of 1960. Fourthly, there is the new competition for the Thermal Efficiency Cup, which will be decided on a formula which relates speed to weight and fuel consumption.

In addition to the profuse array of awards and cash prizes (totalling over £30,000), *The Motor* Challenge Trophy goes to the entrant of the British car which finishes highest in the main results, with souvenirs to the two drivers.

Order of Battle

Some of the traditional regulations for this unique race have been dropped as being obsolete in modern conditions, but the main structure of the rules remains. The cars must be genuine sports or touring cars with proper bodywork, seats, wings, hoods, lamps and screens. Manufacturers are allowed to enter their cars of the future, the prototypes of projected production models. The fuel is provided by the club, supplied to each pit through pressure hoses fed from reservoir tanks in the paddock, and is a commercial type fuel of between 95 and 100 octane. Fuel, oil and water may only be taken on at intervals of 30 laps (just over 250 miles), the filler caps being sealed each time. Only two men may work on a car at the pits, although a third mechanic may operate the fuel hose—and do nothing else. No one else may set foot on the road, which means the driver must leave his seat and get into his pit if he is not one of those working on the car.

The starting system remains unchanged. The cars are ranged in line tail-on to the pits in descending order of engine-size so that the fastest cars can get away on their own without having to thread a way through the " traffic." The drivers who are to work the first stint (wearing dark blue armlets to distinguish them from their co-drivers who wear orange armlets) stand on the opposite side of the road. When the flag falls at 4 p.m. they race to their cars, jump in, press the starter and move off into the first of the long 24 hours of the race.

The circuit lies about three miles out of Le Mans on the road to Tours. The main approach route for cars is past the station, under the railway bridge and through the suburban streets which are sign-posted, out on to the Arnage road. Then, just after leaving the built-up area, the entrance to the circuit is seen on the left, by the aerodrome. Spectators can wander from enclosure to enclosure from the main grandstands round to Tertre Rouge on both sides of the circuit. The car parks are so arranged that it is possible to enter or leave and come back again at any time. There are buffets and restaurants, shops, kiosks, a post office, a bank, barbers' shops, showers, bars—and even a chapel. *The Motor* has arranged an English commentary to be given over the loudspeakers every hour, augmenting the French commentaries, and a vast, floodlit scoreboard above the pits shows the number of laps covered by every car. Behind the paddock, reached from the grandstand enclosures by the tunnel at one end of the pits or the bridge at the other, is The Village—a garden with pavilions and exhibition stands and a restaurant and bars.

The whole scene is a welter of colour and sound. Flags, captive balloons, banners, the ceaselessly flowing tide of spectators . . . the whine of passing cars, the strident, amplified voices of the commentators, blaring music, the fair with swings and roundabouts and jugglers and " le night club " . . . and by night the whole stage floodlit from end to end. A whole township with a brief annual population greater than Le Mans city— 7½ miles of standing-room ramps, a quarter of a mile of pits, parking for 24,000 cars and 1,000 caravans, 1,200 gendarmes to keep order and as many officials running the race, 55 starters, 110 drivers, about 1,000 pit attendants, and a race for 24 hours.

For Spectators

Grandstand seats (opposite the pits and scoreboard): Tribune Sommer, £5 19s. 5d. Tribune Benoist, £3 14s. 8d. Tribune Singher, £4 9s. 7d. **Pits Balcony**, £3 7s. 3d. **Car Parks:** reserved space, £1 9s. 11d. Unreserved, 15s.

Information

Syndicat d'Initiative, Place de la Republique. Race tickets: Automobile Club de l'Ouest, Place de la Republique.

XXVIIᵉ Grand Prix d'Endurance
des 24 HEURES du MANS

PHOTOS BY D. DOROT

ONCE AGAIN we were at Le Mans, scene of the most important sports-car race in the world and the fourth round of the World's Championship for Constructors.

• Ferrari had won the first round at Sebring with Hill and Gendebien, who took over the Gurney/Daigh car after their own had dropped out with mechanical trouble. The Behra/Allison Ferrari, finishing in 2nd place, gained Ferrari no points but a further psychological lead at the beginning of the season.

The second round was not so happy for Ferrari: Porsches finished in the first 4 places at the Targa Florio, putting them ahead of Ferrari on points (due also to a 3rd place at Sebring) and far ahead in subjective rating.

Then, to add spice to the pudding, an Aston Martin driven by Moss and Fairman won the 1000 km of Nurburg, making it one race each for three of the major constructors. The point standings, though, still had Porsche first with 15 points, Ferrari 2nd with 14 points, Aston Martin 3rd with 8 points and Maserati 4th with 2 points.

Jaguar, the only other constructor with a chance of winning a major race of this type, had no official factory cars at any of the first three races. Private Jaguars were entered at Sebring and Nurburg and now at Le Mans as well.

Speculation was rampant. The over-all winner was expected to come from one of the 3-liter cars, and odds were in favor of Ferrari. Everyone assumed they had licked the bugs that had put their cars out at Sebring and the Targa, and Le Mans is an excellent circuit for Ferrari to show up to its best advantage. The odds were further increased when newcomer Dan Gurney, of Riverside, Calif., turned in the fastest lap in practice in the Ferrari he was to share with da Silva Ramos. (Later the teams were shuffled around. Gurney co-drove with Behra, while Allison teamed with da Silva Ramos.)

Some of the faster, smaller cars could not be discounted, but were more favored to win the Index of Performance than over-all first place. Porsches were entered in the 2-liter and 1.5-liter classes and would certainly have to be figured as strong contenders for the Index, along with France's only entries, five DB-Panhards.

Four races actually went on at the same time at Le Mans this year, though world-wide attention naturally focused on the outright winners. The distance cup goes to the car which, irrespective of class, goes the greatest distance in the 24 hours. This carries a cash award of just under $14,000. The Index of Performance, a handicap race based entirely on engine size and distance covered, carries a cash prize of the same amount as the outright winners. Third this year was the final of the 25th Biennial cup, which is competed for only by the manufacturers whose cars finished the race the previous year and are competing again. (The makes that finished this year are eligible for the Biennial cup of 1960.) The Index of Performance formula decides this competition. Finally there is the Thermal Efficiency cup, a new category, which determines the winner with a weight, speed and fuel consumption formula. The total cash prizes, coupled with various awards, totaled over $84,000.

The customary immense crowd that assembles for Le Mans was utterly quiet. The drivers had taken up their positions across the track from their cars. The pit crews had withdrawn from the track. The photographers jammed every available vantage point. And at 4:00 P.M. sharp, M. Maurice Herzog dropped the flag.

Stirling Moss, ace sprinter, was not the first man to his car but he was the first off the line, followed at varying distances by Ireland, Trintignant, Flockhart, Bueb and Salvadori.

Behra finished the first lap in 16th place after a slow start, but the other Ferraris—Gendebien's and da Silva Ramos' in particular—had moved up in the pack and were just behind Moss and ahead of Ireland, Trintignant, Flockhart, Bueb and Graham Hill.

Behra was in 12th position after 2 laps, 10th at 3 laps, 9th at 4 laps, and by the 7th lap he had moved up to 4th place. Moss was pulling away from the Gendebien and da Silva Ramos Ferraris, but the crowd was comparing Moss's time against the flying Behra's.

Moss turned in a lap of 4 min 7.9 sec and Behra, by now a traditional Moss rival and apparently more at home in a sports car than in a Grand Prix car, had moved into 3rd place and recorded a lap time of 4 min 3 sec.

Behra moved into 2nd place on the 15th lap, and on the 17th he passed Moss on the long Mulsanne straight. Then he cut down his lap time to 4 min 1.9 sec and 4 min 1.1 sec.

Gurney had started his stint at the wheel and now Fairman took over the Moss car, which had passed into first while the Ferrari was in the pits, but he quickly lost the lead to Gurney, who proceeded to gain 10 sec per lap on Fairman in the bargain. Following these two were Phil Hill, who had taken over from Gendebien; Allison, who relieved da Silva Ramos; and Gregory, who took over for Ireland, all on the same lap with the leader. A lap behind came Lawrence, Frère, Halford, Naylor and Blond.

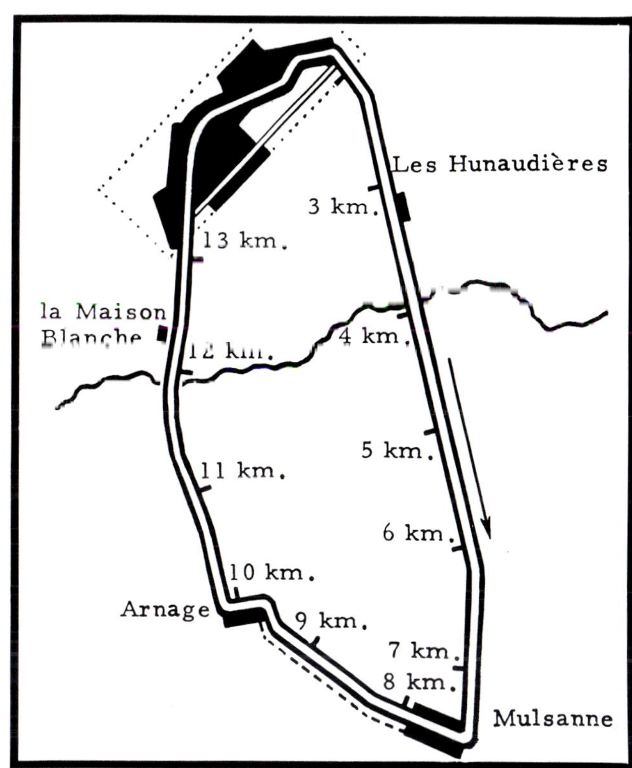

The familiar shape of the Le Mans circuit.

The Allison Ferrari then stopped at the pits and was wheeled into the dead car park, where Peter Bolton's Triumph TR-3-S joined it. This area was becoming quite popular.

After 46 laps (16 at the wheel), Gurney led Fairman by a minute. The gap was widening, but it was more evident that Fairman was getting into the swing of things. At the 49th lap Hill passed Fairman into 2nd place, but on the 53rd he pulled into the pits and lost 2 places in the process. Hill went back onto the course, made one more lap, and then pulled the Ferrari back in for another check.

America's Carroll Shelby and England's Roy Salvadori . . .

. . . Win a previously elusive Le Mans victory for Aston.

At the 4-hour mark, Gurney still led (by over 2 min), followed by Fairman, Gregory, Shelby and Lawrence; 2 laps behind came Halford and Frère. The Stacey/Greene 750 Lotus was leading the Index.

The sandbanks on some turns collected a variety of cars. Some went on and others stayed. A Ferrari hit a dog at Mulsanne but continued.

Just at dusk, the lead Ferrari shot into the pits and Gurney handed over to Behra, who resumed the race in the refueled car less than a minute behind Fairman in the Aston. Shortly after 8:30, Fairman pitted to complain about an ailing oil pressure gauge (at least he hoped it was the gauge), and before he got back in, Behra came by and into the lead. This hurt the Aston's chances seriously because it hadn't yet made its routine stop.

Then came drama. Behra brought the leading Ferrari into the pits and spent some time while the mechanics worked on it. Fairman came into view but instead of going on into the lead, he too stopped at the pits. This time it was for a routine refueling and driver change.

A lap later Moss brought the Aston back into the pits, this time for good. The engine was running very roughly and the gauge registered no oil pressure.

Meanwhile disaster had struck near Whitehouse corner. Russell's Cooper was attempting to lap Faure's Stanguellini when the Stanguellini's engine quit, causing Russell to smite it soundly in the stern sheets. The cars careened off the track and into the Whitehead/Naylor Aston Martin, which had overturned about the same time the Moss Aston retired in the pits. All three drivers suffered minor injuries, and the cars were totally demolished in the fire that followed the second crash.

The 2nd-place Jaguar (Gregory/Ireland) stopped at the pits for good and the lead Ferrari pitted and roared off, still in the lead, with Gurney at the wheel. This was not to last, however. A series of pit stops followed and the car dropped to 2nd and then 3rd.

Shortly after midnight, 8 hours after the start of the race, the Gurney/Behra Ferrari was sounding rough and the Bueb/Halford Lister-Jaguar retired to the dead car park. The order was now Shelby/Salvadori, Hill/Gendebien, Trintignant/Frère, Behra/Gurney and the Bonnier/von Trips Porsche, but calamity awaited three lead cars.

The fuel system of the Hill/Gendebien Ferrari failed just when it appeared they would make it two in a row.

At 1:30 A.M. the Behra/Gurney Ferrari retired for good; official dispatches attributed it to "gear lever trouble." True, the shift knob was missing, but the cockpit was bathed in oil, suggesting something more critical.

The Hill/Gendebien car was the only remaining factory Ferrari, but it sounded very healthy. The leading Aston made a 5-min pit stop just before 2:00 A.M. for some unknown reason, and the Ferrari shot into the lead. By the time the Aston got back into the race, the Ferrari was only a minute from lapping it.

The Tojeiro-Jaguar (Flockhart/Lawrence) came to a halt after running slower and slower, and with its retirement all Jaguar-engined cars were out of the race. The lead Ferrari made a pit stop and re-entered the race, with the 2nd-place Aston now within 2 min of it.

At half distance (4:00 A.M.), the Hill/Gendebien Ferrari was 2 laps ahead of the 2nd-place Aston and nearly 4 laps ahead of the 3rd-place car, the Trintignant/Frère Aston. The 4th-place, Bonnier/von Trips Porsche was 7 laps behind the leader at this point, although it was leading its 2-liter class and the Index of Performance.

Shortly after 5:00 A.M. the leading Ferrari came into the pits so Hill could hand over to Gendebien, with a

Ecurie Ecosse's Tojeiro-Jaguar, driven by Ron Flockhart and Masten Gregory, in the pits for minute-man service.

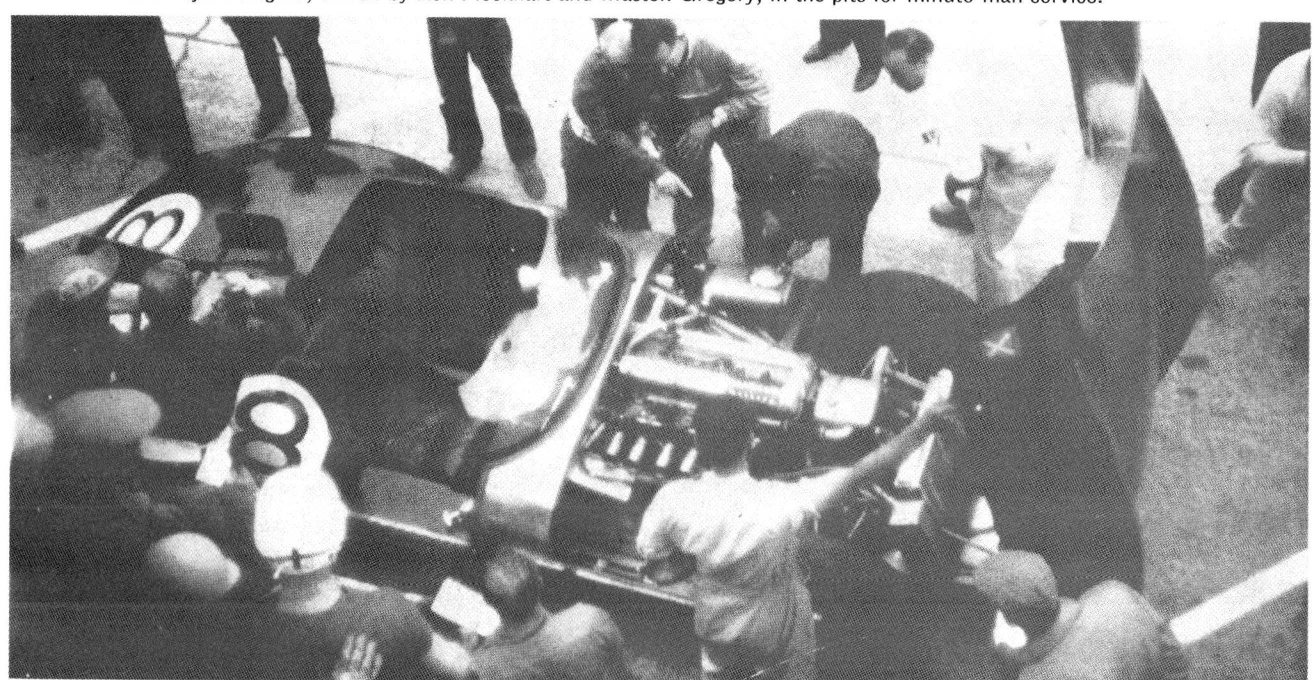

secure lead of 4 laps over the Shelby/Salvadori Aston. Shelby passed while the Ferrari was in the pits, and when Gendebien got going, the Aston was 13 sec ahead (not quite 4 laps in arrears). Gendebien cut this down to a few seconds and held his position just behind the green car.

Trouble hit the 4th- and 6th-place Porsches almost simultaneously. The Barth/Seidel car made a 15-min pit stop, and the von Trips/Bonnier car limped into the pits with a broken crankshaft. The lone remaining Triumph spent 5 min in the pits and resumed racing, but the two Porsches joined the other cars in the *parc fermé*.

After 14 hours (6:00 A.M.) the order was Hill/Gendebien, Salvadori/Shelby, Trintignant/Frère, de Beaufort/Heinz, and Hugus/Erickson. The de Beaufort/Heinz Porsche was leading the Index of Performance.

The 750 Lotus (Stacey/Greene) came into the pits and left, pouring steam. Shortly thereafter it retired near the esses and Stacey returned to the pits on foot.

Shortly after 11:00 A.M. the interest picked up. Both the Hugus/Erickson and Kerguen/La Caze Porsches dropped out, and Gendebien brought in the leading Ferrari, which sounded quite sick. He was in the pits for several minutes and then left only to come back in on the subsequent lap. After consultation with the mechanics and team manager he went back into the contest, the Ferrari sounding worse than ever and only 2 laps ahead of the Aston.

Within a few laps the Ferrari had lost the lead to the leading Aston, driven by Shelby; after putting 2 min between himself and Gendebien, he had come into the pits and turned the wheel over to Salvadori. Gendebien came into the pits again on the following lap and Salvadori flashed past, now a lap in the lead with no other car within striking distance. His lot was made even happier when the Ferrari mechanics pushed the ailing car to the dead car park with 4 hours and 10 minutes of the race left to run.

With only 2 hours to go, the remaining Triumph came to a stop out on the course, reportedly with oil pump trouble (the other two TR-3-S's had poked their fans through their radiators). The two Astons started a procession with less than an hour and a half to go, and with their nearest competitor (the Beurlys/"Eldé" GT Ferrari) 26 laps behind and hardly a reason for concern.

The other competitors could not afford the leisure of relaxing their speed, and the last hour took its toll of cars. Two DB's—the Masson/Vinatier and the Jaeger/Bartholoni entries—retired on the course, but the latter car stopped on the rise to the Dunlop bridge and the driver coasted backward to the pit to be retired.

As 4:00 P.M. drew near, the drivers started watching the clock, hoping to time their finish just past the time limit so they would not have to do an extra lap. The first car across the line after 4:00 was the ultimate winner of the Index of Performance, the Cotton/Cornet DB Panhard. Shelby misjudged his time and had to do another lap, probably as much to his delight as not.

The race *may* go to the swiftest, but it *always* goes to the car that finishes. Lucky or not, racing manager Reg Parnell, general manager John Wyer, owner David Brown and the Aston Martin drivers all deserve much credit.

At the end of this fourth round for the World's Championship of Constructors, Ferrari still leads with 18 points, Aston Martin is 2nd with 16, Porsche 3rd with 15.

A wonderful entry list can be expected for the British Tourist Trophy at Goodwood. The fight should be a close one right up to the last, with anyone still able to win.

ORDER OF FINISH

	Drivers	Car	Miles	Speed
1	Salvadori/Shelby	Aston Martin	2720	112.5
2	Trintignant/Frère	Aston Martin	2684.5	112
3	Beurlys/Dernier	Ferrari	2487	103.5
4	Billet/Arents	Ferrari	2480	103.1
5	Grossman/Tavano	Ferrari	2462	102.5
6	Fayen/Munaron	Ferrari	2455	102
7	Whiteaway/Turner	AC-Bristol	2229	95.1
8	Lumsden/Riley	Lotus Elite	2225	94
9	Cotton/Cornet	DB	2465	90.1
10	Clark/Whitmost	Lotus Elite	2150	89.5
11	Consten/Armagnac	DB	2070	86.3
12	Bengston/Nottorp	Saab	1945	80
13	Lageneste/Guiraud	Stanguellini	1845	76.5

CLASS WINNERS

Class	Drivers	Car
3000-cc	Salvadori/Shelby	Aston Martin
2000-cc	Whiteaway/Turner	AC-Bristol
1500-cc	Lumsden/Riley	Lotus Elite
750-cc	Cotton/Cornet	DB

Index of Performance won by Cotton/Cornet in a DB.

One of the most famous tires in the world and, just beyond the king-sized champagne bottle, the pits.

1959 le Mans 24-hour race

'59 seems to be the year for all bogies of British cars to be broken. First the B.R.M. has won a grande épreuve and now, after nine years of strenuous effort and heart-breaking disappointments, Aston-Martins have won the greatest prize in sports car racing, if not in motor racing as a whole, the le Mans 24-hour race. To appreciate fully the significance of this result it is necessary to have attended le Mans for many years and to have seen high hopes constantly dashed, with the culmination last year when the Aston-Martin had proved its extreme reliability and was also the fastest car in the race by a comfortable margin.

For 1959, prospects looked nothing like so rosy for the David Brown équipe. The surprise win of Stirling Moss and Jack Fairman in the Nurburgring 1,000 km. race, where only one car was entered, looked promising but the two circuits could hardly be more different and le Mans gives much less scope for driving virtuosity than the wicked Ring. Three cars had been entered for le Mans, supported by the privately-owned, DBR.1 of Graham Whitehead, and the short-chassis DB.4 which appeared at Silverstone and was entered by the Swiss drivers, Patthey and Calderari of the Ecurie Trois Chevrons. Against the Aston-Martins were ranged a formidable assortment of Ferraris, headed by three works Testa Rossas to be driven by Behra/Gurney, Gendebien/Hill, Allison/da Silva Ramos, supported by the 2-litre car which went so quickly during earlier trials at le Mans driven by Cabianca and Scarlatti. Apart from the works cars there were no less than seven other cars of the marque entered by private owners. Other contenders for the distance prize were the Jaguar-engined machines: two Listers from Brian Lister, a D-type from the Ecurie Ecosse and a Tojeiro from the same stable. Although of considerably smaller capacity, the Porsches could not be ruled out for an outright win on past record. The index of performance looked likely to rest between Porsche, the two 742 c.c. Lotuses and the usual gaggle of D.B. Panhards. Supporting cast in the 55 possible runners was made up from a Cooper, three works Triumphs, an A.C., an M.G., three Lotus Elites, two Saabs, two OSCA's, two Stanguellinis and a Frazer-Nash.

Scrutineering took place on Monday and Tuesday, as is usual for this event, and the first practice session was on Wednesday evening. It was soon apparent that the works Testa Rossa Ferraris were the fastest vehicles in the race. Last year's winners, Gendebien and Hill, did not venture forth on Wednesday but da Silva Ramos and Gurney put in some fast laps, recording 4' 5.4" and 4' 8.7", a good ten seconds per lap faster than the average practice time achieved by these cars last year. Conversely, the Aston-Martins were slower than in 1958. Moss, Salvadori and Trintignant achieving, respectively, 4' 10.8", 4' 12" and 4' 14.8" as against best times of 4' 7.3", 4' 8.3" and 4' 11.1" for the cars last year. For Thursday's practice session Aston-Martin did not send out the Salvadori/Shelby car, partly because Salvadori was not feeling too well and also because both drivers knew the course and required no more than a brief refresher. Stirling Moss and Trintignant, with their co-drivers, did put in a few laps but were obviously not motoring with tremendous seriousness. The Ferrari team, on the other hand, were motoring as if there were grid positions at stake and Jean Behra got down to 4' 3.3", with team mates Hill and Allison at 4' 4.7" and 4' 3.6". In view of the fact that most of the Ferraris had been over-revved in practice on the previous day by as much as 1,100 r.p.m. it was a slightly bewildering performance. Nobody needed any convincing that they were extremely fast motorcars and the usefulness of the proceedings escaped us. Among the small contenders for the index of performance the two 750 Lotuses were comfortably faster than any of the D.B. Panhards, with best times of 5' 11.4"

and 5' 16.4" by Stacey and Taylor against 5' 18.1" by de Tomaso and 5' 18.9" by Masson in an 850-engined D.B.

As usual in recent years, there was no practice session on the Friday, allowing drivers to have a good rest before the race and mechanics to finish their preparations in peace. There was no doubt that Aston-Martins were disturbed by the great speed of the works Ferraris and laid their plans accordingly. Naturally the red cars could not be allowed to dictate the pace of the race entirely and it was equally obvious that if the Aston-Martin team attempted to keep up with them at a high race average their lives were likely to be short. The solution decided upon by Astons was to attempt to use Stirling Moss as a pace maker, giving the others a slow but steady schedule to adhere to. Reg Parnell, working on the basis that the race average was not likely to be considerably higher than 1958, set the time-table at an average lap speed of 4' 20".

The weather had been fine for a week before the 20th, although there were a few ominous drops on the evening of Friday, 19th. With last year's experience much in the minds of many, it was seen with real anguish on Saturday morning that the gods had opened the heavens once more and a steady downpour was descending from a leaden sky. As quickly as it arrived, however, the rain departed and by 4 o'clock in the afternoon the dust was rising in clouds from the footpaths and car parks around the circuit. Except for a few hesitant drops on Saturday evening, the weather remained fine for the whole of the race.

Usual fast start by Moss

As always, the time dragged interminably to the start, but eventually the cars were pushed into the position dictated by their engine capacity (a slight farce nowadays since the difference between the 20 fastest cars is only in terms of a c.c. or two), there was the inevitable tussle between an ambitious photographer and a policeman, then suddenly the flag was down and the drivers were scampering across the road to their cars. With lightning precision Stirling Moss was in his seat and moving up the road before this observer had seen any other car in motion. In the departing throng, Jean Behra was boxed in and the Lotus of Stacey and the Cooper of Brabham were both very slow away. Again a long, silent wait, and then one of the most exciting moments at le Mans (although why it should be in a 24-hour race is anyone's guess) to see which was the first car round.. Not surprisingly, since he already had a lead of 100 yards at the Dunlop bridge, Stirling Moss hove into view well ahead of the two Ferraris of Gendebien and Allison. On the second lap the order was Moss (Aston-Martin), Gendebien (Ferrari), Allison (Ferrari), Gregory (Jaguar D-type), Trintignant (Aston-Martin), Flockhart (Jaguar Tojeiro), Salvadori (Aston-Martin), Bueb (Lister-Jaguar), Hill (Lotus) and Whitehead (Aston-Martin). The third lap Moss did in 4' 12.5" and had pulled out on the Gendebien Ferrari. From the back, however, Behra was already starting to motor extremely quickly and moved up the field rapidly. Salvadori, mindful of his team orders, was holding himself in check even at this early stage and made no attempt to keep up with the flying leaders or with the cars of Graham Hill and Behra as they came past. Trintignant also kept a tight grip on himself, with the result that by lap 6 the two Aston-Martins were lying eighth and tenth, behind Moss, Gendebien, Allison, Behra, Gregory, Flockhart and Hill, with Bueb separating the two of them. Stirling Moss had now brought his lap times down to about 4' 8", to pull out a six second lead over Gendebien's Ferrari. Behra, however, was going faster still and closing quickly on his team mate Allison. On lap 10, indeed, Behra

The start that has given its name to motor racing—and the man with the remarkable aptitude at it already clear of the field! As Moss's car disappears it can be seen that No 12, Behra's Ferrari, has not even moved

Task nearing completion. The victorious Aston Martins lying first and second—although Frere is a lap behind Shelby—negotiate the Esses half an hour before the end of the race. Note the covering of the wheels

Disappointment and consolation. Stacey's Lotus, which had been leading comfortably on index before retiring, is passed by the Lotus Elite of Clark/Whitman which finished in 10th position

A tense moment in the pits shortly before mid-day on Sunday. The leading Ferrari was in trouble and mechanics worked feverishly to rectify it, eventually resorting to pouring a bucket of water over the fuel pump!

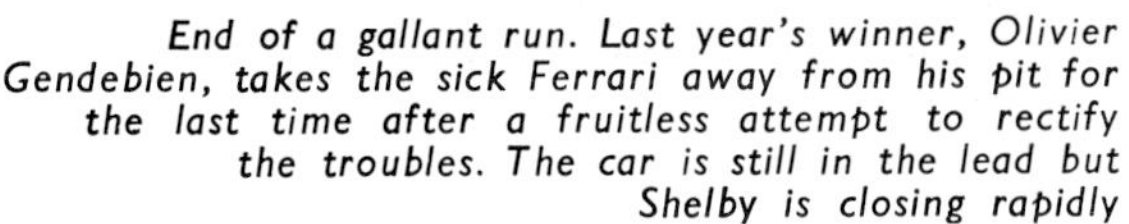

End of a gallant run. Last year's winner, Olivier Gendebien, takes the sick Ferrari away from his pit for the last time after a fruitless attempt to rectify the troubles. The car is still in the lead but Shelby is closing rapidly

circulated at 4′ 3·3″, which took him well past Allison and on to the heels of Gendebien. And so by the end of the first hour, at approximately 14 laps by the leader, the order was: Moss (Aston-Martin) six and a half seconds ahead of Gendebien (Ferrari), two and a half seconds ahead of Behra (Ferrari), who was in turn 21 seconds ahead of Allison (Ferrari). Behind came Gregory (Jaguar), Flockhart (Tojeiro), Hill (Lotus), Salvadori (Aston-Martin), Trintignant (Aston-Martin), Bueb (Lister-Jaguar), Hansgen (Lister-Jaguar), Whitehead (Aston-Martin), Cabianca (Ferrari), Bianchi (Ferrari), Herrmann (Porsche), Bonnier (Porsche), Russell (Cooper).

Behra takes the lead

Behra continued to go faster and faster and rapidly overhauled Moss, to pass him on the 17th lap setting up a new 3-litre course record at 4′ 3″, and passing the stands in the lead to frantic cheers from the French crowd who could not have been more excited if the race had been due to end on the next lap. Moss himself was completely unruffled and, having laid the bait for Ferrari, refused to be drawn in his turn and slowly dropped back. Further down the field the second Aston-Martin of Salvadori was slightly increasing its pace, the driver obviously being a little disturbed at the rate at which he was losing ground at this stage. There had already been a number of pit stops, including the Ferrari of Geithner and the M.G. of Lund which had had the misfortune to hit an Alsatian dog at the end of the Mulsanne straight, causing serious damage to the car and even more serious damage to the dog. The fast Lotus of Hill, complete with 2½-litre Climax engine, had been delayed for a number of laps in its pit but re-started on the 25th lap. Salvadori was, meanwhile, closing on Flockhart's Tojeiro and on Gregory's D-type, and on the 28th lap he passed both and took fifth position. At this stage the whole field had been lapped except for the first seven cars. It was the 29th lap and permissible to stop for fuel or other replenishments on the next appearance at the pits. The cracking pace had given Ferraris a few worries about fuel consumption and Behra came in at this earliest opportunity to let Stirling Moss in the Aston-Martin back into the lead once more. Moreover, not only did Behra come in but on the completion of their 30th lap both Gendebien and Allison brought their cars in, so that three Ferraris were stopped at the pits at the same moment. Not an altogether satisfactory situation! For two laps Aston-Martins were first and fourth, then Salvadori was called in for fuel and to hand over to Shelby, the car dropping well back in the process. For the next ten laps or so there was general chaos as car after car came in at the pits and re-started, having lost a number of places. Aston-Martins had a fair amount of tank space in hand, for Moss carried on to complete 37 laps before refuelling and handing over to Jack Fairman. By the time all the stops were completed the order had resolved itself, at the end of the third hour, to Gurney, driving Behra's Ferrari at only a very slightly abated pace, now well ahead of Fairman in Moss's Aston-Martin, who was lapping considerably slower than the young maestro, followed by Hill in Gendebien's Ferrari, then Innes Ireland in the surprisingly swift D-type Jaguar of the Ecurie Ecosse. These four cars were a lap ahead of the Aston-Martins of Shelby and Frere who were running in company with Lawrence in the Tojeiro and de Changy in the Belgian Ferrari.

Now came the first major casualty when the Ferrari of Allison and da Silva Ramos, which had been at its pit for a lap or two, was wheeled solemnly away to the dead car park. First blood in the Ferrari/Aston-Martin contest had therefore gone to the green cars. In the index of performance the Birtish star was nicely in the ascendant, with the Stacey Lotus comfortably ahead and destined to make its advantage better and better until its eventual retirement.

Not long before 9 o'clock, with nearly five hours of the race run, Jack Fairman came in to hand over once more to Stirling Moss with the Aston-Martin No. 4 still in second position, behind the Ferrari of Jean Behra. Scarcely had Moss taken over than the car was back at the pits again with serious trouble. It appeared that it was valve failure at first but subsequent investigation indicated that some foreign body (possibly and logically part of the Italian Weber carburettor!) had caused the trouble. There was nothing that could be done and gallant No. 4's race was run. At 9 o'clock, therefore, with the Aston newly stopped, the order was: first Behra (Ferrari), second Gregory (Jaguar), third Moss (Aston-Martin), fourth Salvadori (Aston-Martin) two laps behind the leader, fifth Bueb (Lister-Jaguar), sixth Flockhart (Tojeiro), seventh Trintignant (Aston-Martin), eighth Gendebien (Ferrari) who had been having some electrical trouble necessitating two quick pit stops; ninth, and appearing as it were on the leader board for the first time and in sinisterly similar fashion to years before, came the Porsche of Herrmann and Maglioli, tenth a further Porsche of Bonnier and von Trips. The casualties were already fairly considerable, with Brian Naylor having spun the Whitehead-entered Aston-Martin on some oil at White House, damaging the car and being unable to continue. Shortly afterwards Russell's Cooper and a Stanguellini were involved with the crashed Aston-Martin and caught fire. The Stanguellini driver escaped injury but Russell was taken to the local clinic with burns, bruises and some broken ribs. His condition was not serious. A few drops of rain began to fall, then decided better of it, and slowly darkness descended, while in the village behind the pits and at the fairground in the Esses the sideshows changed into top gear. The race was now a third run and was a Ferrari/Aston-Martin/Jaguar struggle as it has been so many times in the past. On the index of performance the Lotus of Stacey was still convincingly in the lead and pulling steadily further ahead.

Now came the long night watches when it was particularly difficult to keep track of the cars' positions owing to the trouble of indentifying them as they flashcd past the pits. Further refuelling stops served to confuse the situation yet again, but it could be seen that the D-type Jaguar of Gregory and Ireland was in mechanical difficulties and before very long it was wheeled away. Not very long afterwards the leading Ferrari of Behra and Gurney had gone too, with all the symptoms of a motorcar which had been pressed beyond endurance. With under half the distance of the race completed, the field was greatly thinned out and had left the Aston-Martin of Roy Salvadori and Caroll Shelby two laps in the lead, with the sole surviving works Ferrari of Hill and Gendebien motoring extremely swiftly in an endeavour to catch up time lost in the pit. Although up to this stage the Jaguar-engined cars had performed extremely well, the retirement of the sole D-type was the signal for troubles to visit the other Jaguar-powered entrants. The Hansgen-Blond Jaguar had thrown a con-rod some time previously; now the Tojeiro of Flockhart and the Lister of Bueb both retired with similar mechanical defects.

Thus well before half the race had been run the Salvadori Aston-Martin was leading the Gendebien Ferrari by just over a lap, with a further Aston-Martin of Trintignant in third position, then the two Porsches of Bonnier and von Trips and de Beaufort and Heins following up. Suddenly Salvadori was coming into his pit for an unscheduled stop, to complain of violent body vibrations. A quick check of the suspension and the transmission indicated nothing amiss and he was pushed back into the race again. On the next lap he took nearly six minutes and even the pit staff could see the car shaking as it went towards the Dunlop bridge. Next lap he was in again and further checks revealed nothing amiss with the car. Just as they were about to send it back into the race once more a mechanic noticed that about 18 inches of tread had stripped from one of the tyres and had not been noticed in all the excitement and with the newly-introduced cowling over the wheels. Salvadori had driven for seven laps on canvas! The slow laps and the two pit stops had let the Ferrari back into the lead once more with the Astons lying second and third. A certain weakening in the braking of the Astons had also been expected and during the course of the long night each car had a change of brake pads, accomplished in approximately five minutes.

And so it was that as the crowds drifted back to the circuit after breakfast the sole surviving works Ferrari had pulled out a 2½-lap lead over the leading Aston-Martin. At almost the same time, the two Porsches, lying third and fourth, driven by Bonnier/von Trips and Barth/von Hanstein both went out with mechanical troubles. By 10 o'clock of a fine Sunday morning, with three quarters of the race completed, the order was: Genedbien (Ferrari) 249 laps, Salvadori (Aston-Martin) 246 laps, Trintignant (Aston-Martin) 245 laps, Hughus and Erickson (Porsche) 228 laps, Elde (Ferrari) 225 laps, Hudson (Ferrari) 222 laps, Grossman (Ferrari) 220 laps, Fayen (Ferrari) 219 laps, Kerguen (Porsche) 217 laps, and Jopp (Triumph) 211 laps. Jopp's car was the last of the works team of Triumph—the other two having suffered from overheating caused by the fan blades cutting the radiator. As a desperate measure, the fan was removed from Jopp's car and he proceeded perfectly satisfactorily through the cooler hours of the morning and only came to grief with the heat of the sun during Sunday. Lund's M.G. was struggling gallantly on in 16th position, after stopping at Arnage for a long time, getting back to its pit to effect reparations and then stopping in nearly the same spot on the following lap. A model of consistency was the A.C. of Whiteaway and Turner which had run without pause, except for refuelling and change of drivers and now occupied 11th position, shortly to take the lead in its class with the retirement of the Triumph.

Exit the last Porsche

Just after 10 o'clock more bad luck struck the Porsche team when, again almost at the same time, their two remaining cars both retired when holding fourth and ninth positions. Their strong challenge of six cars had, therefore, come to nothing. It seemed to us that in this 1959 race, for the first time, Porsche had set their sights at winning the race rather than merely finishing. They therefore maintained a lap speed slightly beyond the capabilities of their cars for such a long period and suffered accordingly. In such a way does consistent success occasionally breed failure.

The race pattern now seemed to be set and there was little likelihood that the Aston-Martins would be able to speed up sufficiently at this juncture to even press the crisp-sounding Ferrari. However, the Italian car had not changed brake pads and even if this did not prove an absolute necessity it was at least reasonable to assume that its braking would be somewhat impaired over the last few hours. Yet it was lapping slightly faster than the Aston-Martin, at this time being driven by Shelby, consistently building its lead with approximately three seconds a lap, so that shortly after 11 o'clock it was nearly three laps ahead, and stop watches were being trained to see whether the Aston-Martin would fight off the Ferrari as it came into the rear view mirror. Strangely enough, on the next lap, the Aston had opened up a bigger gap without increasing its speed appreciably. On the following lap the Ferrari appeared well behind the green car with its lights blazing as it rounded White House Corner. A few seconds later it was in the pits with a hasty investigation afoot to discover the cause of a sudden loss of oil pressure. That something radical was wrong was soon apparent, although the car re-started after two minutes. Two laps more and it was in again for a further investigation, but was once again pushed back into the race—but to motor extremely slowly indeed. Great excitement was caused at this stage by the English announcer giving out that the Aston-Martin was now in the lead but, in fact, it was still two laps behind. The Ferrari was going so slowly, however, that very shortly Shelby was closing to come on to the same lap. This seemed to sting Gendebien into a faster speed which was fatal to the ailing red car. Next lap he was in and had retired with an official explanation of "fuel starvation" although it might have seemed significant that the car had been consistently topped up with water all through the night and had all the symptoms of serious overheating.

Now everything in the garden was lovely and British enthusiasts merely waited the four-and-a-half hours to the finish with crossed fingers. With all opposition suddenly departed, the Astons slowed to such a pace that their team manager was hear to mutter darkly that Salvadori would get sunstroke along the Mulsanne Straight. However, under the circumstances, it was obviously the correct procedure, even though it meant that the outright distance for the race was not improved over 1958. It also forfeited any possibility of the Aston-Martins winning the index of performance.

And so the 24-hour race of le Mans for 1959 ran out. Out of 53 starters there were only 13 cars still mobile at the end of the 24 hours. The two leading Aston-Martins and the gaggle of four privately-entered Ferraris continued to circulate smoothly until the end. Whiteaway and Turner's A.C. never missed a beat throughout the race and the Lotus Elites sounded as crisp as when they started. Moreover, the last three cars mentioned were among the few that were still pressing on with unabated velocity right up to 4 o'clock. Despite a pushed-in tail, sustained during the night watches, the D.B. Panhard of Cornet and Cotton had no trouble in sustaining its lead in the index of performance, ahead of the Aston-Martins.

The delight with which the Aston-Martin victory was finally acclaimed showed that the French crowd appreciated the reward for long years of unflagging effort. A 24-hour race always seems to prove something and it is dangerously easy to over-simplify the situation. This year's race, however, did seem to be a triumph of strategy over speed. Experts estimated the safe lap speed for the Testa Rossa Ferrari at approximately 4' 8". This compared with a safe lap speed for the Aston-Martin of perhaps 4' 12", but probably, more safely, 4' 15". At the worst, therefore, the Ferraris could bank on four seconds per lap faster average for the race, all other things being equal —and when calculating strategy for such a race one must assume this. The Ferraris could therefore bank on gaining approximately one minute per hour, or 24 minutes over the course of the whole race. This would have been a lead of five or six laps. That Behra succumbed to the temptation to show what the Ferrari could do against Moss is obvious enough. In all probability the seeds of later mechanical bothers were sown in the other two Ferraris at this early stage of the race when they were trying to keep the leading Aston-Martin in their sight. Indeed, no less a personage than Paul Frere said handsomely after the race that the real architect of victory was Stirling Moss, who was able to find something like five seconds per lap over the estimated best speed of the Astons by sheer virtuosity of driving. That this can be done on the Nurburgring Paul Frere concedes, but professes it a mystery where these seconds can be saved at le Mans!

Great credit must go to Roy Salvadori for his level-headed driving during the early part of the race and, indeed, for his lion's share (he drove 14 of the 24 hours) of the work when he was still throwing off the traces of a bout of 'flu. This is by far his greatest victory in motor racing and an honour which he richly deserves. During the last two years his driving has achieved a maturity, a consistency, a versatility and a resilience which is second only to Stirling Moss himself. Except for Moss there is no other driver today who is equally brilliant from the bowl of Brand's Hatch to the straights of Le Mans, whether engaged in the cut-and-thrust of a British Formula Two race or driving with his head rather than his heart, to outlast the opposition in a long-distance sports car event. Le Mans has not in the past been the happiest place for the cream of the world's drivers and it is doubly pleasant and significant, therefore, to salute Salvadori on this occasion.

LE MANS—24-hour race.

RESULTS:

1. Salvadori/Shelby*, Aston-Martin, 324 laps, 24: 5' 0·4" 2. Trintignant/Frere, Aston-Martin, 323 laps, 24: 3' 41·8". 3. Burgess/Elde, Ferrari, 298 laps, 24: 3' 40·5". 4. Hudson/Arentz, Ferrari, 297 laps, 24: 2' 25·4". 5. Grossman/F. Tavano, Ferrari, 295 laps, 24: 2' 25·4". 6. Fayen/Munaron, Ferrari, 294 laps, 24: 0' 55·7". 7. Whiteway/Turner*, A.C., 274 laps, 24: 1' 48·1". 8. Lumsden/Riley*, Lotus Elite, 271 laps, 24: 5' 2·1". 9. Cornet/Cotton†, D. B. Panhard, 259 laps, 24: 0' 23·1". 10. Clark/Whitman, Lotus Elite, 258 laps, 24: 5' 3·0". 11. Consten/Armagnac, D. B. Panhard. 12. Nottorp/Bengston, Saab, 13. de la Geneste/Guiraud, Stanguellini.

    *Class winners.

    †Winner on index of performance.

24-HOUR

LE MANS HAS GIVEN ITS NAME TO ANY RUNNING START, AND A FEW DRIVERS HAVE DEVELOPED THE TECHNIQUE TO A HIGH ART.

53 cars start, 13 finish . . . Favorites FERRARI and PORSCHE drop out . . . ASTON-MARTINS take 1-2 for first time . . . Sportscar prototypes predict things to come . . .

SOLID TEAM DISCIPLINE, sound tactics and the brilliance of Stirling Moss (who set a car-breaking pace which lured the Ferraris to destruction in the first three hours)—these were the essential elements that gave Aston Martin a 1-2 victory at Le Mans after 10 years of trying. Ferrari, who had much faster cars and started as hot favorites, seemed to have no coherent strategy. Not a single works car finished, and only the private owners who brought ordinary Gran Turismo models into 3rd, 4th, 5th and 6th places saved the honor of Maranello.

Le Mans still divides itself into two separate events: the unofficial Grand Prix which ends around midnight when most of the sprinters have worn their cars out; and, the real endurance event which is then fought out among the survivors.

The figures speak volumes: 53 cars started and 13 finished. But of the sportscars, including the "prototypes," 32 started and only three finished (nine per cent) while of the Gran Turismo cars in the true Le Mans tradition, 21 started and 10 finished (48 per cent).

Not a single Porsche finished the race, and not a single Jaguar-engined car. The new ohc Triumphs kept up a good pace but two were eliminated by fan blades going through the header tanks. The fan blades were then removed from the third car, which led the two-liter class until three hours' from the finish, when its bearings failed. That is what Le Mans is for, and the production models will be all the better for it.

The little 750 Lotus looked a likely winner of both Performance Index and the new fuel economy category but both cars dropped out with engine failure, leaving the D.B. Panhards to pick up the rich prizes in both categories. Two of the three Lotus Elites put on a fine show. Trimmed and finished as though for a holiday trip, they were first and second in their class and second in the fuel economy event, while a two-year-old, privately-owned A.C. won the two-liter class.

Some very interesting figures emerged from the new fuel consumption category, which takes into account fuel consumption and car weight. Up to half time, the little 750cc Lotus had averaged 22 miles per gallon at an average speed of 87.3 mph. The best Porsche was averaging 12.1 mpg at 105.6 mph, while the Saab GT coupe was using fuel at the same rate of 12.1 mpg at an average 80 mph. —**Gordon Wilkins**

The Bartholoni-Jaeger D. B. tried to restart after a long pit stop to qualify as finisher: died out on first corner.

ENDURANCE RUN

STIRLING MOSS ALWAYS SPRINTS TO HIS CAR LIKE HE'S SHOT FROM A CANNON, GAINS PRECIOUS SECONDS ON EVERY START.

Above: Sunday morning victory. Aston concentrated on perfect preparation; attention to streamlining gave 10 additional mph on long Mulsanne straight. Right: Winning car had double overhead cams, three twin-throat Weber carburetors, cold air box, twin ignition.

Above and right: Triumph entered new TR-3S with double-overhead-cam light-alloy engine, pulled 150 bhp from two-liter displacement. Windscreen encloses all but top of cockpit, body is plastic; disc brakes were fitted all around for Le Mans. Side air intakes duct air to differential. Carburetion is by two siamesed SUs.

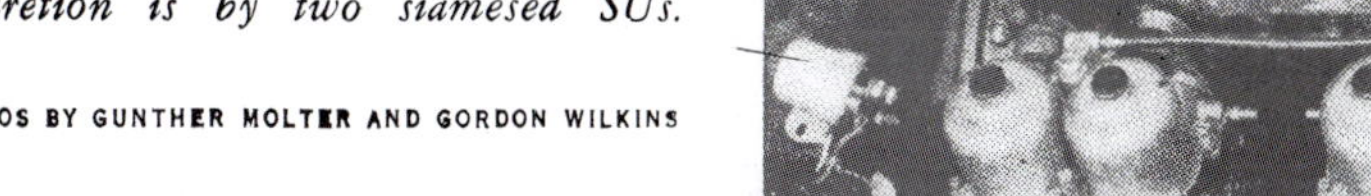

PHOTOS BY GUNTHER MOLTER AND GORDON WILKINS

IT was Aston Martin's day at Le Mans when Roy Salvadori and Carroll Shelby won the Grand Prix d'Endurance at an average speed of 112.57 m.p.h., followed by the similar car of Maurice Trintignant and Paul Frere. Of the 53 starters only 13 were running at the end, and five of those were British.

Scuderia Ferrari's onslaught failed, when all three of the very rapid 3-litre cars failed to stay the course. This was in many ways due to the opening "grand prix" when Stirling Moss set a much hotter pace than the Italians had envisaged. Not a single Porsche managed to reach the finish and a couple of Lotus Elites finished one-two in the 1300 c.c. class—and were also runners-up to the Index winning D.B. Panhard 'in the "Indice Energetique—a fuel consumption race. A really fine effort was that of the Rudd Racing Stable's A.C.-Bristol, which was not only the sole finisher in the 2-litre category, but was seventh in general classification.

Astons Do It At Last!

Superb One-Two Victory for Feltham at Le Mans

by GREGOR GRANT. **Photography by GEORGE PHILLIPS.**

Ferrari dominated Wednesday's practice, da Silva Ramos doing best time with 4m.08.7s. The Walt Hansgen/Peter Blond Lister-Jaguar returned 4m.12.2s. Stirling Moss's best with the Asotn Martin was 4m.10.8s.

Graham Hill did 4m.20s. with the 2-litre Lotus Climax, in which Colin Chapman had decided to install the 2½-litre engine. Ecurie Ecosse's Tojeiro-Jaguar broke part of its Dion tube. Spare bits were available near Namur, Belgium, where the Scottish team's trans-porter had broken down on its way from Nurburgring. Early next day, Ron Flockhart took off in his Auster with John Tojeiro and an Ecosse mechanic, and brought the required spares back.

The Dick Stoop Lotus Elite, to be driven by Doug Graham and Mike McKee was wrecked in an accident returning from the circuit, Jack Britt the mechanic being injured.

With the non-appearance of the Conrero Alfa Romeos, all reserves were called in, including the veteran Frazer-Nash of Dashwood and Wilks. The de Tomaso 750 c.c. Osca was sold to the Rodriguez brothers, so de Tomaso and Colin Davies were in a D.B. Panhard.

Ferrari again made best times on Thursday, Dan Gurney doing 4m.03.3s. (199.176 k.p.h.). Behra, in the same car achieved 4m.03.6s. Gendebien did 4m.5s., whilst Masten Gregory whistled Ecurie Ecosse's D-type Jaguar round to the tune of 4m.9.7s., and Innes Ireland was fractionally slower.

A shock for Ferrari and their 2-litre car was the 4m.13.6s. of the 2-litre Cooper-Monaco-Climax driven by Jim Russell—a car with phenomenal cornering power.

The new twin o.h.c. Triumphs sounded healthy, Ninian Sanderson being quickest of the team with 4m.49.8s. Fastest Porsche was the 1½-litre of de Beaufort with 4m.20.6s. Graham Whitehead's Aston Martin broke its crankshaft, and a spare was flown from England. However, it was not suitable; luckily, Astons had a spare engine, which was installed on Friday.

Saturday dawned dull, but with the promise of sunshine later. An hour or so before the start, it was stiflingly hot, with thunderstorms in the air. Enormous crowds were all round the circuit, and the tribunes were packed to capacity.

As the hands of the clock crept towards 4 p.m., that strange silence fell on the crowd. Down went the flag, and the race was on. Stirling Moss was first

away, followed by Ron Flockhart, Trintignant, Innes Ireland, Patthey (DB4) Bueb Salvadori and da Silver Ramos. Poor Russell lost over 50 secs. trying to start the Cooper. Eventually the 53 starters all got away.

The crowd chattered noisily waiting till the first car would re-appear. Yes, it was a green car in front! Down from Maison Blanche swept Moss, closely followed by the red Ferraris of Gendebien and da Silver Ramos, then Innes Ireland (D-type), Trintignant (Aston Martin), Flockhart (Tojeiro), Bueb (Lister), Graham Hill (Lotus), Salvadori (Aston Martin) and Graham Whitehead (Aston Martin), with Hansgen (Lister) and Scarlatti (2-litre Ferrari) close behind, followed by Bianchi (Ferrari) and de Beaufort (Porsche). Russell steamed through at a tremendous pace, having passed no less than 24 cars.

It was Moss versus the Ferraris with a vengeance, with Ireland of Scotland in 4th place. On lap 2, Behra was in 12th spot, whilst Russell had moved up 4 more places. Moss increased his lead to 4 secs., and Behra advanced to 10th place. Behind Gendebien and da Silva Ramos, Ireland ,Trintignant, and Flockhart were in close company, as were Bueb and G. Hill. Sanderson and Bolton

ALL PRESENT (above) the Ferrari team lines up for scrutineering. ABOUT to overtake Bolton's TR3S (below) is Olivier Gendebien (Ferrari).

a severe blow to Chapman's hopes. Meanwhile Behra continued to close the gap btween himself and the leading Aston. Behind the Ferraris, the Ecurie Ecosse pair circulated steadily, ahead of Salvadori's Aston Martin.

The Escott/Lund M.G. "Twin Cam" was called in by officials for some reason. The Ginther/Carveth Ferrari spent some time in the pits, as did the Swiss-entered Aston Martin coupe of Patthey and Calderari. Minutes ticked on, and still the Lotus remained stationary. At 5.47 p.m. Hill re-started. The trouble was a loose propeller shaft support bearing.

Now the time to re-fuel and change drivers was approaching.

Moss increased his lead to 6 secs., the two Ferraris keeping station behind. Ireland seemed firmly set in 4th place, but Behra was coming through very fast after taking Flockhart, Hill and Trintignant.

The weather dulled, and the fast men were using their headlamps to warn the slower machinery. Salvadori was closing rapidly on Bueb and Trintignant.

With one hour gone, there was the almost unprecedented position of no re-

led the Triumphs, the cars going remarkably well. The Taylor/Sieff "750" Lotus-Climax spent some time in the pits, and was followed later by the Border Reivers Lotus Elite of Clark and Whitmore.

Ferrari put on the pressure, but Stirling still stayed in front. Behra was steadily closing up, whilst Graham Hill had come up pto dispute the issue with Ireland and Flockhart. The Scarlatti/Cabianca Ferrari led the 2-litre brigade by a sizeable margin, with Hermann (Porsche 1600) and Russell (Cooper) fighting it out. De Beaufort's Porsche led the "1500s".

Just after 5.30, the fast Lotus-Climax of Graham Hill came into the pits—

FAST FRENCHMAN. Jean Behra swings the works Ferrari that he shared with Dan Gurney through Tertre Rouge.

ASTONS BOTH. (top) Stirling, in the lead, passes the DB4 at Maison Blanche. BRUCE McLAREN (centre) leaps into the very fast Cooper-Monaco, Jim Russell having relinquished the wheel. ALAN STACEY (below) accelerates the very fast 750 c.c. Lotus out of Tertre Rouge.

tirements. The race order was:
1. Moss (Aston Martin)
2. Gendebien (Ferrari)
3. Behra (Ferrari)
4. Ramos (Ferrari)
5. Ireland (Jaguar)
6. Flockhart (Tojeiro)
7. Hill (Lotus-Climax)
8. Salvadori (Aston Martin)
9. Trintignant (Aston Martin)
10. Bueb (Lister)
11. Whitehead (Aston Martin)
12. Hansgen (Lister).

Behra advanced to second place, returning a shattering 4m.3s. lap (199.342 k.ph..)—a new 3-litre record. The Frenchman was definitely catching Moss, and how the crowd roared when the two cars came through together: they went mad when the PA excitedly announced that Behra had taken the lead at Mulsanne.

Rain was threatening: if it did come down, then Stirling would soon be back in command. On dry roads the Ferrari began to draw away. Behra flashed round in 41.m.1.9s. to do the first ever 200 k.p.h. lap with a 3-litre car. The question now was, "Would Gendebien also take the Aston Martin?"

Just on 6 p.m. Salvadori went into 5th place, ahead of the Ecosse cars. At 6.4 p.m. Behra stopped to re-fuel, and the Ferrari pit was a trifle chaotic when both Gendebien and Ramos came in. This of course put Moss back into the lead. He came through with 81.5 secs. advantage over Dan Gurney who had taken over from Behra. Then came Phil Hill, Innes Ireland, Salvadori and Lawrence who had replaced Flockhart.

Salvadori came in at 6.23 p.m., and handed over to Carroll Shelby. He was then in 4th place. Moss went on non-stop, but 10 minutes later preparations were being made for his pit-stop, and Fairman put on his crash-hat. Rain was now spattering, but the roads still remained dry. Moss had increased his lead to over 1½ minutes. At 6.36 p.m. he came in for a stop which cost just 1m. 8secs. Fairman set off still in front, but next time round Dan Gurney had seized the lead.

With almost 3 hours of racing, there were only three retirements. The position now was:

1. Behra/Gurney (Maserati)	43 laps	2h.58m.48 3s.
2. Moss/Fairman (Aston)	43 laps	2h.59m.30 0s.
3. Gendebien/Hill (Ferrari)	42 laps	
4. Gregory/Ireland (Jaguar)	24 laps	
5. Salvadori/Shelby (Aston)	42 laps	
6. Flockhart/Lawrence (Tojeiro)	42 laps	
7. Allison/Ramos (Ferrari)	41 laps	
8. Trintignant/Frere (Aston)	41 laps	
9. Bueb/Halford (Lister)	41 laps	
10. Whitehead/Naylor (Aston)	41 laps	
11. Hansgen/Blond (Lister)	41 laps	
12. Herrman/Maglioli (Porsche)	40 laps	

After the 4th hour, 10 cars had been abandoned. Brian Naylor turned over with the Whitehead Aston Martin at Maison Blanche, and was taken to hospital with arm injuries. The Hansgen/Blond Lister blew up. Dashwood's Frazer-Nash, the Bianchi/de Changy Ferrari, and the Bolton/Rothschild Triumph were wheeled to the dead park.

At 9 p.m. the order was:

1. Behra/Gurney (Ferrari) 71 laps
2. Gregory/Ireland (Jaguar) 70 laps
3. Moss/Fairman (Aston-Martin) 70 laps
4. Salvadori/Shelby (Aston) 69 laps
5. Bueb/Halford (Lister) 69 laps
6. Flockhart/Lawrence (Tojeiro) 69 laps

The Herrman/Maglioli Porsche "1600", in 9th place headed the 2-litre class, followed by Bonnier/Von Trips Porsche "1600" and the Russell/McLaren Cooper. The "1500s" were led by de Beaufort's Porsche, the Lumsden/Riley Elite headed the "1300s", and the smaller cars were led by the Stacey/Greene Lotus "750".

Fairman, who had 55 secs. lead over the Behra/Gurney car stopped with falling oil pressure, but continued for 3 more laps and then Moss took over. The gremlins immediately swarmed over the Aston-Martin as parts of the air-intake broke up and were swallowed up by the engine. This put the Ecurie-Ecosse D-type into second place.

Fortunately the rain held off, and when darkness fell it was almost perfect motor-racing weather.

Then, just before 10 p.m., sheets of flame shot up near Maison Blanche. The Faure/Guyot Stanguellini crashed, as did the Russell/McLaren Cooper: the wrecked Whitehead/Naylor Aston Martin burst into flames, and both the Stanguellini and the Cooper caught fire. Phillipe Faure and Jim Russell were taken to hospital with superficial injuries.

Not long afterwards the Ecurie Ecosse D-type Jaguar was withdrawn with valve troubles, and the Salvadori/Shelby Aston-Martin moved up to second place behind the Behra/Gurney (Ferrari).

With 6 hours of racing completed the Ferrari led the Aston Martin by 1 lap, with the Bueb/Halford Lister third, and the Gendebien/Hill Ferrari fourth. Not far behind were the Trintignant/Frere Aston Martin and the Flockhart/Lawrence Tojeiro. The Index of Performance was headed by the Stacey/Greene Lotus, closely followed by the Herrman/Von Trips Porsche.

So at 10 p.m., 17 cars had been abandoned, including the fast 2-litre Scarlatti/Cabianca Ferrari which had suffered engine maladies. Index challenger, the Herrman/Maglioli Porsche went out with valve failure.

Not long afterwards, the Behra/Gurney Ferrari stopped at the pits, and the Salvadori/Shelby Aston Martin took the lead. It was now Aston Martin, Ferrari, Ferrari, Lister - Jaguar, Aston Martin, Tojeiro.

The Hermann/Maglioli Porsche 1600

FLYING SCOT. (top) Ron Flockhart, lying sixth in the Ecurie Ecorse Tojeiro-Jaguar, leads Graham Hill (2.5 Lotus) into Tertre Rouge. DOWN to the Esses (centre) go Trintignant (DBR1), Ed Martin (Ferrari) and Ivor Bueb Lister-Jaguar). THIRD car home (below). The Beurlys/Helde Ferrari at Mulsanne.

CLASS-WINNER. The Whiteaway/ Turner A.C.-Bristol leads the de Tomaso/Davis D.B.-Panhard at Arnage.

in eighth place went out with valve trouble. It had taken the lead on Index, now headed by the Stacey/Greene Lotus "750". The Rodriguez brothers abandoned their rear-engined Osca with a fractured oil-pipe. At midnight the Salvadori/Shelby Aston Martin led the Ferraris of Gendebien/Hill and Behra/Gurney, the last-named losing time with electrical bothers. The Bonnier/Von Trips Porsche took the lead in Index from the Lotus. There were now 22 retirements.

The Behra/Gurney Ferrari, which had been stopped by the officials for faulty lights, developed a radiator leak and was abandoned after 129 laps.

During the night the Salvadori/ Shelby Aston Martin spent some time in the pits with vibration trouble, and dropped well behind the Ferrari.

At half-distance (4 a.m.) the position was:

RESULTS

1, **Roy Salvadori**/Carroll Shelby **(Aston Martin DBR1)** 4,347.900 kilometres, 112.57 m.p.h.; 2, Maurice Trintignant/Paul Frere **(Aston Martin DBR1)** 4,337.559 kilometres; 3, Beurlys/Helde (Ferrari) 4,001.601 kilometres; 4, Pilette/Arents (Ferrari) 3,991.447 kilometres; 5, Grossmann/ Tavano (Ferrari); 6, Fayen/Munaron (Ferrari); 7, **Ted Whiteaway/Jack Turner (A.C.-Bristol)**; 8, **Petter Lumsden/Peter Riley (Lotus) Elite)**; 9, Cornet/Cotton (D.B. Panhard); 10, **Jim Clarke/J. H. D. Whitmore (Lotus Elite)**; 11, Consten/Armagnac (D.B. Panhard); 12, Nottorp/Bengtsson (Saab); 13, Langeste/Guiraud (Stanguellini).

Index of Performance:

1, Cornet/Cotton (D.B. Panhard) 1.210; 2, **Roy Salvadori**/Carroll Shelby **(Aston Martin)** 1.181; 3, Maurice Trintignant/Paul Frere **(Aston Martin)** 1.178; 4, Consten/Armagnac (D.B. Panhard); 5, **Peter Lumsden/Peter Riley (Lotus Elite)**.

MAURICE TRINTIGNANT (above) moves out to overtake Ted Lund (M.G.A.) at Maison Blanche. FLEET ELITE (right). The Lumsden/Riley Lotus leads the Gendebien/Hill Ferrari at Mulsanne.

1. Gendebien/Hill (Ferrari)	166 laps
2. Salvadori/Shelby (Aston)	164 laps
3. Trintignant/Frere (Aston)	162 laps
4. Bonnier/Von Trips (Porsche)	159 laps
5. de Beaufort/Heinz (Porsche)	159 laps
6. Barth/Seidel (Porsche)	152 laps
7. Hugus/Ericson (Porsche)	151 laps
8. Beurlys/Helde (Ferrari)	150 laps
9. Pilette/Arents (Ferrari)	147 laps
10. Crossman/Tavano (Ferrari)	145 laps
11. Fayen/Munaron (Ferrari)	144 laps
12. Kerguen/La Caze (Porsche)	143 laps
13. Jopp/Stoop (TR3S)	139 laps
14. Whiteway/Turner (A.C.-Br.)	138 laps
15. Lumsden/Riley (Elite)	135 laps

The weather remained dry. At 3.04 a.m. the Ecurie Ecosse Tojeiro was retired with valve failure; earlier the Bueb/Halford Lister had been abandoned, so there were no Jaguar-powered cars left in the race.

New C.S.I. regulations were introduced from I January 1960 which also applied to the Le Mans race. These were the Appendix C covering sports cars up to three litres, and Appendix J for Group 3 Grand Touring Cars of unlimited capacity. Some of the new regulations were aimed at making the sports cars more 'realistic' - such as the 10 inch depth of screen and the requirement for luggage space - and with the new regulations came a new set of sub-divisions. No longer did the time honoured Classes A to J apply, instead there were 15 new capacity classes, of which class 15 was unlimited above 5,000 cc; going down the scale, 14 was up to 5,000 cc, 13 to 4,000 cc, 12 to 3,000 cc, 11 to 2,500 cc, 10 to 2,000 cc, 9 to 1,600 cc, 8 to 1,300 cc, 7 to 1,150 cc, 6 to 1,000 cc, 5 from 701 to 850 cc. Smaller cars were not seen at Le Mans after 1960, indeed already in 1960 the smallest permitted GT entries were class 7 cars.

Of 55 starting cars, 37 were sports cars and 18 GT cars. Ferrari, as usual, fielded the largest entry - five Testa Rossa sports cars, together with six 250 GT models, all with three-litre engines.

The only other makes to cover both classes were Austin-Healey, with a 996 cc Sprite in the sports car class and a 3,000 GT car; and Alfa Romeo with a Conrero modified 1,147 cc Giulietta sports car and a 1,290 cc SZ GT car. The GT class also attracted two Bristol engined ACs and four Lotus Elites. Rather more unusual was the entry of four Chevrolet Corvettes by Briggs Cunningham and the Camoradi racing team. With massive 4.6 litre V8 engines they were in the GT class.

The sports car - for which one might substitute 'sports prototype' class was better supported. There were two Aston Martin DBR 1/300s, an Ecurie Ecosse entered Jaguar D-type, but more interestingly a Cunningham entered E-type prototype which put in the fastest practice lap. Maserati made a return to Le Mans, with three Tipo 61 models - the notorious 'Birdcage' - which were all entered by the Camoradi team. This completed the three-litre class; there were no 2½ litre cars, and the two-litre class contained two Porsches, three Triumph TRSs, a single Lola and the MGA Twin-Cam which had been entered in 1959 and which now had an engine of 1,762 cc. The 1,600 cc class was a Porsche preserve with four entries. Next, in descending order came three DB-Panhards with 851 cc engines which just put them in the 1,000 cc class: and in the smallest class there were another two DBs, three Fiat based Abarths, two Oscas and a Stanguellini. Abarth, Lola and Chevrolet were all newcomers to Le Mans.

The first car to take the lead was a Maserati Birdcage, driven by Masten Gregory; he was followed by five Ferraris, with the Jaguar D-type in seventh place. While two of the pursuing Ferraris ran out of fuel on the circuit (there was no minimum distance to be covered between fuel stops with the new regulations and presumably the Ferrari team had just miscalculated the cars' consumption), the Maserati gradually fell back permitting the Ferrari Testa Rossa of Paul Frere and Olivier Gendebien to take the lead. There it stayed for the rest of the race, almost equalling the performance of Gonzales and Trintignant in the Ferrari when they led the 1954 race from start to finish. The 1960 race was marked by the lack of effective competition for the Ferraris; the new Jaguar E2A driven by Dan Gurney and Walter Hansgen did not live up to its practice record and was well down the field until it eventually retired, and the D-type broke its crankshaft. Only the Aston Martin driven by Roy Salvadori and Jim Clark kept pace with the Ferraris and in the end finished third after the winning car of Frere/Gendebien and the number two Ferrari driven by Pilette/Rodriguez. Fourth, fifth, sixth and seventh places were all occupied by Ferrari 250 GTs which were followed home by a Chevrolet Corvette and the Baillie/Fairman Aston Martin.

Frere and Gendebien had covered 2,620,644 miles at an average speed of 109.193 mph: fastest lap, however, had been made by Masten Gregory in the Maserati Birdcage at 123.407 mph - before he retired, as did all the Maseratis. The Ferrari in fourth place also won the GT class. Porsche won the 1,600 cc class, the MGA Twin Cam driven by Lund and Escott the 2,000 cc class and there were other British class victories: Lotus Elite in the 1,300 cc class and Austin-Healey Sprite in the 1,000 cc class. A DB-Panhard won the Index of Performance and also won the 850 cc class as well as the Biennial Cup, while another Lotus Elite won the Index of Thermal Efficiency. A total of 25 cars finished this Le Mans but five failed to cover the minimum distance and were therefore not classified - this included the entire team of three Triumphs.

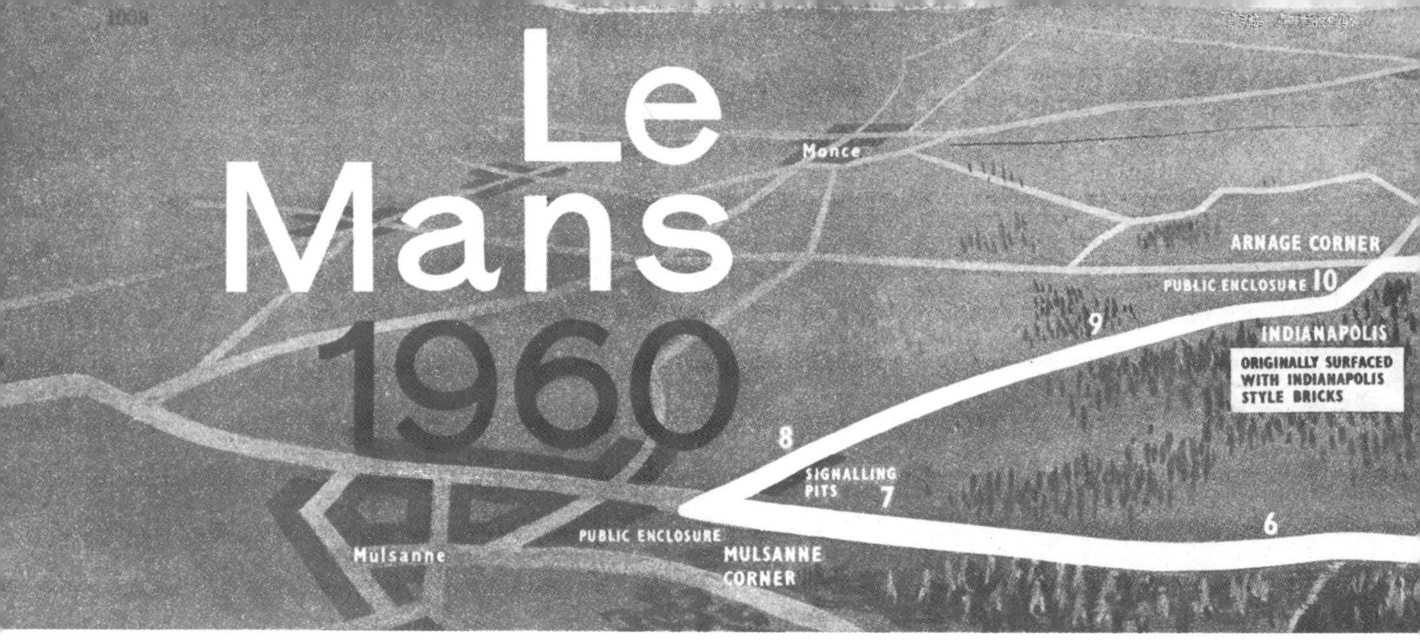

28th G.P. d'Endurance:

Big names missing from entry list

CARS, ENTRANTS

CAR	c.c.	ENTRANT	COUNTRY	DRIVERS
GRAND TOURING CATEGORY				
4,000 to 5,000 c.c.:				
1 Chevrolet-Corvette	4,640	B. S. Cunningham	U.S.A.	Cunningham, Duntov, Forns
2 Chevrolet-Corvette	4,640	B. S. Cunningham	U.S.A.	Thompson, Windridge
3 Chevrolet-Corvette	4,640	B. S. Cunningham	U.S.A.	Grossman, Hugus, Fitch
4 Chevrolet-Corvette	4,640	Camoradi U.S.A.	U.S.A.	Lilley, Gamble
2,500 to 3,000 c.c.:				
14 Ferrari	2,953	Scuderia Serenissima	Italy	Abate, Balzarini
15 Ferrari	**2,953**	**A. G. Whitehead**	**G.B.**	**Whitehead, H. Taylor**
16 Ferrari	2,953	F. Tavano	France	Tavano, Loustel
17 Ferrari	2,953	N.A.R.T.	U.S.A.	P. & R. Rodriguez
18 Ferrari	2,953	N.A.R.T.	U.S.A.	Arents, Kimberley
19 Ferrari	2,953	N.A.R.T.	U.S.A.	Hugus, Pabst
20 Ferrari	2,953	N.A.R.T.	U.S.A.	Publicker
21 Ferrari	2,953	Equipe Nle Belge	Belgium	Beurlys, Blary, Swaters
22 Ferrari	2,953	Ecurie Francorchamps	Belgium	Dernier, Noblet
23 Austin-Healey	**2,910**	**J. C. Sears**	**G.B.**	**Sears, Riley**
1,300 to 1,600 c.c.:				
35 Porsche	1,588	Automobiles Porsche	Germany	Linge, Walter
1,150 to 1,300 c.c.:				
41 Lotus Elite	**1,216**	**D. Buxton**	**G.B.**	**Buxton, Allen**
42 Lotus Elite	**1,216**	**D. Buxton**	**G.B.**	**Wagstaff, Marsh**
43 Lotus Elite	**1,216**	**D. Buxton**	**G.B.**	**Baillie, Parks**
44 Lotus Elite	1,216	R. Masson	France	Masson, Laurent, Gallier
SPORTS CAR CATEGORY				
2,500 to 3,000 c.c.:				
5 Jaguar	**2,997**	**Ecurie Ecosse**	**G.B.**	**Flockhart, Halford**
6 Jaguar	2,996	Jaguar New York	U.S.A.	Hansgen, Gurney
7 Aston Martin	**2,992**	**Border Relvers**	**G.B.**	**Clark, Salvadori, Whitmore**
8 Aston Martin	**2,992**	**Major Baillie**	**G.B.**	**Baillie, Fairman**
9 Ferrari	2,953	Scuderia Ferrari	Italy	P. Hill, Ginther
10 Ferrari	2,953	Scuderia Ferrari	Italy	von Trips, Allison
11 Ferrari	2,953	Scuderia Ferrari	Italy	Frère, Gendebien
12 Ferrari	2,953	Scuderia Ferrari	Italy	Scarfiotti, Cabianca
24 Maserati	2,890	Camoradi U.S.A.	U.S.A.	Shelby, Gregory
25 Maserati	2,890	Camoradi U.S.A.	U.S.A.	—
26 Maserati	2,890	Camoradi U.S.A.	U.S.A.	Jeffords, Schappard, Casner
1,600 to 2,000 c.c.:				
28 Triumph	**1,985**	**Standard Triumph**	**G.B.**	**Sanderson, Rotschild, Boxall**
29 Triumph	**1,985**	**Standard Triumph**	**G.B.**	**Bolton, Becquart**
30 A.C.-Bristol	1,971	Equipe Lausannoise	France	Wicky, Gachang, Gretener

AT the traditional hour on Saturday afternoon, the patter of 110 feet across the tarmac will mark the start of yet another 24-hour Le Mans race, 28th Grand Prix d'Endurance. This year the race is open to Appendix C Sports Cars of up to 3 litres capacity, as has been the ruling for the past two years, and also eligible for 1960 are Appendix J, Group 3 Grand Touring cars of any capacity above 1,000 c.c. Classes for sports cars are all those internationally recognized from 700 c.c. to 3 litres, and for G.T. cars from 1,000 c.c. upwards.

Regulations for Le Mans are amongst the most complicated in the world, and a thoroughly efficient and knowledgeable team manager who knows the book of rules back to front is one of the most important adjuncts for success. Besides the long list of misdemeanours that the standing F.I.A. regulations contain which can result in disqualification, at Le Mans there are a further 33, such as starting to refuel before engine has fully stopped, which carry the same penalty. As well as these, there is a multitude of lesser infringements which carry monetary fines.

Probably the most significant clause in the regulations is the much discussed—and execrated—article which calls for windscreens of 25cm (9·84in.) vertical height. Most drivers consider this to be dangerous—at night and in the wet, or both, extremely so. Other regulations call for a minimum size of luggage boot which is larger than last year's, so that many cars are running with rather ungainly modifications to their tails in order to comply with the new ruling.

Maximum capacity of the petrol tank is also limited—nearly 31 gallons for the largest cars and just over 13 gallons for the smallest—but there is no restriction on how frequently the cars may be refuelled. Oil and water, however, can be replenished only at 25-lap (211-mile) intervals. No driver may be at the wheel for longer than 14 hours out of the 24, or for more than 52 consecutive laps (435 miles).

Only two people may work on the car simultaneously, and spare parts or tools used must either be those carried in the car, or actually available in the pits. Whether tyres or wheels are to be changed, the spare carried in the car must be used—or at least taken out of the car, laid on the pit counter, and finally replaced again. Of particular importance is the regulation stating that the car may leave the pits only after the engine has

AND DRIVERS

(British entries in bold).

CAR		c.c.	ENTRANT	COUNTRY	DRIVERS
1,600 to 2,000 c.c. (continued):					
31	Lotus	1,964	**Lotus England**	**G.B.**	**Ireland,**
32	M.G.	1,762	**Ted Lund**	**G.B.**	**Lund, Escott, Bloor**
33	Porsche	1,606	Automobiles Porsche	Germany	Trintignant, Barth
34	Porsche	1,606	Automobiles Porsche	Germany	Bonnier, G. Hill
1,300 to 1,600 c.c.:					
36	Porsche	1,588	J. Kerguen	U.S.A.	Kerguen, Lacaze, Dewez
37	Osca	1,569	Automobiles Osca	Italy	—
38	Porsche	1,498	G. de Beaufort	Belgium	de Beaufort, Bootz
39	Porsche	1,498	Automobiles Porsche	Germany	Hermann
1,150 to 1,300 c.c.:					
40	Alfa-Romeo Conrero	1,290	Virgilio Conrero	France	de Leonibus
1,000 to 1,150 c.c.:					
45	**Lola-Climax**	1,098	**Lola Climax**	**G.B.**	**Vogele, Ashdown, Honeger**
850 to 1,000 c.c.:					
46	**Austin-Healey**	996	**Donald Healey**	**G.B.**	**Sprinzel, Colgate, Ross**
47	D.B. Panhard	954	Automobiles D.B.	France	Vinatier, Vidilles
48	D.B. Panhard	954	Automobiles D.B.	France	Jaeger, Bouharde
700 to 850 c.c.:					
49	Fiat Abarth	847	Abarth	Italy	Poltronieri
50	Fiat Abarth	847	Abarth	Italy	Cattini
51	D.B. Panhard	750	Automobiles D.B.	France	Cotton, van den Bruwaene
52	D.B. Panhard	750	Automobiles D.B.	France	Bartholoni, de Sait Auban
53	Osca	746	Automobiles Osca	Italy	Laroche, Simon
54	Osca	746	Hugus	U.S.A.	Bentley
55	Stanguellini	741	Stanguellini	Italy	de la Geneste, Revillon
56	D.B. Panhard	701	Automobiles D.B.	France	Laureau, Armagnac
RESERVES					
Grand Touring:					
57	A.C.-Bristol	1,971	J. Rambaux	France	Rambaux
Sports Cars:					
58	Porsche	1,488	C. Goethals	Belgium	Goethals, Pilette
59	**Triumph**	1,985	**Standard Triumph**	**G.B.**	**Leston, Ballisat**
60	Fiat Abarth	850	Abarth	Italy	Davis
61	Stanguellini	741	Stanguellini	Italy	Guiraud, Foury
62	**Lotus Elite**	742	**Lotus England**	**G.B.**	**Sieff,**
63	Alfa-Romeo Conrero	1,290	G. Ubezzi	Italy	Ubezzi
64	D.B. Panhard	750	Automobiles D.B.	France	—
65	E.F.A.C.	741	Société E.F.A.C.	—	—

ON THE ABOVE MAP the figures indicate the distance round the circuit from the start, in kilometres. One lap is 13.461 km (8·366 miles). The lap record, which stands at 125·67 m.p.h., was achieved by Mike Hawthorn (Ferrari) in 1957, before the introduction of the 3-litre limit. Greatest distance ever covered in the 24 hours was 2,732·36 miles by the Ecurie Ecosse Jaguar driven that year by Ron Flockhart and Ivor Bueb

TELEVISION AND RADIO COVERAGE

B.B.C. Sound

June 25

3.50- 4.10 p.m.	The start, in " Out and About "
5.25- 5.30 p.m.	Progress reports
6.35- 6.55 p.m.	,, ,,
8.15- 8.30 p.m.	,, ,,
10.40-10.45 p.m.	,, ,,
11.50-11.55 p.m.	,, ,,

June 26

9.30- 9.45 a.m.	,, ,,
noon-12.01 p.m.	,, ,,
1.40- 1.45 p.m.	,, ,,
2.44- 2.46 p.m.	,, ,,
4.30- 4.45 p.m.	Finish

B.B.C. Television

June 25

10.30-10.45 p.m.	Progress reports by Raymond Baxter

June 26

2.25- 2.40 p.m.	Progress reports by Robin Richards
3.30- 4.10 p.m.	Finish

been restarted by the driver from his seat. To qualify as a finisher, one must cover a minimum predetermined distance during the 24 hours, and complete the last lap in 30min or less. Failure to maintain an average speed within 20 per cent of the required speed worked out at the 6th, 12th and 18th hours can result in disqualification of the competitor.

Although most of the glamour surrounds the car which completes the greatest distance within the 24 hours, to many the Performance Index winner is just as worthy of praise. In the past the Index of Performance has favoured the smaller capacity cars—in fact, many people have considered that it was conceived primarily to help a French win, as there are no large capacity French sports cars these days. The new windscreen regulations will undoubtedly prove a bigger handicap on these

LE MANS WINNERS SINCE THE WAR				
Year	Car	Drivers	Speed (m.p.h.)	Distance (miles)
1949	Ferrari	Chinetti and Selsdon	82·31	1,974·90
1950	Talbot	L. and L. J. Rosier	89·72	2,153·20
1951	Jaguar	Walker and Whitehead	93·49	2,243·87
1952	Mercedes-Benz	Lang and Riess	96·67	2,320·20
1953	Jaguar	Rolt and Hamilton	105·85	2,540·30
1954	Ferrari	Gonzales and Trintignant	105·10	2,524·00
1955	Jaguar	Hawthorn and Bueb	107·00	2,592·91
1956	Jaguar	Sanderson and Flockhart	104·46	2,507·18
1957	Jaguar	Flockhart and Bueb	113·85	2,732·36
1958	Ferrari	Gendebien and Hill	106·21	2,548·94
1959	Aston Martin	Salvadori and Shelby	112·57	2,715·25

A.C. Ace-Bristol, at Le Mans last year

Aston Martin DBR1-300

Triumph TRS

Works-entered Austin-Healey Sebring Sprite

LE MANS 1960...

small cars, and it may well be that the winner in this category will come from a larger capacity class. Cash prize for the overall winner is 50,000 new francs, while the winner of the performance index collects 30,000 new francs.

Since this year a Grand Touring category is included, there is a separate cup for the fastest sports car because only the latter are eligible for the Manufacturers' Sports Car Championship markings. The Index of Performance is based on a formula which requires the minimum estimated distance to be covered by a car in kilometres to be equal to $4{,}000 \dfrac{C-125}{C+150}$ where C equals the cylinder capacity in cubic centimetres. By the amount this estimated distance is exceeded, so much higher is the Index of Performance figure.

Positions for the Biennial Cup are worked out from placings on the Index of Performance. This year is the second round of 26 such competitions and only five cars are eligible—two Aston Martins, two D.B.s and a Stanguellini. For the second time there is a Thermal Efficiency Index, which is calculated from the average speed for 24 hours, weight of car and the actual petrol consumption. This regulation is the sort of thing in which the technically minded members of the *Club de l'Ouest* seem to delight. Its aim is to underline the progress reached from year to year in respect of fuel economy. The weight used in the calculation is without fuel in the tanks but with a full supply of water and oil and with a spare wheel aboard; all cars are weighed thus during scrutineering before this race. Success in this part of the race is also worth 30,000 new francs.

For the team prize only two cars are necessary, but they must be of the same make, and entered by the same entrant. There are hordes of other awards to be won, including special prizes to unclassified and retired competitors—for example, if you cover only one lap, you will still come away with 200 new francs.

There are 35 sports cars out of 55 entries—not including reserves—and this year the largest entries are Italian cars, although a majority of them are American-entered.

It is rather disappointing to see a poorer showing from Britain than has been the case for many years, and particularly the absence of any DB4 GT Aston Martin. Trying to pick a winner out of so many probables would be risky indeed, but with thirteen Ferraris, including four works cars, entered, this marque must be among the favourites. Notable absentees amongst the drivers are Stirling Moss, Jack Brabham and Tony Brooks—at least one of these has been heard to say that he considers the race too dangerous.

GREAT BRITAIN

A.C. Ace-Bristol

LITTLE INFORMATION has been forthcoming on this car, but there is no reason to suppose that it is other than a standard Ace-Bristol, similar to the car which, last year, won its class and finished in seventh position in general classification. This year the entry is a French one; rumours have drifted across the channel that a Ferrari engine—of unknown capacity—has been installed in the chassis, but this story is extremely suspect. Heading the reserves, and therefore almost certain of an entry, is another French

Left: Ecurie Ecosse D-type Jaguar

Below left: Ted Lund's M.G. MGA

Below right: Lola

LE MANS 1960 . . .

entered A.C.—this one, however, is running in the G.T. category and is presumably an Aceca.

Aston Martin

FOLLOWING their withdrawal from sports car racing, Aston Martin have no works car entries this year, and it is regrettable that there is no example of the DB4 G.T. model in the important *gran turismo* category. The privately entered DBR1-300 sports-racing cars are two of the ex-works machines which last year won at Le Mans, and brought the World Championship for Sports Car Constructors to this country.

The Border Reivers' entry, to be driven by Roy Salvadori and Jim Clark, is the car which won the Nürburgring 1000km race last year, and subsequently caught fire when leading the Tourist Trophy.

Ian Baillie's car, which he will share with Jack Fairman, is the machine that Baillie and Edward Greenall drove at the Nürburgring. It is, in fact, last year's Le Mans winner.

Austin-Healey 3,000

THIS CAR, entered by Norfolk farmer Jack Sears—although with the very sincere blessings of the manufacturer—is probably nearer to what can be bought by a moderately wealthy enthusiast than anything else in the race. It is a hard-top model with basic modifications to comply with regulations, including installation of a 25-gallon petrol tank. In the Sebring 12-hour race one of these cars, in the hands of Jack Sears and Peter Riley, was in fifth overall position in the G.T. Category for much of the race until transmission troubles resulted in a long delay at the pits.

Austin-Healey Sprite

THIS is the first time for several years that Donald Healey has actually entered a car of his own at Le Mans; now a Sprite equipped with full Sebring modifications is running under his auspices. Engine modifications, close-ratio gearbox, centre-lock wire wheels and disc brakes on the front are all standard extras that can be bought from the speed equipment division of the Donald Healey Motor Company.

Ecurie Ecosse

BECAUSE OF strong discouragement by Coopers against fitting the deep regulation screen to one of their cars, and the difficulty of providing centre-lock hubs in time for the race, the Cooper Monaco entered by Ecurie Ecosse will not be running. Ron Flockhart and Bruce Halford will share the driving of the other Ecurie Ecosse entry—a D type Jaguar. This car will be competing in its fourth Le Mans race; it finished second in 1957 and ran also in the Monza 500 mile race.

Jaguar are not assisting this year with preparation of the Ecurie Ecosse car, and "Wilkie" Wilkinson has built a new 3-litre engine, basically a modified 2.4 Jaguar unit, with cylinder bores opened out to 86mm and a new crankshaft giving a stroke also of 86mm. Three twin-choke Weber carburettors are used.

Luggage space is provided by a bulge beside the tail fin, and a transparent plastic cover fits between this and the top of the screen to reduce drag.

Lola

THIS IS the first time that a Lola has appeared at Le Mans but the car certainly needs no introduction to British spectators, and even on the Continent the name is not exactly unknown. Power unit for the car is the well-tried 1,100 c.c. Coventry Climax. A regulation-size windscreen makes the car look a little strange.

Although this car is entered by the works it will, in fact, race in Swiss colours since the car used belongs to the Swiss driver Charles Vogele. Co-driving with him is Peter Ashdown, whose name is synonymous with Lola.

Lotus

ALL ENTRIES this year are Elites, including a works car to be driven by Innes Ireland and A. N. Other. This latter is an experimental prototype fitted with a Coventry Climax twin-cam-shaft FPF engine of 2 litres' capacity (actually a modified 2½-litre unit). To withstand a power output in the region of 170 b.h.p. the transmission has been changed, a new close-ratio, four-speed, all-synchromesh gearbox being fitted. The final drive assembly is new, with increased torque capacity and a Z.F. limited-slip differential.

Externally the car appears unchanged, but front suspension is the same as that of the current formula 1 cars, with double tubular wishbones, coil springs and adjustable Armstrong telescopic dampers. At the rear, the strut-type suspension is identical with that of last year's formula 1 cars. Girling disc brakes are of greater diameter, those at the rear being mounted inboard of the drive shafts.

Fuel tank and spare wheel positions have been transposed for more rapid access to the wheel during the race. Fourteen gallons are carried in the tail and five in a tank in the left wing valance, as on the original Elite. Dry weight is about 1½cwt more than the production car.

David Buxton has entered three Elites as a team. These are standard, with engines at stage 3 tune. The fifth Elite is a French private entry by R. Masson, the sixth being on the reserve list.

MGA

LAST YEAR the privately entered M.G. of Ted Lund did extremely well until it had the misfortune to hit a large dog when at high speed on the Mulsanne straight. In spite of considerable damage, the car was able to continue until it retired with lack of gearbox oil. For this year, Ted Lund has entered an MGA again, but the engine has been bored out to 1,762 c.c., with the idea of being able to compete in the 2-litre class rather than the usually hotly contested 1,600 c.c. group. Unfortunately two of the works Porsches have also been bored out to run in this class. An attractive streamlined coupé body has been built on to an existing MGA body, providing sufficient room for a 20-gallon petrol tank and the required luggage space.

Triumph

TRIUMPH are making their second appearance in the race with the experimental TRS, which performed very consistently last year until eliminated by cooling fan failures. Significantly, when the cars appeared at the practice day on 9 April the fan blades had been removed from the end of the water pump spindle. Two cars, to be driven by Sanderson-Rothschild and Bolton-Becquart, with Boxall as reserve driver, are already listed among the acceptances. A third works team car, to be driven by Leston and Ballisat, is third on the reserve list and, therefore, stands a very good chance of gaining a starting place to complete a triple entry as last year.

The glass fibre body for this year's cars is a new design, but rather surprisingly is not strikingly different from the production TR3s. They are powered by the experimental 1,985 c.c. (90mm bore, 78mm stroke) twin overhead camshaft engine. The best lap achieved on the 9 April practice day was 4min 50.4sec (103.65 m.p.h.) compared with the fastest race lap last year of 4min 45.9sec (105.32 m.p.h.).

ITALY

Abarth

THESE SMALL, rear-engined cars from Italy are making their first appearance at Le Mans. Power unit is of Fiat derivation, but Abarths tune the engine and fit it to their own chassis. Two 847 c.c. models have been entered, and in the try-out day last April one of the cars managed to lap very near the 100 m.p.h. mark. They will prove strong contestants for the Index of Performance award.

Alfa-Romeo Conrero

VIRGILIO CONRERO, better known for his rally achievements, has entered one of his specially prepared cars this year. These cars are well known at many of the large sports car races in Europe, but last year they were absent from the 24-hour race, after a rather unsuccessful outing in 1958. Engine is tuned by Conrero and a Zagato body is fitted. At practice last April the car recorded the rather unspectacular speed of 85.75 m.p.h.

Ferrari

Maserati Camoradi

Chevrolet Corvette

Porsche Carrera GTL

LE MANS 1960 . . .

Ferrari

FERRARI has no fewer than 13 entries, four of which are works cars, among the 55 starters. All of these cars will be powered by the 2,953 c.c. vee-12 engine. The works team open sports cars will be as raced at the Nürburgring, 1,000km race, having a wishbone type of independent rear suspension evolved from that used on the current G.P. cars. Team pairings—subject to alteration, of course—are Phil Hill-Ginter, Frère-Gendebien, Scarfiotti-Cabianca, and von Trips-Allison, but a substitute will be necessary for Allison, who will not be fully recovered from his Monaco accident.

The nine private entries will be 250 GT coupés, four of which are entered by the North American Racing Team, and one of these will be driven by the young Rodriguez brothers from Mexico. It would not be surprising if one of these 250 GT entries proved to be the overall winner. Last year they came very close to it, finishing third, fourth, fifth and sixth behind the two winning Aston Martins.

Maserati

AFTER ITS WIN in the Nürburgring 1,000km race when driven by Moss, the Camoradi-entered 2,890 c.c. "bird-cage" Maserati, of which three are entered, must rank as one of the pre-race favourites. Also, driven by Moss, this car, it will be recalled, built up a 30-mile lead after eight hours' racing at Sebring, before it was eliminated by gearbox trouble. It is quite one of the ugliest sports cars ever produced, but it has several intriguing features. The space frame is built up of a multitude of small diameter tubes, and a low bonnet height is achieved by installing the engine at an angle of 45deg. This has enabled the regulation height of windscreen to be obtained with a comparatively low overall height. The rear end with the five-speed, transversely mounted gearbox in unit with the final drive and de Dion rear axle is derived from the Maserati 250F Grand Prix car.

Osca

TWO VERSIONS of Osca have been entered; one is the 2-o.h.c. 1½-litre engine version, and the other a 750 c.c.—two of the latter models are entered. Last year two 1,100 c.c. models were entered for the race but neither lasted the distance. All Oscas have neat twin-tube chassis with forged wishbone front suspension and coil springs, and at the rear a live axle located by radius arms.

Stanguellini

ONE OF THE THREE Stanguellinis entered last year finished, and is eligible for competing in the Biennial Cup. The 750 c.c.-engined version has been entered again, and another one is listed among the reserves. Engine is basically Fiat, with a 2-o.h.c. conversion and downdraught Weber carburettors.

AMERICA

Cunningham

BRIGGS CUNNINGHAM, a charming American, makes a welcome return to the Sarthe circuit after an absence of five years. In the years 1952, 1953 and 1954 he was so near to success with his cars; in 1952 co-driving with Spear he was placed fourth, in 1953 Walter and Fitch brought a Cunningham into third place, and Cunningham himself, driving a similar car with Spear, finished seventh, and the third team car tenth. Again, in 1954 Spear and Johnston finished third, and Briggs co-driving with Bent finished fifth. No one would be a more popular winner in 1960.

His main entry is undoubtedly the experimental new competition Jaguar (fully described on page 1000) which he has inveigled out of Sir William Lyons. This is to be driven by American

D. B. Panhard

sports car champion Walter Hansgen, who will have Dan Gurney as his co-driver. Gurney shared a Ferrari with Behra last year, and was leading the race until eliminated on the 129th lap. In addition to the Jaguar, Cunningham is entering three Chevrolet Corvettes, one of which Briggs will share with Arkus Duntov, who is the General Motors engineer responsible for the development of the Corvettes. The vee-8 engine has a capacity of 4,640 c.c., uses Rochester-type fuel injection, and a more powerful version of the engine than that used on 9 April practice day will be available for the race. The fourth Corvette is entered also by the Camoradi U.S.A. team. Although these cars have glass fibre bodies they are comparatively heavy, and the standard drum brakes may prove to be the weak link in 24 hours of racing.

GERMANY

Porsche

FOUR CARS have been entered by the Porsche company: three RS 60 Spyders to be driven by Barth, Bonnier, Trintignant, Herrmann and Graham Hill, and one new special-bodied Abarth-Carrera GTL coupé, the wheel of which will be shared by Linge and Walter. There are three private entries in addition.

Of the Sixties, two will have a capacity of 1,606 c.c., the third will be a 1500. The larger-engined cars thus will compete in the 2-litre class. Specifications of all Porsche entries—with very few exceptions—will tally with those of the cars that had run in the recent 1,000km Race at the Nürburgring. So far as the sports-racing cars are concerned, engines are identical, except that the bore is 85mm for the smaller and 88mm for the larger units—the stroke being 66mm in both cases. Both types of engines are running on a compression ratio of 9·8 to 1 and are said to develop 166 and 178 gross b.h.p. respectively, at 7,800 r.p.n. The crankshaft of the RS engine, it will be recalled, is of the built-up type, running on three roller- and one ball-bearing. Big-ends are also fitted with roller-bearings. Valves are actuated by four shaft-and-bevel-driven overhead camshafts.

Despite experiments with disc brakes of their own design in the 1,000km race, all the cars entered for Le Mans will be fitted with drum brakes of 11in diameter, heavily turbo-finned.

Bodies are almost standard. The GTL has been lightened by 10-15lb, bringing the total to somewhere near 15·2cwt. The fuel tankage on the GTL is a standard 17 gallons.

The Sixties are, of course, much lighter, turning the scales at roughly 11cwt. They have narrower tracks (50·7in F, 49·2in R), against the GTL's (51·5in. F, 50·0in R), but a wheelbase longer by 3·94in, as they have to accommodate the engine in front of the rear axle-line. The 1500 will be fitted with two fuel tanks with a total capacity of 17 gallons, whereas the 1·7-litre will be able to carry a trifle under 22 gallons.

For Le Mans, the RS 60 model cars will be fitted with a high-tailed body rather on the lines of last year's Lotus sports cars. Early Porsches had such a raised poop, but it was discarded when the lower silhouette was found to be more favourable aerodynamically. Now, after the high and wide windscreens have been made compulsory, this shape has been resuscitated.

FRANCE

D.B.

ALL FRENCHMEN follow keenly the fortunes of the little D.B. Panhards, the only French entries in their most famous motor race. Since the war the record of these little cars in the Index of Performance part of the results has been outstanding. This year two different models are entered—three of the 750 c.c. versions, and two of the 954 c.c. In practice a coupé-bodied 750 c.c. car lapped at 96·78 m.p.h., compared with a fastest race lap last year of 95·8 m.p.h.

Spray spews behind the top-finishing Porsche, the Carrera GTL of Linge and Walter, as it scoots through rain-swept esses to an 11th overall.

Gregory sights over weird Maser windshield blasting to astounding lead.

Ferrari's Tavoni caught napping.

"All of a sudden...poof," says Windridge. Duntov, back to camera, listens.

Endurance is Emphasized

Twenty-four American drivers provided most of the drama at this year's Le Mans race. With this kind of an effort an all-U. S. victory can't be far off.

by Jesse Alexander

▶ The 1960 Le Mans race drew the heaviest American contingent yet seen at the famous Sarthe circuit. The formidable Chevrolet Corvette group led by Briggs Cunningham plus the Camoradi-entered Corvette provided a much-needed degree of interest in the race. Americans were to be found driving everything from Sprites to Oscas to Jaguars to Ferraris, and after all was said and done a North American Racing Team Ferrari finished second overall, ably driven by Rodriguez and Pilette, a Mexican and a Belgian. Hopes for an outstanding Corvette showing faded early and the best the white and blue Detroit iron could do was 8th and 10th, overall. Highest-placed all-American entry was the Arents/Connell Ferrari 250/GT which turned in a creditable fifth overall.

7 a. m. Sunday. Piano, piano!

More than a little pre-race interest centered around the Cunningham Jaguar to be driven by Hansgen and Gurney. The car arrived at Le Mans directly from the Coventry experimental shop and since its last appearance at Le Mans in April, a large fin had been added at the back. Regrettably

Flames belch from Salvadori/Clark Aston in Mulsanne corner downshift.

the car was involved in an accident with Fritz D'Orey's Ferrari on the first night of practice and had to be driven back to the garage for hasty repairs to its beautiful nose. It arrived late at the second session with Dan Gurney taking the car over for the first time. He promptly tried turning some fast laps and found some very serious deficiencies in

No turning back. The start (left) of the longest race in the world. Albert Maher, shown at right with Briggs Cunningham, garnered a place on Corvette team merely by asking Alfred Momo if there was an opening. There was, and he helped refuel. Here they wait during night practice for number two Corvette.

the car's handling. Best Dan could do that night was around the 4'20" mark; he complained of unequal braking, too-soft suspension and a car most unstable on the Mulsanne straight. That was Thursday night, and practice was officially over. At midnight the following evening Dan and Walt were on the road trying the car in its final state after considerable effort had been put into making it handle. Pronouncing it noticeably better, the two drivers decided to race come hell or high water and the Cunningham entourage returned to their hotels, fingers crossed for the morrow.

Walt Hansgen started. He made a good getaway and the sleek Jag was soon screaming around the circuit until mechanical troubles set in. An injector pipe came loose and this plagued the car for hours. During the night with Dan at the wheel the trouble recurred and the car was in the pits almost every lap for a plug change. Eventual cause of retirement was a burned piston and the story of the car came to a close. Insufficient actual race testing on English circuits with either Hansgen or Gurney behind the wheel certainly contributed to the new Jaguar's poor showing. Six months from board to track isn't much and Coventry needed more time, time that wasn't available.

For the first time in years Ferry Porsche did not come to Le Mans. It was just as well for with the exception of the Abarth Carrera driven by Linge and Walter, the Stuttgart cars did very badly. Strangely enough, there was no one universal trouble to which they all succumbed. The Bonnier/G. Hill car had several troubles, strangest of which was a peculiar bump and momentary bang somewhere in the suspension. This usually occurred on the straight and, as Graham Hill related, was most unpleasant and disconcerting. The drivers had no idea what it was and their imaginations ran rampant. Eventually this car burned its copper gasket between cylinder and head; the mechanics sought to find out the extent of the damage on the spot and had the head off the engine in minutes, right in front of the pits, but to no avail. The Trintignant/Herrmann car damaged a piston and although the Barth/Seidel car finished in 12th place it had few gears left and limped over the line. De Beaufort and Stoop lost the hydraulic pump in the clutch-actuating mechanism, the first time such a failure had occurred.

The 1960 RS Porsche was slower than last year's car. In 1959 the best time in the RSK was a 4'17" lap while this year all that could be eked out was a 4'23". Increased drag from the required windshield was felt more by the smaller-displacement cars than by the big boys.

No less than 12 Ferraris started the race. Six of them finished, and two out of the six that retired did so for the most inexcusable reason: they ran out of gas! I happened to be on the spot when the Trips/Hill car coasted to a halt near Tertre Rouge. A wide-eyed Trips could not believe it, but the fuel pump was just not getting anything to pump and ran on — chattering merrily to itself. The car was in perfect condition otherwise and most probably could have finished the 24 hours without difficulty. The Scarfiotti/Rodriguez car conked out for exactly the same reason. And as the eventual winner, Olivier Gendebien, rushed towards White House on his last lap before handing over to Frere he felt the Ferrari begin to cut out. Gendebien actually coasted into the pits!

The reason for the error was apparently this: fuel consumption tests had been made during the practice session in April and the number of race laps that the team cars would be able to do was computed at that time. As it turned out, the pace in the opening laps was hotter than expected and without any kind of reserve tank on board the Ferraris were caught with their petrol down. This was

24 Hours of Le Mans

June 25 and 26
8.36 miles per lap

	Drivers	Car	miles	mph
1	Gendebien/ Frere	Ferrari	2620.7	109.2
2	Rodriguez/ Pilette	Ferrari	2587.3	107.8
3	Salvadori/ Clark	Aston Martin	2558.7	106.6
4	Tavano/ Loustel	Ferrari 250/GT	2520.3	105.2
5	Arents/ Connell	Ferrari 250/GT	2504.4	104.35
6	Elde/ Noblet	Ferrari 250/GT	2503.6	104.31
7	Hugus/ Pabst	Ferrari 250/GT	2498.0	104.08
8	Fitch/ Grossman	Corvette	2350.1	97.92
9	Baillie/ Fairman	Aston Martin	2349.3	97.89
10	°Lilley/ Gamble	Corvette	2307.7	96.16
11	Linge/ Walter	Porsche Carrera GTL	2249.3	
12	Barth/ Seidel	Porsche 1.5 RS60	2207.4	
13	Lund/ Escott	MG Twin Cam	2188.6	
14	Masson/ Laurent	Lotus Elite	2183.0	
15	°Ballisat/ Becquart	Triumph TRS	2149.0	
16	Wagstaff/ Marsh	Lotus Elite	2183.0	
17	Laureau/ Armagnac	D. B. Panhard	2116.1	
18	°Leston/ Rothschild	Triumph TRS	2115.6	
19	°Bolton/ Sanderson	Triumph TRS	2090.6	
20	Dalton/ Colgate	Austin-Healey Sprite	2055.2	
21	Lelong/ Van den Bruwaene	D. B. Panhard	2036.4	
22	°Wicky/ Gachnang	A. C. Bristol	2001.7	
23	Bentley/ Gordon	Osca 750	1982.1	
24	Bouharde/ Jaeger	D. B. Panhard	1906.5	
25	Bartholoni/ Saint-Aubin	D. B. Panhard	1865.1	

°Officially not classified; did not achieve required minimum distance.

Index of Performance

	Drivers	Car	
1	Laureau/ Armagnac	D. B. Panhard	1.257
2	Gendebien/ Frere	Ferrari	1.157
3	Bentley/ Gordon	Osca 750	1.151
4	Rodriguez/ Pilette	Ferrari	1.142
5	Lelong/ Van den Bruwaene	D. B. Panhard	1.130
6	Salvadori/ Clark	Aston Martin	1.128

Index of Energy

	Drivers	Car	
1	Wagstaff/ Marsh	Lotus Elite	1.15
2	Masson/ Laurent	Lotus Elite	1.02
3	Bouharde/ Jaeger	D. B. Panhard	0.97
4	Salvadori/ Clark	Aston Martin	0.94
5	Dalton/ Colgate	Austin-Healey Sprite	0.94

A 250/GT California roadster version of this month's cover and Road Research Report car was driven by Bill Sturgis and Joe Schlesser. The only one of its type entered, it was retired Sunday afternoon.

Porsche sought to give roadsters a coupe effect by revamping the tail structure in line with regulations requiring high windshields.

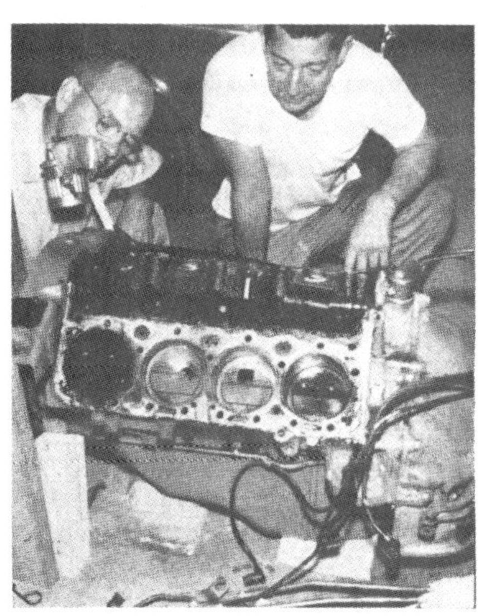

Only a few hours before the start, work continued on the Cunningham-entered Jaguar which features components evolved from the once-successful D-Type, including an alloy engine in body-cum-chassis.

Creative destruction. G.M.'s Frank Burrell and tuner Bill Frick inspect Corvette engine which was deliberately blown up in practice session.

Twin-cam Triumph TRS differs slightly from version which appeared at Le Mans last year.

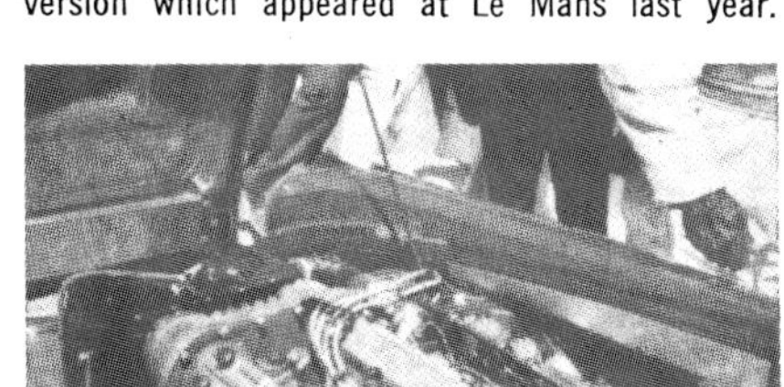

Paul Frere, who shared driving chores and winners' laurels with another Belgian, Olivier Gendebien, signals "seven" as he roars past the Ferrari pits; what he means by cryptic sign is anybody's guess.

ENDURANCE IS EMPHASIZED

something that could only have happened to Ferrari, but sheer weight of numbers saved the day.

The Ginther/Mairesse Ferrari retired with a broken gearbox after Mairesse apparently strained things in the early hours of Sunday morning — actually racing! He increased his tempo so much that Frere had to speed up to stay safely in the lead.

Four of the 12 Ferraris were 3-liter V12 Testa Rossas — Mairesse/Ginther and Scarfiotti/Rodriguez were issued the independent-wishbone-rear cars while the rest had to be content with de Dion rear axles. It was interesting to note that none of the cars used the V6 2.5-liter Dino engine at Le Mans, which may indicate that the power unit has been shelved in favor of the tried and true 12-cylinder, at least for faster races. Interesting to note further that the G.T. Ferraris were just as fast — if not a hair faster — than the factory sports cars on the Mulsanne straight.

The Camoradi Maserati entry was impressive, to say the least. Mort Morris-Goodall replaced Piero Taruffi as team manager, and attempted to weld a certain amount of unity into the crew. Two of the 2.9 Masers were fitted with the biggest piece of plexiglas acting as a windshield that anyone has ever seen. If ever there was a living testimony to the stupidity of the current sports car regulations, this was it. Faired in to the body as much as possible, the windshield terminated at a point parallel to the driver's nose so that he could easily see over the top, proof positive that whatever regulation is thought up, car builders will get around it in one way or another. Masten Gregory set the pace in the opening laps, screaming down the Mulsanne straight so fast that even the jet-powered helicopter couldn't keep up. Short-circuits in the starting motors plagued Maserati and the starter was replaced on at least one car in the pits. The new rear portion of the Maser's bodywork increased its overall length by at least a foot and a half and aerodynamically was slightly more efficient. The Gregory/Daigh Maser eventually broke its engine but left a stirring account of itself, easily the fastest car on the track that day.

The Jefford/Casner Maserati (Casner by the way is the guiding spirit behind the Camoradi Team) was bounced off a sand bank by an embarrassed Casner who forgot to mention the incident when he handed over to Daigh after the latter's car had thrown a rod through its crankcase. Daigh brought it back into the pits after about ten laps with the right front tire worn through from a rubbing fender, and with a gearbox full of sand. This effectively blunted the third and last point of the Maserati trident. It was a harsh blow after the failure of the Scarlatti/Munaron car after two short hours of racing.

Due to a practice accident involving one of its drivers, the two-liter Lotus Elite was withdrawn, a car that could have been as fast as anything at Le Mans this year. Based on the Climax G.P. unit, its twin-cam engine put 170 bhp through a new all-synchro gearbox to a heavy-duty final drive. Front suspension was more rugged, like the current G.P. Lotus, and the disc brakes were appropriately enlarged.

The Chevrolet Corvette effort was impressive if not blindingly successful. One engine was deliberately blown in practice in an attempt to see just what liberties they could take on the gas available. The result was that the cars were reliable enough but were not really sufficiently fast to be impressive, for their engine size. The Cunningham/Kimberley car went out early when Kimberley got into a sudden spot of rain and was just a bit too fast. The car swapped ends before he could do a thing and was smashed up considerably, even starting a fire in the engine room.

Saddest Corvette mishap of all affected the Windridge/Thompson car, after they'd worked hard digging it out of the sand. It ran beautifully till noon on Sunday when suddenly — as Windridge passed the pits — a huge cloud of smoke poured out of the exhaust as the engine blew. Shortage of oil was the basic reason. Even though the crankcase was low on the car's previous pit stop the mechanics were unable to fill it since less than 25 laps had elapsed since the stop before that. Fuel could be put on at any time but water and oil cannot be added at Le Mans in less than 25 laps. The Camoradi Corvette driven by Gamble and Lilley ran regularly as did the Fitch/Grossman car. Buckets of ice for the Fitch/Grossman Corvette were necessary in the final hours to make it finish the race. The ice was packed solidly around head and block and had to be renewed often.

Motor racing *per se* stopped at Le Mans this year as soon as the Gregory/Daigh Maserati turned up its toes. Prior to this the spectacle of the three factory Ferraris charging through the "esses" and out onto the Mulsanne straight was exciting and spine-tingling. The noise of these three cars was more than most ears could take. But in a few hours the race settled down to a regular pace at which everyone tried as hard as he could NOT to strain his car, just to keep station and finish — to finish in the money.

The Ecurie Ecosse D-Type, now ancient and venerable yet still going strong, was a favorite this year in the hands of Flockhart and Halford in the beginning, but destroyed itself during the night. There were two privately-entered Aston Martins, the Border Rievers-sponsored car driven by Clark and Salvadori really being babied on Sunday just to finish — which it did, in third place.

As we noted last year Le Mans needs an overhauling. The present regulations are not realistic and are not the best for motor racing in our opinion. Many feel that this could be the last Le Mans in which sports/racing cars such as the Ferrari and Maserati will participate as the trend towards G.T. and production machinery takes hold. Even at the reduced speed of 20 of the 24 hours this year the pace was too much for many.

A final note: this was Paul Frere's last race. He's "retired" from racing before but presumably he means it this time. It was a terrific ending to a half-time job (he's a journalist) that was envied by many full-time drivers. —*JLA*

FERRARI WINS the 24-hour Race

Clean Sweep by Modena Cars broken by Border Reivers Aston Martin (third). Austin-Healey, M.G., Lotus and Triumph uphold British Tradition at Le Mans

The start is always a tremendous spectacle at Le Mans and here is this year's scene as the field streams out from under the Dunlop Bridge and up the hill towards the Esses. Clark's Aston Martin, after a simply phenomenal getaway, is already out of the picture.

In the lead for the entire race once the "birdcage" Maserati of Gregory and Daigh had stopped with starter trouble, the 3-litre Ferrari driven by the Belgians, Frere and Gendebien, seen here speeding through the wet, was never again really challenged.

FERRARI sports and Grand Touring cars scored an overwhelming victory in the 28th Le Mans 24-hour race last weekend, finishing 1st, 2nd, 4th, 5th, 6th and 7th. Only the Border Reivers' Aston Martin DBR1 with Jimmy Clark and Roy Salvadori sharing the driving, interrupted the triumphant torrent of Ferraris across the finishing line by taking 3rd place.

As the winning Ferrari seized the lead in the second hour and never lost it thereafter, it was a race somewhat lacking in incident but also this includes unfortunate incidents, for no driver was badly hurt during the 24 hours. The first hour of the event, however, was raced at record speed by Masten Gregory driving one of the three Camoradi, U.S.A. 2.9-litre Maseratis but the car was then delayed by an hour-long pit stop and later retired

as did its two team-mates. The new Jaguar built for Briggs Cunningham was in 3rd place in the opening stages but was then relegated to the tail of the field by a long pit stop, and retired during the night. The three new twin-overhead-camshaft Triumph T.R.S.s all finished the race as did the M.G. MGA Twin-Cam, two Lotus Elites (the 2-litre Elite non-started) and an A.C.-Bristol. Two of the four Chevrolet Corvettes entered finished in 8th and 10th positions.

The race began in a grey depressing afternoon, continued in an evening of downpours of tropical intensity and ran the final eight hours on Sunday in blazing sunshine under a blue sky. The relatively slow speeds at which it was run no doubt partly accounts for no fewer than 25 of the 55 starters finishing, an unusually high proportion.

Press Stand, Saturday.

GREY skies did not prevent the usual enormous crowd from pouring to the circuit to take up positions on the terraces hours before the race was due to begin at 4 p.m. Not that they lacked entertainment, for from midday onwards the competing cars were brought to their pits and their tanks filled under official supervision, while friends of the drivers, friends of friends of the drivers and anybody with a box camera and persuasion strolled up and down in front of the pits in the pre-race special parade which is for many people one of the chief charms of Le Mans.

Other diversions included the arrival of an American army band accompanied by the national flags of the competitors, the parade of a Citroen 2 C.V. which had been driven round the world, and the very latest thing in Ferrari 250 G.T. cars which had been brought especially from Modena to act as Course Car in conjunction with a

magnificent drophead Bentley from Crewe.

Then the police formed a human chain across the road at each end of the pits and plodded relentlessly forward, sweeping everyone off the circuit or into the arms of their colleagues.

At two minutes to four, the drivers were requested to take up their positions standing in the white painted circles on the opposite side of the road to their cars, now lined up in decreasing order of engine size with their tails to the pit counters, the massive block of four white and blue Chevrolet Corvettes at the head of the line looking most imposing. Somehow, the start seemed lacking in its usual drama this year. The drivers strolled amiably across to their positions, the President of the Royal Belgian Automobile Club raised his national flag and before he had time to drop it drivers were sprinting back to their cars. Jimmy Clark, who was taking first turn at the wheel of the blue Border Reivers Aston Martin BDR1 was the first to accelerate away from the line of cars and swept past the Corvettes to head the field, thereby repeating his Moss-like performance at the start of the Nurburgring 1,000 km. race last month when he was also first away by a considerable margin.

Hardly was the blue Aston under way when the road was packed with cars rushing along hub to hub, the late starters trying to thrust their way through the very rapid traffic stream, but without much success. When the entire field had swept under the Dunlop Bridge and disappeared from sight in a thunder of assorted exhaust notes, there still remained the usual luckless driver whose car had failed to respond to the starter button. On this occasion it was Feret's squat little red Fiat-Abarth which crept slowly and shamefacedly away long after the rest of the pack had dwindled to a loud noise in the direction of Tertre Rouge.

Comparative peace reigned for three minutes or so, then the roar of the mad pack swelled in volume as it swept into the curve before Arnage, changed down for that difficult slow corner and accelerated away to burst into view just after White House. Masten Gregory already held a handsome lead in one of the low Camoradi U.S.A. white and blue Maseratis. His car with the long, sloping windscreen stretching almost to the nose, whined past the stands at fantastic speed, drawing ever farther away from the works Ferrari 250 T R of Gendebien. To the delight of all the British spectators, the new Jaguar with Walter Hansgen driving streaked past in third position, but close on its tail fin came Mairesse with a second works Ferrari, Ricardo Rodriguez with another Ferrari 250 T.R., Ron Flockhart (Ecurie Ecosse D-type), von Trips (Ferrari 250 T.R.) and Jimmy Clark, already somewhat overwhelmed after his magnificent start.

MAIN PROVISIONAL RESULTS

JUNE 25/26, 28th LE MANS 24-HOUR RACE, SARTHE CIRCUIT   8.36 miles per lap. Weather: Torrential showers on Saturday, dry and hot on Sunday.

GENERAL CLASSIFICATION

1. O. Gendebien/P. Frere (2,953 c.c. Ferrari T.R.), 2,020.7 miles, 109.20 m.p.h.
2. R. Rodriguez/A. Pilette (2,953 c.c. Ferrari T.R.), 2,587.3 miles, 107.81 m.p.h.
3. J. Clark/R. Salvadori (2,992 c.c. Aston Martin B.R.1), 2,558.7 miles, 106.61 m.p.h.
4. F. Tavano/P. Loustel (2,953 c.c. Ferrari G.T.), 2,520.3 miles, 105.02 m.p.h.
5. G. Arents/A. Connell (2,953 c.c. Ferrari G.T.), 2,504.4 miles, 104.35 m.p.h.
6. Helde/P. Noblet (2,953 c.c. Ferrari G.T.), 2,503.6 miles, 104.31 m.p.h.
7. J. Hugus/A. Pabst (2,953 c.c. Ferrari G.T.), 2,498.0 miles, 104.08 m.p.h.
8. J. Fitch/R. M. Grossman (4,640 c.c. Chevrolet Corvette), 2,350.1 miles, 97.92 m.p.h.
9. Major I. Baillie/J. Fairman (2,992 c.c. Aston Martin D.B.R.1), 2,349.3 miles, 97.89 m.p.h.
10. L. Lilley/F. Gambles (4,640 c.c. Chevrolet Corvette), 2,307.7 miles, 96.16 m.p.h.

(Results continued on page 65)

A jammed starter after its first refuelling stop made when the car held a commanding lead put the Gregory-Daigh Camoradi Maserati out of the picture, for it took an hour to rectify the trouble.

LE MANS 1960

Lap 2, and Mairesse (Ferrari) snatched third place, then Rodriguez and von Trips also went by, and on the next lap the Hansgen Jaguar was seen to be making for its pit, there to lose three laps to the leaders while a fuel injection pipe was replaced.

Meanwhile, Masten Gregory was pressing on at a formidable rate, acting the role of pacemaker with a vengeance, so that by the end of the third lap he already led the Ferraris by over 15 seconds, and soon increased it to more than half a minute. For once, however, the Ferrari drivers refused to be drawn into their usual three-hour Grand Prix, and while Masten Gregory was taking the Maserati round consistently in under 4 min. 6 sec., Gendebien in second place with the Ferrari was quite content to hold about 4 min. 13 sec. and await events. And already, even this early in the race, people were having their troubles. The leading Porsche, with which Bonnier had climbed slowly into 11th place, began a whole succession of visits to its pit with a jammed shock absorber which took a long time to diagnose. The Chevrolet Corvette entered by the Camoradi U.S.A. team had a long pit stop with electrical troubles, but these were eventually sorted out and it continued on its way.

By the end of the first hour, Gregory and the Maserati led the race by no less than 1 min. 10 sec., but Ferraris held the next five places, with the Ecurie Ecosse Jaguar seventh. Gregory's two team-mates, Munaron and Jefford, held 8th and 12th positions respectively, the leading Corvette was Thompson's in 14th place.

With the race only one hour and 39 minutes old, the Ferrari team lost their first car when von Trips came to a full stop at Tertre Rouge having run out of petrol, and 15 min. later the same fate overtook the Rodriguez car at White House. This was apparently in part due to the new 1960 F.I.A. regulations limiting 3-litre sports cars to 29½-gallon tanks, and in part to poor mathematics in the Ferrari pit, as this year the race regulations did not stipulate minimum distances between refuelling stops.

These disasters were matched by equal desolation in the Maserati camp; at 5.49

the drivers of the open cars just toured round peering dismally through tall windscreens which were streaming with water on both sides—only Porsche had fitted windscreen wipers acting on the inside of the screen in addition to the normal exterior wipers.

Some cars made unscheduled pit stops at which their drivers urgently demanded cushions to raise them sufficiently to see over the screens. Others just trailed round at a very much reduced rate. When, therefore, the signal lights on the approach to the bend, under the Dunlop Bridge, began flashing their yellow danger warning, most drivers were only too glad to proceed with caution. The disaster in question was the partial blocking of the road by the red G.T. Ferrari coupé of Beurlys which had spun on the approach to the Esses and was now partially on the grass on the left side of the road and facing the wrong way. It was unceremoniously bundled across the road but was out of the race, the driver only slightly bruised.

POSITIONS IN GENERAL CLASSIFICATION
AT FOUR HOURS (8 p.m.)
1. O. Gendebien/P. Frère (Ferrari 250 T.R.), 52 laps, 112.6 m.p.h.
2. W. Mairesse/R. Ginther (Ferrari 250

Lotus Elites were prominent in their class during the early stages of the race, and although most of them ran into trouble later, that driven by Masson and Laurent came second in its class. This is No. 44 car in the above photograph, seen at the Cafe de l'Hippodrome in close company with the sister model of Buxton and Allen.

p.m. Masten Gregory swept into his pit for a routine refuelling and the starter refused to function after the tank had been refilled so that it had to be practically re-built, a process which took 55 min. and left the Maserati 11 laps behind the leader. Moreover, the Maserati driven by Munaron also went missing out on the circuit and had, in fact, stopped for good with complicated electrical bothers.

As a result of these collective disasters, the works Ferrari of Gendebien and Frère now led the race from the other surviving works Ferraris of Mairesse and Ginther, with the Ferrari 250 T.R. entered by the North American Racing Team and driven by Ricardo Rodriguez and André Pilette in third place, so that of the six drivers of the three leading cars, no fewer than four were Belgians.

And then, soon after 6 p.m., down came the rain with torrential violence, so that

T.R.), 51 laps, 108.9.
3. R. Rodriguez/A. Pilette (Ferrari 250 T.R.), 51 laps, 107.5.
4. R. Flockhart/B. Halford (Jaguar D.), 51 laps, 107.4.
5. J. Clark/R. Salvadori (Aston Martin D.B.R.1), 50 laps, 106.9.
6. F. Tavano/T. Loustel (Ferrari 250 G.T.), 50 laps, 103.1.
INDEX OF PERFORMANCE
1. G. Laureau/P. Armagnac (D.B. Panhard).
2. G. Laroche/A. Simon (Osca).
3. M. Trintignant/H. Herrmann (Porsche).
RETIREMENTS
Von Trips and P. Hill (Ferrari 250 T.R.), out of fuel; Scarfiotti/T. Rodriguez (Ferrari 250 T.R.), out of fuel; G. Scarlatti/Munaron (Maserati), electrical; B. Cunningham/W. Kimberley (Chevrolet), crashed; Beurlys/L. Bianchi (Ferrari 250 G.T.), crashed; Spichiger/Feret (Fiat-Abarth); J. Vidilles/J. Vinatier (D.B. Panhard).

Strong upholder of British hopes until its crankshaft broke early on Sunday morning was the Ecurie Ecosse D-type Jaguar, seen here at speed, that was driven by Flockhart and Halford. At the time it retired it was lying third.

After a magnificent drive Salvadori and Clark in a private DBR1 Aston Martin, seen here at Tertre Rouge, split the Ferrari dominance by finishing in a well-deserved third place.

The lap times of the leading Ferrari dropped to around 5 min. 36 sec. and life was thoroughly miserable. Kimberley, who was sharing the wheel of a Corvette with Briggs Cunningham slid off the road and out of the race at White House without personal injury. The Corvette of Thompson and Windridge also shunted at White House but continued to its pit where the wounds to the right side of the body were patched and it went on with the race. The third Corvette of the Briggs Cunningham team, which John Fitch and R. M. Grossman were sharing, was going very well indeed and seemed faster than most in the wet, so that it rose steadily through the field until it had attained tenth place after six hours of racing. The Cunningham-entered Jaguar was also running well once more and was working its way upwards from its position of 31st at the end of the first hour to 18th after two hours and 10th after three hours, but then renewed troubles caused a series of visits to the pits and it lost ground steadily.

A drear dusk fell, the lights were switched on in the pits and in the restaurant the enormous B.P. totem pole displaying the positions of the leaders in lights also lit up and a rival red neon sign about the big score board said, incompletely, "—SSO." On this occasion, there was no need to chivvy errant cars into switching on their headlamps for the drivers had been glad of their illumination for some time past.

The Gendebien/Frère Ferrari continued to lead, but disaster had overtaken the Thompson/Windridge Corvette and the Jefford/Casner Maserati, for both cars were embedded in sand banks.

POSITIONS IN GENERAL CLASSIFICATION
AT 8 HOURS (Midnight)

1. Gendebien/Frère (Ferrari), 101 laps, 105.67 m.p.h.
2. Mairesse/Ginther (Ferrari), 99 laps, 103.85.
3. Salvadori/Clark (Aston Martin), 99 laps, 103.83.
4. Rodriguez/Pilette (Ferrari), 99 laps, 103.46.
5. Flockhart/Halford (Jaguar), 99 laps, 103.40.
6. Whitehead/H. Taylor (Ferrari G.T.), 99 laps, 100.66.

INDEX OF PERFORMANCE

1. Laureau/Armagnac (D.B. Panhard).
2. Condriller/Guichet (Fiat-Abarth).
3. De Beaufort/Stoop (Porsche).

RETIREMENTS

Trintignant and Herrmann (Porsche), piston; Laroche and Simon (Osca); Gregory and Daigh (Maserati), engine.

Leading the 1,100 c.c. class, the Dalton/Colgate Austin-Healey Sprite takes Tertre Rouge ahead of the Thompson/Windridge Corvette.

LE MANS 1960

Press stand, midnight June 25-26.

Due in part to the heavy rain experienced earlier but also to the absence of pressure on the leader after the damaged starter had delayed the Gregory/Daigh Maserati for an hour, the average speed after eight hours was lower than the finishing speeds in the previous three years and was some 7 m.p.h. less than in 1959.

As a marque, Ferrari were in a strong position, for out of their 12 starters, making a total of a gross of cylinders, nine were still runners, occupying 1st, 2nd, 4th, 5th, 8th, 9th, 11th and 14th places and leading both the race and the G.T. class. Despite a brief appearance in 2nd place at 11.30 p.m., last year's winner Salvadori, with Clark in the Border Reivers Aston Martin was generally outpaced, and their teammates Baillie/Fairman were well back in 13th position, some eight laps behind the leader. The Ecurie Ecosse Jaguar "D"-type, with a longitudinal "suitcase" in parallel with the original fin, was running a regular race but the early troubles of the Cunningham entry, plus a constant struggle against the disease of only five cylinders firing, had played havoc with the chances of this much-fancied entry, which was probably the fastest flat-out of any on the course.

The disappearance of the Maseratis had transformed the 28th 24-hour event at that point from a race into a demonstration.

Porsche having put pace before staying power in 1959, had pitted themselves less strenuously against the dynamometer this year but were lying in 10th place at best, whereas one of Cunningham's Corvettes was somewhat surprisingly a close second in the G.T. class, less than a lap down. The last Maserati (Jefford and Casner) which went into the sand at Tertre Rouge was dug out, but retired with grit in the gearbox, handing its position briefly to the Austin-Healey of Sears and Riley which departed at four minutes past midnight with a big-end too big.

The fanless Triumphs were running in a threesome, holding 17th, 18th and 19th positions, the fastest British cars in the 2-litre class, although in the downpour hydro-dynamics added to aerodynamics had cut the maximum r.p.m. on the high top gear from 6,200 to 5,600 r.p.m. The 1.2-litre Lotuses were 23rd, 26th and 32nd, the Lola 25th on 1,100 c.c., and the G.T. model M.G. 27th on 1,700 c.c. and two overhead camshafts. The somewhat quaintly bodied Austin-Healey Sprite stood 35th of the 46 runners remaining from 55 starters, having averaged 83.88 m.p.h.—a winning speed in the 1949 race!

By 1 a.m. the speed of the leader had risen to 106.8 m.p.h. and that of the third-running Aston Martin (2 laps behind) to 104.06 m.p.h. By contrast, the new Jaguar found life too hard to bear owing to a blown cylinder gasket, and it accepted hand propulsion to the dead car park in place of self propulsion around the course at 1.40 a.m., when lying 20th; a sad end to an effort which was perhaps more sporting than judicious. But let us pay tribute to a gallant gesture, even if "Nemesis with halting foot followed not far behind."

As the 10th hour went by the Belgians Gendebien and Frère drove their Italian car ruthlessly, relentlessly and remorselessly in the lead at a slowly increasing

Above: Wolfgang von Trips disgustedly abandons his Testa Rossa works Ferrari after only 1½ hours' racing—through lack of fuel.

Left: Another pit-stop for the Cunningham-entered Jaguar, which finally dropped out of the race in the early hours of the morning.

Right: After its long pit-stop cost it an impressive lead, the Gregory/Daigh Maserati simply slashed through the rain in a vain attempt to pull back with the leaders.

race average (107.2 m.p.h.) to the strains of "Carmen," the warm and passionate music contrasting all too clearly with the calmness of the drivers, who knew that only mechanical frailty stood between them and the palm of victory. But much might happen, as Olivier Gendebien must have been painfully aware after last year's race, in a 24-hours not yet half run.

The night was now dry and warm, but with the lights of the "Village" for the most part extinguished, the pits stood like a luminous river with dark banks behind, and the cars played the part of flickering and noisy fireflies as they sped along the invisible road beneath them. The weaker brethren had by now been weeded out, and after 10 hours the solid core of 40 runners were barking their defiance at their thermal and dynamic foes to, appropriately again, the tune of Colonel Bogey.

Now the main interest lay in the displacement of the Aston Martin's third place by the Ecosse Jaguar in the 10th hour (2 a.m.) when it lay 1min. 19sec. behind the 2nd Ferrari and 27 seconds ahead of the Feltham car. Less than 2 minutes separated all three after 600 minutes of racing.

As the faster open cars recovered from their submarine experiences earlier on, and could use both positive and negative acceleration on the dry roads, they pulled away from the Corvettes, the best of which stood 10th at the 10th hour, with its remaining pair of team-mates 18th and 39th. For drum-braked cars scaling the awe-inspiring figure of 2,900 lb., some 50% more than the Jaguar, Ferrari and Aston Martin, and nearly twice as much as the Maserati, this counts as a creditable achievement, especially as the slowest of the team had been involved in some hedging and ditching which literally shook every fibre in its plastic shell.

The Triumph triplets were deranged when the Leston/Rothschild machine fell four laps (and four places) behind the other two cars, but with a steady average in the region of the 90's despite a top gear chosen in relation to piston speed as well as car speed, they showed great consistency.

Some idea of the torrential rain through which the cars drove on Saturday evening is given by this picture of the Connell/Arents G.T. Ferrari approaching Arnage corner.

Below: Miserable, huddled figures around the stationary Trintignant/Herrman Porsche as the little Austin-Healey sweeps past the pits in the wet, wet dusk.

Highest-placed Grand Touring car to finish, the Tavano/Loustel Ferrari leads the Rodriguez/Pilette Ferrari through White House corner.

In the handicap for the Index of Performance very small cars were in the first four positions, and at 3.15 a.m. the Fiat-Abarth, lying second, came into the pits for replenishment and left with a healthy roar, whereas a minute later the leader got away reluctantly on one cylinder before picking up on all two; a phenomenon the less unnerving because it had done the same thing before, to prove that this was clearly bottom-end mixture staggers and not a major defect. At this phase of the race the most remarkable and significant fact was, however, the pace of the Rodriguez/Pilette Ferrari, which rose from fifth at 2 a.m. to second by 3.30 a.m., so that in less than 100 minutes it had overtaken three cars and was challenging for the lead, which had seemed securely in Frère's and Gendebien's possession. To dispossess them Ricardo Rodriguez was showing what a teenager can do in the dark by lapping at 118 m.p.h.

As half-time was near, slight rain damped the surface and pulled down the speed altering the locations of the leaders so that at 4 a.m. we had:

POSITIONS IN GENERAL CLASSIFICATION
AT 12 HOURS (4 a.m.)
1. Gendebien/Frère (Ferrari), 155 laps, 108.43 m.p.h.
2. Rodriguez/Pilette (Ferrari), 152 laps, 107.00.
3. Mairesse/Ginther (Ferrari), 152 laps, 106.94.
4. Flockhart/Halford (Jaguar), 151 laps, 105.82
5. Salvadori/Clark (Aston Martin), 151 laps, 105.38
6. Tavano/Loustel (Ferrari), 147 laps, 102.53.

INDEX OF PERFORMANCE
1. Laureau/Armagnac (D.B. Panhard), 1.234.
2. Condriller/Guichet (Fiat-Abarth), 1.174.
3. Barth/Seidel (Porsche), 1.166.

The Leston/Rothschild Triumph comes smartly out of Tertre Rouge.

Highest Porsche finisher from a very depleted team was the Abarth-bodied coupe driven by Linge and Swaters.

Although delayed by an excursion into a sandbank, the Baillie/Fairman Aston Martin finished.

A steady drive by Ted Lund and Colin Escott brought their privately-entered M.G. (seen here with the Scarlatti/Munaron Maserati at Tertre Rouge) to a well-deserved finish.

RETIREMENTS

Sears/Riley (Austin-Healey), bearing; Kerguen/Lacaze (Porsche), camshafts; Hansgen/Gurney (Jaguar), gasket; Ubezzi/Rozinski (Alfa Romeo), universal joint; Jefford/Casner (Maserati), gearbox; de Leonibus/Consten (Alfa Romeo), suspension.

At 4.30 a.m., light began to seep through a leaden layer of cloud, to reveal cars as coloured three-dimensional entities stripped of the anonymity conferred by night, although as yet still needing headlamps to outline the way ahead, some 1,250 miles more, or three times the distance from London to Edinburgh.

The leaders had responded so well to the Mexican's sprint that they retained a comfortable margin and Mairesse and Ginther's Ferrari got back to second place. The hours of darkness had passed with 11 cars suffering mechanical trouble and only one driver making a mistake. Although the first three places were securely claimed by Modena it was a sad blow to learn that the Jaguar D-type had retired at 5.30 a.m. with a presumed broken crankshaft at Arnage when lying fourth with 168 laps to its credit. This set the Aston Martin up a place and by 6 a.m. (the 14th hour) it had stolen third place as a consequence of a Rodriguez/Pilette stop lasting some ten minutes.

Nevertheless there were still ten dozen Ferrari cylinders left out of the gross which had started and they occupied nine places in the first 15 the only others being two Aston Martins, two Porsches and two Chevrolets. Taking a wider view at the moment when ten hours still remained, Ferraris held first to third and fifth to eighth places; Chevrolet lay 9th and 15th, and Porsche 10th, 14th, 17th and 19th. Aston Martins ran 4th and 12th and Triumph 16th and 18th. A Lotus Elite was 20th, others 22nd, 24th and 28th, and the Lola 27th. The Twin Cam M.G. stood 21st, and the Austin-Healey Sprite was combining an average of 84.6 m.p.h. with 27 m.p.g. With only private entries of 3-litre cars, the race was not auspicious for Britain, and although looking forward it

seemed that the Aston Martin could repeat last year's win, it was all too likely that the race would go to one of the many Ferraris which were just as firmly placed at the 15th hour as they had been from the moment when Gregory could not restart after making a new 3-litre record lap in the Maserati at 121.66 m.p.h.

At the 15th hour the leader had averaged 109.86 m.p.h.; a modest pace which proved that the Belgians were driving with intelligence as well as with skill.

POSITIONS IN GENERAL CLASSIFICATION AT 16 HOURS (8 a.m.)

1. P. Frère/O. Gendebien (Ferrari), 210 laps, 110.04 m.p.h.
2. R. Rodriguez/A. Pilette (Ferrari), 205, 107.56.
3. W. Mairesse/R. Ginther (Ferrari), 204, 107.12.
4. R. Salvadori/J. Clark (Aston Martin), 203, 106.50.
5. F. Tavano/P. Loustel (Ferrari G.T.), 200, 104.58.
6. G. Whitehead/H. Taylor (Ferrari G.T.), 199, 104.33.

INDEX OF PERFORMANCE

1. G. Laureau/P. Armagnac (D.B. Panhard).
2. Condriller/Guichet (Fiat-Abarth).
3. E. Barth/W. Seidel (Porsche).

RETIREMENTS

Rambaux/Boutin (A.C.-Bristol), holed piston; Flockhart/Halford (Jaguar), broken crankshaft; Buxton/Allen (Lotus Elite); Vogele/Ashdown (Lola-Climax).

By breakfast time on Sunday, with eight hours still to go, Le Mans for the spectators once more became a motor race. They left their tents and caravans and straw bales to cast a bleary eye at the 35 cars still running on this overcast but dry morning. Hopes of a British win still rested with the Salvadori/Clark Aston Martin which at its present lap speeds of a little under four and a half minutes could only be achieved by the retirement or long delay of at least the leading Ferrari, seven laps—about 60 miles—in front. At 8.15 a.m. it came one step nearer to victory when the driver of the Mairesse/Ginther car walked back to the pits after abandoning his car with gearbox trouble. Weaknesses in the transmission have let Ferrari down many times in the past: were the two leaders to suffer a similar fate? The leading car was evidently taking things easy with lap times, on a dry track, of about 4 min. 42 sec.—slower, in fact, than the Fitch/Grossman Corvette (but in no danger of being caught with 15 laps between them), and considerably slower than the second Ferrari which gained about 10 seconds a lap until it caught up to run in line astern before making a routine stop.

By 10 a.m.—with six hours to go—the

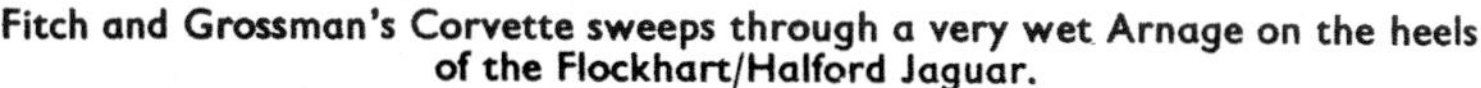

Fitch and Grossman's Corvette sweeps through a very wet Arnage on the heels of the Flockhart/Halford Jaguar.

Winner of the Index of Performance and its class, the Laureau/Armagnac Panhard passes the famous White House in the closing laps.

1. G. Laureau/P. Armagnac (D.B. Panhard), 1.257.
2. E. Barth/W. Seidel (Porsche), 1.183.
3. P. Frère/O. Gendebien (Ferrari), 1.163.

RETIREMENTS

Beaufort/Stoop (Porsche); Baillie/Parkes (Lotus Elite); Condriller/Guichet (Fiat-Abarth); Bonnier/Hill (Porsche), blown head gasket; Thompson/Windridge (Corvette), caught fire; Mairesse/Ginther (Ferrari);

clouds had lifted and Le Mans was once more bathing in wind-swept sunshine. Porsche, normally one of the most reliable cars here, had their fourth retirement when the Bonnier/Hill car that had given so much trouble early on in the race, was abandoned with a blown cylinder head gasket. Although well down in 14th place, the Porsche pit made a do-or-die attempt to get the car back into the race. The engine was whipped out, up-ended and the head stripped down, only to reveal that the cylinder liner was damaged too much for it to continue. This left three Porsches running, in 11th, 14th and 15th places, leading their class and the three 2-litre Triumphs in 16th, 18th and 20th positions. The lone Lola, that had been motoring round steadily but not very quickly by Lola standards, then retired.

The order remained unchanged: Ferrari, Ferrari, Aston Martin, followed by five G.T. Ferraris, the Baillie/Fairman Aston Martin in eighth place and the first of the three remaining Corvettes—Fitch and Grossman—burbling around with its odd-sounding exhaust in 9th place. The leading G.T. Ferrari, incidentally, had only been delivered to its owner, Tavano, on the Monday before the race; and scrutineering took place on Tuesday!

After one of the most gallant and eventful drives that have been seen at Le Mans, the Thompson/Windridge Corvette (it had much of its bodywork removed early on Saturday and spent a long time during the night being unditched from the Tertre Rouge sandbank) suddenly belched smoke on its way past the pits for the 207th time, at 11.15 a.m. Smoke poured from everywhere; the bonnet, the cab, the exhaust. Showing great restraint the driver took to the escape road, stopped with tantalizing slowness, and leapt out to safety, as the smoke subsided.

The index of performance was still being led very comfortably by the Laureau/Armagnac two-cylinder D.B. Panhard, sounding considerably better than the now sick Bolton/Sanderson Triumph. After motoring round unhappily for many laps with a number of pit stops for investigation the Ballisat/Becquart car too began making similar rough noises. But they both motored on regardless.

POSITIONS IN GENERAL CLASSIFICATION
AT 20 HOURS (12 noon)

1. P. Frère/O. Gendebien (Ferrari), 262 laps, 107.74 m.p.h.
2. R. Rodriguez/A. Pilette (Ferrari), 259, 108.37.
3. R. Salvadori/J. Clark (Aston Martin), 256, 107.12.
4. F. Tavano/P. Loustel (Ferrari G.T.), 252, 105.57.
5. G. Whitehead/H. Taylor (Ferrari G.T.), 251,105.07.
6. Helde/Noblet (Ferrari G.T.), 249, 104.45.

At 12.45 p.m. another of the Ferraris retired. After holding first 6th and then 5th place since the early hours of the morning, the Whitehead/Taylor car came to rest on the Mulsanne straight. This car, like that of Tavano, had only been delivered to Whitehead just before the event and considering that neither driver had raced it before, put up a remarkably good performance.

Half an hour later yet another Ferrari went; the American-entered car of Sturgis and Slessor that was holding 12th place. And the best-placed Porsche made a long pit stop before continuing without losing its 10th place.

With two and a half hours to go, 30 of the original 55 starters had retired, the order still being Ferrari, Ferrari, Aston Martin and four more Ferraris. Split into makes there were eight Ferraris, two Aston Martins (the only ones to start), two Corvettes, two Porsches (six started), two Lotus (four started), three Triumphs—two of them not very happy—three D.B.s, and one each of M.G., Austin-Healey, Osca, A.C.-Bristol and Stanguellini. All the Fiat-Abarths and Maseratis had retired.

As the race entered its closing stages it was interesting to analyse the maximum speeds reached by the various cars down the Mulsanne straight. Traditionally Jaguar laurels, this year's fastest car was easily the Gregory/Daigh Maserati. With its long, gently sloping windscreen extending down to the nose of the car, the Maserati's maximum speed was a shade under 170 m.p.h. Others were as follows: Ferrari (Scarfiotti/Rodriguez), 162 m.p.h.; Ferrari GT (Whitehead/Taylor), 157 m.p.h.; Jaguar (Flockhart/Halford), 157 m.p.h.; Jaguar (the new one of Gurney and Hansgen), 153 m.p.h.; Corvette (Thompson/Wind-

Left: In bright Sunday afternoon sunshine, the Salvadori/Clark Aston Martin completes its final laps.

Right: A sea of people on the track as the "thermal efficiency" Lotus, driven by Marsh and Wagstaff comes in.

ridge), 151 m.p.h.; Aston Martin (Salvadori/Clark), 149 m.p.h.; Porsche (Trintignant/Herrmann), 145 m.p.h.; Austin-Healey 3000 (Sears/Riley), 129 m.p.h.; Triumph (Leston/Rothschild), 128 m.p.h.; Lotus (Buxton/Allen), 128 m.p.h.; A.C.-Bristol (Wicky/Gachnang), 123 m.p.h.; Fiat-Abarth, 119 m.p.h.; Osca, 115 m.p.h.; D.B. Panhard, 111 m.p.h.

As the clock moved round to 3 p.m.—one hour to go—there were 25 cars still running. The leading Porsche, that of Barth and Seidel, finally came to rest at Tertre Rouge after a long pit stop; the car was obviously restarted simply to finish the race. The overall position altered very little during the last few hours and remained at two Ferraris, one Aston Martin and four G.T. Ferraris; the Fitch/Grossman Corvette had moved up to 8th place, the Baillie/Fairman Aston Martin had dropped to 9th and the Lilley/Gambles Corvette was 10th in front of the first Porsche, now that of Linge and Swaters.

As the race ran into its final hour many of the survivors stopped at their pits. Some, of course, were purely routine changes of driver, as were made by the two leading Ferraris to enable the Belgian drivers Paul Frère and André Pilette to take over, easily distinguishable by their helmets in Belgian racing yellow. Others, however, such as the Chevrolet Corvette of Fitch and Grossman paused for long, anxious consultations round their raised bonnet before resuming the race somewhat hesitantly to encouraging cheers from the big crowd which had assembled to watch the finish with all its traditional ceremonial.

With but a quarter of an hour to go the Porsche of Barth and Seidel which had been parked on the right side of the road just before the pits with what is known in France as *ennui*, set off to limp round on what it hoped would be its final lap.

With a few minutes to go the leading Ferrari made the error of crossing the finishing line so had to set off on another lap to Paul Frère's intense disgust. It was therefore a mixed bunch of D.B.s and three Triumphs in line abreast formation which were the first cars to receive the chequered flag at 4 p.m. So ended a Le Mans notable for the high number of finishers rather than for great drama or close racing.

A grandstand finish by the Ferraris in line astern: Gendebien/Frère (1st), Rodriguez/Pilette (2nd), Tavano/Loustel (4th) and Arents/Connell (5th)

The most happy fellas. Olivier Gendebien waves his cowboy hat and Paul Frère tries to steer as the team-laden Belgian-driven winner is cheered at the finish of the race.

RESULTS

(continued from p. 57)

GENERAL CLASSIFICATION

11. H. Linge/J. Swaters (1,588 c.c. Porsche), 2,249.3 miles; 12. F. Barth/W. Seidel (1,498 c.c. Porsche), 2,207.4 miles; 13. E. Lund/C. Escott (1,762 c.c. M.G. M.G.A.), 2,188.6 miles; 14. R. Masson/C. Laurent (1,216 c.c. Lotus Elite), 2,183.0 miles; 15. K. Ballisat/M. Becquart (1,985 c.c. Triumph T.R.S.), 2,149.0 miles; 16. J. Wagstaff/A. Marsh (1,216 c.c. Lotus Elite), 2,183.0 miles; 17. G. Laureau/P. Armagnac (702 c.c. D.B. Panhard), 2,116.1 miles; 18. L. Leston/M. Rothschild (1,985 c.c. Triumph T.R.S.), 2,115.6 miles; 19. N. Sanderson/P. Bolton (1,985 c.c. Triumph T.R.S.), 2,090.6 miles; 20. J. Dalton/J. Colgate (996 c.c. Austin-Healey Sprite), 2,055.2 miles; 21. P. Lelong/Van den Beruwaen (851 c.c. D.B. Panhard), 2,036.4 miles; 22. A. Wicky/G. Gachnang (1,971 c.c. A.C. Bristol), 2,001.7 miles; 23. J. Bentley/J. S. Gordon (746 c.c. Osca), 1,982.1 miles; 24. R. Bouharde/J. Jaeger (841 c.c. D.B. Panhard), 1,906.5 miles; 25. R. Bartholoni/P. de Saint-Auban (851 c.c. D.B. Panhard), 1,865.1 miles. (Last five finished but did not qualify as below set speeds.)

INDEX OF PERFORMANCE

1. G. Laureau/P. Armagnac (702 c.c. D.B. Panhard), 1.257; 2. O. Gendebien/P. Frère (2,953 c.c. Ferrari T.R.), 1.157; 3. J. Bentley/J. S. Gordon (746 c.c. Osca), 1.151.

INDEX OF "THERMAL EFFICIENCY"

1. A. Wagstaff/A. Marsh (1,216 c.c. Lotus Elite), 1.148; 2. R. A. Masson/C. Laurent (1,216 c.c. Lotus Elite), 1.021; 3. R. Bouharde/J. Jaeger (841 c.c. D.B. Panhard), 0.968.

LE MANS 24-HOUR RACE

HOUR-BY-HOUR POSITIONS

DRIVERS	CARS	HOURS																							
		1	2	3	4	5	6	7	8	9	10	11	12	13	14	15	16	17	18	19	20	21	22	23	24
Cunningham—Kimberley	Chevrolet	24	21	—																					
Thompson—Windridge	Chevrolet	14	15	37	30	40	43	44	45	42	39	37	34	32	30	28	27	*	*	*	*				
Fitch—Grossman	Chevrolet	18	13	15	13	11	10	8	7	9	10	9	9	11	9	10	10	9	9	9	10	9	8	8	8
Lilley—Gambles	Chevrolet	41	38	28	26	25	24	23	21	19	18	16	16	16	15	15	15	13	13	13	13	12	11	10	10
Flockhart—Halford	Jaguar	7	4	4	4	4	5	4	5	4	3	4	4	*	*	*	*								
Hansgen—Gurney	Jaguar	31	18	10	10	9	15	14	20	*	*	*	*												
Salvadori—Clark	Aston Martin	10	6	5	5	5	3	3	3	3	4	5	5	5	4	4	4	3	3	3	3	3	3	3	3
I. Baillie—Fairman	Aston Martin	21	11	13	16	14	4	13	13	12	13	13	13	12	12	11	12	8	8	10	9	8	9	9	9
Von Trips—P. Hill	Ferrari	3	32	—																					
Mairesse—Ginther	Ferrari	4	2	2	2	3	4	5	2	2	2	2	3	2	3	3	3	*	*	*	*				
Frère—Gendebien	Ferrari	2	1	1	1	1	1	1	1	1	1	1	1	1	1	1	1	1	1	1	1	1	1	1	1
Scarfiotti—P. Rodriguez	Ferrari	6	33	—																					
Whitehead—Taylor	Ferrari GT	11	9	7	6	6	6	6	6	7	7	7	7	7	6	6	6	5	5	5	5	—			
Tavano—Loustel	Ferrari GT	9	7	6	7	8	7	9	8	6	6	6	6	6	5	5	5	4	4	4	4	4	4	4	4
R. Rodriguez—Pilette	Ferrari GT	5	3	3	3	2	2	2	4	5	5	3	2	3	2	2	2	2	2	2	2	2	2	2	2
Arents—Connell	Ferrari GT	23	19	17	17	15	13	12	12	13	12	11	10	10	8	8	8	7	7	7	7	6	6	6	5
Hugus—Pabst	Ferrari GT	17	20	16	15	13	11	11	11	11	11	12	12	13	11	12	11	10	10	8	8	7	7	7	7
Sturgis—Slessor	Ferrari GT	20	17	11	12	16	16	16	14	14	14	14	14	14	13	13	13	12	12	12	12	11	—		
Beurlys—Bianchi	Ferrari GT	13	12	—																					
Helde—Noblet	Ferrari GT	16	14	9	8	7	8	7	9	8	8	8	8	8	7	7	7	6	6	6	6	5	5	5	6
Sears—Riley	Austin-Healey	30	28	24	23	20	19	17	15	*	*	*	*												
Gregory—Daigh	Maserati	1	5	46	40	33	28	21	29	*	*	*	*												
Jefford—Casner	Maserati	12	8	12	11	12	12	15	37	33	35	39	39	*	*	*	*								
Scarlatti—Munaron	Maserati	8	34	—																					
Ballisat—Becquart	Triumph	29	27	21	21	22	20	18	17	15	16	18	18	18	18	19	20	18	17	18	18	17	15	15	15
Bolton—Sanderson	Triumph	28	25	22	22	23	22	22	19	16	17	17	17	17	16	17	18	16	15	15	16	15	17	19	19
Wicky—Gachnang	A.C.	35	35	29	37	39	37	32	31	28	27	27	32	37	35	35	33	28	26	26	25	23	22	22	22
Lund—Escott	M.G.	34	31	30	35	31	32	29	27	21	20	23	22	22	21	21	21	19	18	17	17	16	14	14	13
Bonnier—G. Hill	Porsche	54	54	48	43	38	30	24	22	18	15	15	15	14	14	14	*	*	*	*					
Trintignant—Herrmann	Porsche	15	10	8	9	*	*	*	*																
Linge—Swaters	Porsche	26	24	18	20	21	21	33	28	24	22	21	21	20	19	18	17	15	14	14	14	13	12	12	11
Kerguen—Lacaze	Porsche	25	23	19	19	19	18	19	16	*	*	*	*												
De Beaufort—Stoop	Porsche	19	22	20	18	17	17	37	36	26	23	20	20	19	17	16	16	*	*	*	*				
Barth—Seidel	Porsche	22	16	14	14	10	9	10	10	10	9	10	11	9	10	9	9	11	11	11	11	10	10	11	12
Leonibus—Consten	Alfa Romeo	38	47	41	42	46	45	43	41	*	*	*	*												
Wagstaff—Marsh	Lotus	37	36	26	27	26	25	35	32	30	32	32	30	29	28	27	26	22	21	21	20	18	16	16	16
Buxton—Allen	Lotus	33	29	27	29	29	27	27	26	22	25	25	24	24	22	25	31	*	*	*	*				
G. Baillie—Parkes	Lotus	52	55	49	47	45	39	36	34	27	28	28	26	26	24	22	25	*	*	*	*				
Masson—Laurent	Lotus	32	30	25	25	27	26	25	23	20	19	19	19	21	20	20	19	17	16	16	15	14	13	13	14
Vogele—Ashdown	Lola	36	37	31	31	30	31	28	25	25	26	26	27	27	27	32	35	*	*	*	*				
Dalton—Colgate	A.-H. Sprite	49	48	40	39	37	36	34	35	32	31	30	31	30	29	29	28	24	23	23	22	21	20	20	20
Lelong—Van der Bruwaene	D.B. Panhard	45	45	35	38	41	38	38	38	39	38	34	35	34	32	31	30	25	24	24	23	22	21	21	21
Laureau—Armagnac	D.B. Panhard	44	43	34	33	35	34	30	30	29	29	29	28	28	26	26	24	21	22	22	21	20	19	18	17
Spichiger—Feret	Fiat-Abarth	47	44	33	36	36	46	46	46	43	41	40	40	*	*	*	*								
Condriller—Guichet	Fiat-Abarth	39	39	32	28	28	29	26	24	23	24	24	25	25	25	24	22	*	*	*	*				
Vinatier—Vidilles	D.B. Panhard	48	50	43	—																				
Bartheloni—De Saint-Aubun	D.B. Panhard	50	51	42	41	44	40	39	40	36	34	36	37	36	34	34	34	29	28	28	27	26	25	25	25
Laroche—Simon	Osca	43	42	39	34	*	*	*	*																
Bentley—Gordon	Osca	51	49	44	45	42	42	40	39	35	33	33	33	33	31	30	29	26	25	25	24	24	23	23	23
Quilico—Reis	Stanguellini	53	52	50	48	48	47	45	44	41	40	38	38	38	36	36	36	31	29	29	28	*	*	*	*
Bouharde—Jaeger	D.B.	55	53	47	46	47	44	42	42	38	37	35	36	35	33	33	32	27	27	27	26	25	24	24	24
Rambaux—Boutin	A.C.	42	41	38	32	34	35	31	33	31	30	31	29	*	*	*	*								
Leston—Rothschild	Triumph	27	26	23	24	24	23	20	18	17	21	22	23	23	23	23	23	20	19	20	19	19	18	17	18
Rigamonti—Cattini	Fiat-Abarth	46	46	36	—																				
Ubezzi—Rosinski	Alfa Romeo	40	40	45	44	43	41	41	43	*	*	*	*												

N.B.—Between 4th and 20th hours retirements listed at 4-hour intervals only. Asterisks indicate 4-hour period in which car retired. This table is compiled from official figures. The fact that some cars are shown as holding a position when, in fact, they were out of the race is because they may not have been declared retired by the entrant.

Arguably, the modern Le Mans racing car was born in 1961. There was nothing new about rear or mid-engined cars - indeed, up to 1961 and for many years afterwards, Porsche had never built or raced anything else - but the presence at Le Mans in 1961 of a new breed of mid-engined sports racers from Ferrari, Maserati and other makes was an important pointer to future developments. The regulations were largely unchanged from 1960 and 35 sports cars came to the start together with 20 GT cars. Jaguar was a notable absentee, for the first time since 1950. Ferrari again entered 11 cars; four were works entries in the sports car class and included two V12 three-litre Testa Rossas, the mid-engined 2¹/₂ litre six and (just to confuse matters) a prototype 250 GT. There was also an American entered Ferrari Testa Rossa driven by the Rodriguez brothers and, in the GT class, six 250 GT coupes, one of which was driven by Stirling Moss and Graham Hill - Moss' last Le Mans; he retired from racing following his accident at Goodwood at Easter 1962.

Maserati had no works entries but entrusted three new mid-engined Tipo 63s with three-litre V12s to Scuderia Serenissima (one car) and Briggs Cunningham (two cars)- Cunningham also entered a two-litre Birdcage which he co-drove. Aston Martin had two DBR 1/300s; also a DB 4 and two Zagato bodied DB 4 GTs with 3.7 litre engines which ran in the GT class. The last cars with engines over two litres were an Austin-Healey 3000 (GT class) and a Cooper Monaco 2¹/₂ litre (sports class). The two-litre class was much better supported: apart from the Birdcage Maserati, it contained three Porsches, three Triumph TRSs and the MGA Twin-Cam appearing for the third time at Le Mans. All of these ran in the sports car class but there were also two AC Ace GTs among the two-litre cars.

There were two 1,600 cc Porsches and two Sunbeam Alpines, entered by Rootes, a late return to Le Mans for a famous name - had not the three-litre Sunbeam come second in 1925? - even if the name was the only similarity between the 1925 and the 1961 entries. Of the Alpines, one was open and the other a fastback coupe by Harrington. Four Lotus Elites were the only cars in the 1,300 cc class, and the one-litre class was not well supported with two Austin-Healey Sprites and a single Osca. By contrast, there were no less than 13 cars in the 701-850 cc class: six DB-Panhards, five Abarths, an Osca and a Lotus which had a 750 cc engine in an Elite body.

Ferrari was again the dominant force in the race; this might have led to a relatively uninteresting Le Mans, but this was not so due to two factors: the spirited performance of the Rodriguez brothers driving in opposition to the works entries, and the appearance of the 2.4 litre mid-engined car driven by Ginther/von Trips. These two cars, together with the works Testa Rossas of Gendebien/Hill and Mairesse/Parkes regularly filled the first four places on the scoreboard throughout the race, with the Ferrari GTs yapping at their heels. The Aston Martin DBRs were not effective challengers; the clutch of the Flockhart/Jim Clark car gave in, although the Salvadori~Maggs car was lying fourth when the fuel tank split. The GT Astons did not fare any better; the two Zagato bodied cars were among the earliest retirements with blown gaskets due to overheating, while the third DB 4 had to stop in the last hour of the race when the electrics failed. Nor were the mid-engined Maseratis able to break Ferrari's hold over the race; two of the Tipo 63's had retired early on, and only one of the Cunningham entered cars (driven by Pabst and Thompson) survived the race.

As the mid-engined Ferrari ran out of fuel and the Rodriguez brothers blew up their engine (though not before Ricardo had put in a lap at 125.020 mph), it was a second victory for Gendebien and Phil Hill (it was in fact Gendebien's third) with the Mairesse/Parkes Testa Rossa in second place, followed by the first Ferrari GT in third place (this car also won the GT class). Pabst and Thompson drove their Maserati up through a depleted field to finish in fourth place, followed by the first of the Porsches which also won the two-litre class. In addition Porsches won the 1,600 cc class, while among British successes was a win for the Lotus Elite in the 1,300 cc class, and the team prize was awarded to the three Triumphs which finished ninth, eleventh and fifteenth. There were no finishers in the one-litre class, and an Abarth took the 850 cc honours.

The Index of Performance went to a DB-Panhard, but the Index of Thermal Efficiency was won by the Sunbeam Alpine Harrington, mainly because it was 50 per cent heavier than most of the other contenders for this Index. This fastback coupe version of the Sunbeam Alpine was immediately re-named Le Mans. A total of 22 cars finished the race, and the highest placed British car to finish was the Triumph in ninth place. Ferrari, celebrating the fifth victory for the make, had equalled the record of Bentley and Jaguar.

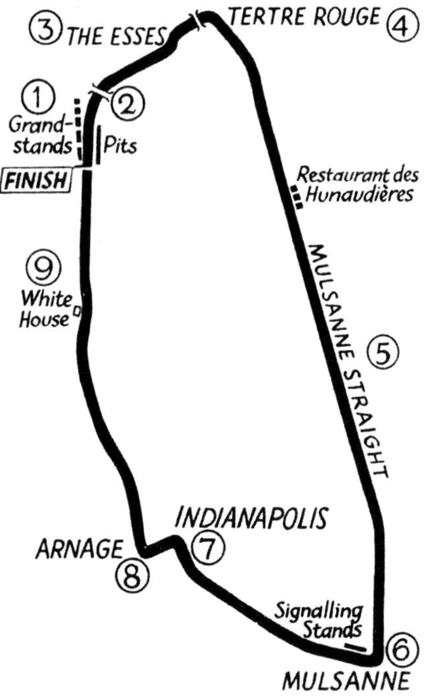

1. Starting on the straight with pits (hidden) on their right and packed terraces and stands on their left, cars plunge immediately into a fast right-hander . . .

2. . . . under the first of Dunlop's two famous bridges which carry spectators across the track.

A Corner-by-corner Lap of the

Le Mans

New Race Records in Prospect, with Ferrari

WILL the 1961 Le Mans 24-hour race be the fastest ever run? If the weather remains fine throughout most of the 24 hours between 4 p.m. next Saturday and the same hour on Sunday afternoon, then the answer will almost certainly be yes, for the new breed of rear-engined sports cars which are such a feature of the 1961 season are very rapid indeed. Inspired by the success of the Cooper Monaco—and its great rival, the Lotus 19—both Ferrari and Maserati have produced new rear-engined sports cars, in spite of the fact that this is probably the last season in which such cars will be able to compete in the classic long-distance sports-car races, for the Commission Sportive Internationale has recommended that such races next year should be restricted to Grand Touring cars. Which is not to say that the sports-racing cars will vanish from the scene, for they may well take the place of the still-born Intercontinental Formula.

However, in what is probably their last appearance on the Sarthe circuit, they should go out in a blaze of glory, for there is every prospect of an intensely exciting battle for outright victory between the four Ferrari works entries and the four Maseratis, two entered by Briggs Cunningham and two by the Italian Scuderia Serenissima. Ferrari have entered three of the latest three-litre V-12 TR models with their new, streamlined bodies and one of the 2.4-litre V-6 rear-engined cars. The four Maseratis will be finally selected from the front-engined Type 61 model and the rear-engined Type 63 which exists in four-cylinder, V-8 and V-12 versions.

British hopes of an outright victory are slender indeed this year; to oppose the latest Continental sports machinery we have only two Aston Martin DBR1s and a Cooper Monaco, for the sole Lotus 19 entered is running with a two-litre engine.

Among the Grand Touring cars, however, the two Aston Martin Zagato DB4GT cars may well give the many Ferrari 250GT models a run for their money. Other British G.T. entries include an Austin-Healey 3000, two A.C.-Bristols, numerous Lotus Elites and two works Sunbeams.

9. Gentle curves and undulations bring the cars to the sometimes under-rated right-and-left zig-zag at the White House, taken at about 100 m.p.h. by the experts. From here it is uphill to the pits to complete the lap.

3. A short straight, uphill and down, brings cars to the tight curves of the Esses (*above*).

4. The exit from the Esses is just visible at the top of this picture (*right*); cars then come down the brief straight under the second Dunlop bridge and into the right-handed Tertre Rouge.

Famous 8.36-mile Sarthe Circuit

and Maserati the Favourites

Le Mans Timetable

Tuesday, June 6.   7 a.m.-6 p.m. Scrutineering at circuit.
Wednesday, June 7. 7 a.m.-4 p.m. Scrutineering at circuit.
                                 7 p.m.-11 p.m. First practice session.
Thursday, June 8.   6 p.m.-11 p.m. Second practice session.
Saturday, June 10.   12 noon. Cars to be at their pits.
                                 4 p.m. Start of the race.
Sunday, June 11.   4 p.m. Finish of the race.

The Three Principal Awards

First in General Classification . . . 50,000 new francs (about £3,750).
First in Index of Thermal Efficiency (based on distance covered, weight of the car and its fuel consumption per 100 km.) . . . 30,000 new francs (about £2,250).
First in Index of Performance (based on capacity and distance covered . . . 25,000 new francs (about £1,875).

The Circuit

Situated five miles south of Le Mans on N.158 to Tours and D.139 to Laigne. One lap = 8.36 miles or 13.48 kilometres. Lap record: J. M. Hawthorn (4.1-litre Ferrari), 3 min. 58.7 sec., 126.17 m.p.h. in 1957 race.

Result of 1960 Race

1, O. Gendebien/P. Frère (2,953 c.c. Ferrari), 2,620.7 miles, 109.20 m.p.h. 2, R. Rodriguez/A. Pilette (2,953 c.c. Ferrari). 3, J. Clark/R. Salvadori (2,992 c.c. Aston Martin). Index of
(*Continued overleaf*)

7. (*Right*) There is a fast right-hand curve just before the circuit's sharpest left-hander at Indianapolis, seen at the top of this picture, linked by a short straight to . . .

8. . . . the severe right-hand corner at Arnage (*below*).

5. Then follows the long Mulsanne straight (*above*) where the faster cars will be reaching over 160 m.p.h. The slight kink about three-quarters of the way down on the map can just be discerned as an appreciable corner in the distance.

6. The Mulsanne straight ends abruptly in a sharp right-hander of the same name (*above*) and cars leave it (*below*) for a mildly twisty section leading to Indianapolis corner.

Le Mans

The Type 63 Maserati (*left*) is the rear-engined version of the Type 61 "birdcage" model. It may be fitted with either an inclined four-cylinder engine, a V-12 or a new V-8. Much development work has gone into the Type 61 Maserati (*right*), victor in the Nürburgring 1,000 kilometre sports-car race for two years in succession.

Performance: Laureau/Armagnac (D.B. Panhard). Index of Thermal Efficiency: Wagstaff/Marsh (Lotus Elite).

BROADCASTING

The B.B.C. Light Programme will describe the start of the race and will follow this up with several progress reports up to midnight. On Sunday morning at 8.30 the Light Programme will give a summary of the first 16½ hours of the race followed by periodic progress reports until the finish at 4 p.m.

On B.B.C. television there will be a direct transmission of the closing stages of the race.

There is likely to be a keen struggle between the Aston Martin Zagato DB4GT (*above*) and the Ferrari 250GT (*below*) which has hitherto reigned supreme in G.T. racing. In the Le Mans trials in April, a G.T. Ferrari lapped at over 120 m.p.h.

LE MANS ENTRIES

Car	Capacity	Entrant	Drivers
Sports Cars			
Aston Martin	2,992	Essex Racing Team	R. Salvadori/X
Aston Martin	2,992	Border Reivers	J. Clark/R. Flockhart
Ferrari	2,953	Ferrari works	O. Gendebien/P. Hill
Ferrari	2,953	Ferrari works	W. von Trips/R. Ginther
Ferrari	2,953	Ferrari works	R. Rodriguez/P. Rodriguez
Maserati	2,890	B. S. Cunningham	W. Hansgen/B. McLaren
Maserati	2,890	B. S. Cunningham	A. Pabst/Dick Thompson
Maserati	2,890	Sc. Serenissima	M. Trintignant/L. Maglioli
Maserati	2,890	Sc. Serenissima	X/X
Cooper Monaco	2,496	Ec. Ecosse	T. Dickson/B. Halford
Ferrari	2,417	Ferrari works	W. Mairesse/F. Tavano
Maserati	1,989	B. S. Cunningham	B. S. Cunningham/J. Kimberley
Triumph	1.985	Standard-Triumph	M. Becquart/M. Rothschild
Triumph	1,985	Standard-Triumph	L. Leston/R. Slotemaker
Triumph	1,985	Standard-Triumph	K. Ballisat/P. Bolton
Porsche	1,980	Porsche works	J. Bonnier/X
Porsche	1,980	Porsche works	D. Gurney/H. Herrmann
Porsche	1,980	Porsche works	E. Barth/X
Lotus 19	1,960	Team Elite	W. Allen/P. Arundell
Porsche	1,588	A. Veuillet	P. Monneret/X
Osca	1,100	N.A.R.T.	X/X
Austin-Healey	994	Donald Healey	J. Colgate/P. Hawkins
Fiat-Abarth	982	Abarth works	B. Consten/X
Fiat-Abarth	982	Abarth works	J. Rosinski/X
Fiat-Abarth	982	Eq. National Belge	C. Dubois/Langlois
D.B.-Panhard	954	D.B. works	Bartholoni/X
Austin-Healey	948	Ec. Ecosse	N. Sanderson/W. Mackay
D.B.-Panhard	848	D.B. works	X/X
D.B.-Panhard	848	D.B. works	X/X
Fiat-Abarth	846	Abarth works	Condriller/X
Osca	742	Osca works	Laroche/A. Simon
Lotus	742	UDT/Laystall	C. Allison/M. McKee
D.B.-Panhard	702	D.B. works	G. Laureau/P. Armagnac
D.B.-Panhard	702	D.B. works	Vinatier/Bouharde
D.B.-Panhard	701	R. Masson	Masson/Richard
Grand Touring Cars			
Aston Martin	3,670	J. Kerguen	J. Kerguen/Dewez
Aston Martin	3,670	Essex Racing Team	Tony Maggs/X
Aston Martin	3,670	Essex Racing Team	A. F. Davison/B. Stillwell
Ferrari	2,953	P. Noblet	J. Guichet/P. Noblet
Ferrari	2,953	Ec. Francorchamps	Beurlys/Heldé
Ferrari	2,953	Sc. Serenissima	X/X
Ferrari	2,953	N.A.R.T.	S. Moss/G. Hill
Ferrari	2,953	N.A.R.T.	J. Surtees/M. Parkes
Ferrari	2,953	Eq. Nationale Belge	M. Bianchi/Vandevelde
Austin-Healey	2,912	Ec. Chiltern	J. Bekaert/R. Stoop
A.C.-Bristol	1,971	Chardonnet	Alexandrovitch/Magne
A.C.-Bristol	1.971	Eq. Lausannoise	de Sibenthal/Wicky
Sunbeam Alpine	1,592	Sunbeam-Talbot	P. Harper/P. Procter
Sunbeam Alpine	1,592	Sunbeam-Talbot	P. Jopp/P. Hopkirk
Porsche	1,588	Porsche works	H. Linge/X
Alfa Romeo	1,292	Sq. Conrero	X/X
Lotus Elite	1,216	Team Lotus	D. Buxton/X
Lotus Elite	1,216	Team Lotus	J. Dalton/Walker
Lotus Elite	1,216	Ec. Edger	Boyer/Kosellek
Lotus Elite	1,216	Los Amigos	J. F. Malle/X

The Aston Martin DBR1 was victorious at Le Mans in 1959 and was highest placed British car, in third position, last year. One or both of the two cars entered privately this year may well finish high up in the field through sheer reliability.

The latest V-12 front-engined Ferrari TR1 (*right*) carries a new streamlined body and is shorter in the wheelbase than the TR1s that won here in 1958 and 1960. Based to a considerable extent on last year's Grand Prix cars, the rear-engined Ferrari (*left*) is powered by a V-6 engine. It has already won the Targa Florio this season. Note the turned-up tails on both cars, designed to prevent fumes being drawn forward into the cockpit.

(*Left*) Making their third successive appearance at Le Mans, the team of three twin-overhead-camshaft Triumphs has been modified in certain details, now being wider in track and fitted with rack and pinion steering gear.

(*Above*) The Cooper Monaco entered by Ecurie Ecosse will be the sole representative at Le Mans of a car which has exerted considerable influence on Continental sports-car design.

(*Above*) Porsche have made a most careful study of the streamlining of their cars in an attempt to offset the disadvantage of sheer lack of litres on so rapid a circuit as Le Mans. The result of their studies is this very smooth coupé with the air intakes behind the rear window but under the extended roof.

(*Below*) One of the two Sunbeam Alpines will be this Harrington-bodied G.T. model with a very smooth front, and the second will be a normal hardtop. Both cars are equipped with special 22-gallon fuel tanks.

A number of Lotus Elites (*above*) have been entered, and will be attempting to win the Index of Thermal Efficiency for the second year in succession. Austin-Healey are represented by two Sprites and this very standard 3000 G.T. model (*below*) entered by the Ecurie Chiltern.

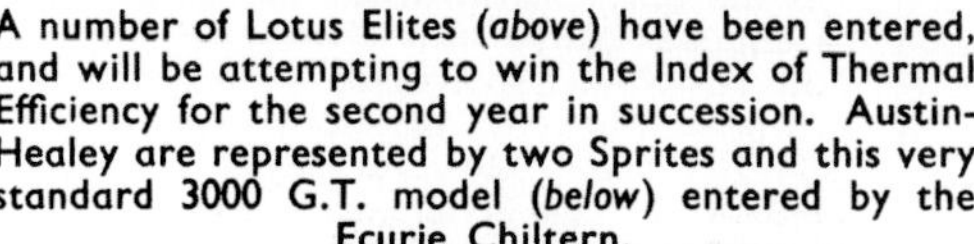

Le Mans 1961

OUTRIGHT WIN FOR HILL-GENDEBIEN (FERRARI) : THERMAL EFFICIENCY INDEX TO HARPER-PROCTOR (SUNBEAM ALPINE)

SAVE for the first part of the opening lap, when Jimmy Clark's Aston Martin led the field, Ferraris dominated the Le Mans 24-hour race last weekend, occupying at least the first two places, and more frequently the first five, throughout the race.

At first the Hill-Gendebien and the Ginther-von Trips works cars battled for the lead, treating the long race as though it were a sprint. Then, when the Ginther-von Trips car retired, the Rodriguez brothers took over the challenge in their privately entered Ferrari, the two leading cars being separated by only 5sec even after 15 hours of racing. All the time, the crowds were rooting for the young Mexicans, and showed their disappointment unrestrainedly when, very near the end, the car came in to retire; unfortunately, their cheers and encouragement could not get the Ferrari back in the race—but without the Rodriguez boys it would have been a considerably duller Le Mans.

All this time, the works Ferrari driven by Mairesse and Michael Parkes was up among the leaders, eventually taking second place to the Hill-Gendebien car in the general classification. The Index of Performance was again won by a D.B.-Panhard, Laureau driving the winner for the third time, this year with Bonharde.

It was not Britain's good day, at least so far as the general classification was concerned. For some time, the U.D.T.-Laystall 742 c.c. Lotus-Climax led on Index of Performance, however, until it retired with a faulty oil pump. A very fine performance indeed, and some compensation to the great numbers of British spectators present, was the win for Peter Harper's and Peter Proctor's Sunbeam Alpine in the Thermal Efficiency Index.

● ● ● ● ● ● ● ● ● ● ● ● ● ● ● ● ● ● ● ●

Le Mans, Friday 9 June.

SHORN of its sideshows, its fairground atmosphere, and its colour, the Le Mans 24-hour race would be no more than the fourth round in the battle for the Sports Car Championship for 1961; yet, in fact, it is the most glamorous, the best publicized, and perhaps the best attended, event of the racing year. Other races are fought and won in an afternoon, or a day at most; but Le Mans itself involves a full day' and night with, above all, the thrill of racing in darkness; and, if you care to lose yourself completely in the atmosphere that builds up beforehand, there are the four days of preparation and practice before ever the race begins.

Somehow, in an age of unquestioned reliability, when the most mundane car driven by an average driver can cover great journeys without uncertainty as to its safe arrival, Le Mans has retained, and continues to provide the romance and glamour of great distances covered against the clock, and of travel in the mode of the " heroic age " of motoring.

The scrutineering, weighing, and checking the cars in compliance with the rules took all of Tuesday and Wednesday, starting each day at 7 a.m. There were anomalies, as is usually the case with Le Mans; a Morgan, low on the list of reserves, was turned down on the grounds that it was an outdated type, and did not comply with the spirit of the event, despite the first-class performance put up by the car at Spa and the Nürburgring.

Practice is of less importance in this race than in a Grand Prix, where grid positions have to be fought for; here, the cars are lined up against the pits in descending order of engine capacity.

There were newcomers to the scene, in one or two cases making their debut at Le Mans, such as the rear-engined Abarths, described fully in last week's issue of *The Autocar*; another was the 746 c.c. rear-engined Osca with swing-axle rear suspension, and converted from a 1958 front-engined car by its No. 1 driver, J. Laroche of Dijon; second driver was Colin Davis. There was also a brand-new, rear-engined D.B.-Panhard, and an outstanding new Ferrari coupé with coachwork by Farina (instead of the Scagliatti creations on the Berlinettas) and 300-plus b.h.p. vee-12 engine. This uses six double-choke Weber carburettors, and is identical with the motors of the big front-engined sports-racing Ferraris; being the sole example of its type, the car was running in the sports category.

Ferrari Newcomer

Of the likely winners on maximum distance covered, Mike Parkes, honoured as the only British driver in the Ferrari team, was paired with Mairesse in one of the 12-cylinder sports cars, somewhat as a surprise when he had been expecting a 250 Berlinetta. However, despite his newness to the car, he lapped in 4min 6·4sec, fourth fastest! Fastest of all (also during the first practice periods in early April) was the Ritchie Ginther-von Trips rear-engined 2½-litre vee-6 Ferrari, with a time of 4min 2·8sec—124·02 m.p.h.

Among the Gran Turismo cars, the 250 Berlinetta Ferrari—painted in Rob

Above: Before the tightly packed stands, and the crowded pit counters, the cars streak up towards the Dunlop bridge during the early stages of the race. Below: Stirling Moss and Graham Hill put up a superb performance by keeping this Ferrari Berlinetta up among the leading sports-racing cars for the first few hours, until it was retired. It is followed here by the Salvadori-Maggs Aston Martin—also a fine performer until it retired—and the Stoop-Bekeart Austin-Healey 3000

Olivier Gendebien, on the way to victory in the 12-cylinder, front-engined, 3-litre Ferrari he shared with Phil Hill. Gendebien now shares with Woolf Barnato and Luigi Chinetti the honour of having been co-driver in the winning car on three occasions in this gruelling race

Left: The Peter Harper-Peter Proctor Alpine which, by winning the Thermal Efficiency Index, did much to console the British crowds—a fine performance in this car's first outing at Le Mans. Right: The 2-litre Porsche, driven by Masten Gregory and R. Holbert, which won its class

Walker's colours, owned by Dick Wilkins, entered by Chinetti's North American Racing Team, and driven by Stirling Moss and Graham Hill—lapped in 4min 16·1sec. Moss, after only two laps in a total of three, was seventh fastest of all 55 entries, and the car took second place in the GT category to the Berger-Pilette 250 Berlinetta, which lapped in 4min 15·9sec.

Briggs Cunningham, always a staunch supporter of the 24-hour race, brought two rear-engined Type 63 Maseratis with 3-litre, vee-12 engines, which were said to be reaching 300 k.p.h. (around 185 m.p.h.) along the Mulsanne Straight. As well as these, he had a front-engined Type 61 four-cylinder, 2-litre car which he drove himself. Scuderia Serenissima,

Count Volpi's costly plaything, was also using a 2-litre Type 61 and a 12-cylinder 3-litre Type 63, a model represented as well in Chinetti's North American Racing Team. Unfortunately, the Camoradi Maserati Type 61 was a non-starter, having broken its frame after its very successful outings at the Nürburgring and Rouen.

Despite their official absence from all forms of racing, Aston Martin were represented by five privately-owned cars— a couple of Zagato-bodied DB4-GTs entered by John Ogier's Essex Racing Team, a standard DB4-GT entered by Kerguen, a DBR1-300, also from the Essex Racing Team, and the Border Reivers DBR1-300 which did well last year.

At scrutineering, the ground clearance

rule caught out several entries, including one of the two Sunbeam Alpines, which had to have its undershield removed to clear the wood block. Also caught were the works Porsches, which were saved by tightening up their torsion bars, and the Kerguen Aston Martin which was given a few added millimetres of clearance by pumping its tyres up to unprecedented pressures!

* * *

THE MORNING of race day was dull, overcast and cold: occasional showers kept the streets of Le Mans glistening wet. As the traditional starting time of 4 p.m. approached, the rain stopped and the

Heroes of the race were the Mexican Roderiguez brothers who at one time looked as though they might beat the works cars with their Ferrari which led the race for many hours

Study in concentration: The Guilhaudin-Jaeger D.B.-Panhard coupé is overtaken by the Linge-Bon 1,600 c.c. Porsche

Le Mans 1961

track dried out, but the other climatic conditions remained, plus a wind to make it colder. After the Le Mans traditional ceremonies of an "offensive sweep" by the *gendarmerie* to clear the start area, and a display by their motorcycle-mounted colleagues, the drivers took up their positions opposite the cars, led by Moss, who remembered something and wandered

back to his Ferrari. Promptly at 4 p.m. a vast *tricolore* set the race in motion—and the 24-hour battle was on.

SO FAR AS the start was concerned it was an Aston Martin benefit, with Clark leading off in the Border Reivers' car, followed by Salvadori in John Ogier's DBR1, and the French entered DB4-GT driven by Kerguen. The Davison-Stilwell DB4-GT was off late, and Pabst's very fast Type 63 Maserati even later; it finally left the pits around two minutes after the rest had gone.

By the end of the lap, 8.3 miles completed, Ginther's 2½-litre rear-engined Ferrari, and Phil Hill's 3-litre front-engined car were in front, well clear of Hansgen's 12-cylinder Type 63 Maserati,

the Rodriguez brothers' 12-cylinder Ferrari, the Border Reivers' Aston, and Moss in the GT Ferrari, leading his category and sixth overall. Behind Moss came Salvadori's Aston.

Before long, the Rodriguez Ferrari had moved up to join the leading two cars of the same make, and there began the sort of "Grand Prix" that often lends so much excitement to the opening hours of this long race. The three scarlet cars lapped in close company for a while, swopping places, but in a few more laps, the Rodriguez N.A.R.T. entry had pulled away from the two works cars.

Behind all this excitement came Mike Parkes, going splendidly on his first drive in the fast, 12-cylinder Ferrari works car, and McLaren in the Cunningham-entered 12-cylinder Maserati. After a small interval were the two DBR1-300 Aston Martins (Clark and Salvadori), and Moss's GT Ferrari, keeping close together, and swopping places. Pabst (Maserati) was steadily working through the field, making up for a bad start.

Leading the Porsche contingent was Bonnier's car, 19th overall, and running extremely well was Bolton's Triumph, in 23rd position, heading several other potent Porsches. The Ecurie Ecosse Cooper was 10th, and steadily gaining ground; and the Ted Lund M.G. coupé, brought in from the reserve list, was lying around 30th, going well and obviously very beautifully prepared—only to retire a few laps later on the Mulsanne Straight with a broken connecting rod.

By a little before 5.30 p.m., the routine fuel stops and driver changes began because of the maximum fuel-tank capacity limits imposed this year. The Rodriguez Ferrari opened the bowling, and at the same time, the Parkes-Mairesse Ferrari came in; then followed the two Cunningham Maseratis driven by Hansgen and Pabst, the Pabst car now up with its team mate which had made an earlier pit stop.

Moss came in and handed over to Graham Hill, while the Salvadori and Clark Aston Martins went on ahead, one exciting battle over, temporarily at least. Phil Hill brought in his Ferrari when the other team cars had vacated the pit, but Ginther, with the 2½-litre car's lower fuel consumption, carried on and so took over the lead once more. Soon the news came through that Jack Fairman's Aston Mar-

Personnel at the signalling pits, immediately following Mulsanne Corner, watch as the leading Hill-Gendebien Ferrari and the 2-litre Porsche accelerate out of the corner

Through the Esses: the Stoop-Bekaert Austin-Healey leads the Giancarlo-Rigamonti
Fiat-Abarth, a couple of D.B.-Panhards and the Davison-Stilwell Aston Martin

Le Mans 1961

Nocturne: A lone spectator watches the cars, headlamps blazing, as they sweep through the curve to the Dunlop bridge. Though the hour is late, there are still many spectators in the stands opposite

tin had stopped at the Hippodrome, following a pit stop; subsequently it came round to the pits for another stop.

By 6 p.m. rain began to blow towards the pits from the direction of White House corner, and turned into a grey, dank drizzle that made the circuit extremely slippery, reducing the race speed considerably. Soon after this, with all the leaders having made routine fuel stops, Ginther brought in the 2½-litre Ferrari; von Trips took over, and rejoined the race in second place, with the Rodriguez Ferrari (now driven by Ricardo) in the lead. Shortly after, von Trips was passed by Gendebien; the Mairesse-Parkes car held third place, and the Moss-Graham Hill Berlinetta Ferrari by now was fourth, a remarkable performance by a GT coupé.

Slowly the circuit became soaked. The Ecurie Ecosse Cooper, which had been doing so well, made a three-minute stop and rejoined the race with Halford driving. Within a short time, running up to the Dunlop Bridge corner after the pits, the car went into a wide, sweeping slide, clouted the outside barrier and spun. The car had been going very fast, and it looked an ugly accident; it seemed ages before the yellow flags went out, and the flashing light signals operated at the start of the corner.

Of the first 11 cars at this stage, eight were Ferraris, two Aston Martins, and one Maserati, with Ferraris occupying first five places. By now the McLaren-Hansgen Maserati, the Davison-Stilwell Aston Martin, and, of course, the Ecurie Ecosse Cooper Monaco, were out of the race—fewer retirements than usual after 2½ hours' racing. Hansgen had hit the sandbank at Tertre Rouge, and had been taken to hospital with a broken arm and cracked vertebræ.

By 8 p.m., with one-sixth of the race over, the drizzle continued and clouds had obliterated much of the landscape; many cars were already running with their headlamps on. News came through from the hospital that Bruce Halford had sustained facial injuries, less than had been feared.

With the second crop of pit stops completed—save for the 2½-litre Ferrari, which was refuelling every two hours, to the 1½ hours of the 3-litre cars—the race order was: Ferrari (von Trips), Ferrari (Pedro Rodriguez), Ferrari (Phil Hill), Ferrari (Mike Parkes), Aston Martin (Salvadori), Ferrari (Moss), Ferrari (Tavano), Ferrari (Noblet) and Aston Martin (Clark). The latter had been held up by a longish pit stop, and had raced for several laps with its boot lid missing. The Fairman-Consten Aston Martin had abandoned its leisurely short-of-water progress round the circuit, and retired. Six cars were now out of the race, and only five cars were on the same lap as the leader.

However, despite the Ferrari domination on "distance classification," the little 742 c.c. Lotus Elite, driven by Allison and McKee and entered by U.D.T.-Laystall, was leading on Index of Performance, with the Ginther-von Trips Ferrari second, and a couple of Fiat-Abarths third and fourth. It was not until 8.18 p.m. that von Trips brought the 2½-litre Ferrari in. It was refuelled and handed over to Ginther, to rejoin in third place behind the Phil Hill-Gendebien and Rodriguez' Ferraris. In the wet and slippery conditions, the Ferraris looked steady and extremely fast, going through the curve under the Dunlop Bridge appreciably faster than even the Maseratis.

Already by now it was becoming easy to recognize the cars by their exhaust notes—the raucous blasts of the Ferrari

Left: The unfortunate Kerguen Aston Martin DB4-GT Zagato which, until a couple of hours before the finish, was lying ninth. It came in for a scheduled stop and the crew were unable to restart the engine. Right: One of the new rear-engined Fiat-Abarths, driven by Zecoll and Vinatier, tries to rejoin the race after leaving the road at Arnage. Beyond, an injured photographer receives attention

and Maserati sports-racing cars, the melodious boom of the Ferrari Berlinettas, and the positively ferocious crackle of the little Index-leading Lotus. A few were identifiable, in the failing light, by the fact that they raced with their direction indicators flashing—a left-over from when they last pulled away from the pits; it seems that even racing drivers commit the sins of their workaday counterparts!

This was not to be a lucky race for Ecurie Ecosse—one-time winners—for at about eight o'clock their second car, the Austin-Healey Sprite, driven by Sanderson and MacKay, left the road and capsized at White House corner; MacKay was taken off to join Bruce Halford in hospital, with a broken arm.

As dusk changed to darkness, the neon lights asserted themselves against the heavy sky. With this background the cars and drivers circulated, each a deafening, sliding little world of its own, a driver's only contact with the outside world being the regular cryptic signals to and from his signalling station at Mulsanne.

A light drizzle, barely sufficient to wet the track, was creating problems of decision for the team managers. To fit or not to fit rain tyres was the subject of a standing conference between Ferrari and Dunlop experts. At 9.30, calculations revealed that the Allison-McKee Lotus, number 51, had dropped back to fifth place in the Index of Performance and the Condriller-Foitek Abarth had come into the lead. Subsequently it was found that the I.B.M. electronic calculating apparatus was playing up, so that these announcements were taken with a pinch of salt. The Lotus, still running perfectly, had made no un-scheduled stops. We assumed it still led on Index. In the general classification the Rodriguez car had taken the lead from Gendebien and there was the appearance of a duel developing between the two, but team manager Tavoni seemed unmoved, so all must have been in order.

The Ferrari position suddenly became less secure when, at about 10.30, Ginther came in for a long pit stop with the Vee-6 car, and Mike Parkes began to slow, letting the Moss-Hill Berlinetta through into fourth place. This left Ferrari with two sound cars out in front racing against each other—one of them a private entry.

In keeping with the thoroughly suspect positions announced on the official scoreboard—suspicions had been aroused by the remarkable changes in the Index classification—the Moss-Hill Ferrari was credited with seventh place, having completed 94 laps; the Parkes-Mairesse Ferrari, however, having completed only 93 laps, was credited with third position.

The rear-engined DB-Panhard, which for some time had assumed a decidedly down-by-the-bow attitude, was by now making repeated pit stops to have the front wings hammered upwards, and further upwards, to cater for the sagging spring. The Scarfiotti-Vaccarella Type 63 Maserati went to the dead-car park with a blown gasket.

LATER, when the overall positions at 11 p.m. were announced, it seemed that

The slightly faster Hopkirk-Jopp Sunbeam Alpine leads its team mate, driven by Harper and Proctor, towards Arnage Corner

the electronic device had had second thoughts; Moss and Hill were back in fourth place astern of the Rodriguez brothers, Phil Hill and Gendebien, and Ginther and von Trips. Behind Moss-Hill came Parkes-Mairesse and the Salvadori-Maggs Aston Martin—a Ferrari benefit indeed, with the Prancing Horse in the first five places. So far as the Index classification was concerned, the computers stood their ground until, approximately a quarter of an hour later, they yielded on this score too. They gave the Index lead to Laureau and Bouharde, in their D.B.-Panhard, and second place jointly to the Allison-McKee Elite and the Condriller-Foitek Fiat-Abarth.

By now, the rain had stopped, the track dried out and the night became relatively mild. The surviving 45-odd cars roared on through the darkness, their progress punctuated by routine pit stops for fuel and a change of drivers. Still the leading car, driven by the Rodriguez brothers, was lapping in around 4min 2sec to 4min 3sec, only two or three seconds slower than in daylight. It must have been a great relief to the drivers of the fast cars that the little BMW had not been allowed to start.

AT 1 A.M., with the race nine hours old, the Rodriguez brothers still held their lead over Hill-Gendebien, each car having completed 123 laps; in third place came Mairesse-Parkes, with 120 laps completed, then Ginther-von Trips, Moss-Hill, and Salvadori-Maggs, each with 118; in seventh place lay the Pabst-Thompson Maserati, with 116. Still not much more than a pocket handkerchief covered the two leading cars.

Then suddenly, on the big scoreboard, the leaders' lap-scores began to build up—but the Moss-Hill Ferrari Berlinetta's figure stood at a steady 118 laps. Both the Rodriguez and the Hill-Gendebien cars continued to roll off the laps until, when they had completed 128, Moss re-joined the race, 10 laps behind and lying 9th. The Berlinetta completed another lap, a radiator hose broken, and it returned to the pits to take on more water. Next time round it came in and retired, a cylinder-head gasket gone—the end of a superlative drive.

In the early hours of Sunday the Lotus which many of us thought was still leading the Index, solved a possible dilemma for the electronic computer by losing most

Parkes, on his excellent first drive with Scuderia Ferrari, takes the big 12-cylinder car through Arnage on the way to second place

Though it made a poor getaway at the start, the Pabst-Thompson Type 63 Maserati, entered by Briggs Cunningham, worked its way up to fourth place by the finish; here the once white car is seen looking very travel stained

Le Mans 1961

Ron Flockhart, in the Border Reivers Aston Martin DBR1-300, which held a high place during the early stages, leads the Cunningham-Hugus Osca (entered by Chinetti's North American Racing Team) and the Allen-Taylor Lotus Elite into Tertre Rouge corner

of its oil pressure and retiring. The Malle-Carnegie Lotus had also stopped out on the circuit with a split fuel tank.

Two unforeseen setbacks had overtaken the Triumph team. On the sprint at the start Les Leston tore a ligament in his leg—fortunately he was able to drive though walking was difficult—and soon after his co-driver, Robbie Slotemaker, took over the ignition coil failed. Four laps passed before Slotemaker could trace the trouble, connect to the spare coil and get going again. Bad luck for Ken Richardson, for these were some of the best prepared cars in the race.

The Border Reivers' Aston Martin was now becoming a frequent visitor to the pits, with a malady of the clutch withdrawal mechanism. As the leaders went through on their 136th lap the trouble was thought cured and Jimmy Clark shot back into the race, but only for a lap; the car came back in and was mournfully pushed into the park.

On a track slightly damp again the three leading cars lapped consistently at speeds around 4m 6sec, changing places almost for the fun of it or when they came in for their regular pit stops. Only the Pabst Maserati and the Salvadori Aston Martin offered any real threat to them.

The lone entry from Donald Healey had gone out after 64 laps and Peter

Harper in the Sunbeam Alpine was now 10 laps behind its sister car. Mixed with two of the Triumphs and Linge's Porsche, the Ecurie Chiltern Healey, too, was being conducted with great consistency by Dicky Stoop and John Bekeart.

AT 4 O'CLOCK in the morning, as the sky was beginning to lighten—and reveal the same heavy rain-clouds—the order on distance covered was as follows: 1, Ferrari (P. and R. Rodriguez); 2, Ferrari (Hill and Gendebien); 3, Ferrari (Mairesse and Parkes); 4, Ferrari (Ginther and von Trips); 5, Aston Martin (Salvadori and Maggs); 6, Maserati (Pabst and Thompson); 7, Ferrari (Noblet and Guichet); 8, Ferrari (Tavano and Baghetti); 9, Porsche (Bonnier and Gurney); 10, Ferrari (Trintignant and Abate); 11, Porsche (Gregory and Holbert); 12, Ferrari (Grossman and Pilette); 13, Porsche (Barth and Herrmann); 14, Aston Martin (Franck and Kerguen); 15, Maserati (Cunningham and Kimberley).

At this stage of the race, when the leaders had covered 1,378 miles, only 30 cars remained of the original 55. These included the full complement of Triumphs, both Sunbeams—though Hopkirk's was shortly to retire (for no other reason than that it was disqualified when the gearbox was topped up before the imposed interval of 25 laps)—and three Lotus Elites, as well as the 3-litre Austin-Healey. Never once had the name of Ferrari been missing from the futuristic B.P. "totem pole" which, throughout the race, announced in coloured lights the leading car, its race speed and lap times. All five of the Porsches that started the race were still running, as were the six D.B.-Panhards.

By 5 a.m. it was fully light, though a few cars were still running with lights on. The night-driving part of the 24 hours was over, and with it the intermittent drizzle and showers had ended, leaving the circuit dry. Still the Panhard of Masson and Armagnac led the Index of

Performance, with the Condriller-Foitek Abarth second. After 13 hours' racing the two leading Ferraris were running within 10 seconds of each other, and lapping at 122 m.p.h. A pit stop for Rodriguez put the Hill-Gendebien Ferrari into the lead, but in less than a minute young Rodriguez was away in pursuit. The Osca of Cunningham and Hugus and one of the Fiat-Abarths (Giancarlo-Rigamonti) were added to the ever-growing list of retirements, while Trintingnant and Abate were out of the race.

AT 6 A.M. Hill-Gendebien's Ferrari made its routine pit stop, so the Rodriguez car regained the lead. On the subsequent lap, now after 14 hours' racing, still only 10 seconds separated the two leading cars. Soon they were running in formation until the Rodriguez car came in for its routine pit stop and the Hill-Gendebien Ferrari took its turn in the lead. Running with them, but four laps behind, the Mairesse-Parkes Ferrari had stepped up its lap speed to match the leaders'. In the ensuing dice Rodriguez touched the Parkes car and denied the tail.

At around 7 o'clock Richie Ginther handed the vee-6 car over to von Trips. Fate now stepped in, for after one more lap the Rodriguez car was back into the pits with a misfire. As the ensuing investigation lengthened into five minutes, then 10 minutes and 20 minutes, while the other team cars flashed past with monotonous regularity, Hill and Ginther quietly hugged themselves while young Pedro's face grew longer and longer. Finally the fault was traced to a faulty condenser and the Mexicans' car went back into the race 27 minutes late. Almost at the same time Phil Hill took over from Gendebien.

Among the lesser fry the Becquart Triumph had slowed and was trailing a smoke cloud, and Wyllie's Team Lotus Elite had slackened off to a slow touring speed.

Moment of victory: Phil Hill takes the winning Ferrari past the packed enclosures, the long race over for another year

24 Hours of Ferrari Domination

At eight o'clock the positions were Hill-Gendebien, 223 laps; Ginther-von Trips, 219 laps, Parkes-Mairesse, 219 laps, Rodriguez-Rodriguez 218 laps; Salvadori-Maggs, 214 laps; Noblet-Guichet (Ferrari 250GT) 210 laps; Bonnier-Gurney (Porsche) 207 laps; Pabst-Thomson (Maserati) 204 laps.

The main interest now lay in the Rodriguez' battle to recatch first Parkes and then Phil Hill. With 27 min between Hill and their North American Racing Team car the Mexican boys would need to better Hill's time by 10 seconds a lap, to finish first; this with a car which had been driven remorselessly from start to finish. So the private entry started to lap in times of 4 min 4 sec, a fantastic speed at this stage of the race. The Hill-Gendebien reply was to step up their pace until the Ferrari TR61 was circulating in a carefully judged 4 min 8 sec.

After 243 laps the only real British contender, Roy Salvadori in the Aston Martin, pulled into the pits with a split fuel tank. After a lengthy examination it was decided to withdraw the car.

There was drama, too, for the French. At 11.30 the bright blue D.B.-Panhard, leading the Index of Performance classification, puttered slowly into the pit area, and was pushed the last few yards by Armagnac. It was immediately withdrawn, and the Condriller-Foitek Abarth assumed the lead on Index for a brief hour before dropping behind Laureau's DB.

BY NOON, the circuit looked surprisingly underpopulated, with only 28 cars still running. Then, 40 min later, the Bonnier-Gurney Porsche, lying fifth overall, retired because the flywheel had come adrift—first of the Porsches to go. This allowed the Pabst-Thomson Maserati into fifth place—astern of the GT leaders, Noblet and Guichet in their Ferrari Berlinetta. The Maserati had been piling on speed, and was now two laps behind the Berlinetta. At this stage, the electrical computers clattered out their answers to the formidable Thermal Efficiency Index calculations, and gave the Peter Harper-Peter Procter Sunbeam Alpine in the lead. This was great news indeed, both for the British crowds, and the Rootes pit crews.

With only 2½ hours to go, the last surviving Aston—the DB4-GT entered by Kerguen—was lying ninth; two Triumphs were running well in 13th and 14th positions, but the 3-litre Healey, lying 15th, suddenly went on to five cylinders. The two surviving Elites lay 18th, 19th, and the D.B.-Panhards were occupying the last five places. Gendebien, now driving the leading Ferrari, continued unchallenged, four laps ahead of the Mairesse-Parkes car, sounding as fit as when it had started. His Ferrari was running at an average speed 3.5 m.p.h. higher than the previous race record.

Then suddenly, with only two hours to go, the Rodriguez Ferrari came streaking in to the pits trailing a cloud of oil smoke. The crowds rose and peered down the pit-line; mechanics and well-wishers swarmed round the car, and eight minutes later it was wheeled away, its great run over. The 3-litre Healey, too, which had also been trailing smoke and running on five cylinders, came in and retired.

Even at this late hour there were still to be retirements and changes of fortune. The Buchet-Monneret Porsche dropped out with engine trouble at Les Hunaudières; the French-entered Aston-Martin called in for a routine pit stop, when apparently running well, and was still at the pit an hour later. The Becquart-Rothschild Triumph, after smoking its way round for several laps, came in to have a camshaft oil-seal replaced. The Condriller-Foitek Abarth retired with engine trouble in the last hour.

And then, so that things should finish as they had begun, it started to rain. The Triumph, after its long stop, rejoined the race. Everyone had reduced speed considerably on the wet track, for it was too late to risk leaving the road now. The crowds flocked to the pit area, and the final minutes dragged by, but still the French Aston stood at its pit.

Then, as is the way with Le Mans, the race ran out, like a spring finally unwound. There were few cheers; the cars crossed the finish slowly, to turn off abruptly. The crowds swarmed from the enclosures and ran after them; and the *gendarmes*, dominating the scene as they had at the beginning, 24 hours before, held them back. The French-entered Aston Martin, which had done so well right up to its final scheduled stop, still stood at its pit, abandoned.

Le Mans: RESULTS

CLASSIFICATION ON DISTANCE COVERED
(Lap distance: 8.36 miles)

	Make	c.c.	Drivers	m.p.h.	miles
1	Ferrari	2,961	P. Hill and Gendebien	115.90	2,781·75*
2	Ferrari	2,953	Parkes and Mairesse	114·93	2,758·22
3	Ferrari	2,953	Noblet and Guichet	110·25	2,645·93
4	Maserati	2,984	Pabst and Thomson	108·28	2,598·63
5	Porsche	1,968	Gregory and Holbert	107·57	2,581·58
6	Ferrari	2,953	Grossman and Pilette	107·46	2,579·00
7	Porsche	1,606	Barth and Herrmann	106·47	2,555·38
8	Maserati	1,989	Cunningham and Kimberley	105·43	2,530·41
9	Triumph	1,985	Ballisat and Bolton	98·91	2,373·34
10	Porsche	1,588	Linge and Bon	98·87	2,372·93
11	Triumph	1,985	Leston and Slotemaker	97·18	2,332·27
12	Lotus	1,216	Allen and T. Taylor	93·13	2,235·02
13	Lotus	1,215	Kossellek and Massenez	92·97	2,231·20
14	Fiat Abarth	847	Hulme and Hyslop	91·45	2,194·77
15	Triumph	1,985	Becquart and Rothschild	91·25	2,190·03
16	Sunbeam	1,592	Harper and Procter	90·92	2,182·18
17	AC Bristol	1,971	Magne and Alexandrovitch	90·80	2,179·43
18	DB Panhard	702	Laureau and Bouharde	89·51	2,148·41
19	DB Panhard	848	Moynet and Vidilles	84·64	2,031·34
20	DB Panhard	848	Guilhaudin and Jaeger	84·64	2,031·27
21	DB Panhard	848	Rollin and Bartholoni	83·25	1,997·86
22	DB Panhard	848	Caillaud and Mougin	82·55	1,981·24

*New race record.

TEAM AWARD : Triumph.

CLASSIFICATION ON INDEX OF PERFORMANCE

	Make	c.c.	Drivers	INDEX
1	DB Panhard	702	Laureau and Bouharde	1·265
2	Ferrari	2,961	P. Hill and Gendebien	1·228
3	Porsche	1,606	Barth and Herrmann	1·219
4	Fiat Abarth	847	Hulme and Hyslop	1·219

CLASSIFICATION ON THERMAL EFFICIENCY INDEX

	Make	c.c.	Drivers	
1	Sunbeam	1,592	Harper and Procter	1·07
2	Lotus	1,215	Kossellek and Massenez	1·03
3	DB Panhard	848	Guilhaudin and Jaeger	1·03

Grand Touring cars: 1, Ferrari (Noblet and Guichet); 2, Ferrari (Grossman and Pilette); 3, Porsche (Linge and Bon); 4, Lotus (Allen and T. Taylor); 5, Lotus (Kossellek and Massenez); 6, Fiat Abarth (Hulme and Hyslop); 7, Sunbeam (Harper and Procter); 8, AC Bristol (Magne and Alexandrovitch); 9, DB Panhard (Guilhaudin and Jaeger); 10, DB Panhard (Caillaud and Mougin).

Sports cars: 1, Ferrari (P. Hill and Gendebien); 2, Ferrari (Parkes and Mairesse); Maserati (Pabst and Thomson); 4, Porsche (Gregory and Holbert); 5, Porsche (Barth and Herrmann); 6, Maserati (Cunningham and Kimberley); 7, Triumph (Ballisat and Bolton); 8, Triumph (Leston and Slotemaker); 9, Triumph (Becquart and Rothschild); 10, DB Panhard (Laureau and Bouharde); 11, DB Panhard (Moynet and Vidilles); 12, DB Panhard (Rollin and Bartholoni).

Class awards: Grand Touring cars: 701 to 850 c.c.: 1, Fiat Abarth (Hulme and Hyslop); 2, DB Panhard (Guilhaudin and Jaeger); 3, DB Panhard (Caillaud and Mougin). **1,151 to 1,300 c.c.:** 1, Lotus (Allen and T. Taylor); 2, Lotus (Kossellek and Massenez). **1,301 to 1,600 c.c.:** 1, Porsche (Linge and Bon); 2, Sunbeam (Harper and Procter). **1,601 to 2,000 c.c.:** 1 AC Bristol (Magne and Alexandrovitch). **2,001 to 3,000 c.c.:** 1, Ferrari (Noblet and Guichet); 2, Ferrari (Grossman and Pilette).

Sports cars: 701 to 850 c.c.: 1, DB Panhard (Laureau and Bouharde); 2, DB Panhard (Moynet and Vidilles); 3, DB Panhard (Rollin and Bartholoni). **1,601 to 2,000 c.c.:** 1, Porsche (Gregory and Holbert); 2, Porsche (Barth and Herrmann); 3, Maserati (Cunningham and Kimberley); 4, Triumph (Ballisat and Bolton); 5, Triumph (Leston and Slotemaker); 6, Triumph (Becquart and Rothschild). **2,001 to 3,000 c.c.:** 1, Ferrari (P. Hill and Gendebien); 2, Ferrari (Parkes and Mairesse); 3, Maserati (Pabst and Thomson).

The Thermal Efficiency Index is based on the relationship between the car's engine capacity, weight and quantity of fuel used during the 24 hours. The calculations are as follows, the Thermal Efficiency Index being Ir:

$$Ir = \frac{Em}{Er}$$

where Er is the actual fuel consumption of the car in litres per 100 kilometres (62·15 miles), and Em is calculated from the following formula:

$$Em = \frac{P - 300}{100} + \frac{V}{25} + \frac{(V - 95)^2}{600} + \frac{(V - 140)^3}{21,000}$$

V being the average hourly speed of the car for the 24 hours, and P being the **weight** of the car in kilogrammes (1 kg = 2·2 lb).

Les 24 Heures du MANS

BY HENRY MANNEY III

HENRY MANNEY PHOTO

To THOSE OF US WHO FOLLOW the competition season here in Europe, each race has its own flavor and personality, which are derived from the countryside, the attitude of the organizers, weather, memories of past performances and, of course, the character of the track itself. For this reason, most of my friends and I look forward to the Monaco GP, which has all the best attributes and then some; conversely Reims and Monza are not too eagerly anticipated, as not only is the occasional good race their only recommendation, but we are often actively hampered from getting on with our job. Now, these of course are Grands Prix, but the long-distance sports car races which determine the Constructors' Championship vary even more, due to the presence of large numbers of people on the business side of the paddock gate who normally have little to do with racing in a professional sense.

This sort of thing has reached its zenith at Le Mans, where a quite useful endurance race for touring cars has been padded out by book, magazine, and newspaper publicity into an Event, much as a sunken Spanish cannon is encrusted and transmuted by parasite coral. Over the years great grandstands have grown up, as well as permanent concrete pits, and the relevant sections of the Tours and Angers Routes Nationales, plus the necessary connecting links, have been paved and widened to within an inch of their lives. And, except for the odd manifestation like a section of the Tour de France, all this grandeur—rather like Indianapolis—is for one event: the 24 Hours of Le Mans.

There is no denying that the race definitely has atmosphere. Early in race week, usually in June to coincide with the maximum amount of daylight, hordes of enthusiasts and the entourages of competitors begin to filter into Le Mans. This ancient market town, sometimes referred to by American visitors as the Sebring of France, absorbs the visitors into numerous furnished rooms, and pocketbooks. The concurrents, however, generally vanish into the surrounding small towns, seeking out one of the now-traditional hostelries which are accustomed to people with dirty hands trailing in at all hours shouting loudly for refreshment, ham-and-eggs for breakfast, a proper pot of tea, and which can put up with loud bangings in the middle of the night. Tuesday the first cars present themselves for scrutineering (this year, at the course); both mechanical, to ascertain that they are really production cars, and then the Mickey Mouse business where ground clearance is checked by passing over little boxes. One of the Aston GTs needed to blow up its tires to pass the ground-clearance test and the Halford/Dickson Cooper Monaco, which was wearing wire wheels on the back and disc on the front, found that it had to change to the same all around to conform with the rule which states that at any tire change, the spare wheel on the car must be used first.

More and more cars arrived and the space behind the pits began to fill up with that curious mixture of cars, transporters, trucks big and little, advertising and component manufacturers' vans, and the converted buses so often used for workshop/sleeping quarters by your touring competitor.

However, it is the Wednesday evening practice which really starts the ball rolling as the first hopefuls splutter out onto the track for a few cautious and experimental laps before the car is turned over to those who have not driven at Le Mans before, hoping that they will learn it before night clamps down or some time-wasting derangement strikes the automobile. There is only one more practice on Thursday, from 6 P.M. to 11; after that, Friday is free for preparation. Of course on Saturday, at 4 P.M., comes the deluge.

Practice is not too terribly indicative at Le Mans, for times have no bearing on the starting position as at the Nurburg Ring. Most people just check out the gearing, carburetion, headlamp settings, pit signaling, and general creature comforts.

Just as an added attraction rain was thoughtfully laid on by the organizers for one of the sessions, thus fortunately pointing out that there was a newly paved section 200 meters before Mulsanne that could be extremely slippery in the wet. Richie Ginther discovered this when the nose of his Ferrari, which was already well dipped under braking, suddenly rose up of its own accord as the tires ceased to grip. Similar conditions were likely to prevail—the Sarthe region had had 38 straight days with some precipitation up to Saturday. But, rain or not, the Ferraris were out charging around and Ginther topped the list with a respectable 4 min 02.8 sec, which works out to 199.586 kph, the Rodriguez Ferrari being next with 4:03, and Hansgen/Thompson Maserati third with 4:03.8 ahead of four other Ferraris.

Although Le Mans as a spectacle has been built up to its present stature as a sacred cow by the English (and most of the people in the pits seem to be of that nationality), there were no really serious contenders from that green and pleasant land for the over-all prize, for the famous 3.8 D Jaguars had been legislated out of existence and the new E wasn't ready. This honor fell to the legions of Italy, more specifically Scuderia Ferrari, which led the Championship standings with wins at Sebring, Targa Florio, and a 2nd at the Nurburg Ring. Playing safe, the factory brought two of the fast and reliable front-engined 3-liter 12s for Phil Hill/Gendebien and Mairesse/Parkes—this latter with a slightly older model engine—plus one of the rear-engined V-6 2.4s, which Ginther/Trips were to drive. In addition, factory mechanics supervised another 12-cyl sports, entered for the Rodriguez brothers by NART, which organization also filled its hand by backing Graham Hill/Stirling Moss (Ferrari GT) and Reed/Arents (Ferrari GT). Other Maranello coupes were for Noblet/Guichet, Trintignant/Abate, Berger/Bianchi, Grossman/Pilette, and Tavano/Baghetti, this last having a special wind-cheating Farina body and sports engine.

Opposing the Ferraris were three rear-engined 12-cyl Maseratis; two of these belonged to Briggs Cunningham (Hansgen/McLaren and Pabst/Thompson) and the other, a rough red banger with millions of holes cut in it, was a Scuderia Serenissima entry for Vaccarella/Scarfiotti. Of incredible complexity, these fascinating machines looked from the rear like B-29 gun turrets, with their four megaphoned exhaust pipes, and sounded not unlike one, too. The engine, developed from Maserati's wonderful but unsuccessful GP engine, was hidden well down inside, and because the construction program had been evidently engine-wheels-frame-body, hatches of various sizes gave access to critical parts of the machinery; not too much help, really, as all one saw at first glance were tubes going everywhere and then—oh, yes!—down inside, the beady eye of $800 worth of Webers.

Ranged against this aggregate of 156 little cylinders and 10 big ones, Essex chicken magnate Ogier brought two GT Aston Martins (Davison/Stilwell and Fairman/Consten) plus a DBR-1 for Salvadori/Maggs. Another GT was entered by Kerguen/Franc and the Scottish Border Reivers stable showed up once again with a dark blue DBR-1 for Clark/Flockhart. As a token tie with the past, Ecurie Ecosse also mustered up a 2.5 Cooper Monaco for Bruce Halford and Tom Dickson, the Mutt and Jeff of motor racing. That was all the serious English and Scottish competition, but Porsche was there in force as well. The Germans had gotten the message from last year's Le Mans, the Targa, and 1000 km and provided only a 2-liter Spyder for Gregory/Holbert and two of the chopped-top coupes of 1679 (Bonnier/Gurney) and 1606 (Barth/Herrmann) plus the privately entered Abarth Carerras of Monneret/Buchet and Linge/Bon.

Traditional at Le Mans these days, perhaps because the flat-twin Panhard engine is the only French one that will stand the stresses of competition, are a raft of small blue-painted machines in various unusual shapes, mostly powered by this engine and competing for the Index of Performance prize, which is almost as lucrative as an absolute distance win. It favors small capacity cars and, as far as I can remember offhand, has been carried off only five times since 1949 by non-French machinery; the most successful of these was Chinetti's Ferrari which took both distance and Index. However, hope springs eternal and, while Ginther's very fast 2.4 Ferrari was entered with an eye on this prize, two open and three shut Fiat Abarths (all except one around 700 cc), two special Sprites, and two Oscas were closer to the mark. One of these Oscas had been modified to a rear-engined car by the time works driver Colin Davis came to practice in it, a fact which caused great surprise both to him and the factory. Also in the oddities category was the Elite of UDT drivers Cliff Allison/Mike McKee, powered by a new 750-cc twin cam Climax that is actually half of the projected GP V-8.

By the time 3:30 P.M. rolled around on Saturday afternoon, all the surrounding car parks were full, and the paddock was stuffed to repletion with personal transportation of the drivers, friends of the Club, pit personnel, advertising trucks, trade vans, and all the usual stuff we

Happy man: Olivier Gendebien—co-winner with Phil Hill.

LE MANS 24 HOUR

mentioned before. The stands were stiff with spectators who had paid not inconsiderable prices to be there and indeed they seemed to be lined all around the course along the earth barricades. Advertising balloons flew, advertising voices were heard over loudspeakers everywhere, but the biggest concentration of people was right in the pits, falling all over the brightly shining cars, which were arranged in echelon by cylinder capacity, the largest (the Aston GTs) at the end toward the Dunlop bridge. Last minute revvings up were done, last minute clonks with hammer on hub nuts, and soon the traditional wave of *vaches* or cops turfed perhaps 50% of those who had no right to be there out of the pit area.

The associated Vespa Clubs of western Camargue came by in a haze of blue smoke, the off-key drum and bugle band marched up and down, a wreath was presented at the plaque which marks the 1955 disaster, the race director made a final tour in his Ferrari, and a great hush fell over the crowd as drivers nervously took their places in the little painted circles.

Four o'clock ticked off, M. Paul Panhard dropped the flag, and the 55 drivers hurried across the road as if only one lap were ahead of them, not 24 hours. Another moment of agonizing silence, Clark's Aston burst into its frenzied bellow, and he was off and away once again, car-lengths in front of the nearest competitor. . . . It seems he starts twiddling things before he is even in the car. But perhaps Astons just start more easily, as Salvadori and Kerguen were next out, followed by Fairman, Ginther, Moss and Gendebien. As they disappeared under the Dunlop Bridge, we turned our attention to those unfortunates who were left at the post, including Davison's Aston GT, Allison's Elite, and finally Thompson's Maserati, which had perhaps cooled off a little too much by this time. Its getting under way was a perfect example of the classic Italian formula of no torque and a fierce clutch . . . wowwwow-eeek-wowwwow-eeekwowowow-eek, leaving a succession of black marks like a dotted line. Almost as soon as he had left, two red specks appeared from the direction of White House and blasted by the stands at a shocking rate, leaving a whirlwind of dust and flying scrap paper in their wake; Ginther and Gen-

A Ferrari GT leads an Aston Martin past a slower car.

debien had blown by Clark and the other Astons on the long Mulsanne straight and so were first to mark up the name of Ferrari on the scoreboard, a name which was not to be taken down for the remaining 24 hours.

As the race settled down, the pattern which would last for so long developed. Ginther, dutiful team man, let Gendebien through into the lead and then hung on behind, watching first for any threatening move from the third-place Maserati of Hansgen and then, as Rodriguez came knifing up from his place in the middle of the pack with Mike Parkes in the other team car following, Ferraris took over the first four places. Behind Hansgen, the dark blue GT Ferrari of Moss was locked in a fierce struggle with the Astons of Clark and Salvadori, all three scrapping as if everyone would quit at eight o'clock and go to supper. However, the Rodriguez boys underlined their status as a private entry by moving past Ginther and Gendebien on the 9th lap to take the lead, with the other two Ferraris immediately latching on to watch.

This three-car train rumbled on, steadily pulling away from the rest of the field, until 5:30, when the somewhat thirsty 12s came in for fuel, leaving Richie out on his own for a half hour or so in the lead until he pitted in his turn. As he pulled out, the Rodriguez No. 17 passed to assume first place again, with Gendebien never

A study in chassis construction (both rear engined) . . .

letting the Mexican boy out of his sight.

The grey clouds which had persisted all day intensified the gathering dusk and soon a fine rain began to sift down through the pine trees, making conditions even more difficult for the drivers of the faster cars. Ferrari had learned at least one lesson from the rainy Nurburg Ring and had installed glass windscreens, as well as plastic sheeting over the engine of the V-6, but trouble still was experienced with water blowing through various crannies onto the inside of the screen.

Pushed by a strong wind, the rain laid a thorough film on top of the existing oil-and-rubber coating; Hansgen's Maserati, which was moving up, possibly due to a little better visibility, was the first to go as it went straight into the Tertre Rouge sandbank. Shortly afterward, the Ecurie Ecosse Cooper, which had been cornering with great verve, commenced to gyrate under the Dunlop Bridge and caromed off the earth bank, throwing pilot Halford out in the road. Fortunately, neither driver was hurt badly, although the usual vicious rumors flew around the pits. Mairesse narrowly escaped joining their number when he did a surfboard act at the Tertre Rouge sandbank, avoiding the very twitchy Swiss AC, but carried on at unabated speed.

A wet and soggy darkness fell and with it arrived a special set of problems for the big cars. As if smeared

HENRY MANNEY PHOTOS

82

windscreens, a slimy road, inefficient wipers, reflections from water droplets, squashed bugs, and the sudden appearance of small cars traveling anything like 70 mph slower in unexpected places were not enough, Gendebien and Ginther also had to deal with the NART Ferrari which had slackened its pace very little and was lapping at around 4:15, or 120 mph, a tremendous rate with three quarters of the race still to go. Obviously one of the team cars had to stay with it for safety's sake even though they would have preferred not to circulate that quickly so soon and, likewise, the other must stay within striking distance. Thus it was that Nos. 17 and 10 roared through the night swapping places from time to time, generally in each other's slipstream. A hell of a situation in a one-make walkover.

Otherwise it was a pretty good race with, surprisingly, quite a few retirements and the usual number of strange and wonderful ailments. The first MG to lap Le Mans at over 100 mph, Lund's coupe had also been the first to retire as a rod went out the side at full revs.

The Elites, which generally do well at Le Mans, were delayed by a variety of piddling troubles and so it came to pass that the highest placed one was the 750 being driven by Allison and McKee. Since it was running up with much larger cars, this information was fed to the

And a study of front engined cars: Maserati and Ferrari.

. . . on the Porsche and the V-12 "gun turret" Maserati.

IBM machine which calculates index and it promptly got indigestion, first giving the Lotus as first and then 7th, although it had made no unusual stops. Eventually, the machine rallied its French blood and announced Masson/Armagnac (D-B) as the leader, whereupon the Elite lost all its oil pressure in disgust and went to bed.

At midnight, with 16 hours to go, the Grand Prix was still in progress; Gendebien/Hill and Rodriguez/Rodriguez occupied the first slot intermittently, with the Ginther/Trips car, slowing a little because of increased oil consumption, in 3rd a lap behind. Surprisingly enough, the Moss/Hill GT had gotten by the Mairesse/Parkes team car and was on the same lap as Ginther, thus giving NART two cars in the first four.

Midnight at Le Mans is where most of the so-called magical atmosphere comes to pass and if one *has* to be there, midnight to 4 A.M. is the time. Surprisingly, the spectator terraces and grandstands still hold a reasonable number of people to hear the remaining runners flee past the pits; the GT Ferraris with their well-bred, muffled purr compared with their raucous sports sisters, the acrid crackle of the D-Bs, Salvadori's bellowing Aston, or the thin snarl of an Elite. Many more spectators still wander among the vast and vulgar village of beer gardens, "greasy spoons," shooting galleries, wrestling bouts, nude shows, and dance halls hastily erected by traveling showmen to occupy the scarcely sophisticated locals and mulct them of their pig money.

Open-mouthed and red-faced, they listen to the barker's pitch, while barely feet away the driver of an Abarth coupe motors by in his own private, noisy little world. Negotiating the pit area with its floodlights and scoreboards, he shoots under the Dunlop Bridge, tops the hill, and descends the esses and its short straight thereafter to Tertre Rouge, looking on each side at the twirling fortune wheels, nougat stands, and monsieurs croquing *croque*—monsieurs, all with their heads turned resolutely away from the race. He may reflect, as he rounds Tertre Rouge and heads down the darkness of the Mulsanne Straight, that nobody out there cares that his throttle is sticking, that there is a pool of water in his seat, that his pit crew all seem to have gone to sleep, or that there is a horrid vibration which may mean that a tire is about to deflate and send him into a lamppost, dead as a doornail.

Just before Mulsanne, the tiny lights in his mirror suddenly grow large and everything suddenly contracts and jumps sideways as a Ferrari rockets by, the taillights dwindling into one in a few seconds, and splattering the screen with spray and dirt. I'd really show them, he reflects through Indianapolis, so called because it used to be paved with bricks. No I wouldn't, he decides as another Ferrari blasts by and gets slightly sideways through White House. And back by the pits again, driving into the floodlit glow, wondering when the next gas stop is.

In the pits there is something of the atmosphere of a hospital, partially, at least, because of the white-waist-coated *plombeurs* standing around to seal oil and fuel tanks, but mostly because when a car sweeps in from time to time, all hands rush to it with all manner of shining tools and lights and whip out its entrails, the driver and entrant meanwhile standing by with waiting-room expressions.

The ACO occasionally scrapes the bottom of the barrel in recruiting its pit marshals and one of these set the police on German photog Weitmann when he tried to take a photo—by their request—of Gendebien and Hill. It would be well for the ACO to remember and pass on to its minions that not only are 95% of us in the game there just because we have to be, not from choice, but that without the press it would slide back to a purely regional attraction.

In the middle of all this hoo ha, nevertheless, Graham Hill suddenly pulled into the pits with no oil pressure showing on the 4th place Ferrari GT. Moss went out, came in, work was done on the ball-check valve in the oil line, the car was revved up and quantities of steam came out. Finito. A blade of the freewheeling fan had come off and cut the lower radiator hose, letting all the water out and thus running the bearings. Everybody moved up a notch as the two leading Ferraris, nose to tail, roared by the pits.

Dawn came with its usual complement of bleary eyes, creaky joints, and listless searches for what passes for coffee in that benighted place, accompanied if possible by solid hot food. The remaining cars still went around, presenting a strangely depleted and travel-stained sight to those lucky types who appeared, freshly shaven and sparkling, from a tranquil night in bed. With just over half the race run, the works Ferrari drivers were becoming worried that Gendebien was being towed along too fast and his car would not last; on the other hand it was not beyond the realm of possibility that some Machiavellian arrangement had been concluded between Ferrari and the wealthy Rodriguez family, as persistent slow-down signals had been hung out for Gendebien. He was paying scant attention, however, and soon would come in for Hill to take over.

About this time, another sort of danger presented itself as the two leaders lapped Parkes for the fourth time; in trying to shake off his tow, Rodriguez cut in a mite sharply and dealt the Parkes car a belt on the nose. Wouldn't that have been a dilly, with all three Ferraris up in the stands. However the problem resolved itself rather dramatically when No. 17 suddenly pulled into the pits, the young Mexican driver complaining of a rumbling or misfiring. On the premise that there might be a fuel shortage, the car was topped up and the other brother went out in it, only to return a lap later. The experienced Ferrari mechanics then gathered up their tools and started digging while the seconds ticked away. Gendebien extended his lead, Parkes and Ginther gradually unlapped themselves, and Father Rodriguez stood there in his shades and fedora hat darting significant glances at his sons.

Never say die, though, and after 24 min in the pits the NART car jumped back into the fray and, lapping at the astonishing rate of 4:2, commenced to pull up on the Parkes car again although a lap behind, obviously intent on win or bust. Soon afterward, it automatically moved up a place as Ginther's V-6 coasted to a stop on the Mulsanne straight with a split gas tank and then it was not too much longer before the Parkes/Mairesse No. 11, troubled with grabbing brakes, was passed once more. Although 4 laps behind, there was a bare possibility that the Rodriguez car, driven flat out, might just catch Hill/Gendebien before the checked flag flew but the canny partners, unmoved by slow-down signals from the pits or any information from the signals at Mulsanne, speeded up just enough to make the margin impossible to resolve.

However, with two hours to go, the small red No. 17 Ferrari, trailing a very large cloud of smoke, appeared down the deceleration lane from White House, and it was hardly necessary to examine it to diagnose a broken piston. Gendebien immediately slackened speed, knowing the hard way that not even a Ferrari can be thrashed for 24 hours without penalty. And his car was still in the lead when he turned it over to co-driver Phil Hill to finish the race.

Three fifty nine again and another shower of rain had swept the circuit. Jacques Loste stood there with the flag as various types motored slowly by looking hopefully at him and at their watches. The millions of real motor racing photographers whom one never sees at any other event crowded the finish line and pit area, while the millions of harassed policemen, most of whom couldn't care less for a motor race, treated sheep and goats indiscriminately. Pits were packed with the same yo-yos in curly-brimmed trilbies and decorative popsies in tight pants that were in evidence from 3:30 to 4:30 P.M. the previous day, and some of them were even looking at the cars. Almost unnoticed at one end was the remaining Aston-Martin GT of Kerguen/Franc, held at its pit after a routine stop by a short in the electrical system somewhere. Zaps and blue flashes appeared from inside, where a mechanic was working. But nothing happens when you press the starter button, after 24 hours.

The flag fell, happily for the English, on the Sunbeam, sole salver of their national pride. All the other cars, having formed up in odd groups on the last lap, crept slowly into thunderous applause, a beaming Phil Hill screened behind the three Triumphs. As he motored gently down into the grandstand area to pick up a mechanic and return for the customary fuel and seal check, the capacity crowd leapt the barriers and in a second filled the track. Four-oh-five P.M. Suddenly we all felt very tired.

Walt Hansgen starts his irrevocable slide toward the sand bank and digs in while two Triumph twin cams and a Ferrari drive carefully by.

Another complete change of regulations banned sports cars but promptly substituted a new category of 'Experimental' cars - if the intention had been that these should be GT prototypes, the outcome was instead some 'bigger and better' sports prototypes, especially as the capacity limit was increased to four litres for the experimental class. The Italian manufacturers were quick to exploit the new rules and Ferrari had two 330 models with four-litre V12 engines - an open 330 LM model driven by past winners Hill and Gendebien, and a closed 330 GT driven by Parkes and Bandini. Maserati countered with three Tipo 151 V8 four-litre coupes, entered by Briggs Cunningham and Maserati France. Ferrari were out in force with one of their biggest ever entries totalling 15 cars; apart from the two four litre cars, works experimental entries included two mid-engined cars, a 2.6 V 8 and a 2.4 V6 (the latter in the hands of the Rodriguez brothers). There were also two Testa Rossas, an experimental 'bread van' coupe and in the GT class eight 250 GT models.

Aston Martin had the 212 GT prototype driven by Graham Hill and Ritchie Ginther, backed up by two DB.4 GT Zagato bodied cars. Jaguar made a return to Le Mans with three privately entered E-type coupes and there was a single Chevrolet Corvette with a 5.3 litre engine. Ecurie Ecosse fielded a Tojeiro coupe with a Coventry Climax Grand Prix 2.5 litre engine in the experimental class, and the only remaining big car was an Austin-Healey 3000 run in the GT class. There were a mere three cars in the two-litre class, all GTs: an AC Ace (the final appearance at Le Mans of the venerable Bristol engine), Chris Lawrence's Morgan Plus Four (which had been rejected by the Le Mans scrutineers in 1961 as 'old fashioned') and finally there was a T.V.R. (Blackpool's only Le Mans entry) with an MG engine of the unsuitable capacity of 1,622 cc.

In the smaller classes, Abarth had four 1,300 cc cars with Simca based engines and three with 701 cc Fiat engines. Alfa Romeo fielded two 1,300 cc coupes, and Lotus had two Elites, also in the GT class. Lotus would have entered the 850 and 1,000 cc experimental classes with two Type 23s but these were rejected by the scrutineers under the infamous 'contrary to the spirit' clause, causing a lot of bad feeling in the British camp against what was seen as French favouritism for their own small cars. These were divided among two makes as the long-running DB partnership had been dissolved - Charles Deutsch had three 702 cc Panhard based cars, while Rene Bonnet in a change of allegiance used Renault Gordini engines in his cars, one of 706 cc and two of 996 cc. The total number of cars was 55, of which 25 were GTs and 30 experimental.

As expected, the main battle was between the experimental Ferraris and the Maseratis; the only other car that kept pace with the leaders was the Aston Martin 212. In a virtual repeat of the 1961 race, the Hill/Gendebien car took turns to lead with the mid-engined Ferrari of the Rodriguez brothers, until the latter was forced to retire with transmission failure around half time. It turned out that neither the Aston Martin nor the Maseratis had the stamina to last the race; the Aston was out after six hours with engine trouble and by half time the last of the Maseratis had also retired. For most of the rest of the race Ferraris filled the first four or five places on the scoreboard; it was only in the last few hours that the E-type Jaguars of Cunningham/Salvadori and Sargent/Lumsder managed to squeeze past into fourth and fifth places, helped by the retirement of the other mid-engined Ferrari.

The result was victory for Hill and Gendebien their third together and Gendebien's fourth. Their total distance was 2,765.876 miles at an average speed of 115.244 mph; and lapping at 126.884 mph, Hill finally broke Hawthorn's 1957 lap record. They were followed home by the GT class winners, Guichet/Noblet in a Ferrari 250 GTO, a similar car was third and then came the two Jaguar E-types. Porsche took the 1,600 cc class, but Britain could score two class wins. the Morgan (which won the thirteenth car home) in the two-litre class and the Lotus Elite in the 1,300 cc class. Small car honours went to France, Bonnet in the 1,000 cc class and Panhard-CD in the 850 cc class; this car also won the Index of Performance, while the Index of Thermal Efficiency went to the class winning Lotus Elite which combined an average of 100 mph with a fuel consumption of 20 mpg. A total of 18 cars finished the race.

Le Mans . . .

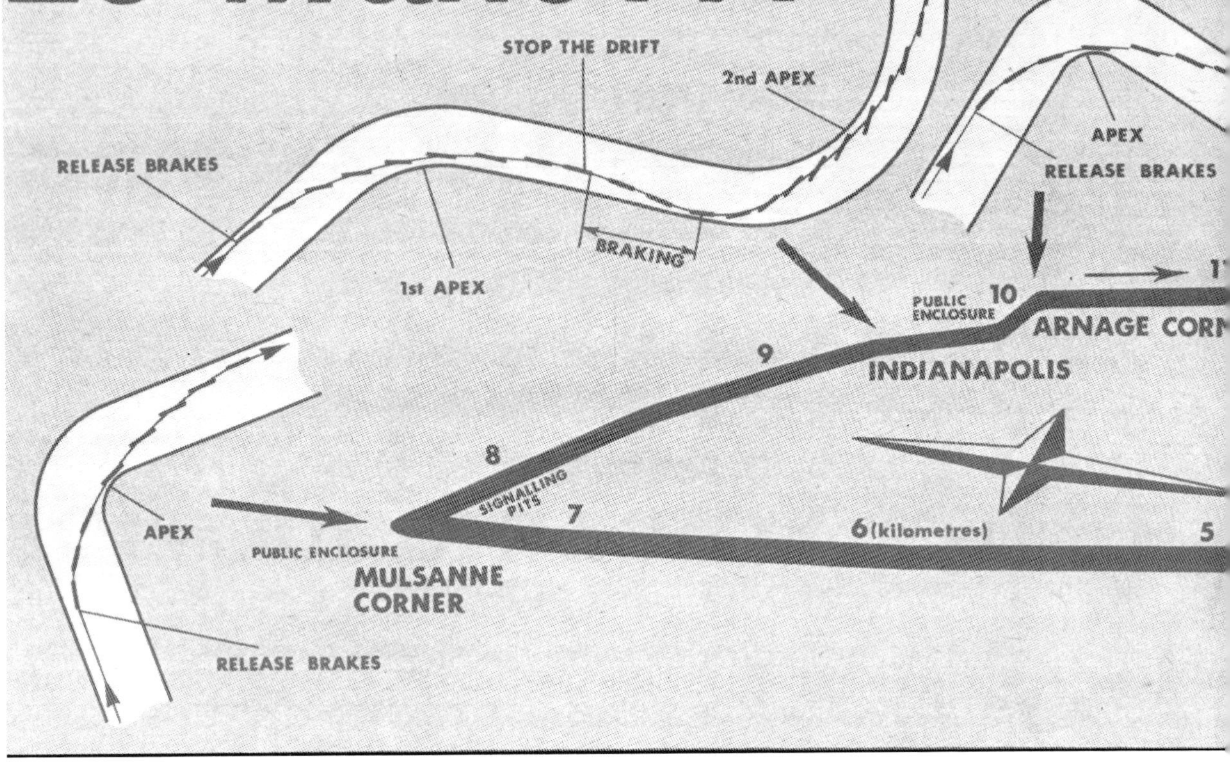

Previous instalments in this series have taken readers on a high-speed lap of the Goodwood and Silverstone circuits with Tony Brooks at the wheel—in each case in anticipation of a major British meeting. Now he takes them abroad, to the famous 8·46-mile *Circuit Permanent de la Sarthe* where, at 4 p.m. tomorrow evening, 55 cars will set off on the famous Le Mans 24-hour race—the most glamorous and publicized race of the motoring calendar. In conjunction with the details of the race and the B.B.C. broadcasts which follow, Brooks' article gives readers a clear insight into the tremendous task that faces the drivers and cars.

By TONY BROOKS

BLAZING headlights, the drone of engines at White House Corner a mile away, rising to a crescendo as the pencils of light approach the illuminated pits, with eager yet tense personnel straining forward to identify their cars—this is Le Mans.

Bleary-eyed drivers stagger into the pits from their caravans to see how their co-driver is getting on, having given up the unequal struggle between sleep and the noise, excitement and indigestion. Cups of coffee by the hundreds are consumed, mechanics refuse to be relieved but can be found in the very early hours standing up against the pit walls, caps pulled well down, and nodding. As dawn breaks the aroma of bacon and eggs quenches the smell of petrol and hot engines as Le Mans slowly comes to life, the drivers breathe a sigh of relief, and all look forward with renewed vigour to the racing ahead, the hard luck stories, and the finish.

For some International drivers the race at Le Mans has meant "who can get back to the hotel first" rather than a challenge of restraint, with 24 hours of steady motoring as the aim. Drivers have been known to be able to follow the second half of the race on radio and television from the comfort of their fireside at home, many hundreds of miles away, some through hard luck, others through bad driving.

The two-hour Grand Prix from 4 p.m. to 6 p.m. on the Saturday never fails to be a feature of the race and all the careful instructions of the team managers may be thrown to the wind. International class drivers find it difficult to resist the challenge for the lead and some push the cars too hard. Manufacturers put tremendous effort and money into their bid for honours at Le Mans as it carries more publicity than any other race. A driver owes it to the team to drive sensibly with a view to finishing.

The fact is that few International class drivers look forward to the race. The speed differential between the cars at Le Mans—often as much as 80 m.p.h.—presents a constant overtaking problem, particularly at night, in the early morning mist, or in the rain. The problem is considerable when a combination of these conditions occurs. There are also many inexperienced drivers taking part as over 50 cars start in the race so that more than 100 competent and experienced drivers are required but are not available. Another aspect of the race that the top class driver does not like is the need to drive within his maximum performance, perhaps by as much as 10 to 15 seconds a lap. This increases the chances of lapsed concentration and fails to give him the impression that he is really motor racing.

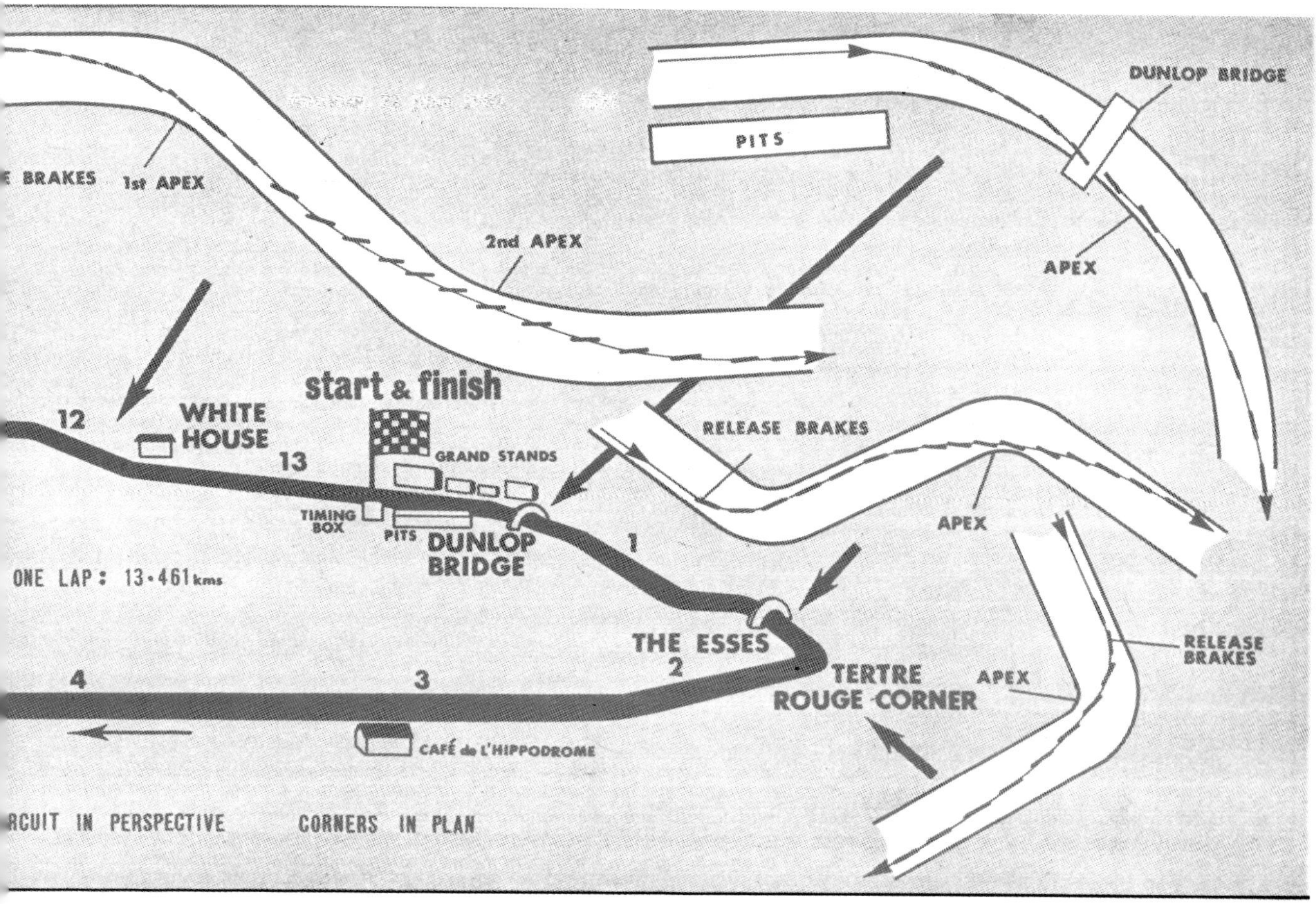

The lap is 8·36 miles which is covered well over 300 times in the 24 hours by the leaders. There are 13 main corners that vary in speed from 165 m.p.h. to 35 m.p.h. and the straight of just over 3½ miles allows the faster cars in the race to reach speeds of around 180 m.p.h. The surface is very smooth but between Arnage and White House corners it does collect puddles through some gentle curves.

For this race, axle ratios are a little on the high side to keep the engine revolutions down on the long straight. Intermediate gear ratios are not very critical in such a long event, although it is surprising how many cars start practice with second gears too high for Mulsanne and Arnage corners yet are unable to use first because of a complicated gate on the gearbox or inherent weakness in what is really only a " starting gear."

Power plays a very big part at Le Mans and overshadows the importance of roadholding. Five easy seconds gained on the straight each lap take a lot of catching up by less fleet competitors, and if the straight line performance is matched by equally good acceleration the driver need do little more than take corners on a geometrical line for the 24 hours. With the almost universal adoption of disc brakes, braking no longer presents a problem at Le Mans.

The record lap stands to the credit of the late Mike Hawthorn in a Ferrari, with a time of 3min 59·6sec (125·67 m.p.h.). If you were a driver needing to get a move on to catch a competitor in the closing stage of the race with a car such as the 3-litre DBRI Aston Martin using a five-speed gearbox, you would try consistently to stick to the following routine, lap after lap.

Passing the pits in fifth gear at around 155 m.p.h. on the left-hand side of the road, watching carefully for cars rejoining the race, you would start to guide the car into the fast Dunlop Bridge right-hander, straightening out the corner as much as possible. You develop a small drift as the car travels towards the apex, there being no need to ease back the accelerator. Tyre scrub drops the speed by about 10 m.p.h. and on the exit you allow the car to drift to within a few feet of the edge of the road as it goes up the rise. You breast the rise, the car becoming light on the back, before rushing downhill to the left-hander of the Esses,

The famous **Esses,** which occur shortly before Tertre Rouge after the downhill swoop from the " blind " crest after the Dunlop bridge

Le Mans . . .

braking hard on the right of the road from about 145 m.p.h. and taking third at the marker board.

You take the left-hander close with very little drift as the right-hander follows immediately. The best line for the left turn is sacrificed so that the car is well positioned on the left of the road for you to swing it across to the apex, setting up a drift at about 80 m.p.h. as you turn on the power progressively. This gives punch to the exit from the Esses as you slide the full width of the road, finishing within a foot of the grass verge.

Hard acceleration in third gear to Tertre Rouge, approached on the extreme left. You brake hard, take second gear and turn into the corner a little late so that you can see the full width of the road around the blind apex before turning on the power to produce what is in the main a 65 m.p.h. tail slide with a little left lock correction, so positioning the car for maximum acceleration.

As the car stops sliding just short of the sandbank you really become lead-footed as the straight opens up. Maximum permissible revolutions in all the gears, taking fifth as you pass the Hippodrome Café and wish you could join the spectators around the tables with long, cool drinks in front of them. You fight distractions and take quick glances at your instruments, perhaps using the left foot to keep the accelerator depressed as your hot and tired right foot cries "enough." You watch the slower cars for pulling out and overtaking each other, and check that no one is in your slipstream.

Flat Out

You achieve maximum revolutions in fifth—165 m.p.h.—at the 5-kilometre post and hold them to the 6-kilometre post where there is a flat-out right-hander. It must be straightened out, avoiding a drift as far as possible because the engine revolutions drop by 200 even if the corner is just straightened out.

Ahead of you is a brow which signifies the approach to the Mulsanne right-hander and as you take the brow at 165 m.p.h., having regained the lost revolutions, you prepare to brake just over the other side, after the "300" marker board. Really hard braking; but you do not go through all the gears to select second so as to avoid unnecessary gearbox loading. You swing the car from the extreme left of the road, feed on the power as the off-side wheel clips the apex at about 40 m.p.h., and apply a little corrective lock to catch the tail sliding under power. A glance at your signalling pit on the right as you take third at 85 m.p.h., then fourth at 115 m.p.h., an easy right-hander, then another a little more difficult but still flat, taking fifth at 145 m.p.h.

You start braking from about 150 m.p.h. into the right-hander at Indianapolis, selecting third, then clipping the corner very close, allowing the car to drift out no farther than the centre of the road so as to be correctly placed for the left-hander immediately following. You stop the drift at about 80 m.p.h., brake again, take second, and throw the car into the left-hander which seems to go on longer than expected, turning the power on before you make your apex and slide to the right-hand grass verge. You accelerate in a short burst to the slow Arnage right-hand turn, taking third briefly.

Brake, back to second, swing in from the left side of the road, make the apex on the inside turn on the power and accelerate away from about 35 m.p.h. with a little corrective lock. Through the gears and a couple of flat-out left-handers, one right-hander, straightening them all out and into fifth. You also take the next right-hander over a brow "flat" before rushing down towards the fast right and left at White House corner.

You brake from 150 m.p.h., take fourth, sacrifice the best line for the right-hand curve using a very small angle of drift, so as to get on line for the left-hander, then set up a bigger drift as soon as you line up on the second apex at around 135 m.p.h. As you initiate the drift you turn on the power and then drift rapidly to the right-hand side of the road after almost touching the grass at the apex on the left. You have gained two or three hundred revolutions on the exit at the expense of a very slightly slower entrance and you have an excellent start to the run up to the pits through a number of slight "kinks" which are straightened out and taken "flat." Fifth is taken soon after White House and you sweep through the curves to the start and finish line, accelerating up to 155 m.p.h. to start yet another lap.

By Night

For the night spell it is essential for a driver to find braking markers that are immovable and are easily picked up by the headlights or spotlights. In addition he needs to find equally immovable sighting markers such as trees, posts, or reflector sticks which help him to turn into a corner at the right moment. He also needs apex markers, and careful positioning of the spotlights during night practice pays big dividends. He drives by his markers, for lights even today do not illuminate the road sufficiently at speeds of over 160 m.p.h. to eliminate the need for "blind driving." Careful study during night practice can enable a driver to put in laps within two to four seconds of his best daylight time.

The passing of rivals at Le Mans does not present any great difficulty for the road is a good width and "out braking" another driver into the Esses, Mulsanne, and Arnage, together with the slight differences in maximum speeds on the long straight, provide ample opportunity. The slower cars are a problem and the only safe maxim about overtaking is "if in doubt don't" which costs time but is much preferable to the alternative. If it rains at night, the spray thrown up by the slower cars can be such as to obscure their rear lights. Approaching such a car at about 80 m.p.h., as if it were stationary, can be extremely hazardous and Le Mans winners are cautious in such circumstances.

Le Mans tests the endurance of the cars, the endurance and self control of the drivers, at the same time offering the public a 24-hour spectacle that is unique. When the drivers dash across the road, jump into their cars, and press the starters at 4.0 p.m. tomorrow, the 30th Le Mans race will be under way. The eventual winner may be the last to start but when he sees the chequered flag both he and his co-driver will have earned their victory and after the champagne, the congratulations, a hot bath and an enormous meal, they may be heard to murmur "Never again—well not this year anyway."

*A trio of Ferraris—two racing-sports cars and a Berlinetta—crowds into **Arnage** corner, with the left-handed Indianapolis in the background*

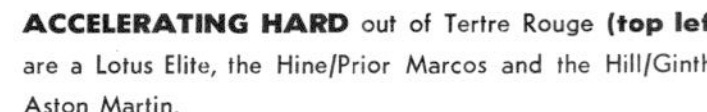

ACCELERATING HARD out of Tertre Rouge **(top left)** are a Lotus Elite, the Hine/Prior Marcos and the Hill/Ginther Aston Martin.

*

SUN AND SHADE (top centre). The Cunningham/Salvadori E-type is followed through the Esses by the Consten/Rosinski Bonnet, the Fulp/Ryan Ferrari and the Arents/Behra Osca.

*

"ENZO'S BREAD VAN". The peculiar hard top Testa Rossa Ferrari of Abate and Davis is chased through Tertre Rouge by the rear-engined machine of Baghetti and Scarfiotti **(top right)**.

*

MORE MONSTERS. Two of the three new 4-litre Maseratis are seen here mid-way through the Esses. The Trintignant/Bianchi car is leading the Thompson/Kimberly machine **(bottom left)**.

*

RIVALS FROM MODENA (bottom right). Lucien Bianchi (4-litre Maserati) leads the Rodriguez brothers' 2½-litre rear-engined Ferrari through Mulsanne.

F E R R A R I
LES TROIS PREMIÈRES

Phil Hill and Olivier Gendebien head a 1-2-3 Victory at Le Mans — Lotus Elites one-two in Thermal of Efficiency — Class Successes for Morgan, Porsche, Lotus, Bonnet, Panhard and Ferrari — "Index" Goes Again to Panhard — New Lap Record by Phil Hill at over 127 m.p.h.

BY GREGOR GRANT

PHOTOGRAPHY BY GEORGE PHILLIPS

THAT incomparable partnership of long-distance specialists, Phil Hill and Olivier Gendebien, won the Grand Prix d'Endurance at Le Mans for the second successive year. Heading a Ferrari 1-2-3 benefit, they covered over 4,451 kilometres in the 24 hours; not such a great distance as their 1961 record, but a new record for the 4-litre class. Their V12 experimental Ferrari had a front-mounted V12 engine, and all-independent suspension with Dunlop disc brakes, and an open body. In the third hour, Phil Hill established a new lap record for Le Mans at 127.6 m.p.h.

Runner-up was the French-entered Ferrari of Noblet and Guichet, which, although entered and announced as an experimental machine, somehow managed to win the Grand Touring category in front of a more normal G.T.-type driven by the Belgians Elde and Beurlys. Into fourth place came the E-type Jaguar of Briggs Cunningham and Roy Salvadori, which moved up over the splendidly prepared and driven E-type of Peter Sargent and Peter Lumsden, which had engine bearer trouble right at the end, and had to be driven comparatively slowly.

Lotus had tremendous satisfaction after their unhappy experiences with the A.C.O. in regard to their "23" models. The Elites of David Hobbs/Frank Gardner and Clive Hunt/John Wyllie were first and second in the highly remunerative Thermal of Efficiency, and also took third place in the Index of Performance, to a Panhard and a René Bonnet—awards which more or less keep French small-capacity racing cars in business from year to year.

Actually only 18 of the 55 starters completed the distance—six of them being British built. Despite their success, Ferrari had a high mortality rate, for only four of the 15 starters finished. In point of fact, Italian and Franco-Italian machines had a poor reliability record. Of the 31 which started, only half a dozen survived. All three V8 Maseratis fell by the wayside, only the Hansgen/McLaren car lasting for more than half the distance.

Graham Hill/Richie Ginther put up tremendous opposition during the early stages, their 4-litre Aston Martin showing great promise, and leading the race for a few laps. Unfortunately, in curing a dynamo fault, an oil pipe was damaged and the car had to be withdrawn after six hours of racing.

The Morgan of Chris Lawrence and Richard Shepherd-Barron won the 2-litre class, and the other British car to finish was the Sunbeam Alpine of Peter Harper/Peter Procter.

After the elimination of the big Aston Martin and the Maseratis, only the spirited challenge of the Rodriguez brothers in their 2.4 Ferrari kept interest alive in the general category. Unlucky yet again, the Mexicans had to abandon with broken transmission at 4.30 a.m., when disputing the issue with the Hill/Gendebien machine.

The refusal of the A.C.O. technical committee to accept the Lotus 23s of Jim Clark/Trevor Taylor and Les Leston/Tony Shelly was an unfortunate affair altogether. When the cars were presented for scrutineering, they were turned down because the front wheels had four-stud fixing, and the rears six-stud. It was alleged that the spare wheel could replace only one pair of wheels. In consequence, Colin Chapman arranged to have the rear wheels modified to a four-stud fixing. Thereupon the officials adopted an extraordinary attitude, to the effect that since the wheels had originally been designed for a six-stud location, modification to four-stud rendered the machines unsafe. Moreover, they refused point blank to examine the cars, insisting that they had already been turned down.

How the A.C.O. can take the decision that a layout is unsafe without submitting the components to a destruction test passes comprehension. Colin Chapman naturally protested strongly, even going to the trouble of bringing Dean Delamont of the R.A.C. over from England to present the case, which Harold Parker, in spite of a perfect command of the French language, was apparently unable to do earlier. Also, "Jabby" Crombac tried everything possible to have the officials listen to reason, but it was obvious from the start that the A.C.O. people had made up their minds to ban the cars, and that was that. Thus, Great Britain's strongest contenders for the Index of Performance were eliminated, no doubt to the great relief of the supporters of Bonnet and Panhard.

Behind this unsavoury "affaire Lotus" was the dictatorial attitude of the A.C.O., which, more or less, amounted to: "We couldn't care less—and the heck with F.I.A. rules and regulations!"

It is understood that the entrants are seeking to institute court proceedings against the organizers.

During Wednesday evening's practice, Phil Hill, in the open, front-engined 4-litre Ferrari with all-independent suspension, unofficially lowered the Le Mans circuit record, with a time of 3 mins. 55.1 secs., 206.123 k.p.h. (128.08

THE START: The flag has dropped, the drivers have sprinted to their cars and, after a few seconds, the 55 cars are away. Leading the pack are Tony Settember's Chevrolet Corvette (left) and Graham Hill's Aston Martin Project 212 which led on the opening lap.

ABOVE: The Bruce McLaren/Walt Hansgen Maserati (right) passes the Giancarlo Sala/de Luca di Lizzano Alfa Romeo coming into Tertre Rouge.

BELOW: The Paul Armagnac/Gerard Laureau Bonnet leads the Tony Settember/Jack Turner Corvette and the Jack Fairman/Tom Dickson Ecurie Ecosse Tojeiro at Arnage.

The car that was not allowed to start—the works Lotus 23 of Jim Clark and Trevor Taylor.

m.p.h.). This was 2.2 secs. faster than Mike Hawthorn's existing record with the 4.1-litre Ferrari. Next best was Mike Parkes in the G.T. prototype 4-litre, with 4 mins. 0.9 secs., then Pedro Rodriguez (2.4 Ferrari) with 4 mins. 2.2 secs.

The V8, 4-litre Maseratis were fantastically quick on the Mulsanne straight (over 180 m.p.h.), but were a trifle tricky to handle in the bends. Bruce McLaren did 4 mins. 5.5 secs. in one of the Cunningham coupés. Fastest British car was the 4-litre Aston Martin driven by Graham Hill, with 4 mins. 16 secs.

The SSS Venezia Ferrari No. 16 was a strange-looking device, rather like a Ferrari pick-up. The three Sunbeam Alpines looked most unfamiliar with their chopped-off tails.

Ecurie Ecosse produced just one Tojeiro, fitted with a 2.5-litre Coventry-Climax engine. Porsche withdrew the "flat-eight" and substituted a 1.6-litre Abarth-Carrera, so Dan Gurney and Jo Bonnier accepted the offer to drive a Venezia sports Ferrari. French driver Bouharde crashed his Bonnet at White House, wrecking the car completely. He was taken to hospital with a knee injury.

Enormous crowds turned up for Thursday's training, during which British hopes were raised high by the performance of Graham Hill in the Aston Martin, who recorded 3 mins. 59.8 secs., the green car sounding really magnificent. Dick Thompson did 3 mins. 59.1 secs. with the big Maserati. Roy Salvadori was due to co-drive with the American, but could not fit into the

cockpit comfortably. He switched to Briggs Cunningham's E-type Jaguar.

Mike Parkes hurtled the big G.T. Ferrari prototype round in 3 mins. 58.6 secs., and co-driver Bandini achieved 4 mins. 1.3 secs., which was equalled by McLaren in the other Cunningham 4-litre Maserati. Trintignant, in the French-entered version, returned 4 mins. 3.3 secs. Phil Hill was again fastest of all, this time with 3 mins. 55.2 secs.

John Coundley, in Maurice Charles's E-type, shook the G.T. Ferrari brigade with a time of 4 mins. 2.3 secs., whilst the 1,300 c.c. Simca-Abarth of Bianchi/Harris was credited with the remarkable time of 4 mins. 34.3 secs. Coundley's time, though issued by the timekeepers, was thought to have been achieved by another car—possibly the Thompson/Kimberly Maserati No. 3—the Jaguar being No. 8.

* * *

IN bright sunshine, enormous crowds gathered to watch the start of "Les Vingt-Quatre Heures". In front of the packed tribunes they were scores deep, many of them provided with periscopes, and all wearing a strange variety of headgear to protect their heads from the dazzling sun.

There was the traditional parade of the colours of the competing nations, accompanied by the usual discordant band which, somehow, never seems to be able to keep in step. This temporarily replaced the raucous P.A. equipment over which "Twist Again" was being given big licks. As the hour hand approached 3.30 p.m., the official 2 Plus 2 Ferrari went round to close the circuit, followed by the astonishingly quiet pre-production Rover gas-turbine saloon, which was given a motorcycle escort.

The field included no fewer than 15 Ferraris out of the 55 starters, the largest number of any one make ever to appear at Le Mans. The Marcos was the first wood-built machine to start a race there, and its Ford power-unit was the first engine of Dagenham origin at Sarthe since the o.h.v. Arden in the Allard.

British cars numbered 16, comprising three Aston Martins, three Jaguars, two Sunbeams, two Lotus Elites and one each of A.C.-Bristol, Morgan, Marcos, Tojeiro-Climax, Austin-Healey and T.V.R. As the 55 cars were lined up in order of start with the big-capacity cars nearest the Dunlop Bridge, headed by a Chevrolet Corvette, one could see the first drivers taking up their position opposite the pits. Amongst those having been selected to take the first stint

were Olivier Gendebien, Graham Hill, Pedro Rodriguez, Bruce McLaren, Maurice Trintignant, Mike Parkes, Dan Gurney, Mike Salmon, Maurice Charles, Tom Dickson, Bill Kimberly and Briggs Cunningham.

Behind the cars there was a sea of faces, every pit jammed solid with human beings. All along the banks, photographers crouched in the hot sun, awaiting the "off". The hands of the official clock moved slowly towards 4 o'clock, then down went the flag and the race was on. Several engines fired at once, and Settember got the unwieldy Corvette on the move, but before reaching the Dunlop Bridge Graham Hill had taken the lead with the Aston Martin, followed in quick succession by the Ferraris of Parkes and Gendebien, Charles's E-type and Kerguen's Aston Martin. Parkes and Gendebien closed up on the green Feltham car, and the latter snapped into second place on the Mulsanne straight, cutting in front of Parkes as they approached the corner. The unfortunate Parkes had to do some last-minute wheel-twiddling, partially lost control, and ended up in the sand banks. He ruefully climbed out of the big G.T. prototype, and studied ways and means of extricating the red car.

Meanwhile Graham Hill was keeping in front, hotly pursued by Gendebien. To the huge delight of the big British contingent, the Aston Martin whistled round "Maison Blanche" first, and held its advantage all the way down the

LEFT: The V8 Ferrari of Giancarlo Baghetti and Lodovico Scarfiotti (left) and the winning 4-litre V12 of Hill/Gendebien. Note the different exhaust systems and the strange aerodynamic "shelves" behind the drivers.

RIGHT: Massive machinery! The V8 Maserati engine. All three 4-litre cars retired.

shimmering road to the pits. However, the Ferrari was closing up rapidly, and out of the Esses, Olivier was making to pass. So quickly had the two leaders got off their marks that fully 14 seconds passed before the next group passed the pits, in the order Guichet (Ferrari), Pedro Rodriguez (Ferrari), Tavano (Ferrari), McLaren (Maserati), Vaccarella (Ferrari), Trintignant (Maserati), Grossman (Ferrari), Baghetti (Ferrari) and Fulp (Ferrari)—one lone British car amongst a horde of Italian machines.

At Mulsanne Gendebien was in front of Hill, and when the pair appeared for the second time the Belgian had increased his advantage to six seconds. Rodriguez had moved up to third, and Kimberly pushed the big white Maserati into sixth place, ahead of Baghetti and Tavano. Next British car to the Aston Martin was the ultra-low Ecurie Ecosse Tojeiro of Tommy Dickson, chased by Peter Sargent's E-type Jaguar. John Whitmore had moved up to 22nd place with the Ecurie Chiltern Austin-Healey, but Oreiller's tiny blue Abarth Simca was on his tail.

Charles made a brief pit-stop with his Jaguar, and the T.V.R. race came to an abrupt end when Peter Bolton found that all the water had boiled away in less than three laps. Thus already the British cars had lost one of their number. Peter Procter was also in trouble with the Sunbeam, and had to stop to have a sticking throttle fixed, after the engine had shot up to nearly 7,000 r.p.m. without doing any apparent harm.

Speeds were already high on the timed section at Mulsanne, with Kimberly's Maserati registering 281 k.p.h. (173.6 m.p.h.), and Hill's Aston Martin, 270 k.p.h. (167.8 m.p.h.). Masson's 700 c.c. Fiat-Abarth was clocked at 188 k.p.h. (117.4 m.p.h.).

To a storm of cheering from the French, Trintignant scorched past Rodriguez to take third place with the red Maserati coupé, the two Cunningham Maseratis closing up on the Mexican, followed by a perfect fury of Ferraris, no fewer than seven of the Maranello products being led by Baghetti, and then Abate in the Venezia "delivery-van". Gendebien was steadily increasing his lead over Hill, and there were 18 secs. between them at the end of six laps. All three Maseratis had overtaken Rodriguez, running in line astern, but losing ground to the leaders.

An exhausted Parkes completed the herculean task of digging out the Ferrari and, bathed in sweat, he returned to the pits to hand over to Bandini. Already the leaders had doubled the Austin-Healey, all three Porsches and the fastest of the Abarth-Simcas (Oreiller's). Dan Gurney was beginning to move his

The gallant Aston Martin which alone upheld any British chance of an outright victory. Graham Hill in the Esses in the early stages when it went so well.

Ferrari up the leader board, closing fast on Baghetti and Abate.

The three Maseratis were far faster than anything else on the Mulsanne straight, but were losing seconds on the bends to the far superior handling of the Ferraris, and Hill's superb Aston Martin. The presence of David Brown's newest machine was certainly adding spice to the contest, and it was the only non-Italian car capable of dealing with the Ferraris and Maseratis. Yet Gendebien was gaining about 5 secs. a lap, and Hill was doing likewise to the Maserati trio. Gurney's spurt brought him up to seventh place after 10 laps, right on the tail of the Rodriguez sister-car. Innes Ireland was going like an express train with the light-green U.D.T.-Laystall Ferrari GTO, and Dickson was putting up a splendid show with the 2.5-litre Tojeiro, keeping in front of Sargent's E-type. Speeds were rising again, and de Lageneste's tiny 1,300 c.c. Abarth-Simca was timed at 222 k.p.h. (140 m.p.h.), and McLaren at 285 k.p.h. (177 m.p.h.).

Gurney shot past Rodriguez to take sixth place, gaining seconds a lap on the Maseratis. This was just after the first hour positions were announced, which were: 1, Gendebien; 2, G. Hill; 3, Kimberly; 4, Trintignant; 5, McLaren; 6, Rodriguez; 7, Gurney; 8, Baghetti; 9, Abate; 10, Guichet.

A spirited tussle between Ireland's GTO Ferrari and Bob Fulp's sports-racer ended when the American had to make a pit stop. Leading small car was Oreiller's Abarth-Simca, then in 26th place, having passed the two leading Porsches. Both Sunbeams were running consistently, and Whitmore, in 24th place, kept the Austin-Healey in front of Coundley's E-type.

First of the faster cars to refuel was the Tojeiro, and Fairman took over. At 5.27, with only 20 laps completed, the leading Ferrari came in to refuel and have a tyre examined. Phil Hill was not prepared for such an early change, so off went Gendebien again. Trintignant handed over his Maserati to Lucien Bianchi. This put the Aston Martin into the lead, by some 30 secs. from Rodriguez, who had earlier retaken Dan Gurney, and then the Maseratis, when they stopped to refuel. McLaren changed with Walt Hansgen, Kimberly with Dick Thompson, and Gurney with Bonnier. Then in came Pedro to hand over to Ricardo, and Graham Hill now had 77 secs. in hand over Gendebien. Demetz's Fiat-Abarth was stuck at Arnage, the driver setting off for the pits.

Hill led with the Aston Martin till the 26th lap, when he handed over to Richie Ginther, the stop pushing the green car down to fourth place. The Gurney/Bonnier Ferrari was in trouble with a broken throttle, remaining stationary at the pits for some considerable time. The Parkes/Bandini coupé was also in trouble, circulating slowly with abnormally high water temperature and a suspected leaking radiator. With Olivier Gendebien back in the lead, a furious struggle developed between Dick Thompson and Rodriguez for second place. The Ireland/Gregory GTO Ferrari had advanced to 10th position.

Down into Tertre Rouge from the Esses come an Osca, an Abarth-Simca, and two sports Ferraris.

By the second hour, Gendebien, Thompson, Rodriguez, Ginther, Hansgen and Scarfiotti had all completed 28 laps, with Gendebien 45 secs. ahead of the Maserati. The race average had gone up to over 118 m.p.h., and there were all the makings of a real Grand Prix, particularly with Ricardo Rodriguez driving his 2.4-litre car round at an astonishing pace, giving Thompson no respite.

Ferrari supporters had a shock when Gendebien came in again at 31 laps, but this was to take on petrol and oil. World Champion Phil Hill restarted at 6.10 p.m., down to fifth position. Vinatier abandoned his Bonnet with serious overheating, and the Bentley/Gordon 1.6 Osca was retired for no specific reason, but with something wrong with the transmission. The leading Ferrari's stop put a Maserati into the lead for the first time (Thompson), but the American was having quite a time of it holding off the eager Rodriguez.

Parkes was circulating slowly with the ailing Ferrari, many, many laps in arrears. Obviously the writing was on the wall for the big experimental coupé, which could quite well have been disputing the lead with the others. Rodriguez tried everything to take Thompson, but just could not match the tremendous speed of the white Maserati on the straight. Walt Hansgen closed right up on Ginther, who was worried because his dynamo had ceased to charge. Shortly before 6.30 p.m., Venezia's strange "delivery-van" ceased to function, and was abandoned with back axle maladies. Balzarini's Abarth-Simca came to a grinding halt, which brought the list of retirements up to six.

With 40 laps completed, and the scoreboard showing the Aston Martin with the wrong number of laps to its credit, Thompson stopped to refuel and Kimberly took over. The race order then was 1, Rodriguez; 2, Hansgen; 3, Phil Hill; 4, Ginther. This was the order at 3 hours, but Hill moved up when Hansgen handed over to McLaren.

Kerguen, coming in with his Aston Martin to have the gearbox seen to, spun in the slow-down area, and arrived at his pit backwards. Retirements included the Berger/Darville Ferrari, the Charles/Coundley Jaguar, which had developed a serious engine fault, and the Pon/de Beaufort Abarth-Porsche, which had axle bothers. The Austin-Healey was still going well, with Bob Olthoff now at the wheel, whilst Dickson was back in the sleek Tojeiro, which did not seem to have its full complement of gears. Abarth-Simca's numbers were further reduced when Oreiller's very fast blue car blew up.

Rodriguez refuelled and handed back to brother Pedro. Phil Hill, driving very fast indeed, covered his 49th lap in the new record time of 3 mins. 57.3 secs., 204.212 k.p.h. (127 m.p.h.). The Aston Martin was then in second place, with Rodriguez third after his stop. So fast had Hill gone that, when he handed over to Gendebien at 52 laps, Ferrari No. 6 restarted still in the lead. However, Ginther's Aston Martin was in trouble with the dynamo, and it was decided to repair this before darkness set in. Graham Hill rejoined the race, over five laps in arrears, down to 14th place.

When the fourth hour was registered, Gendebien and Rodriguez had covered 57 laps, with just half a second separ-

The winning Ferrari of Phil Hill and Olivier Gendebien at the Esses. Olivier Gendebien has now won Le Mans three times in succession.

ating them. McLaren lost time with a burst tyre, falling well down the list, and restarting in eighth place. Chief challenge to the Ferraris came from Kimberly, who handed over to Thompson at 8.21 p.m., after refuelling and changing brake pads. Shortly afterwards the big Maserati crashed at the Esses, burst a petrol tank and had to be abandoned. Trintignant, in the red V8, was over a lap behind the leading Ferrari when he handed over to Lucien Bianchi. The offside rear wheel was fouling a damaged wing. and this had to be straightened. All four tyres were changed. Magne's A.C.-Bristol was wheeled away with a burnt-out clutch, leaving the Morgan in complete command of the 2-litre class. Fulp's Ferrari required some minor panel-bashing, and Pete Ryan took over. British car positions at this stage were: 12th, Sargent/Lumsden (Jaguar); 14th, Hill/Ginther (Aston Martin); 16th, Salmon/Baillie (Aston Martin); 18th, Cunningham/Salvadori (Jaguar); 19th, Fairman/Dickson (Tojeiro); 20th, Whitmore/Olthoff (Austin-Healey); 23rd, Hobbs/Gardner (Lotus); 24th, Hunt/Wyllie (Lotus); 29th, Hine/Prior (Marcos); 30th, Hopkirk/Jopp (Sunbeam); 31st, Lawrence/Shepherd-Barron (Morgan) and 34th, Harper/Procter (Sunbeam). Forty-four cars still remained in the race.

At 5 hours, Hill/Gendebien were a lap ahead of the Rodriguez brothers, and two in front of Baghetti/Scarfiotti. The Noblet/Guichet "G.T." car was in fourth place, 1½ mins. in front of the Hansgen/McLaren Maserati. Then came the Tavano/Simon Ferrari, and the Ireland/Gregory Ferrari. Salmon's Aston Martin was a lap ahead of the Hill/

Ginther car. Fairman took over the "Toj", losing over a lap whilst the gearbox was sorted out. Parkes handed over to Bandini, but the car was in the pits for over 10 minutes.

It was now almost dark, after a lovely twilight, but with a suggestion of mist at White House. Several cars, obviously in trouble electrically, had been circulated to the last possible moment with just side lights. The Hunt/Wyllie Lotus had its dynamo repaired.

With the sixth hour coming up the Hill/Ginther Aston Martin was retired with no oil pressure. In repairing the dynamo, an oil pipe had been damaged, so it was goodbye to a gallant British effort for an outright win. The Parkes/Bandini car was finally withdrawn with a badly leaking radiator.

Ferraris occupied the first five places, with Hill/Gendebien and the Rodriguez brothers on the same lap, a couple of minutes separating them. The Trintignant/Bianchi Maserati was three laps adrift, and the Hansgen/McLaren car five. Best-placed British machine was the Sargent/Lumsden E-type, in 11th place, a couple of laps ahead of the Salmon/Baillie Aston Martin. The Index of Performance was headed by the Masson/Zeccoli Fiat-Abarth, with the Rodriguez Ferrari in second place.

The battle went on between the two leading Ferraris, and at the seventh hour the Rodriguez brothers led Hill/Gendebien by a couple of minutes, each having completed 99 laps—two ahead of Noblet/Guichet. The Whitmore/Olthoff Austin-Healey had advanced to 17th, and Hobbs/Gardner (Lotus) in 18th place headed the Barth/Herrmann Porsche, and the Bianchi/Harris Abarth-Simca, which had been having plug troubles, but was now on all four again. The Marcos was in trouble with the engine, spending much time being repaired.

Dickson, in the Tojeiro, spent many horrifying minutes sitting in the middle of White House with the car jammed in gear. Cars whizzed past to the left and to the right—fortunately all missing the unlooked-for road block. Herrmann's Porsche required 20 minutes for clutch adjustment, and Trintignant was in trouble with the rear suspension of his Maserati.

The Marcos had lost most of its oil through the speedometer drive, and despite an effort to keep going till oil could be added, the engine cried "enough", and Le Mans's first wooden car had to be abandoned.

At midnight (after eight hours), the Hill/Gendebien car was back in the lead, with more than a lap in advance of the Rodriguez boys. Salmon's Aston Martin was now 12th, in front of the Jaguars of Cunningham/Salvadori and Sargent/Lumsden. The Ireland/Gregory Ferrari GTO, going splendidly in seventh place, ran out of lights, and brushes had to be replaced in the dynamo, amongst other jobs. Gregory restarted, having lost nearly two laps. At 1 a.m., Rodriguez had completed 127 laps, to the 126 of Hill/Gendebien. Ferraris were in the first six places, with Trintignant/Bianchi (Maserati) seventh and Hansgen/Mc-Laren ninth. The Rodriguez brothers had taken over the lead from the Fiat-Abarth in the "Index", and Guilhaudin/

ABOVE: Grand Touring cars. At Mulsanne Corner, the Fernand Tavano/André Simon Ferrari leads the similar car of Leon Dernièr Ede/Jean Beurlys and the Tony Settember/Jack Turner Corvette.

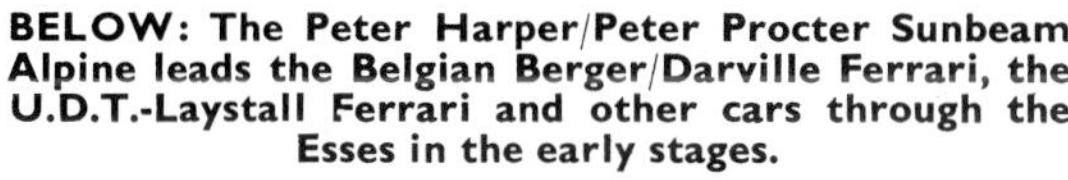

BELOW: The Peter Harper/Peter Procter Sunbeam Alpine leads the Belgian Berger/Darville Ferrari, the U.D.T.-Laystall Ferrari and other cars through the Esses in the early stages.

Bertaut were third with their Panhard.

Trintignant's Maserati was withdrawn with suspension and transmission failure, and the surviving American-entered V8 was eight laps behind the leader. Up into 10th and 11th places went the Jaguars of Cunningham and Sargent, but the Salmon/Baillie Aston Martin had developed a serious-sounding misfire, as had the Austin-Healey. At 1.27 a.m., Salmon retired with a holed piston. Hansgen lost a rear light, which had to be replaced. Masten Gregory lost over 30 minutes whilst the dynamo was again repaired. Kerguen (Aston Martin) stopped for the umpteenth time, on this occasion to change all six spark plugs.

At 2.48 a.m., McLaren took over the Maserati from Hansgen, but the transmission was making funny noises. The car was then in sixth place. Simon was called in to have his lights checked on the Ferrari, and left after replacing a light unit and a blown fuse. Kerguen finally abandoned his Aston Martin with transmission failure.

At half-distance (4 a.m.), the Rodriguez brothers were back in the lead, having completed 170 laps. However, Hill/Gendebien were just 30 secs. behind. Sargent had advanced to 10th place, a lap ahead of Salvadori. George Reed had to change a headlamp bulb on the Ferrari, and Ed Hugus took over in 12th place.

At 4.30 a.m., after a fine performance, the Rodriguez brothers had to abandon with final drive trouble. It was a blow to the Mexicans, and many tears were shed in their pit. The departure of the "2.4" gave Hill/Gendebien a four-lap lead over Noblet/Guichet, and Ferraris still held the first four places. The Maserati was being circulated hopefully, but the noises from the rear-end per-

ABOVE: The gallant Austin-Healey 3000 of John Whitmore/Bob Olthoff leads the Peter Harper/Peter Procter Sunbeam Alpine at the Esses.

BELOW: The Index of Performance winner, the André Guilhaudin/Alain Bertaut 701 c.c. Panhard.

sisted. It was being threatened by the Simon/Tavano car, and also by the Vaccarella/Scarlatti machine. With the approach of daylight, more than a few of the 32 survivors breathed freely, for several cars had dodgy lights and batteries in a low state of charge.

Shortly after 5 a.m., the Hansgen/McLaren Maserati had its transmission pack up, and it was abandoned, leaving Ferraris in the first six places followed by the two Jaguars, with the Sargent/Lumsden car three laps in front of the Cunningham entry. The Austin-Healey was back on to six cylinders, but smoking rather excessively. Hopkirk/Jopp ran the big-end bearings on their Sunbeam, and mechanics set about replacing the shells—a tricky job, especially when the oil from the sump had to be saved, and none could be added. The commissar had his beady eyes on the operation from start to finish.

The morning was a fine one, but by 7 a.m. only 25 cars were circulating. Whitmore/Olthoff had advanced the Austin-Healey to 10th position, and the Morgan was 15th. Abandonments included the Ireland/Gregory Ferrari, the Fulp/Ryan Ferrari and the Vaccarella/Scarlatti Ferrari. Not long afterwards, the Tavano/Simon Ferrari was abandoned. The repaired Hopkirk/Jopp Sunbeam struggled along last but one, with little hope of completing the required distance before exclusion.

The crowds began to take notice of the race once more, after the serious business of taking "petit dejeuner". In the pits area, the odour of eggs and bacon came from the British camps, mixed with the pungent smell of strong coffee. Dust was everywhere, rising in clouds from the car parks, as vehicles returned from Le Mans and its environs to the circuit.

All the time, the Hill/Gendebien Ferrari circulated, sounding as healthy as ever. If anything should happen to it, why there were four more to take its place. At 8 a.m., the British picture was not quite so dismal, for Sargent/Lumsden had taken their dark green Jaguar up to sixth place, followed by the Cunningham/Savadori car, and then the admirable Austin-Healey of Whit-

ABOVE: The Bruce McLaren/Walt Hansgen 4-litre Maserati coming in to its pit, with one front lamp dangling. This was the longest-surviving Maserati.

BELOW: Thermal of Efficiency victors, the two Lotus Elites of David Hobbs/Frank Gardner and Clive Hunt/Dr. M. R. J. Wyllie.

more/Olthoff. The Morgan had lost part of its exhaust system, but was still chuffing round merrily at nearly 100 m.p.h. average. A splendid tonic was the sight of the two Elites, not quite so clean as they were, but sounding in mighty fine nick.

The leader had been slowed down considerably, but still kept five to six laps in front of the G.T. car. Baghetti/Scarfiotti abandoned just before 10 a.m., when in third place. This let the Jaguars into fifth and sixth places, and the Hobbs/Gardner Elite into eighth.

Unhappily for Chiltern hopes, the Austin-Healey had obviously done in a piston, but it was too much to hope that it could be made to last out for six more hours The Hopkirk/Jopp Sunbeam had been abandoned with engine trouble, so 21 cars were all that were left at 10 a.m. on a bright Sunday morning. The Foitek/Ricci Alfa Romeo had no clutch, and the Arents/Behra Osca sounded very ribby.

The gallant Austin-Healey run came to an end around 10 a.m., when the engine finally gave up its struggle against unequal odds. Sargent and Lumsden were now attacking the Elde/Beurlys Ferrari, being only 3½ minutes behind at midday. They had advanced to four laps ahead of the Cunningham car. Porsche and Lotus Elite were fighting a stern battle for G.T. honours in the 2-litre class, with Herrmann in front of Gardner by just over a lap.

Lunch-time came and went, and Hill/Gendebien still circulated their now very dirty looking Ferrari. Sargent and Lumsden were in pursuit of the Belgian-driven car, gaining about 15 secs. a lap. Gardner and Hobbs had overtaken the Herrmann/Barth Porsche. Foitek had trouble restarting his Alfa Romeo without a clutch, struggled along to the Dunlop Bridge, only to stall the engine and have to abandon on the grass with a flat battery. Bob Grossmann/Fireball Roberts were also in trouble with the starter of their Ferrari, made to push the car, but fortunately for them it did not start. Finally, they got it away on the starter, and the commissar took no further action.

The closing stages were unlucky for Sargent/Lumsden and Hobbs/Gardner. With fourth place almost in the bag the Jaguar had a rear engine bearer collapse, requiring a strict rev. limit in order to finish. The Elite went on to three cylinders, and immediately began to be overhauled by the Porsche. Eventually Cunningham/Salvadori displaced the British-entered car, and Herrmann just managed to catch and pass the Hobbs/Gardner car. The Osca was retired in the final hour, and so only 18 machines were still running when the 4 p.m. maroon sounded. Elites achieved a well-deserved first and second in the Thermal Efficiency Index, and Chris Lawrence's supporters went wild with excitement when the Morgan completed the race, to win the 2-litre class.

No one could possibly begrudge Phil Hill and Olivier Gendebien their success, nor Ferrari their overwhelming superiority. The 4-litre was built with the express purpose of winning the G.P. d'Endurance, and the closed cars to take the G.T. category. Nevertheless, it should be explained just how Noblet and Guichet managed to have the car transferred from experimental to G.T., without other entrants being notified of the change!

HOW THEY FINISHED . . .

General Classification

1. Phil Hill/Olivier Gendebien (3,967 Ferrari), 4,451.255 kiloms., 185.469 k.p.h.
2. Noblet/Guichet (2,953 Ferrari G.T.), 4,384.133, 182.673.
3. Elde/Beurlys (2,953 Ferrari G.T.), 4,213.875, 175,578.
4. **Briggs Cunningham/Roy Salvadori (3,781 Jaguar "E" G.T.),** 4,166.617, 173.609.
5. **Peter Sargent/Peter Lumsden (3,781 Jaguar "E" G.T.),** 4,163.417, 173.476.
6. Grossmann/Roberts (2,953 Ferrari), 3,997.810, 166.575.
7. Barth/Herrmann (1,588 Porsche G.T.), 3,858.532, 160.772.
8. **David Hobbs/Frank Gardner (1,216 Lotus Elite G.T.),** 3,847.066, 160.295.
9. Hugus/Reed (2,953 Ferrari G.T.), 3,779.317, 157.472.
10. Sala/de Luca (1,290 Alfa Romeo G.T.), 3,774.655, 157.278.
11. **Clive Hunt/John Wyllie (1,216 Lotus Elite G.T.),** 3,733.458, 155.561.
12. Buchet/Schiller (1,588 Porsche G.T.), 3,655.696, 152.321.
13. **Chris Lawrence/Richard Shepherd-Barron (1,991 Morgan G.T.),** 3,629.288, 151.220.
14. Bianchi/Harris (1,288 Abarth-Simca), 3,603.165, 150.132.
15. **Peter Harper/Peter Procter (1,590 Sunbeam Alpine),** 3,601.467, 150.061.
16. Guilhaudin/Bertaut (702 Panhard), 3,427.026, 142.793.
17. Consten/Rosinski (996 R. Bonnet), 3,421.551, 142.565.
18. Armagnac/Laureau (706 R. Bonnet), 3,396.906, 141.538.

G.T. Championship

(Above 2,000 c.c.)

1. Ferrari (Noblet/Guichet), 9 pts.
2. Ferrari (Elde/Beurlys), 9.
3. Jaguar (Cunningham/Salvadori), 4.
4. Ferrari (Hugus/Reed), 4.

(1,001-2,000 c.c.)

1. Porsche (Barth/Herrmann), 9.
2. Lotus (Hobbs/Gardner), 6.
3. Alfa Romeo (Sala/de Luca), 4.
4. Lotus (Hunt/Wyllie), 4.
5. Porsche (Buchet/Schiller), 4.
6. Morgan (Lawrence/Shepherd-Barron), 1.
7. Sunbeam (Harper/Procter), 1.

Index of Thermal Efficiency

1. **Lotus (Hobbs/Gardner),** Index 1.27, speed 160.3 k.p.h., consumption 14.4 litres/100 kiloms, weight 630 kg.
2. **Lotus (Hunt/Wyllie),** 1.17, 155.6, 14.3, 630.
3. Panhard (Guilhaudin/Bertaut), 1.15, 142.8, 11.4, 590.
4. Alfa Romeo (Sala/de Luca), 1.10, 157.3, 17.5, 820.
5. Porsche (Barth/Herrmann), 1.06, 160.8, 19.5, 840.
6. **Jaguar (Sargent/Lumsden),** 1.04, 173.5, 29.4, 1,220.
7. Bonnet (Armagnac/Laureau), 1.00, 141.5, 12.3, 520.
   Jaguar (Cunningham/**Salvadori**), 1.00, 173.6, 30.6, 1,220.

Index of Performance

1. Guilhaudin/Bertaut (Panhard), 1.265.
2. Armagnac/Laureau (Bonnet), 1.251.
3. **Hobbs/Gardner (Lotus Elite),** 1.204.
4. Noblet/Guichet (Ferrari), 1.203.
5. P. Hill/Gendebien (Ferrari), 1.192.
6. Hunt/Wyllie (Lotus Elite), 1.169.

Class Winners

Up to 4,000 c.c. (13): Hill/Gendebien (Ferrari), 4,451.255 kiloms. (Record).
Up to 3,000 c.c. (12): Noblet/Guichet (Ferrari), 4,384.133.
Up to 2,000 c.c. (10): **Lawrence/Shepherd-Barron (Morgan),** 3,629.288.
Up to 1,600 c.c. (9): Barth/Herrmann (Porsche), 3,858.522.
Up to 1,300 c.c. (8): **Hobbs/Gardner (Lotus Elite),** 3,847.060.
Up to 1,000 c.c. (6): Consten/Rosinski (Bonnet), 3,421.551 (Record).
Up to 850 c.c. (5): Guilhaudin/Bertaut (Panhard), 3,427.026.

Retirements

Bolton/Sanderson (T.V.R.), 16.35 hrs., lack of water.
Bentley/Gordon (Osca), 17.00 hrs., transmission.
Demetz/Sigala (Fiat Abarth), 17.43 hrs., engine trouble (valves).
Vinatier/Vidilles (Bonnet), 17.55 hrs., overheating.
Balzarini/Albert (Abarth-Simca), 18.27 hrs., transmission.
Berger/Darville (Ferrari), 18.37 hrs., engine.
Charles/Coundley (Jaguar), 18.47 hrs., engine.
Pon/de Beaufort (Porsche), 19.00 hrs., transmission.
Magne/Martin (A.C.-Bristol), 20.28 hrs., clutch.
Gurney/Bonnier (Ferrari), 20.30 hrs., engine.
Oreiller/Spychiger (Abarth-Simca), 20.30 hrs., engine.
Abate/Davis (Ferrari), 18.15 hrs., transmission.
Thompson/Kimberly (Maserati), 21.04 hrs., accident.
G. Hill/Ginther (Aston Martin), 22.01 hrs., damaged oil pipe.
Parkes/Bandini (Ferrari), 22.12 hrs., split radiator.
De Lageneste/Rolland (Abarth-Simca), engine.
Prior/Hine (Marcos), 01.00 hrs., engine.
Salmon/Baillie (Aston Martin), 01.27 hrs., piston.
Kerguen/Franc (Aston Martin), 03.28 hrs., transmission.
R. Rodriguez/P. Rodriguez (Ferrari), 04.45 hrs., transmission.
Boyer/Verrier (Panhard), 05.04 hrs., engine.
Freysinnet/Condrillier (Fiat Abarth), 05.41 hrs., piston.
Settember/Turner (Corvette), 05.55 hrs., piston.
Hansgen/McLaren (Maserati), transmission.
Trintignant/L. Bianchi (Maserati), transmission.
Fulp/Ryan (Ferrari), clutch.
Ireland/Gregory (Ferrari), electrical.
Dickson/Fairman (Tojeiro), gearbox.
Lelong/Hanrioud (Panhard), crash.
Baghetti/Scarfiotti (Ferrari), transmission.
Olthoff/Whitmore (Austin-Healey), engine (piston).
Hopkirk/Jopp (Sunbeam), engine.
Foitek/Ricci (Alfa Romeo), clutch.
Tavano/Simon (Ferrari).
Vaccarella/Scarlatti (Ferrari).
Arents/Behra (Osca).
Masson/Zeccoli (Fiat Abarth).

LIKE HAY FEVER, every summer the 24 Hours of Le Mans rolls around, causing discomfiture and even pain to many, but providing an inexhaustible subject of conversation. As the calendar creeps toward the summer solstice and nights grow shorter, the consumption of midnight oil increases by inverse proportion as strange and wonderful machinery takes form; in typical racing tradition, the less time there is left in the year since the last Le Mans, the more things there are to do. Entries have long since rained in on a haughty Auto Club de l'Ouest, which has allotted the much-sought-after places in accordance with its own curious ideas, and a full week before the event strange and tatty caravans commence to congregate at Le Mans. And for what?

Racing for 24 hours is a slightly more serious matter than two times 12, for example. On the mechanical side, all parts of the automobile must be put together as if you were going into the Gobi desert for a year—anything not checked, wired and viewed with a beady eye will most assuredly let you down. On one hand, all susceptible components must be waterproofed while, conversely, the same ones may require a supply of fresh air to keep them operating properly.

Nothing can be taken for granted, least of all the driver, who must be protected against himself by a sufficiently long rear-end ratio, but nevertheless can destroy six months' preparation by a dose of he-can't-do-that-to-me. A momentary pique is to be excused by the conductors, though, as Le Mans must be simultaneously one of the most boring and dangerous races in the world. Perforce running at a speed below the normal level and overcome with either sleep or doubtful noises from underneath, the driver may at any moment run across rain, mist, three cars abreast, or an almost invisible tiddler doing something like 75 mph slower.

If he survives these, the 4 to 6 P.M. GP, the aching hours of the night, and the French gasoline (which seems to include mice), then he still has to face the long drag from 9 A.M. to 4 P.M. on Sunday, when all reason for racing seems to have passed and pit crews sit around in a stupor. The obstinate machinery often chooses this moment to give its last gasp or, more often, manifest some irritating little trouble that takes ages to fix and is from an accessory, anyway. After all this, he has a splitting headache, a worn-out motor car and, unless he is very lucky indeed, about $20 in French currency to pay a $200 hotel bill. So who needs it?

Apparently lots of people, including the minions of Enzo Ferrari, who seem to have had a strangle hold on the event in recent years. In spite of the fact that the Maranello firm has won every important sports event in 1962, it made a really big effort and brought the 2.4 twin-cam V-6 roadster for the Rodriguez brothers, the 2.7 sohc V-8 for Baghetti/Scarfiotti, the 4-liter V-12 coupé seen at Nurburg Ring for Parkes/Bandini, and a similarly engined roadster already noticed at the Le Mans trials for Hill/Gendebien. A little further fining-up had been done on these two Superamerica variants; a glass windshield had been inserted into the plexi on the roadster and, because the Ferrari tuners were apparently not content with the nominal 400 horses seen formerly, 6 double-choke Webers fitted instead of the original 3.

THE 24 HOURS OF LE MANS

The Noblet/Guichet Ferrari GTO swings through the esses followed by a lone E-type Jaguar.

The factory, as befits a racing business, was backstopped by numerous customers who, curiously, never seem to be quite as fast. Scuderia Serenissima showed up with the Sebring-winning 12-cyl TR, hastily rebuilt after its shunt at the Nurburg Ring, for Bonnier/Gurney; Gendebien's old Tour de France Berlinetta, changed into a startling "station wag on" for Davis/Abate; and a normal GTO for Vaccarella and Scarlatti. North American Racing Team provided two blue and white cars, a front-engined TR and a GTO, to be driven by Ryan/Fulp and Grossman/Roberts, this last gentleman y-clept Fireball of stock-car fame. To wind up the Ferrari list, there were GTOs for Noblet/Guichet, Ireland/Gregory (UDT), a Bertone-bodied one for Reed/Hugus, Eldé/Beurlys, Tavano/Simon, and one of last year's for Berger/Darville.

So who was going to bell the cat? Briggs Cunningham looked as if he would have a good try at it by appearing with an E Jaguar coupe (Cunningham/Salvadori) plus two of the delicious V-8 Maserati coupes (Kimberly/Thompson, McLaren/Hansgen). Salvo originally was going in a Maser but wouldn't fit. No matter what blather the FIA makes about GT racing, these low-browed and intimidating hot rods are real crowd pullers. Of 3944-cc capacity (91 x 75.8 mm) with the cylinders disposed in a 90° vee mit four Webers in between, they recall the hairy Maserati Le Mans coupes of several years ago in line as well as mechanical design, the power being piped through the gearbox/differential at the back and thence to the road via a de Dion arrangement of some complexity. Two oil radiators decorated the chopped

tail, extra lights festooned the front, and altogether it was a lovely shopping car. The drivers seemed happy with them even if there was a general feeling that there could be more power and, for that matter, brakes; one conductor said that his Maser felt better at 180 than the E Jag did at 100, so with a year's more development we anticipate grand possibilities.

Anyway, Maserati France entered another one of these, finished in its normal red, for Trintignant/Bianchi, and to bring up a little more opposition to Cunningham's Jag in GT there were two more E types, resplendent in British Racing Green and driven by Lumsden/Sargent and Charles/Coundley, respectively. To finish off, as well as spearhead, the English challenge, Aston Martin returned to racing with a new 4-liter, 6-cyl prototype four-seater for G. Hill/Ginther. Of more or less normal design Astonwise, it is considerably more handsome than the present production range and, for that matter, quicker. Keeping it company on the grid were two Zagatos (Kerguen/Franc, Salmon/Baillie), an Austin-Healey 3000 (Whitmore/Olthoff), and Ecurie Ecosse's Tojiero for Dickson/Fairman. Of ovoid shape, this vehicle seemed to be rather pointedly based on an old F I Cooper with rear-mounted 2.5 Climax engine and was considerably detuned to try for distance. Also in GT but bearing No. 1 was the Settember/Turner Corvette, completely showroom stock and thus not really competitive.

In the regretted absence of Porsche's 2-liter eights, three normal Abarth Carerras (Pon/de Beaufort, Barth/Herrmann, Buchet/Schiller) appeared, giving rise to remarks like

HILL/GENDEBIEN & FERRARI

Darkness comes, and with it, Hill's lights.

Dragoni briefs Gendebien before the start.

The altered Lotus rear hub (see text).

LE MANS

von Hanstein must not trust the new engine. A sad mistake. One Morgan (Lawrence/Sheperd-Barron) and an elderly AC disputed the middle GT with two highly modified Sunbeams (Harper/Procter, Hopkirk/Jopp), two flatback Giulietta SVZs (Sala/di Lucca, Foitek/Ricci), and two Elites (Hunt/Wyllie, Hobbs/Gardner). The prototypes in this category turned out to be an MG-engined (out to 1623) TVR coupe (Bolton/Sanderson), a plywood Marcos with modded Ford (Hine/Prior), two bubbletop Osca 1600 coupes (Bentley/Gordon, Arents/Hamill/Behra) and four Abarth-Simcas (de Langeneste/Rolland, Oreiller/Spychiger, Dubois/Harris, Balzarini/Albert).

No small GTs being allowed, the tiddler-hafen was full of moving chicanes like the Freyssinet/Condrieler, Demetz/Bianchi, M., and Masson/Zeccoli 701-cc twin-cam Fiat Abarths, and three 702-cc Panhard coupes for Gilhaudin/Bertaut, Lelong/Henrioud and Boyer/Verrier. If that wasn't enough driftwood to plow through, three Bonnets appeared after another was wrecked in a practice shunt; two coupes and one roadster, for Consten/Rosinski, Vinatier/Vidilles and Armagnac/Laureau. Renault-based, they are naturally rear-engined with the first (996 cc) and last (706 cc) of these having twin-cam engines, Vinatier's originally being slated for a cooking rocker arm but inheriting the wrecked Bouharde's 706 twin-cam as well.

There is no point of going into practice, beyond observing that P. Hill broke the course record at 3 min 55.1 sec or 128 mph with the big roadster and that G. Hill of moustache fame was the only other to get under 4 min. What does need some airing, though, is the pre-race scrutineering by the Auto Club de l'Ouest. Regardless of the dictates of the FIA, which God knows is bad enough anyway, the Le Mans club busies itself with pettifogging little regulations which apply to its race, and its race only. In 1961, as you will remember, the Morgans were turned down, allegedly because their bodywork was "outdated," but the same style was okay this year. Before the race, the so-called technical experts bellyached about the Maserati visibility, making them plasticize the carburetor dome; moaned about the Ferrari glass windshield insert and tried to take measurements from the top of the insert itself, and then really made themselves popular by banning the two Lotus 23s, to be driven by Clark/Taylor and a UDT pair. Citing lack of turning circle, ground clearance, too large a reservoir, and dissimilar fixing of front and rear wheels, they told Lotus to go home or fix it. Because the rear wheels were fixed by six studs and the front by four, a new four-stud hub was made up, flown over, and the team car presented again, the other details having been cleared up as well. Oh no, says the examiner, barely taking a look at the Lotus, if there had to be six studs before, then four studs aren't strong enough!

Now six studs were on the back of this 23 because it had been run at the Nurburg Ring with a 1500 Ford and also because a BRM V-8 was going in for Clermont-Ferrand. The

Shortly after the start: the Ecurie Ecosse Tojiero-Climax sweeps past the pits, passing a Sunbeam and about to be passed by a Ferrari.

engine for Le Mans was a 1000-cc Ford-based twin-cam unit, while the UDT one was a 750, both obviously much lighter than even the 1500. When this was pointed out to the inspecting *commissaire,* who I understand delivers trailers for a living, he backed down on the safety angle but finally said that the "spirit of the regulations" was against it. The regulations, for prototypes, mean that the car must be habitable, not solely a sports/racing car, and look like being a prototype GT car. What did enter, then, as a prototype GT car? The Tojiero was allowed to run, the open sports Ferraris, the Maserati coupes, the Serenissima *wagone,* the Bonnet spyder, and the Panhards.

Now this Lotus had not taken the Club by surprise as photos and drawings had been submitted with the entry and had been conditionally approved. In the meantime, though, the ancient house of Panhard had decided to make a big propaganda effort and introduce its CD coupe, entered in the race, as a possible production car. The Lotuses were certainly the perfect car to win the Index of Performance, being considerably lighter than the Panhards and also more powerful. The Bonnets were French but were new, the Abarths not likely to finish, so the Lotuses had to go. Therefore with Italy's Lurani complaining and Britain's representative not being any help, it appears that the Lotuses were sacrificed to city hall. Pretty smelly.

Race day was sunny and very hot, for once, but old Le Mans hands viewed the occasional tiny cloud with suspicion, as if it would suddenly reach out and throw a bucketful of water at them. There was a last-minute scurry as somebody protested the Rodriguez Ferrari for lack of ground clearance, and a bit of hammering was done . . . another highly technical Club *commissaire* commanded team manager Dragoni to notify him in an hour that the work was done, whereupon the Ferrari rep stated that if he weren't told in 10 minutes that the cars would start, he would take them straight off to Modena! Further down the line, Tony Settember was doing a bit of tuning on his very stock Corvette—as it would not run above 5000 rpm—but eventually shut the lid. The millions of odd types that one sees in Le Mans on these occasions, from leather-shorted wonders to lydies dressed as for Ascot or a Young Thing looking like Marcel Marceau in drag, walked around on each other's feet and inadvertently got in each other's pictures. Finally the vague *des vaches* cleaned things out a little bit, the Rover turbine car made a lap of the circuit, the nervous drivers took their places in their numbered circles, and a deathly hush fell over the shirtsleeved crowd, peering busily through its periscopes.

Patterpatterpatter and to lift the hearts of thousands of Americans present, if only temporarily, Settember's white Corvette lurched out of line and led the field toward the Dunlop bridge, its brief moment of glory being cut short by Graham Hill's Aston, which accelerated by into the lead, followed by a flock of Ferraris, Maseratis, Jags, *et al,* both Cunningham and McLaren getting away rather late, and the rear being brought up by a couple of the blue French vehicles which always seem to occupy that slot. Down through the Esses and around Tertre Rouge, on to the Mulsanne straight, and Parkes pulled past Graham Hill into the lead as the sports iron was flitting past the Chevrolet. Watchers at Mulsanne corner, though, got a bit of a thrill as Parkes arrived with all four locked up and plopped into the infamous sandbank, giving himself a bit of Sunday digging and letting Graham out front once more. Through Indianapolis, Arnage, White House, and the straining multitude saw Graham still leading through a flurry of dust and paper but Gendebien in the big 4-liter roadster was making great strides down the straight. They passed under the Dunlop bridge and then . . . nobody . . . until Noblet's GTO

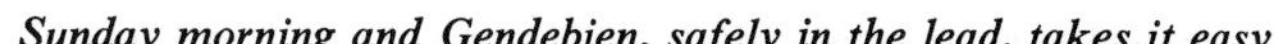

Sunday morning and Gendebien, safely in the lead, takes it easy.

LE MANS

Ferrari came screaming through, closely pursued by the Connecticut mob and the Rodriguez V-6. Even as the luckless Bolton TVR pulled into the pits, gaining the doubtful honor of being the first car to retire (from a water leak), Gendebien rushed past the green Aston and took over a lead that Ferrari was to hold from the 2nd to the 330th.

Behind him, Noblet held grimly onto his place, making time while he could, until he was swallowed by the Rodriguez car, the big Masers and then finally dropped a few more spots avoiding Parkes' feet sticking out from under the coupe. At any rate, the race was breaking up into dices within dices and soon it settled down to Gendebien well out in front, then Graham Hill, Pedro pursued by Trint, McLaren and Kimberly, Tavano leading Baghetti who looked rather flustered and then Fulp, Vaccarella plus Noblet plus Abate, then Gurney pulling away from Grossman and Ireland. The Jags were further back, Sargent and Charles battling with Dickson, and the other GT Astons not much better.

The good Jellybean, thrice winner of this event, was not about to be caught by Graham or the rumbling coupes, much less his teammate whom they soon pushed down to 6th, and although clocking a modest 4 min 5 sec or thereabouts he was all too soon lapping the slower stuff and pulling away from the Aston as well, promoting a 2-min cushion by the end of the first hour. Kimberly had shouldered by the other two Masers, doing 177 mph down to Mulsanne and banging mightily on the overrun to take 3rd, but fanciers of other makes had the depressing sight of 11 Ferraris in a row from 6th through 16th, Rodriguez looking nervously over his shoulder for Gurney who was traveling at a tremendous pace. Alas, after Bonnier took the V-12 over from Dan, it began handling somewhat peculiarly and was eventually retired with something loose in the rear suspension, just about the same time that Serenissima's chic "shooting brake" came to rest on the back straight with no final drive.

We went down to the Esses about 6 P.M., when the sprint is still on, and some of the antics were tremendous. Rubber and a large quantity of oil had been laid down, enough to cover the white line, and many were the narrow moments. Ryan and Gregory were having a nice go, the young NART pilot getting more than a little sideways, de Langeneste's Abarth-Simca, soon to make a long halt with a broken generator mounting, almost lost it hurrying to beat a Berlinetta, Hobbs' Lotus and the plywood Marcos seemed evenly matched, Cunningham was taking it in a courteous manner, waving his own Maser through, Vinatier was boiling and soon retired, and the Jags and the Corvette as well rolled excessively. One felt sympathy for the drivers of quicker GT cars, though, as in the slanting rays of the sun it was plain that their windshields were practically opaque with oil, squashed flies, rubber dust and general debris. Strangely enough, the new Maser coupes were better than the Ferraris in this respect, Ireland finally stopping to have a bug deflector put on his Ferrari.

As the evening wore on, we walked back up the hill, watching the faster cars jump at the top, took aboard a liter or so of Perrier at the hospitable Martini stand, and trudged down to White House corner. This rather special S-bend, scene of some gaudy accidents (including the Darville/Berger Ferrari later that night), requires a good technique and better nerves to get through quickly as it is next-to-flat but impossible to see around. Scarcely had we re-acquainted ourselves with the marshals when Parkes arrived at a moderate pace . . . he had dug himself out of the sand and turned over the car to Bandini after a long stop at the pits, but evidently the radiator had sprung a leak. Unable to refill with water before a specified time, he was coasting around the downhill portions, but didn't quite make it. This seemed to be the witching hour, as Pon came trickling through to retire his Porsche, Spychiger's Abarth was cutting in and out and eventually died on the other side of Arnage, and poor Thompson, getting new brake pads in the Maserati, gave one too few pumps going into the esses and hit the wall, damaging the car too badly to continue.

The first refueling stops had come and gone, most drivers electing not to change, but at the second ones new pilots took over what undoubtedly seemed to them at the time a worn-out motor car. Phil Hill apparently had no such thoughts as he promptly went out and, in the process of getting some distance between himself and the Maseratis, incidentally lowered the course lap record to 3 min 57.3 sec (126.849 mph). This put him comfortably ahead of the Rodriguez car, which for all intents and purposes was being treated like a Cyclops, for example. That seemed to be the signal for Ferrari fortunes to take an especially good turn as Phil, headlights blazing, rushed through the still considerable traffic; Maser stock dropped another point as the persistent McLaren, after being as high as second, threw a tread on the backstretch and wiped out the connections to his clearance lights. Then the other bogey man, G. Hill/Ginther's big Aston, made a long halt to repair the generator before night fell and pulling back time, the unfortunate Graham grabbed 3rd instead of 5th gear and bounced a valve. Therefore at quarter distance it was Phil, Rodriguez, Baghet', Noblet, Tavano, and then Trintignant before more Ferraris of Grossman, Ireland, Vaccarella, Eldé, and Lumsden's E-type.

There were already 13 cars missing, the attrition being highest among the Abarth variants percentagewise, and many more were to follow.

Back to the pits, and after a dreadful meal at one of the dreadful restaurants nearby, out front to see what was going on. Phil and/or Gendebien was still circulating in the lead. Henrioud dropped his Panhard under the bridge without harm, thus making one less dimly lit obstacle, but aside from that and the Ferrari at White House there was very little action.

Suddenly we noticed that Trintignant's Maserati, running strongly in 8th, seemed to be coming in rather often. Peering around the back, we were met by definite graunch marks and a second-hand rear tire with big chunks out of the tread. Sliding on some oil, the Maser had thumped the left rear wheel and bent the rear suspension. Since nothing could be traced, much less straightened, and it ate tires, the big red Maser was out.

Thus at 4 A.M. (wot an 'orrible thought!) with the race only half through (more 'orrible), the Rodriguez V-6 led as it had from time to time by virtue of shuffling caused by pit stops and by going up under the Dunlop bridge flat out. Second, of course, was the big No. 6 roadster of Hill/Gendebien, 3rd Baghetti-Scarfiotti's V-8 four laps behind, then Noblet, Grossman, McLaren, Tavano, Eldé, Vaccarella, and then the first Jag of Lumsden/Sargent. The Austin-Healey, understeering furiously, was trundling along in 14th, with the class-leading Elite of Hobbs/Gardner just behind, the first Porsche (Barth) was in 15th and Schiller had had to change a valve spring, letting Sala's Alfa in front.

Comes the dawn and with it a cool breeze provoked by the Queen of the Wilis; she waved her myrtle branch and Zip! things started to happen. The 2nd-running Rodriguez Ferrari came in for a normal pit stop but when it tried to restart, the most horrible noises came forth as if the starter dog refused to disengage. The engine was shut off, some frenzied banging took place, and the V-6 was fired up again. Same noise, like someone killing a ham-slicer. Incredibly, the car was sent off again, great handfuls of blip being used to try to free this apparatus. Four minutes went by. Five. Six. No Rodriguez. A long walk home, overall 2nd place thrown away, and a first on Index. Poor Rodriguez. The engine note of Gendebien's Ferrari passing by dropped 500 rpm.

The evil spells were not through, by

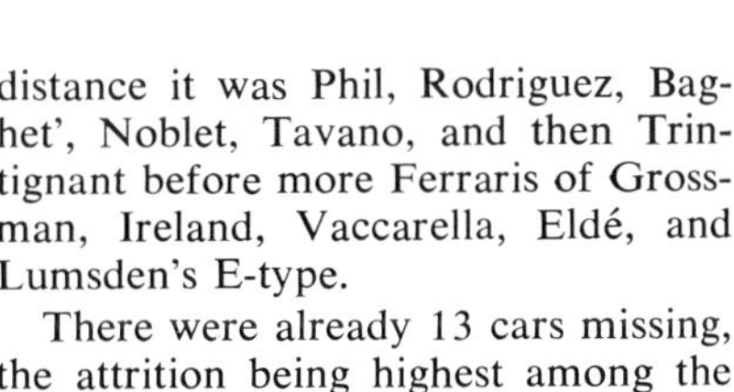

LE MANS

any means. The earth-shaking beat of McLaren's Maserati coupe, still charging though 8 laps behind, suddenly ceased as a piston collapsed and that left only the thin purr of Ferraris populating the circuit. Even this grew thinner as Vaccarella's Serenissima GT broke its propshaft, Grossman made a long stop to tinker with the gearbox, Tavano dried up the read end, and Ryan stuffed the NART barchetta into Parkes' private sandbank, eventually leaving it there in spite of much shoveling and bracing.

The heat grew as the sun rose and everybody tiptoed around very gently except Baghetti, who was trying for an Index placing and paid the price when the V-8 started jumping out of gear after Scarfiotti took over. At that it's an ill wind as the Index-leading Masson/Zeccolli Fiat-Abarth, which was very sick indeed with a broken engine mount and various leaks, was forced to hurry and finally expired in a large cloud of smoke, leaving Bertaut's Panhard in possession of the prize and only one other Abarth running out of eight.

The morning, the endless morning drew on . . . the race had been over when Rodriguez retired and even if the Feel Heel had a dubious clutch, both he and Jellybean were good at nursing and Noblet was many laps away. But for some the clock never stopped ticking . . . both Elites were in with generator problems once again, tinkering under the inquisitive noses of suspicious *commissaires* who have seen their switching act before, Grossman made another long stop and lost a 3rd by starter trouble this time, and Foitek's Alfa clutch refused to do that. The gallant Healey, running in 8th, lost a piston, had the rockers and plug wire disconnected and carried on only to blow another piston, and Hugus' Ferrari disappeared from 7th in the last hour. Salvadoris' smoking Jaguar gradually overhauled a gearless Lumsden, putting two Jags in 4th and 5th. Eighteen running out of 55. *Quel* long day.

Jacques Loste waved the flag at Grossman, whose Ferrari immediately acquired a crust of happy mechanics. Then came the limping yellow Abarth, which got roses thrown at it by Belgian friends, and next Phil Hill. No race record but then the racing really stopped at 5 A.M. Lap record, though. Third win for him and 4th for Gendebien. Not so bad for a country boy. Much applause and what did he get thrown at him? Roses? Not on your life. Cartons half full of melted ice cream. Lovely people in Le Mans.

Roy Salvadori in the fourth place getting Jaguar E-type accelerates past beached Ferrari.

Cunningham team's 4-litre Maserati coupe and Jaguar E-type being prepared before the beginning of the race.

ferrari's le mans hat trick

Repeating last year's victory, Hill and Gendebien cleaned up again, leading a Ferrari contingent that took top three places.

WHAT Ferrari lacks in Grand Prix winning ability, it made up for by a resounding Le Mans hat trick.

World champion Phil Hill and Olivier Genderbien repeated last year's victory by bringing the big, front engined 4-litre Ferrari into first place at an average speed of 115.2 mph, having covered 2766 miles in the 24 hours.

The big sports car was followed up — 42 miles behind — by a 250GTO coupe. There was another in third place and another sixth with a GT in ninth spot.

However, British cars were well represented, for Jaguar E-type coupes were fourth and fifth and a Lotus Elite, driven by David Hobbs and Australia's Frank Gardiner, was eighth. The Elite also won the Index of Thermal Efficiency and was third in the Index of Performance.

Fifty five cars started the race, but when it finished 24 hours later, there were only 18 left in the fray, and many of them were sick, too. There were some surprises down among the back markers, for it was a Morgan that won the 2000 cc GT class and a Sunbeam Alpine did incredibly well to make 16th place.

Ferrari had to work hard to gain its victories, for in the first few hours Hill and Genderbien were pursued by the lone Aston Martin 212 until its driver, Graham Hill, accidentally selected third instead of fifth gear which sent the revs to nearly 7000 and put the car out of the race. This was the only serious British challenge for outright victory.

At the drop of the flag, Graham Hill made a superb start and quickly overtook the Chevrolet Corvette that was the first of the 55 cars to get away. At the

end of the first lap the Aston Martin was still in the lead with Genderbien in the massive open Ferrari not far behind, but the rest of the field had been more or less outpaced. The next three cars were Ferraris of assorted shapes and sizes, with Bruce McLaren in the first of the Maserati V8 coupes.

This year the opening hours of Le Mans were different. Instead of the drivers having an all-out battle and ultimately blowing their cars up, they drove cooly, recording lap times considerably slower than those of practice. The Ferrari soon worked its way past the Aston Martin which was still holding second place fairly comfortably. Then it was forced to make several pit stops because of dynamo trouble and consequently dropped right back in the field.

After four hours of racing no less than 11 cars had been retired, including two of the very fast Abarth-Simcas — one with a broken gear lever and the other with suspension trouble. One of the Jaguars had lost its oil and the Bonier/Gurney Ferrari had broken its transmission.

So, with fours hours gone the Hill and Genderbien Ferrari was first, with the rear-engined 2.4-litre Ferrari of the brothers Rodriguez second and the Thompson/Kimberley 3.9-litre Maserati coupe third.

At midnight, the Aston Martin broke its valves whilst in 13th place and retired. The two Lotus Elites were motoring very well until the Hunt/Wyllie car lost 40 minutes in pit stops to cure dynamo trouble. They were well in the lead of the 1200 cc class besides being in front of bigger cars, including the Corvette.

The two works-entered Sunbeam Alpines were going very nicely, lapping consistently at more than 90 mph and holding 31st and 34th places. In front of the Sunbeam was the Marcos unitary construction wooden car powered by a 1502 cc version of the Ford Classic engine.

Gradually the Maseratis slipped back. At four hours they were in third, fifth and ninth places, but after

The winning Ferrari in full flight. It was the only open car in the first 10. Note "flying-bridge" wind channel behind driver.

that they began to loose ground. The fastest of them had a nasty accident in the esses and was eliminated, but whilst they were at their peak, they proved very fast indeed and were the only cars able to match the winning Ferrari's 180 mph maximum down the straight.

By dawn on the Sunday there were 33 cars remaining in the race. The Rodriquez brothers had taken a 31 second lead from Hill and Genderbien, but it was short lived; the transmission failed completely, so the big Ferrari got its lead back and Baghetti and Scarfiotti's 2.6 Ferrari moved in to second slot with the Noblet/Guichet GT Ferrari third.

The Corvette retired with transmission failure when in 20th place. After a pit stop the UDT-Laystall entered Ferrari GTO refused to start and the Jopp/ Hopkirk Sunbeam Alpine spent nearly an hour in the pit while the big end bearings shells were replaced.

There had been 31 retirements by 8 am and the only cars that looked as though they could do anything

about breaking the Ferrari formation up front were the two Jaguars in sixth and seventh places.

By mid-Sunday morning there were six laps between the big Ferrari and its nearest rival, the Baghetti/ Scarfiotti Ferrari which was running badly and finally came to rest on Mulsanne straight with transmission failure.

Twenty one left, with Jaguar now fifth and sixth and the Hobbs/Gardiner Elite in a remarkable eighth place. Then disaster struck the best Jaguar. It came into the pits for fuel and would not re-start because of a burnt-out starter motor — something similar had happened to several of the other Jaguars.

The Lumsden/Sargent Jaguar was now in difficulties the suspension bushes having worn, making it unsafe to drive really fast and its lap times got 30 seconds longer.

The leading cars were going strongly with little chance of anything happening that could upset the Ferrari hat trick.

Cunningham and Salvadori got past the unstable Jaguar easily and moved into fourth position at seven minutes to four.

Suddenly, the race was over and Hill and Genderbien were the winners again. It was world champion Hill's tenth run at Le Mans, but he had only finished the race once before — and that was in first place. #

THE FIRST TEN — GENERAL CLASSIFICATION

1. P. Hill/Gendebien (3,967 cc Ferrari 330/LM), 2,766.0 miles, 115.2 mph.
2. Noblet/Guichet (2,953 cc Ferrari GTO), 2,724.3 miles, 113.5 mph.
3. Elde/Beurlys (2,953 cc Ferrari GTO), 2,618.5 miles, 109.1 mph.
4. Cunningham/Salvadori (3,781 cc Jaguar E), 2,589.1 miles, 107.9 mph.
5. Sargent/Lumsden (3,781 cc Jaguar E), 2,587.1 miles, 107.8 mph.
6. Grossmann/Roberts (2,953 cc Ferrari GTO), 2,484.2 miles, 103.5 mph.
7. Barth/Herrmann (1,588 cc Porsche Abarth), 2,397.7 miles, 99.9 mph.
8. Hobbs/Gardner (1,216 cc Lotus Elite), 2,390.5 miles, 99.6 mph.
9. Hugus/Reed (2,953 cc Ferrari GT), 2,348.5 miles, 97.9 mph.
10. Sala/de Luca (1,290 cc Alfa Romeo), 2,345.6 miles, 97.7 mph.
11. Hunt/Wyllie (1,216 cc Lotus Elite); 12. Buchet/Schiller (1,558 cc Porsche Abarth); 13. Lawrence/Shepherd-Barron (1,991 cc Morgan); 14. Dubois/Harris (1,288 cc Abarth-Simca); 15. Harper/Procter (1,590 cc Sunbeam Alpine); 16. Guilhaudin/Bertaut (702 cc Panhard); 17. Consten/Rosinski (996 cc R. Bonnet); 18. Armagnac/Laureau (706 cc R. Bonnet).

INDEX OF PERFORMANCE

1. Guilhaudin/Bertaut (702 cc Panhard), 2,129.6 miles, 88.7 mph, 1.265.
2. Armagnac/Laureau (706 cc R. Bonnet), 2,110.8 miles, 87.9 mph, 1.251.
3. Hobbs/Gardner (1,216 cc Lotus Elite), 2,390.6 miles, 99.6 mph, 1.204.

LE MANS 24-HOUR RACE

HOUR-BY-HOUR POSITIONS

DRIVERS	CARS	1	2	3	4	5	6	7	8	9	10	11	12	13	14	15	16	17	18	19	20	21	22	23	24
Settember—Turner	Chevrolet Corv.	30	25	28	27	26	25	23	22	24	23	22	20	19	—										
Hansgen—McLaren	Maserati	5	5	2	9	11	13	12	11	9	8	7	5	—											
Thompson—Kimberley	Maserati	3	2	6	3	17	—																		
Trintignant—Bianchi	Maserati	4	8	7	5	5	6	8	9	7	—														
P. Hill—Gendebien	Ferrari	1	1	3	1	1	1	2	1	6	1	2	2	1	1	1	1	1	1	1	1	1	1	1	1
Parkes—Bandini	Ferrari	53	50	47	43	43	42	—																	
Charles—Coundley	Jaguar	25	32	49	—																				
Sargent—Lumsden	Jaguar	18	13	14	12	12	11	11	14	14	11	10	10	9	7	7	6	6	5	5	5	5	4	4	5
Cunningham—Salvadori	Jaguar	22	21	18	18	15	16	14	13	13	10	11	11	10	8	8	7	7	6	6	6	6	5	5	4
G. Hill—Ginther	Aston Martin	2	4	4	14	14	15	—																	
Kerguen—Franc	Aston Martin	20	16	39	41	36	33	28	26	23	21	20	—												
Salmon—Baillie	Aston Martin	19	18	15	16	13	12	13	12	11	14	24	—												
Bonnier—Gurney	Ferrari	7	31	44	—																				
Abate—Davis	Ferrari	9	7	43	—																				
Grossmann—Roberts	Ferrari	14	14	15	10	8	7	6	6	6	6	6	5	4	4	4	4	4	3	3	3	4	6	6	6
Fulp—Ryan	Ferrari	15	17	16	15	20	17	16	16	16	13	12	13	17	25	—									
Noblet—Guichet	Ferrari	10	9	9	6	4	4	4	4	4	4	4	3	3	3	3	2	2	2	2	2	2	2	2	2
Ireland—Gregory	Ferrari	13	12	11	8	7	8	7	7	12	17	21	17	16	13	—									
Hugus—Reed	Ferrari	21	20	17	17	16	14	15	15	15	12	13	12	11	9	9	9	9	7	7	7	7	7	9	9
Elde—Beurlys	Ferrari	16	15	13	13	9	10	10	8	8	7	8	8	6	6	5	5	4	4	4	3	3	3	3	3
Tavano—Simon	Ferrari	11	10	10	7	6	5	5	5	5	5	5	7	6	5	5	—								
Olthoff—Whitmore	Austin-Healey	24	23	19	20	19	18	17	17	17	15	14	14	12	11	10	8	8	10	—					
Dickson—Fairman	Tojeiro	17	19	21	19	18	23	33	36	—															
Baghetti—Scarfiotti	Ferrari	8	6	5	4	3	3	3	3	3	3	3	3	2	2	2	2	3	—						
Rodriguez—Rodriguez	Ferrari	6	3	1	2	2	2	1	2	1	2	1	1	—											
Lawrence—Shepherd-Barron	Morgan	43	38	37	32	30	30	26	28	27	25	26	22	21	17	15	14	14	13	12	12	13	13	13	13
Pon—de Beaufort	Porsche	34	33	29	—																				
Bolton—Sanderson	T.V.R.	—																							
Harper—Procter	Sunbeam	45	42	36	34	32	29	27	27	28	27	27	24	23	18	16	15	15	14	13	15	14	14	14	15
Hopkirk—Jopp	Sunbeam	41	39	32	31	31	28	25	25	26	26	25	23	22	23	24	23	22	—						
Barth—Herrmann	Porsche	27	24	20	21	21	19	19	23	22	22	19	19	15	14	12	11	11	9	9	8	9	9	7	7
Buchet—Schiller	Porsche	28	26	22	22	24	22	21	20	20	19	17	16	24	22	19	18	17	16	14	13	12	12	12	12
Bentley—Gordon	Osca	37	53	53	—																				
Behra—Arents—Hamill	Osca	40	37	34	33	34	32	30	30	30	30	29	27	25	19	20	17	18	17	16	17	15	19	—	
Hine—Prior	Marcos	44	40	33	30	29	31	37	37	—															
Sala—de Luca di Lizzano	Alfa-Romeo	36	34	26	25	25	24	22	21	21	20	18	18	14	15	13	12	11	10	10	10	10	10	10	10
Foitek—R. Ricci	Alfa-Romeo	38	35	31	29	28	27	24	24	25	24	23	21	18	20	17	16	16	15	15	14	17	20	—	
de Lageneste—Rolland	Abarth-Simca	32	47	45	42	40	40	40	40	—															
Oreiller—Spychiger	Abarth-Simca	26	43	51	—																				
Dubois—Harris	Abarth-Simca	28	23	23	26	23	20	20	19	19	18	16	26	27	24	21	19	19	18	17	16	16	15	15	14
Hobbs—Gardner	Lotus Elite	33	30	25	23	22	21	18	18	18	16	15	15	13	12	11	10	10	8	8	9	8	8	8	8
Hunt—Wyllie	Lotus Elite	35	29	27	24	33	36	31	31	31	28	28	25	20	16	14	13	13	12	11	11	11	11	11	11
Consten—Rosinski	R. Bonnet	39	36	30	28	27	26	29	29	29	29	30	28	26	21	18	21	21	20	18	19	18	17	17	17
Armagnac—Laureau	R. Bonnet	54	51	48	44	42	41	39	38	36	34	34	32	30	28	25	24	23	21	20	20	20	18	18	18
Fraissinet—Condrillier	Fiat Abarth	49	46	40	37	37	38	35	35	35	35	35	33	32	—										
Demetz—M. Bianchi	Fiat Abarth	47	54	54	46	—																			
Guilhaudin—Bertaut	Panhard	48	45	50	39	38	35	36	33	33	32	32	30	29	27	23	22	20	19	19	18	19	16	16	16
Lelong—Henriaud	Panhard	51	48	41	38	39	37	34	39	—															
Boyer—Verrier	Panhard	52	49	42	40	41	39	38	34	34	33	33	31	31	—										
Masson—Zeccoli	Fiat-Abarth	46	44	38	36	35	34	32	32	32	31	31	29	28	26	22	20	—							
Vaccarella—Scarlatti	Ferrari	12	11	8	11	10	9	9	10	10	9	9	9	7	10	—									
Berger—Darville	Ferrari	23	22	24	—																				
Magne—Martin	A.C. Bristol	42	41	35	35	—																			
Vinatier—Vidilles	R. Bonnet	50	52	52	45	—																			
Balzarini—Albert	Abarth-Simca	29	27	46	—																				

The table shows the hour at which cars are officially posted as retired, even though they may have stopped racing some time before.

The experimental cars now became unashamedly proto-type again, but were still divided from the GT cars; restrictions on engine size were, however, removed from both classes. A great number of prerace withdrawals gave a small field of 48 cars to which was added the experimental Rover-B.R.M. gas turbine car which ran outside competition. Ferrari was in a virtually unassailable position with 11 cars entered; four four-litre 330 LM prototypes, but more interesting, three mid-engined 250 P prototypes with three-litre engines and finally, four 250 GTs with three-litre engines. Maserati had a single five-litre version of the Tipo 151 entered by Maserati France; Aston Martin tried to contend with the 215 prototype with a full four-litre engine, as well as three DB.4 GTs. Three lightweight Jaguar E-types were entered by Briggs Cunningham in the GT class, and there was a Jaguar engined Lister prototype as well. The last big engined cars all used American Ford V 8 engines of 4.7 litres capacity but were otherwise widely different; they were two front-engined AC Cobras and a mid-engined Lola prototype.

Porsche was back in force in the two-litre class with their flat-eights, of which two were entered in the prototype category, together with two four-cylinder two-litre examples in the GT class. The only other entry in this class was a solitary MGB driven by Paddy Hopkirk and Hutcheson and looking very ordinary. Nor was there much support for the 1,600 and 1,300 cc classes; two Sunbeam Alpines and an Alfa Romeo in the former, another two Alfas and a pair of Lotus Elites in the latter. All these ran in the GT category. An Austin-Healey Sprite countered two Bonnets in the 1,150 cc prototype class. There was more interest among the smallest cars; in the 1,000 cc class two Bonnets, an Abarth, a new British name - Deep Sanderson with a BMC based engine - and the first appearance of a famous French name- three Alpine Renaults. Among the 850 cc cars was another Abarth, the last Bonnet and a C.D. which this year forsook the Panhard engine in favour of DKW power. The total field was made up of 26 prototypes and 22 GTs.

And then there was the Rover-B.R.M. Since 1953 there had been a formula equating gas turbine with piston engined cars and the A.C.O. had created a special prize to be awarded to the first turbine car to complete Le Mans. Rover had run the world's first gas turbine car in 1950 and by 1963 were confident enough about the future of the gas turbine to enter a car for Le Mans, in collaboration with B.R.M. - the resulting car could be described as a Rover turbine engine in a B.R.M. chassis. The reason why the car ran outside classification at Le Mans was that without a heat exchanger, the fuel consumption of the turbine car was so great that it would have been impossible to run with a regulation size fuel tank. But under the equating formula, the turbine car was set a minimum average speed of 150 kph (93.2 mph). The drivers were Graham Hill and Ritchie Ginther.

The big Maserati soon took the lead but was only able to retain it for a few hours before going out with transmission problems; it just outlasted the Aston Martin 215 which succumbed to the same trouble. From then on there were no further threats to the same to the Ferraris. The Parkes/Maglioli 250 P briefly took the lead replaced by the sister car of Surtees/Mairesse; when this caught fire and burned out in the Esses on Sunday morning, the Scarfiotti/Bandini 250 P which had been lying second for a long time, simply took over the lead to finish. For the first time a rear-engined car had won at Le Mans; furthermore it was Ferrari's seventh win, and their fourth in a row. While it was the eleventh time an Italian car had won, it was the first time that both drivers had been Italian. The winning car averaged 118.104 mph for a total distance of 2,834.509 miles which was a new record; another new record was Surtees' fastest lap at 129.067 mph. The Scarfiotti/Bandini car also won on Index; the first time since 1950 that a big car had won the Index, and not since 1949 had the same car won the race both on distance and Index.

Apart from anything else, the next five places in the finishing list were also occupied by Ferraris; the GTO in second place won the GT class. Only from seventh place did other makes get a look-in; an A.C. Cobra was seventh, followed by a Porsche prototype (which won the two-litre class), an E-type Jaguar, a Lotus Elite (winner of the 1,300 cc class), a Bonnet which won the Index of Thermal Efficiency in addition to the 1,150 cc class, while twelfth and last was the MGB. Many of the retirements had been caused by accidents, particularly after oil was spilt on the track; the worst accident claimed the life of Bino Heinz when his Alpine Renault crashed and burned.

The Rover-B.R.M. finished too, and at an average of 107.71 mph (distance covered 2,592.92 miles) handsomely exceeding the minimum required of it. This performance would have placed it eighth had it been running in competition with the other cars, and would have won Le Mans as late as 1958. The result of the 1963 race was one of the most convincing demonstrations of the superiority of one make ever witnessed at Le Mans; many contemporary pundits were however convinced that the Rover-B.R.M. performance was more important in heralding a new era, and only with the benefit of hindsight 20 years after is it possible to understand why there was no wholesale revolution after the introduction of the gas turbine in the world of motor racing.

A GUIDE TO THE 24-HOUR RACE THIS SATURDAY-SUNDAY

FOR the 31st time since the race was first held on 26 May, 1923, the Automobile Club de l'Ouest is busy putting the finishing touches to the Circuit Permanent de la Sarthe where, at 4 p.m. on Saturday, 15 June, the Le Mans 24-Hour Race is due to start. In those early days the 33 starters—of which three had closed bodywork—were quite simply production sports cars. They had to comply strictly with the description published in the manufacturer's catalogue; they had to carry *bona fide* touring bodywork, be submitted to a jury, and be fitted with wings, running-boards, head, tail, and side lamps, hood, horns, and rear-view mirror; and, save for cars of under 1,100 c.c., which were permitted to have only two seats, all entries had to have full four-seater bodies.

Things have " progressed " a long way since then. Now, the race is open to the following: Grand Touring cars running in Classes 7 to 15 of Appendix J of the International Sporting Code (that is, of not less than 1,000 c.c.), and complying with the requirements of this Appendix; Touring Cars assimilated to G.T. cars, as defined in Appen-

dix J, are not admitted. The race is also open to Prototype Grand Tourers, with an engine capacity of not less than 700 c.c., as defined in the 1963 regulations for this class.

All this, needless to say, makes the race very much more difficult to follow—but it is necessary in fact to realize that two types of car are competing: Those " sports cars " which, open or closed, you can buy (or *could* buy in some cases, if you were very, very rich); and those sports-racing cars (the Prototypes) which it would be very difficult—if not impossible—to buy since they are almost all one-offs, built for this class of racing.

As well as two entirely distinct types of car, Le Mans includes several entirely separate competitions. The first —and the one that appeals to the public for its sheer glamour—is the " distance covered," the overall winner who in the 24 hours of the race has completed the greatest number of laps of the 8.37-mile circuit. Then there is the Index of Performance classification, which is somewhat more complicated. Each car, in order to be classified, must keep running for the entire 24 hours. Each car is given a minimum distance figure D1, based on its engine capacity; again, in order to qualify as a finisher it must complete not less than this distance. To calculate its Index of Performance figure, the actual distance covered by the car, D, is divided by the figure D1, the answer being its Index figure, which is seldom much more than 1.

These two classifications, the Distance Covered and the Index of Performance, are open to every car in the race— G.T. or G.T. Prototype; also open to both categories is the Thermal Efficiency Index, or more officially the *Classement à l'Indice au Rendement Energétique (the Coupe du Progrès vers l'Economie)*, which was inaugurated on the occasion of the 27th Le Mans 24-Hour Race in 1959. It is based, in its complex calculations, on the car's average speed achieved throughout the 24 hours, its weight, and its fuel consumption (expressed in litres per hundred kilometres) during the 24 hours. To be classified, the car must still be running at the end of the 24 hours, and must have covered the minimum required distance D1. For those who like playing with slide-rules, here are the formulae:

$$Ir = \frac{Em}{Er}$$

where Ir is the Thermal Efficiency Index figure, and Er the fuel consumption in litres per 100 kilometers. Em is found from the following formula:

$$Em = 1 \cdot 5 + \frac{(P+1)\,V^3}{4 \times 10^5}$$

where V is the average speed in k.p.h. during the 24 hours;

Ferrari: *Firm favourites for an overall win are the 250P prototypes. Each is powered by a rear-mounted 3-litre vee-12 engine and at the practice days early in April the fastest recorded a lap time of 3min 45·7sec—11·6sec better than the existing record made by Phil Hill in the 4-litre Ferrari last year*

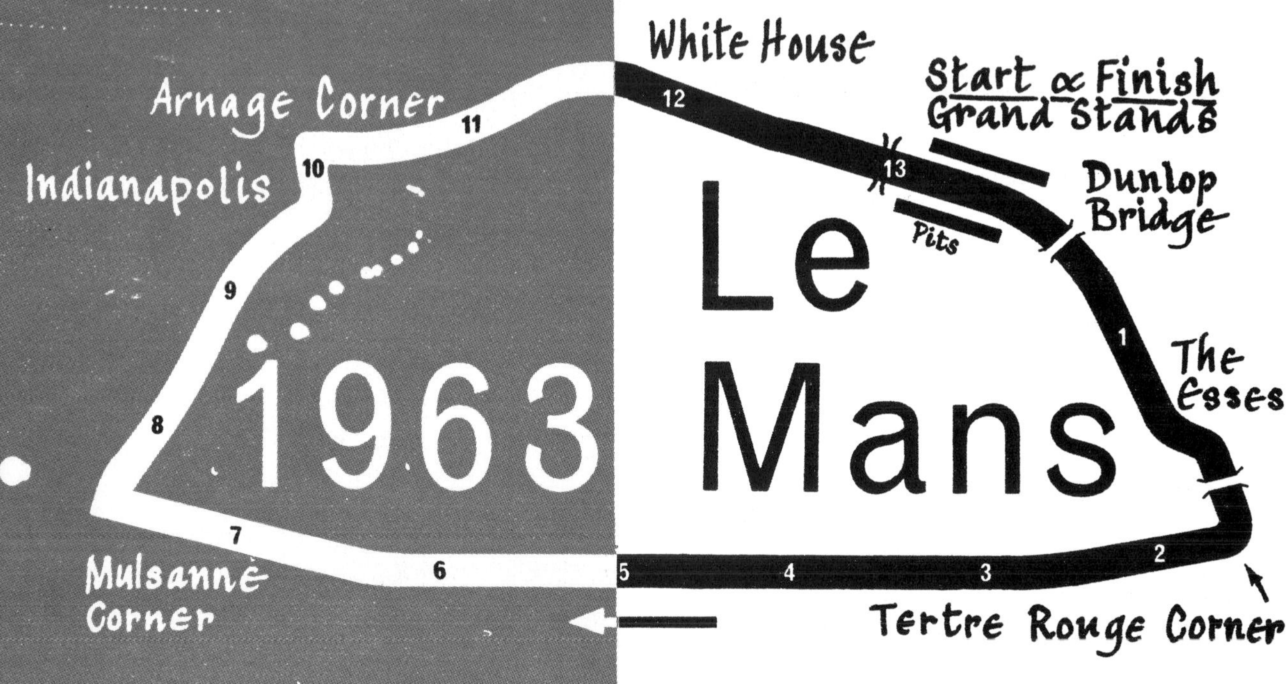

P the car's weight in metric tonnes—with the fuel and oil tanks full and one spare wheel. This formula is applied equally, and without modification to supercharged cars and gas turbines, as well as those with normal engines.

Then there is the Grand Touring classification, according to which marks are awarded in the International G.T. Manufacturers' Championship; there is also the G.T. Prototype classification in which points are awarded towards the various *Trophées Internationaux des Prototypes;* there is the *Challenge Mondial de Vitesse et d'Endurance,* which is a competition involving both the G.T. and G.T. Prototype categories in the Sebring 12-hour race, the Targa Florio, the Nürburgring 1,000km race, and Le Mans; Le Mans being the last of these events still to be held, we shall know the results of this competition by Sunday night; finally, there is the French Championship of G.T. drivers.

The entry is limited to 55 cars—plus the Rover-B.R.M. gas-turbine car, an extremely important entry which is as it were, supernumerary to the normal entry list, and cannot compete for any of the classifications listed above; even if it were to finish first, it would not qualify as winner on distance covered. It is, however, competing for a special 25,000-franc prize put up by the A.C.O. for the first turbo-car to finish the race having covered a minimum distance of 2,238 miles (an average speed of 93·2 m.p.h.). This car is to be driven by Graham Hill and Richie Ginther.

The race is governed by many interesting rules—several of which are not too realistic, being leftovers from the "100 per cent production" days, when the drivers did a lot of the pit work and the cars carried most of their permitted spares. The start is traditionally, and was once exclusively, Le Mans—drivers standing across the road

Lister-Jaguar: The Sargent-Lumsden entry has a modified front suspension and this completely new body, designed by Frank Costin. The screen has been moved forward considerably since the April practice days

THE ENTRIES

Car	c.c.	Category	Entrant	Drivers
1 Chevrolet	5,359	G.T.	Alan Green	Campbell—Grant
2 Maserati	4,941	P.	Maserati France	Simon—Cassner
3 A.C. Cobra	4,728	G.T.	A.C. Cars Ltd.	Boldon—Sanderson
4 A.C. Cobra	4,728	G.T.	Hugus	Hugus—P. Hill
5 Lola	4,637	P.	Lola Cars	Love—Maggs
6 Lola	4,637	P.	Lola Cars	Attwood—Hobbs
7 Aston Martin	3,996	P.	David Brown	McClaren—Ireland
8 Aston Martin	3,750	G.T.	David Brown	
9 Ferrari	3,967	P.	Pierre Noblet	Noblet—Guichet
10 Ferrari	3,967	P.	N.A.R.T.	Rodriguez—Penske
11 Ferrari	3,967	P.	N.A.R.T.	— —
12 Ferrari	3,967	P.	Colonel Hoare	Piper—Salmon
14 Jaguar	3,781	G.T.	Briggs S. Cunningham	Hansgen—Pabst
15 Jaguar	3,781	G.T.	Briggs S. Cunningham	MacLaren —
16 Jaguar	3,781	G.T.	Briggs S. Cunningham	Cunningham—Salvadori
17 Lister-Jaguar	3,781	P.	Peter J. Sargent	Sargent—Lumsden
18 Aston Martin	3,750	G.T.	David Brown	Schlesser—Bianchi
19 Aston Martin	3,750	G.T.	J. Kerguen	Kerguen—Dervez
20 Ferrari	2,953	P.	S.E.F.A.C.	Surtees—Scarflotti
21 Ferrari	2,953	P.	S.E.F.A.C.	Parkes—Bandini
22 Ferrari	2,953	P.	S.E.F.A.C.	Mairesse—Vaccarella
23 Ferrari	2,953	P.	S.E.F.A.C.	Abate —
24 Ferrari	2,953	GTO	Equipe Nationale Belge	Beurlys —
25 Ferrari	2,953	GTO	Tavano	Tavano —
26 Ferrari	2,953	GTO	N.A.R.T.	Grossman —
27 Porsche	1,981	P.	Porsche System Ltd.	Walter —
28 Porsche	1,981	P.	Porsche System Ltd.	Bonnier —
29 Porsche	1,967	G.T.	Porsche System Ltd.	Barth —
30 Porsche	1,967	G.T.	Porsche System Ltd.	Linge —
31 MGB	1,803	G.T.	Hutcheson	Hutcheson-Hopkirk
32 Sunbeam Alpine	1,590	G.T.	Sunbeam-Talbot	Lewis—Ballisat
33 Sunbeam Alpine	1,590	G.T.	Sunbeam-Talbot	Harper—Procter
34 Alfa Romeo	1,570	G.T.	Scuderia St. Ambroeus	Giancarlo—Romolo
35 Alfa Romeo	1,570	G.T.	Scuderia St. Ambroeus	"Kim"—Giampero
36 Alfa Romeo	1,570	G.T.	Scuderia Filipinetti	Foitek—Schaefer
37 Osca	1,568	P.	Automobiles Osca	— —
38 Lotus	1,216	G.T.	Team Elite	Taylor—Hunt
39 Lotus	1,216	G.T.	Team Elite	Hobbs—Wagstaff
40 Lotus	1,210	G.T.	Equipe Nationale Belge	Harris—Dubois
41 Rene Bonnet	1,108	P.	Rene Bonnet	— —
42 Austin-Healey	1,100	P.	Donald Healey Motor	— —
43 A.S.A.	1,032	P.	Scuderja Filipinetti	Muller—Thuner
44 Deep Sanderson	997	P.	Lawrence Tune Co.	Lawrence—Spender
45 Deep Sanderson	997	P.	Equipe Lausannoise	Collomb —
46 A.S.A.	996	P.	Scuderia A.S. Elmo D'Argento	Condriller —
47 A.S.A.	996	P.	Scuderia A.S. Elmo D'Argento	Bassi—Facetti
48 Alpine	996	P.	Sté Automobile Alpine	Heins—Richard
49 Alpine	996	P.	Sté Automobile Alpine	Rosinski —
50 Alpine	996	P.	Sté Automobile Alpine	Boyer—Verrier
51 Rene Bonnet	996	P.	Rene Bonnet	Bouharde—Masson
52 Rene Bonnet	996	P.	Fabre	Rolland—Manzon
53 Rene Bonnet	716	P.	Rene Bonnet	Monneret—Vinatier
54 Rene Bonnet	716	P.	Rene Bonnet	P. Beltoise—Laureau
55 Fiat Abarth	701	P.	Sarayac	Sarayac—Barthe
56 DKW	701	P.	Auto-Union	Guilhaudin—Bertaut
00 Rover-B.R.M.		Turbine	Owen Racing Organisation	G. Hill—Ginther

British entries in **bold type.**

Le Mans

Aston Martin: *The latest 4-litre has a new chassis frame and a double-wishbone type of independent rear suspension*

Maserati: *Represented by only one car this year. It is a private entry to be driven by Simon and Cassner and is powered by a 5-litre vee-8 engine fitted with Lucas fuel injection; the de Dion rear axle has been simplified considerably from the original complicated " birdcage " type*

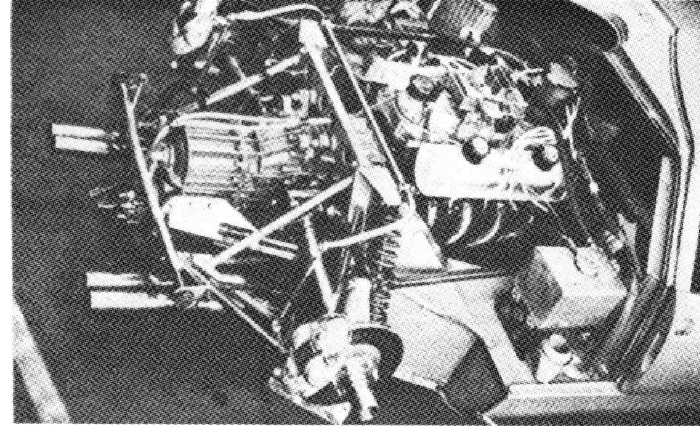

Lola: *A most exciting entry is that of the two G.T. rear-engined prototypes, which have suffered teething troubles in earlier races this year. Originally, it was intended to use one Ford and one Chevrolet Corvette engine, but both entries will have Ford 4·7-litre vee-8 units developing around 350 b.h.p.*

opposite their cars, engines dead, doors closed; at the signal to go, they rush across the road, jump in and start up—placing an empasis on the production nature of the cars, the accessibility of their seats, the efficiency of their starters. . . . No driver may push his car on the circuit—save in the deceleration zone alongside the pits. Drivers who have broken down on the circuit may not walk (or procede by any other means) to the pits to obtain spares or tools with which to repair the car. . . . If a car stops at the pits for repairs, the work may be done by only two people—the two drivers, a driver and mechanic, or two mechanics. . . . All repairs or replacements must be effected with tools and parts carried either in the car or at the pit when the car is at the pit . . . with tools and spares carried on board if the car is out on the circuit . . . replacement of mechanical assemblies, such as the engine, gearbox, rear axle, or dynamo is forbidden . . . and batteries may not be recharged by any external means. . . Fuel may be replenished only when the car is standing at the pit, and a special commissar—the *plombeur*—is responsible for affixing a seal to the tank each time a car refuels, and for checking that the seal has not been broken each time it comes in for fuel. . . .   P. G.

Réné Bonnet: *With the non-appearance of Panhard, French hopes of a win in the coveted Index of Performance will depend largely on the rear-engined Réné Bonnet above, and the Alpine*

A.C. Cobra: *Two will run, one of which is a works entry to be driven by Bolton and Sanderson. They are powered by 4,728 c.c. Ford vee-8 engines*

Porsche: *Le Mans, a much faster course than that of the Targa Florio, will be less favourable to the Porsche and thus the Stuttgart firm have little hope of repeating their recent outright win over the torturous Sicilian circuit. They will be represented by the same cars, which include the 2-litre flat-8 prototype (left), and the 2000 GS four-cylinder car equipped with a new body (right)*

24 HOURS OF
LE MANS

STORY AND PHOTOS BY HENRY N. MANNEY III

O HUM, BACK AT LE MANS for the 24-hour sports car race, and never mind the malarkey about GTs and GT prototypes. I have never been able to understand why spectators came to this blasted heath to have their senses assaulted by noise, dust, and half digested garlic, though with the competitors it is a little easier to comprehend, as there is always Money. (The English will mutter things like "Bentley Boys, Show the Flag, Tradition, BRG, and Send a Gunboat," but then they are daft anyway.) The only trouble is that in recent years a firm called Ferrari has won all the gelt by covering the most distance, and left precious little for anyone else.

There is a subsidiary prize of some value, called the Index of Performance, which ties in average speed with cylinder capacity and the driver's phone number. Since the war this has seemed at times to be reserved for small French cars of limited usage and indeed the organizers took pains so that the world might *think* that they were protecting home talent. Last year, as you will remember, the ACO excluded the Lotuses on a very smelly technicality and this year the French-influenced FIA made things so unpleasant for Abarth's cars at the Nurburg Ring that he got the message and withdrew his whole entry. Chauvin, after all, is a French word. Besides making a few more enemies, all this monkey business did them no good, as Ferrari copped both prizes! But yet another trick prize, the so-called Energetic Index (tied in with fuel consumption) fell to a Renault-based René Bonnet.

We digress. The purpose of the whole race is to cover as many laps of the 8.357-mi circuit as possible in 24 hours. By human standards this is not a very long time, and can be spent sleeping, eating, boozing, watching the telly, making love, or daydreaming about Bardot. For machinery it is a very long while, indeed, as many drivers over the years have found out to their cost, although, human nature being what it is, the machines would have a rather better finishing record if they were driven by automatic pilots.

The public, however, fondly imagines that it can see whoever is encased in aluminum and fiberglass (at least when he emerges at the end), and won't pay to watch black boxes being perfect. And no money, no Ferraris, which would be rather a pity, as the combination of their past successes and the withdrawal of Abarth (see above), the Chevrolets, the Chaparrals, and so forth meant that there was room for all the reserves, and thus more Ferraris. Originally, the number was held to eight, but a glance at

The start—and Phil Hill's Aston Martin is leading the pack . . . for awhile.

starting list shows eleven and very little else by way of competition.

There was a magnificent 5-liter V-8 Maserati coupe, developed from last year's examples, but it was not expected to stay the distance. There was a 4-liter, dry sump, 6-cyl Aston Martin with wishbone rear suspension that might finish.

LE MANS

There were two GT Cobra - Fords which would be considerably hampered by their shape down the long Mulsanne straight; there was the super-low Lola that wouldn't, but had an engine bought from Shelby who makes the Cobras; there were three light-alloy Jaguar Es, which hadn't been too reliable over long distances so far; three Aston GTs, now much faster with their new boattail shape, and two Porsches, which were quick enough in hilly country but couldn't look at the Maranello products in full flight. These last comprised three 250-P, 12-cyl, rear-engined roadsters of 3 liters plus a NART 4-liter front engined model, three 4-liter and seven 3-liter coupes, three of these last having the pipes out under the doors and doing Enzo's SNAP sales no good at all. Apparently it gives more power that way.

Altogether, there were 49 starters occupying a permitted 55 places and I for one hope this is an indication that Le Mans for "Prototypes and GT" is going out of style. This number, of course, contained the well publicized Rover-BRM turbine car, which was really not supposed to be racing against the other 48 but just competing for a special prize. Neatened up and inconspicuous enough in dark green, it made a noise like Buck Rogers and smelled like a fried fish shop, but got through the corners a lot quicker than you would think, considering that there is only one gear. Anyway, the Rover occupied the bottom end of the starting line, as a Le Mans start (laughter) was used and it takes a few seconds longer to get perking. For a change, the runners were lined up according to practice times rather than strictly by engine size, with Rodriguez (3 min 50.9 sec) at the head, a comfortable chunk under P. Hill's 3:57.3 race record last year. Following down were Scarfiotti and Parkes in the 51s, but P. Hill himself, in an Aston this time, was next with 52 and a thundering speed down the back straight of 186.42 mph. The Maserati, then the Ferraris of Surtees and Gurney were next, as the only other ones under 4 min.

Under a brilliant sun, would you believe it, four o'clock rolled around and once again we saw the humiliating spectacle of grown men, all togged out in funny suits and bone domes, actually running across the track. For some odd reason, Astons are very good at this sort of thing and, with

Grossman hits the hay . . .

. . . and drives back out of the escape road . . .

. . . and parks to phone the pits.

Above: The Rover-BRM gas turbine "out for a Saturday/Sunday drive" trails the big Maserati coupe past a René Bonnet, and at left, the GT chases an Alfa Zagato and a Porsche. Below, Bandini overtakes a Renault Alpine.

a resounding bellow, both P. Hill and McLaren were well away, just ahead of Pedro Rodriguez in the intimidating NART Ferrari. The stream poured past the pits for what seemed ages, giving the dense crowds a chance to hear every sort of cylinder note except a twin one (no Panhards this year), and of course we all thought that we had suddenly gone deaf as the Rover glided by, bearing a dignified G. Hill in state like the swan boat in Lohengrin. In spite of having to wait in the armchair (no running for him) until the turbine got up to fifty thou plus, he was by no means the last away as a couple of the little French tin cans stuttered away after. The good Phil managed to hold his lead until after Mulsanne, but the Maserati in the hands of Simon had been knifing through traffic and gobbled him up.

True to form, there are always some people who never learn about Le Mans; Hutcheson took the MG-B off in the sandbank on the outside of Mulsanne to stay a while, and the streamlined Mantzel-tuned DKW did the same at Indianapolis, to become the first retirement. Finding themselves out of elbow room, both Sears and Noblet in their Ferrari coupes carried on down the escape road to Mulsanne, but at least they didn't have to dig.

A heavy throbbing noise announced the arrival of the marvelous Maserati coupe past the stands, and even if it looked a bit sawtoothed up under the Dunlop bridge it was no worse than the horde of Astons, Ferraris, and Jags that came after. The leading group for the first few laps comprised Simon, Rodriguez, Surtees and Parkes, P. Hill, and McLaren (taken in an arbitrary order) with various GTOs like Gurney and Gregory hanging on.

As they entered the fifth round, they lapped one of the Renault-based René Bonnets just at the top of the hill past the pits, and it hit the bank and rolled over under everyone's feet. P. Hill, lying about fourth at the time, whanged down through the gears and stood on everything trying to miss this object while Whitmore in the "GTO" special Sprite went the other side. Phil ran over some pretty solid bits of car, as did Sargent's streamlined Lister-Jag coupe, and both had to pit to investigate body and undershield damage. Later on, unfortunately, their gearboxes finally gave up as a result of that unexpected strain. Now, as there was a whole raft of these little teakettles entered and by 22 minutes after the start four of them had shunted something, I would like respectfully to suggest that henceforth they run a race of their own and quit getting in the way.

As one would expect, Simon kept using the power of the big Maserati to out-torque the Ferraris of Rodriguez, Surtees and Parkes. The young Mexican, who is looking better than he ever did before, was lurking about waiting for Simon (who used to drive for Mercedes, as you may remember) to make

The silent spectre: Hill and gas turbine.

Hill waits while Ginther is interviewed.

The Rover-BRM exposed.

Coupe bodywork is now the fashion: A Renault Alpine.

The Simon/Casner Maserati.

The Basini/Bouharde René Bonnet-Renault.

The Hobbs/Attwood Lola-Ford.

The Hutcheson/Hopkirk MG-B.
The Whitmore/Olthoff Austin-Healey Sprite 1100.

LE MANS

a mistake and the two rear-engined Ferraris were waiting for Simon and Rodriguez to break something. At that, they were all moving along, Surtees and Rodriguez taking turns lowering the lap record (practice times don't count as records) until Surtees finally wound up with 3 min 53.3 sec or 129.071 mph.

After them, there was a sort of a gap before Gurney came dicing with the prudent Scarfiotti, McLaren motoring busily by himself in the enormous Aston, Abate with Hansgen (whose Jag shortly retired with cooked synchromesh) and Noblet's big Ferrari. Bonnier's dishcover Porsche coupe was being hotly pursued by Gregory's GTO, Bolton's Cobra led Attwood's Lola and Richards' E Jag, next came a trio of Barth, Sears, and Kerguen's blue Aston, and then Kimberly's Aston, Beurly's GTO, and Elde's ditto well spaced out. All the little stuff was busily trying to keep out of the way, except Whitmore, who was engaged in eating everything in sight; one of the Elites had already stopped with ignition difficulties, Foitek's bored-out Giulietta SZ had blown its head gasket, the other two Alfas looked terrible, and one almost caused a shunt by getting sideways in the Esses, but the two production-racing Porsche Carreras were circulating in line ahead.

Eventually, of course, the expected happened. Shortly after Casner took over the big Maser, it began to drop back as less and less revs were used and soon it retired with loud grumbles from the rear end. Almost at the same time, Penske relieved Rodriguez and, in spite of some sideways motoring, began to lose two to four seconds a lap to the two works Ferrari roadsters. Parkes led at first, then as the experienced Maglioli sent the Englishman to the showers and Mairesse did the same for Surtees, the Ferrari No. 23 took over a lead that it was to hold most of the race. Wisely avoiding the usual fratricidal scuffle, the Parkes/Maglioli car was later afflicted with a mysterious misfire which resulted in long pit stops to tinker with the ignition and gasworks but Scarfiotti/Bandini gently moved up to hold down second spot in their stead.

As the race is held around the summer equinox for maximum daylight, the dusk lingers on forever. About this time Parkes was lapping in 3 min 58 sec, Surtees or Mairesse about 3:57.5, Penske at 4 min, Maggs 4:11 with the Porsche eight coupe, Hobbs in the Lola 4:13, Hugus' Cobra 4:13.1, Noblet's 4-liter coupe 4:06 with lots of body english (he later retired when the oil filter came unscrewed), Ireland or McLaren's GT Aston 4:04, Gurney's 4-liter the same, the "Roover" 4:25 with Ginther aboard, and Hopkirk using full opposite lock in the MG-B 4:51, trying to make up time after the sandpile episode. Suddenly, one of those things happened that are the worst part of motor racing because they simply cannot be helped; on the fast bend just before the end of the Mulsanne straight McLaren's engine went up with a bang and liberally anointed the track with countless liters of hot engine oil. He freewheeled to a stop on the straight beyond but the cars immediately following found all adhesion gone. Sanderson's Cobra spun like a top but stayed on the road, Kerguen's Aston took to the ditch, Salvadori's Jag spun, overturned, and burst into flames, the driver only being extricated by the Breton's bravery. A few seconds later Manzon's Bonnet capsized as well, throwing the driver out on the road, and just as the fire laddies had used their only extinguisher on the flaming Jag, Bino Heins' Alpine crashed into a phone pole, lit up, and burned the unfortunate driver to death. By this time the commissaires up the road had got the yellow signals working, which saved yet further carnage, but the section remained slippery for some time to come. Yet the race went on.

As dusk faded into night the remaining runners threaded their way around the circuit, the lights of the village's sideshows and the spectator's cigarettes lining it all the way. An occasional black bulk or plodding driver showed up in speeding headlights, witness to the increasing number of retirements. By midnight, 18 of the 49 were already out and many more were to come as a result of the bitter battle being waged in the GT category. Shortly after taking over from Tavano, the exuberant Abate threw away third overall and the GT class by getting two wheels of the GTO off on the grass at White House and thumping the bank. A few minutes later, South African Olthoff lost a good position as Head Tiddler (and one well up in the 2-liter prototypes), putting himself into the hospital in the bargain.

Soon afterward, Penske blew up the NART roadster at full bore between Mulsanne and Indianapolis corners. Blinded by the smoke, he parked the Ferrari in the trees as did Bonnier, leading the 2 liters with his Porsche. It was to be a bad night for Stuttgart as the two Carreras shortly expired as well, with no oil pressure. Gurney in the NART 4-liter coupe had managed to outrun the surprisingly fast Kimberly/Schlesser Aston GT for third, after Abate went out, in spite of slinging chunks from its Goodyears; this was cured by fitting rubber with a thinner tread, but shortly after Hall took over there was a loud thump and a halfshaft went. Poor Hall coasted to the deceleration area and pushed in, distinctly against regulations, but there was nothing else to do. And just to cap everything, an exuberant Schlesser in the last bulbous Aston, with a new third place and GT lead in its glove box, blew a piston down the back straight and never appeared again. The remaining furrin challenge was 18 laps behind.

At the 'orrible hour of four A.M. the race is only half over, if you can imagine such a thing. Mairesse/Surtees had turned 189 laps at an average of 121.837 mph, leading a careful Bandini/Scarfiotti by one tour. Both these roadsters were recognizable by a funny little lump on the back which housed the outrigger clutch. Ten laps back was the next V-12, Gregory/Piper's NART GTO with Mickey Thompson in interested attendance, then, in descending order, Dernier/Dumay's GTO, Beurlys/Langlois silver ditto, Sears/Salmon's 4-liter coupe in trouble with water losses and an odd clutch, and in seventh Barth/Linge's 8-cyl Spyder going strong. Cunningham/Grossman's Jag was eighth, Parkes' Ferrari going like a rocket after effecting a cure for the misfire, the Bolton/Sanderson Cobra under the aegis of S. Moss and the *London Sunday Times* (Hugus/Jopp's had gone down trailing smoke from one engine), Boyer's spaceframe Renault Alpine coupe with Gordini dohc, Sala/Rossi's Giulietta making grating noises, the surviving Sunbeam Alpine of Lewis/Ballisat (the other had got too hot), and Beltoise/Bobrowski's pigeon-toed Bonnet.

The Lola, which had had endless trouble to make scrutineering and had to alter the carburetor air feeds to gain rear vision, was making a long pit stop. A bolt had come out of the gear selectors and graunched things inside; it finally got going again but about dawn jumped out of gear in the Esses and shunted. Still motoring, though, were the two delayed Elites (sandbank and ignition), although Wagstaff's soon ran its rods, Basini's slow Bonnet, and the sputtering Deep Sanderson coupe (Mini in the back) which had done too much sand time to make up. The Rover-BRM was still hissing on its way with an occasional hiccup from the kerosene stove from which it was getting some 7 mpg, driver Hill looking remarkably like a city gent with a muffler around his neck, as the heat doesn't get forwards. After a bit of rumble in scrutineering as well about ground clearance, which was cleared up by the Rover boys measuring the scrutineers' checking block and finding it 1 cm too high (!), it was more than repaying its backers by running without trouble, using no tires and as yet no brake pads, thanks to oversize discs, and if it had been racing with the

boys would be holding down tenth place on distance.

Fortunately for tired eyes, the usual morning mist did not appear and gradually, one by one, the headlights winked out, just in time in some cases, as certain types were doing a bit of crafty slipstreaming on sidelights down the unobserved parts of the course. Gregory made a halt to fix the generator, which put him a bit behind; charging again, he overcooked it and went into the sandbank at Arnage. After the digging out, straightening of opprompled bodywork and handing over to the slower Piper, it had dropped to tenth behind the Cobra, which had had its little ennuis too, what with fanbelts jumping off and the exhaust system coming unstuck from time to time. Grossman also had his little bit of drama, when he put his foot on the brake approaching Mulsanne corner and found a void. Sailing majestically through three rows of haybales, he did the bodywork and rad no good at all. After a call to the boss, he crept back to the pits, arriving with two flats, much steam, and enough grating noises to last the rest of the year, but eventually got going again after cannibalistic efforts on the part of Cunningham's men.

The morning and afternoon of Sunday seem endless. Most of the pits are vacant of their proper occupants and the lonely drivers are sure that their own crews have gone home. But mechanics are forever haunted by Kelly's Law of

The Bolton/Sanderson AC-Cobra had a removable hard top.

Motion, "If Anything Can Happen, It Will."

Nobody knows it better than veteran Edy Barth. As he enters the deceleration lane, a rear wheel breaks off the Porsche Spyder just outside the hub carrier and he has to carry the car to his pit, acting as a human crutch. A new halfshaft is fitted and the jolly Linge carries on. At this point the Dumay Ferrari suffers ennuis of the clutch, losing third place to the Belgian team of Langlois/Beurlys, who carry on their countrymen's fine record in this event. The Roover has an oil change, all 600 cc of it, and front brake pads as a precaution, as it is now running "seventh." And finally bad luck catches up with Willy Mairesse again, as with five hours to go and a 2-lap lead, the Ferrari lights up from an overfull tank, entering the Esses. He has to crash the bank and abandon, burned badly enough so that he will miss his next two Formula I rides as well. Poor Willy.

Thus, first place drops in the lap of the Scarfiotti/Bandini duo, two young men driving even a record distance with a restraint rare in Maranello. Second is the Belgian GTO, and third Parkes/Maglioli, after pulling up from the lower half of the entry. Ferraris run down through the first six places, taking both index and overall, prototype and GT. The Cobra, the Porsche, the Jaguar, the Lotus, the Bonnet, the MG, all consider themselves lucky to finish, but the Rover-BRM comes sighing in, sounding as if it would go on forever. At that, it might, but the drivers are bored stiff. Wonder what will happen next year?

FERRARI DOMINATES AT THE

Rover-BRM Demonstrates Magnificently

TO say that Ferrari dominated the 1963 Le Mans 24-hour race is no overstatement. Only in the opening hours was any car other than a Ferrari in the lead, a lone 5-litre Maserati heading the pack of Ferraris after the latest Aston Martin had sped away from the line. Behind the winning rear-engined 250 P 3-litre prototype driven by Lorenzo Bandini and Ludovico Scarfiotti, who also won the Index of Performance, came five other Ferraris, then the A.C. Cobra, with Ford V8 engine, driven by Peter Bolton and Ninian Sanderson. The race was saved for Britain by the outstanding performance of the Rover-B.R.M.

gas turbine car, which not merely covered the set distance required of it to win the special gas turbine award but finished at a higher speed than any Le Mans winner before 1957. If, in fact, the Rover-B.R.M. had been competing in the race as a whole, it would have been placed eighth.

A Lotus Elite and M.G. B both won their classes, as also did a Jaguar and the A.C. Cobra, but otherwise it was not a particularly successful race for British cars; none of the Aston-Martins finished and only one of the three Jaguars entered by Briggs Cunningham, survived the full 24 hours.

The Days Before

THE big drama during the two days of scrutineering on Tuesday and Wednesday was the failure of the two new Lola G.T.s to arrive in time. Chief designer Eric Broadley and his little organization worked night and day for five days on end and then were beaten by the fog which greatly delayed air services across the Channel. The Lolas' appointed hour for scrutineering was on Tuesday afternoon, but late on Wednesday they still had not arrived, though it was said Broadley himself was driving one car as hard as possible across France while the second followed in the M.R.P. transporter. The commissaires kept the scrutineering open long after it should have officially ended on Wednesday; then, by a most sporting gesture, granted the hard-pressed Lolas a special scrutineering session of their own on Thursday morning. But even then the team's troubles were not over, for only one car could be completed in time and that one was rejected by the scrutineers. Not without reason, the scrutineers objected that the large diameter trunk behind the driver, from the rooftop air intake to the carburetters, gravely obscured rearward vision. Broadley was still not defeated, and his tired men set

Car No. 9 (Guichet/Noblet 4-litre prototype Ferrari) slides off at Mulsanne to let the winning Bandini/Scarfiotti Ferrari through. In the background is the Kimberley/Schlesser Aston Martin.

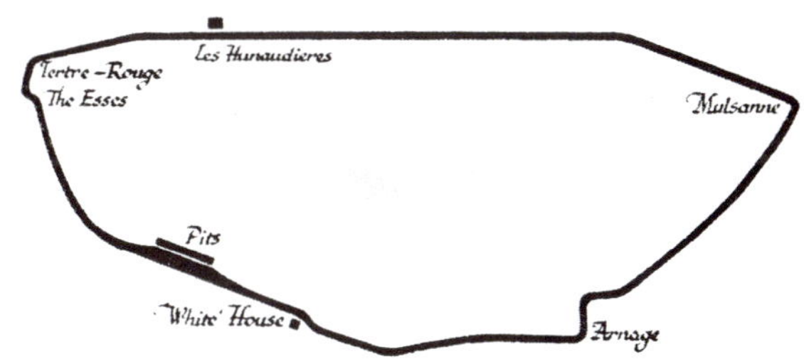

Packed stands, bright sunshine and the field let loose at 4 p.m. last Saturday. The leading car is the Ireland/McLaren Aston Martin followed by the Ferraris of Scarfiotti/Bandini and Surtees/Mairesse. The Rodriguez/Penske Ferrari and the Hill/Bianchi Aston Martin have already got away.

THE FIRST EIGHT ● GENERAL CLASSIFICATION

1. L. Bandini/L. Scarfiotti (Ferrari 250P), 2,834.6 miles, 118.1 m.p.h.
2. J. Beurlys/G. Langlois (Ferrari G.T.O.), 2,700.8 miles, 112.5 m.p h.
3. M. Parkes/U. Maglioli (Ferrari 250P), 2,700.7 miles, 112.5 m.p.h.
4. Elde/P. Dumay (Ferrari G.T.O.), 2,692.4 miles, 112.2 m.p.h.
5. P. M. Salmon/J. E. Sears (Ferrari 330 L.M.), 2,622.1 miles, 109.3 m.p.h.
6. M. Gregory/D. Piper (Ferrari G.T.O.), 2,608.7 miles, 108.7 m.p.h.
7. P. Bolton/N. Sanderson (A.C. Cobra), 2,592.0 miles, 108.0 m.p.h.
8. F. Barth/H. Linge (Porsche), 2,516.8 miles, 104.9 m.p.h.

Index of Performance
Bandini/Scarfiotti (Ferrari), 1.236.

Index of Thermal Efficiency
Beltoise/Bobrowski (René Bonnet), 1.25.

Gas Turbine Award
G. Hill/R. Ginther (Rover-B.R.M.), 2,593.0 miles, 107.8 m.p.h.

SARTHE

to work to make a new air intake from an inlet on the left rear flank, and this having been accomplished, the car for Attwood and Hobbs was finally accepted.

On a lighter note, when the Rover-B.R.M. failed for the second time to pass the ground clearance test, a Rover boffin produced a rule, measured the wooden box over which the car had to pass and denounced it as being two millimetres too high. Collapse of stout French parties.

For the first time, the order in which the cars were lined up at the pits for the start was decided by their practice times and not by their capacity. Head of the line was the open two-seater Ferrari 330LM with its four-litre engine mounted at the front, which lapped in 3 min. 50.9 sec. with Pedro Rodriguez at the wheel on Wednesday evening. Next to it were two of the three rear-engined Ferrari 250P open two-seaters, the Bandini/Scarfiotti car having lapped in 3 min. 51.3 sec. and the Parkes/Maglioli car in 3 min. 51.6 sec.

Then came the fastest British car, the new Aston Martin 215 of Phil Hill and Lucien Bianchi in 3 min. 52 sec. One of the latest Aston Martin DB4GTs was stated to be the first car in Le Mans history to be officially timed at more than 300 k.p.h. on the Mulsanne straight, with a recorded speed of 307 k.p.h., or 190.761 m.p.h.

No car during practice approached the fantastic 3 min. 45.8 sec. of John Surtees during the April test days, although the faster cars were well below Phil Hill's official lap record of 3 min. 57.3 sec. Fastest of the three Briggs Cunningham Jaguar competition Es was the Richards/Salvadori car with a lap in 4 min. 6.6 sec. One of the Jaguars had covered 150 miles in the hour while under test at Lindley, but the Jaguar drivers were, on the whole, disappointed in the straight line performance of their cars; this was possibly because the addition of fog-lamps and additional ventilators had resulted in some increase of head resistance.

Innes Ireland hustles his Aston Martin, in seventh place, through the Esses. Not long afterwards the car broke a connecting rod on the Mulsanne straight.

The First Four Hours

IN complete contrast to the cool, showery weather of the days before the race, Saturday was warm and sunny with plenty of blue sky, so that the massed might of Italy, in gleaming red, glowed in the sunshine as the cars lined up for the start. The crowd seemed larger than ever and every spare inch of space overlooking the starting area seemed crammed solid with people.

The Lola continued to provide pre-race drama almost up to the start, for only 15 minutes before 4 p.m. Dunlop's technician, Vic Barlow, spotted a cracked wheel on the car, which was changed just in time. After all this excitement, it came as quite a relief when the flag fell and

48 of the 49 first drivers pattered across the road to their cars. The 49th, Graham Hill, sat in the Rover-B.R.M., for he was to start 30 seconds after the other cars as he was not in direct competition with the rest of the field but only for the special Gas Turbine Award.

Easily first away was Phil Hill with the new 215 Aston Martin. He made a splendid start and led by a fair margin as he disappeared under the Dunlop bridge with a pack of Ferraris on his tail. Then, to the surprise of most people, it was the big five-litre Maserati with Simon at the wheel which was leading when the fast-moving cars came into sight again as they accelerated out of the White House bend.

With a pack of Ferra[ris] and (with striped bo[n]net) the lone Maser[ati] snarling at his hee[ls] Phil Hill takes the n[ew] Aston Martin 2[15] through Mulsanne [on] the first lap.

LE MANS

Just 1.5 seconds behind the leader was Surtees' rear-engined Ferrari, followed by Phil Hill's Aston, Rodriguez (four-litre Ferrari), Parkes (four-litre Ferrari), McLaren (Aston Martin) and Bandini (rear-engined Ferrari).

The Maserati maintained its lead for almost the first hour of the race, but its driver could never ease the pressure, being hounded the whole time by the Ferraris of Surtees, Rodriguez and Parkes. Behind the leaders some cars were already in trouble. After not much more than ten minutes, Kimberley's Aston Martin came into its pit for carburetter trouble to be rectified, and at 4.30 p.m. the yellow lights flashed on, for Masson's René Bonnet had got into trouble just before the Esses and had rolled several times, fortunately without injury to the driver. Hansgen's Jaguar came into its pit with gearbox trouble, neutral proving very hard to find owing to synchromesh bothers. It returned to the circuit for a spell but later retired. Peter Sargent had narrowly avoided the crashing René Bonnet, having to brake very hard indeed and even so slightly damaging the front of the Lister-Jaguar which was attended to at its pit. But its return to the circuit was not to last very long for early in the race it retired with clutch trouble. Both Fergusson's Lotus Elite and Hutcheson's M.G. B embedded themselves in the sand at Mulsanne, managed to free themselves —after spending an hour and a quarter there in the case of the M.G.—and rejoined the race.

Turn-about lap records

Meanwhile, out on the circuit the Ferraris were breaking the lap record time and again in the pursuit of the bold Maserati. First, Rodriguez reduced Phil Hill's record of 3 min. 57.6 sec. to 3 min. 57.1 sec.; then Surtees brought it down to 3 min. 56.7 sec., to which Rodriguez replied with a lap in 3 min. 56.2 sec. Finally, for the time being, Surtees regained the record with a lap in 3 min. 53.3 sec.

At 5.30 began the first refuelling stops, some of which were full of sound and fury while others were fairly well managed;

the brief pause of the Noblet/Guichet Ferrari was an object lesson in how it should be done. Some teams changed drivers at this first stop, but the Ferrari team had decided to change only every three hours.

By the end of the second hour, the Maserati still led, but was running neck and neck with Parkes' Ferrari which in turn was closely followed by the similar car of Surtees. Rodriguez (Ferrari) was fourth, Bandini (Ferrari) fifth, Noblet (Ferrari) sixth, Gurney (Ferrari) seventh, Abate (Ferrari) eighth, and McLaren (Aston Martin) ninth.

Just before 6 p.m., Phil Hill heard strange and most unwelcome noises from the transmission of the Aston Martin 215, and stopped at the pits to discuss them. He continued, but retired within the next half-hour with the gearbox gone—a

delayed result of hitting fragments of the crashed Bonnet.

During the third hour, however, the Maserati began to wilt, and after being passed on several occasions by Surtees' Ferrari, Casner who had taken over the Maserati came into his pit just before 7 p.m., the rear was jacked up, and the transmission tested, then after some rather half-hearted work on the gearbox, the car was retired. And with it, went much of the interest of the race which now promised to be a Ferrari benefit. During the 7 p.m. pit stops, the Parkes/Maglioli car took the lead, followed by the Surtees/Mairesse Ferrari and the Rodriguez car now driven by the American driver, Penske. Astons had already lost their flyer, the new 215, and of the two remaining Jaguars, Salvadori's was now suffering from the same gearbox troubles which

Full Provisional Results

General Classification

1. L. Bandini/L. Scarfiotti (2,953 c.c. Ferrari 250P), 2,834.6 miles, 118.1 m.p.h.
2. J. Beurlys/G. Langlois (2,953 c.c. Ferrari G.T.O), 2,700.8 miles, 112.5 m.p.h.
3. M. Parkes/U. Maglioli (2,953 c.c. Ferrari 250P), 2,700.7 miles, 112.5 m.p.h.
4. "Elde"/P. Dumay (2,953 c.c. Ferrari G.T.O), 2,692.4 miles, 112.2 m.p.h.
5. P. M. Salmon/J. E. Sears (3,967 c.c. Ferrari 330 L.M.), 2,622.1 miles, 109.3 m.p.h.
6. M. Gregory/D. Piper (2,693 c.c. Ferrari G.T.O.), 2,608.7 miles, 108.7 m.p.h.
7. P. Bolton/N. Sanderson (4,728 c.c. A.C. Cobra), 2,592.0 miles, 108.0 m.p.h.
8. F. Barth/H. Linge (1,982 c.c. Porsche), 2,516.8 miles, 104.9 m.p.h.
9. B. Cunningham/R. Grossmann (3,781 c.c. Jaguar E), 2,372.6 miles, 98.9 m.p.h.
10. P. Fergusson/J. Wagstaff (1,216 c.c. Lotus Elite), 2,257.0 miles, 94.1 m.p.h.
11. J. P. Beltoise/C. Bobrowski (1,120 c.c. René Bonnet), 2,255.0 miles, 94.0 m.p.h.; 12, A. Hutcheson/P. Hopkirk (1,803 c.c. M.G. B), 2,207.2 miles, 92.0 m.p.h.

Fastest lap: J. Surtees (2,953 c.c. Ferrari 250P), 3 min. 53.3 sec., 129.00 m.p.h.
Index of Performance: Bandini/Scarfiotti (Ferrari), 1.236.
Index of Thermal Efficiency: Beltoise/Bobrowski (René Bonnet), 1.25.
Gas Turbine Award: G. Hill/R. Ginther (Rover-B.R.M), 2,593.0 miles, 107.8 m.p.h.

Class Winners

G.T. Cars 1,151-1,300 c.c.: P. Fergusson/J. Wagstaff (1,216 c.c. Lotus Elite), 94.10 m.p.h. **1,601-2,000 c.c.**: A. Hutcheson/P. Hopkirk (1,803 c.c. M.G. B), 92.0 m.p.h. **2,501-3,000 c.c.**: J. Beurlys/G. Langlois (2,953 c.c. Ferrari G.T.O.), 112.5 m.p.h. **3,001-4,001 c.c.**: B. Cunningham/R. Grossmann (3,781 c.c. Jaguar E), 98.90 m.p.h. **Over 4,000 c.c.**: P. Bolton/N. Sanderson (4,728 c.c. A.C. Cobra), 108.0 m.p.h. **Prototype**: L. Scarfiotti/L. Bandini (2,953 c.c. Ferrari 250P), 118.1 m.p.h.

to finish and hoping fervently for no final heart-break. Even the leading Ferrari had slowed to a lap time of 4 min. 18 sec. The Rover B.R.M. continued its rounds at just over 4 min. 30 sec. as it had done for most of the race. The Gregory/Piper Ferrari was really hurrying, however, lapping at around 4 min. 9 sec., the fastest car on the course, as its drivers strove to make up for time lost in the sand: and to good purpose, for the Ferrari overtook first the Cobra for sixth place and then set off in pursuit of the overheating Salmon/Sears Ferrari.

However, even this effort was abandoned and the final hour of the race was almost farcical as the surviving 13 cruised gently round on their Sunday afternoon run in the country. A blue-jeaned member of the somewhat sparse crowd that remained to watch the finish expressed the whole situation rather wickedly as he climbed over the fence and, stretching full length on top of the embankment by the Dunlop Bridge, pretended to fall into a deep sleep.

Then as the final quarter of an hour ticked away, the police deployed in front of the pit, the lame René Bonnet went off into orbit for the final lap to the plaudits of the multitude and the Ferraris busily arranged themselves in line ahead formation, the M.G. somehow getting caught up in the middle of them. At last with the Bandini/Scarfiotti car at the head of the column, the brigade of Ferraris poured across the finishing line to take the first six places. But the loudest cheers of all greeted the Rover-B.R.M. at the conclusion of its triumphant demonstration.

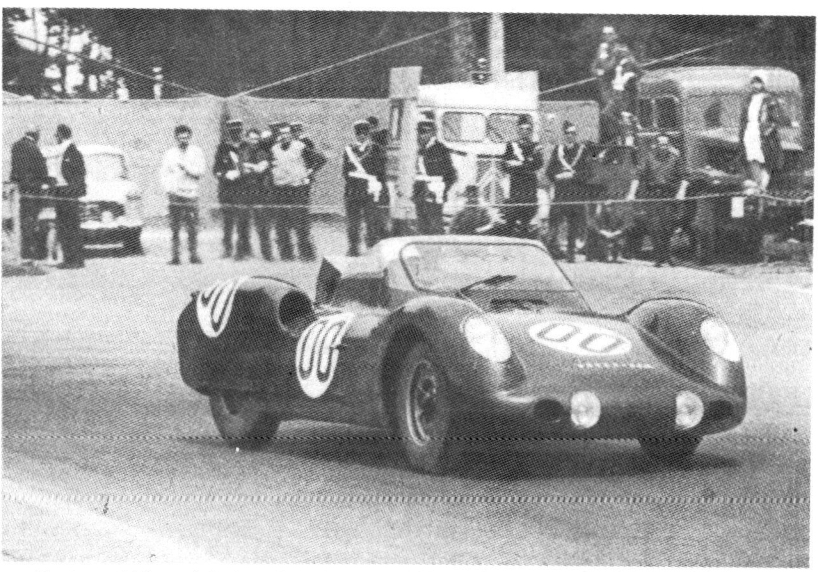

Graham Hill and Richie Ginther had a comfortable 24 hours swishing around in the Rover-B.R.M., seen above at Tertre Rouge. After the race (*below*) Hill and Ginther are as pleased with the outcome as the winners, Scarfiotti (*left*) and Bandini.

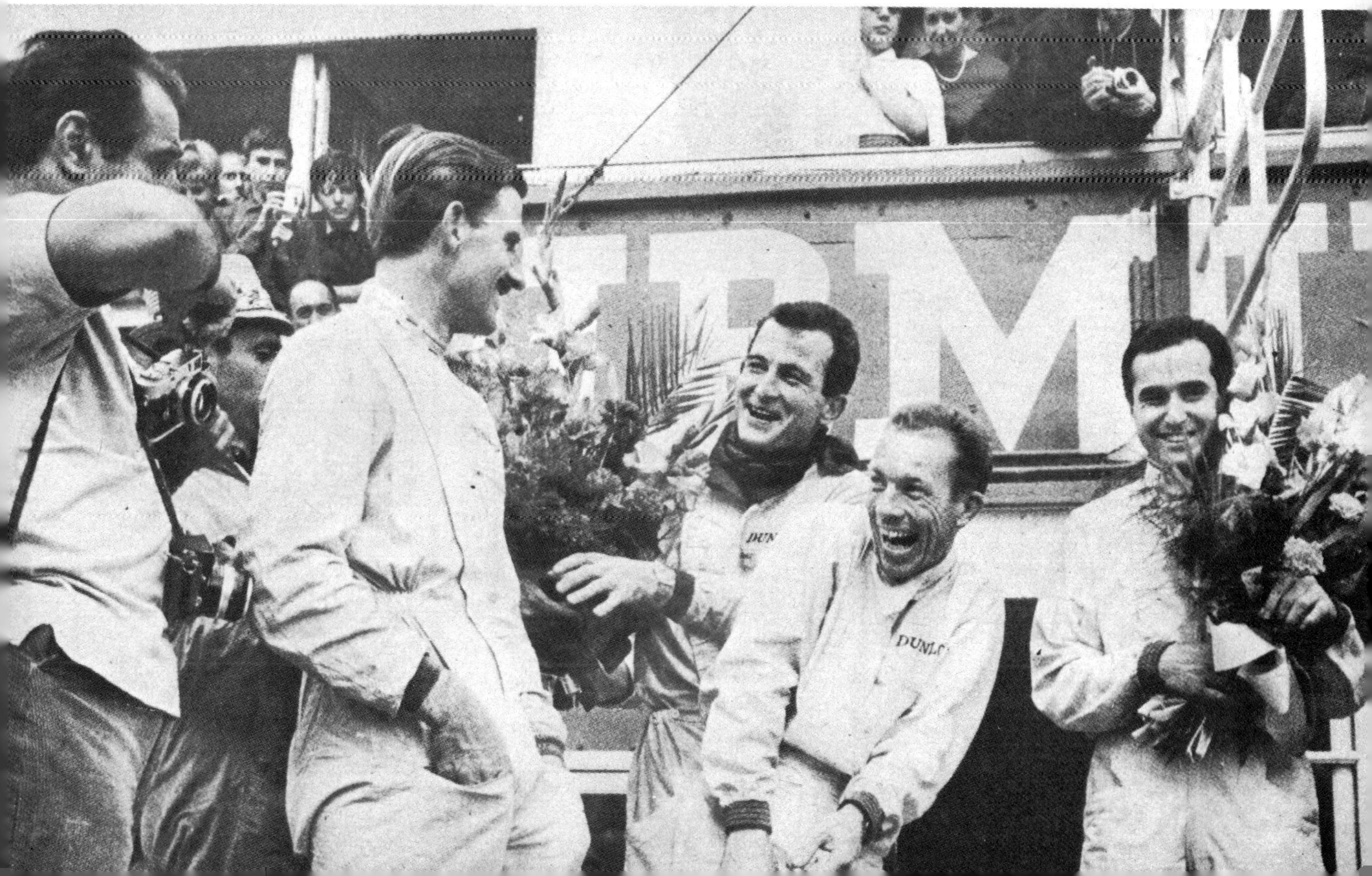

Page in the Pits
At Le Mans
15
AUTOSPORT
COPYRIGHT
THEO PAGE M.S.I.A.

IT is a curious fact that, on the whole, Italian drivers have been conspicuously unsuccessful at Le Mans. Lodovico Scarfiotti and Lorenzo Bandini have set a precedent by being the only all-Italian pairing ever to win the 24-hour race. Looking back on the history of the race, we find that the only Italians to have received the chequered flag were: Luigi Chinetti (1932, 1934, 1949) and Tazio Nuvolari (1933). Chinetti's co-drivers were, respectively, Raymond Sommer, Etancelin and Lord Selsdon, whilst Nuvolari shared with Sommer.

Italy has done a great deal better with her cars, for the scoreboard shows that Alfa Romeo had four victories, and Ferrari now have seven. The British total is made up of Bentley, 5; Jaguar, 5; Lagonda, 1; Aston Martin, 1. France's score is : Lorraine, 2; Chenard-Walcker, 1; Bugatti, 2; Delahaye, 1; Talbot, 1. Germany has had one victory with a Mercedes-Benz. So, since the race was inaugurated in 1923, we have a sort of league table:

1. Great Britain   12
2. Italy   11
3. France   7
4. Germany   1

France has had it all her own way in the Index of Performance, which began in 1925. Her total of 17 is made up of Salmson, 2; Chenard-Walcker, 1; Talbot, 1; Bugatti, 1; Simca, 2; Monopole, 2; Panhard, 3; D.B.-Panhard, 5. Great Britain's six comprises Bentley, 1; Riley, 2; Aston Martin, 2; Lotus, 1. Italy's six were O.M., 1; Alfa Romeo, 2; Osca, 1; Ferrari, 2. Germany's only win was with a Porsche.

It may mean something, but the most successful marques at Le Mans are still very much in business, Bentley, of course, now being made by Rolls-Royce. The only car of under 2-litres to win the Grand Prix d'Endurance was the Ferrari of Chinetti/Selsdon in 1949.

It is probably the realization that the most publicity at Le Mans goes to the winners of the "Endurance" or the "Index," which has caused a gradual dropping in support of the intermediate capacities. It is interesting to note that this year the entry comprised:—

3 litres and over   23
2 litres   6
1,600 c.c.   3
1,300 c.c.   4
Up to 1,000 c.c.   12

Porsche, Alfa Romeo and Sunbeam were, of course, very much concerned in the G.T. Championship class, but it would appear that the tendency is either to enter cars with a chance of winning outright, or to concentrate on the two "Indexes." Class victories mean very little at Le Mans,

Le Mans in Retrospect

BY GREGOR GRANT

how brought to the pits, and mended from parts taken from the two abandoned machines. As no complete components are permitted to be replaced, even the bonnet had to be built up from pieces cut out of the Hansgen/Pabst car, and a major repair job done on the radiator, instead of merely having to replace it. After an hour and fifty minutes, the Jaguar returned to the fray—and finished in ninth place.

Bruce McLaren was terribly upset when he returned to the pits after Aston Martin No. 8 blew up, and oil vapour possibly precipitated the multi-car pile-up on the Hunaudières section. No one could possibly put any blame on McLaren for this; few drivers save their engines like the New Zealander does, and it was just another of those unfortunate incidents which are amongst the hazards of motor-racing.

In the paddock and village areas the trade people vied with each other to offer hospitality to their guests. One of the most delightful spots during the race was the International Martini Club, which also extended its welcome to visiting journalists and photographers. Shell Berre was another focal point, and in the pits area Dunlop, K.L.G. (Club Soixante-Douze), Trico, Lucas, Castrol and others had a constant stream of visitors.

Prior to and after the race the "Globe"

FIRST ALL-ITALIAN win at Le Mans after many years of Ferrari wins with "foreign" drivers. Lodovico Scarfiotti and Lorenzo Bandini drove a calculated race in their 250P Ferrari seen leaving the Esses (above). INDEX OF ENERGY winner, the Jean-Pierre Beltoise/Claude Bobrowski René Bonnet nearly overdoes it at the same spot (right).

Theo Page at Le Mans

1. **Sketch of the independent rear suspension of the Lola G.T.**

2. **View of the carburetters of the Ferrari**

3. **Rear suspension of the successful Rover-B.R.M.**

4. **Front suspension of the Lumsden/Sargent Lister-Jaguar which unfortunately retired**

5. **Air intake to the cockpit of the ill-fated E-type Jaguar of Roy Salvadori**

6. **Rear suspension of the Aston Martin 215**

7. **Cockpit of the Ferrari**

and I believe that it was only recently that the A.C.O. recognized categories by cylinder capacity, prompted by the fact that a few specialized periodicals included class results. They are used mainly to record distance records.

This was the first Le Mans to be won by a rear-engined machine. There were a record number in this year's event, made up of Alpine, 3; René Bonnet, 5; Fiat-Abarth, 2; Deep Sanderson, 1; Lola, 1; Porsche, 4; Ferrari, 3—a total of 19, plus, of course, the Rover-B.R.M.

One cannot over-praise the sheer determination of the Cunningham équipe in getting Jaguar No. 15 back into the race. Bob Grossman mowed down several straw bales due to losing his brakes going into Mulsanne. The Jaguar was badly damaged, with a split radiator, the bonnet bent beyond repair, and sundry other parts battered. Grossman telephoned team manager John Baus at the pits to announce his retirement, but Baus and the two Jaguar works mechanics organized a most remarkable cannibalization job, the car was some-

in the Place de la Republique was the meeting place for many enthusiasts, and it was quite amusing to watch Bill Jones, the landlord of the famous "Star" near Lord's cricket ground, helping out behind the bar during one of the many rush hours.

It may not have been one of the most exciting Le Mans races, but more people seemed to enjoy themselves than in other years. Perhaps the fine weather which held out for the entire 24 hours had something to do with this.

THE scrutineering period of this year's race was dominated by the shadow of Colin Chapman. Last year the Lotus cars were unjustly excluded, and Chapman very rightly boycotted the 24-hour race of 1963. The club received such a bad press in this connection that a change of heart was necessary if the race was to continue. The alterations which the Lola team were asked to carry out were entirely reasonable, and the final acceptance of the car was both humane and just. Indeed, the scrutineers were far too lenient with the D.K.W., which was a single-seater, because the passenger would have shared his space with the vast exhaust system and the gear-change mechanism. However, this car was the first retirement.

Easily the most outstanding car technically was the Rover-B.R.M., and the applause which it received at the finish proved that the crowd realized its importance. It was perhaps the only car in the race which demanded no mechanical adjustments, and it could certainly be developed to out-perform any of the piston-engined cars of 1963. Superbly driven, it demonstrated Grand Prix roadholding among many less effective chassis, in spite

The faster Ferraris had no synchromesh in their gearboxes, this mechanism also being absent from the 4-litre Aston Martin, though John Wyer regretted the impossibility of incorporating it. The extremely high maximum speed of the Astons underlined their clean aerodynamic lines, but to race big six-cylinder engines against 12-cylinder Ferraris is asking too much. The lower stresses of the multi-cylinder unit render it a certain winner in such a very long race.

One was surprised that the officials permitted the rear-engined Ferraris to leave the pits repeatedly with fuel pouring from the tank overflow pipes. This was evidently due to over-filling and resulted in the elimination of the leading car when driven by Mairesse. He had to jump while the machine was still in motion because his seat was on fire. Other pits were noticeably lax about fire precautions during refuelling, in which respect the British teams were certainly the most careful.

The Lola was extremely impressive after arriving late and suffering some changes as a result of the edicts of the scrutineers. It was sad indeed that a defective gearbox caused David Hobbs to enter a corner in

some clots in the cockpits there were also some careless fellows in the pits. What about the French car that was allowed to run out of petrol or the Italian one that was eliminated because the mechanic failed to screw home the oil filler cap? Let us be charitable, though, for 24-hours is a long time and both drivers and mechanics were utterly weary long before the end.

Certainly the finest improvisation was achieved by the Deep Sanderson boys. During a practice period which was largely wasted by maddening disasters, the main oil pump drive failed. It was essential to get back on the course and motor at racing speed, for time was running out and the car had not qualified. The dry-sump engine was converted to wet-sump, using the scavenge pump for pressure. With minutes to spare, this jury-rig sufficed to secure a position at the start for the little rear-engined car. In the race, the engine proved completely reliable and gave a splendid performance. Unfortunately, some minor bothers in the chassis department caused the car to fall below the minimum distance requirement. After adjustment, it went as never before and got well ahead of schedule but the short lapse had been noticed by the officials and it was necessary to withdraw the Deep Sanderson when it was running perfectly.

Before the race, Ed Roy appeared with his glorious 1913 opposed-valve Delage, with four cylinders · and 6.2 litres. Very rightly, Lord Montagu was in the passenger's seat and the blue Grand Prix two-seater thundered up to the starting line. Then—and if my eyes were not entirely dry I make no apology—an ex-world

TECHNICAL ASPECTS OF LE MANS

BY JOHN BOLSTER

of its delayed response to the accelerator pedal. It also underlined the fundamental reliability of the alternator, compared with several orthodox D.C. dynamos of different makes which wilted during the hours of darkness.

The most efficient engine in the race was the Renault Gordini unit which was found in the Alpine (pronounced "Alpeen") and René Bonnet cars. This five-bearing, four-cylinder unit was producing 98 b.h.p. from 996 c.c. at 7,800 r.p.m. The performance of the ill-fated Rosinski/Heinz car proved that this power was certainly being maintained, though in most other cases the unit was slightly de-tuned for greater fuel economy, the valuable thermal efficiency prize being very much in mind.

The twin-cam Renault engine is based on the R8, but it has the over-square dimensions of 71.5 mm. × 62 mm. Curiously enough, the camshafts do not operate the valves directly through inverted pistons, but impart their motion via rocking fingers with roller-type cam followers—an apparently archaic solution. The technical details of these engines are not willingly given, but it is extremely interesting that two of the René Bonnet cars had an entirely different power unit.

This engine, though possessing a valve cover of "twin-cam" appearance, is in fact a push-rod job. It has inclined valves in hemispherical combustion chambers with orthodox push-rod and rocker gear, the dimensions being 70 mm. × 72 mm. (1,108 c.c.). The Basini/Bouharde and Beltoise/Bobrowski cars were fitted with these units, which were notably reliable. The Alpines incorporated many Lotus suspension parts and a Hewland (VW) five-speed gearbox. The René Bonnets used the four-speed, all-synchromesh gearbox of the Renault Estafette van, and the very advanced aerodynamic body design was by the aircraft firm, Bréguet. Both makes were phenomenally quick but lost time on the faster corners, due to insufficiently rigid chassis.

REAR VIEWS of three cars at Tertre Rouge. They are: (left to right): the Bruce McLaren/Innes Ireland Aston Martin DB4GT, the Giancarlo Sala/Romolo Rossi Alfa Romeo Giulietta and the Dan Gurney/Jim Hall Ferrari 330LM.

neutral, but the car earned golden opinions before the accident eliminated it. The A.C. Cobras, with similar Ford V8 engines, were particularly well driven, having regard to their somewhat "hairy" handling characteristics. The rear suspension of the Lola, with its positive location of the wheels, perhaps gave a hint to the engineers at Thames Ditton? Nevertheless, resounding applause must be given to the A.C. as the first British car to finish, and with some cleaning up of body details it would go even faster down the Mulsanne straight.

This is a technical article, but the standard of driving must be mentioned. A few drivers were wild and irresponsible, behaving as though they were in a club sprint instead of a 24-hour endurance race. Ask Ninian Sanderson how he (rather unwillingly!) saved the life of a Porsche driver. Ask any of the big car pilots, in fact, what they thought of the conductors of certain little blue cars, which raced neck and neck while much faster machinery was being braked violently behind. If there were

champion flagged the car on its way. The great René Thomas, an octogenarian on two sticks, released his old Grand Prix car, crying "doucement, doucement", as it accelerated away.

One cannot conclude without referring to the deplorable accident. Safety precautions have done much to prevent the spreading of oil on the road, but what remedy is there for a connecting rod through the sump? While the piston engine lasts, the danger of a major blow-up will remain. Obviously, a dry-sump engine is to be preferred, but any unit which smashes to pieces must deposit some lubricant on the road. Perhaps there is an answer to this problem, but I have been pondering it ever since I saw Dick Seaman lose the British Grand Prix because a "non-competitive" car spread its inside over the Donington circuit.

Let us end by repeating the lesson of Le Mans. To compete against 12 cylinders you need 12 cylinders. It's as simple as that!

LE MANS
1964

In many ways this was a watershed in Le Mans history: 1964 saw the last entry of Jaguar and Aston Martin for many years, and the first entry from Ford. The rules were as before but there was now a minimum engine size of 1,000 cc, instead of 700 cc which had been the previous limit. The Rover-B.R.M. had been expected to return, with sleek coupe bodywork designed by Bill Towns and fitted with a heat exchanger to reduce its voracious appetite for paraffin: but the car was damaged in transport on the way back to Solihull after the April practice session, and could not .be ready in time for the race itself.

The number of starting cars was back up to 55 and again Ferrari filled the lion's share of places with 12 cars entered: three four-litre and five 3.3 litre prototypes as well as four three-litre GTs. The biggest engine on the track was found in another Italian car, a new make that made its appearance, the Iso Rivolta which disposed of 5.3 litres - courtesy of Chevrolet. This car ran in the prototype category, as did a five-litre Maserati. If a Chevrolet V 8 was found in the Iso, Ford V 8 engines were favoured by no less than three competitors: the four AC Cobras in the GT category had 4.7 litre Ford engines, while the Sunbeam Tiger prototypes used the 4.2 litre size; slightly bigger than the engines used in Ford's own trio of GT 40 prototypes. These in fact used dohc engines originally developed by Ford for the Indianapolis race, and were conceived in Anglo-American collaboration between Ford and Lola. The first GT 40 had been completed less than three months before Le Mans and there had only been one race appearance (at the Nurburgring) prior to the 24-hour race.

Aston Martin fielded one car, and Jaguar two; they shared a common engine capacity of 3.8 litres and all ran in the GT category. As the $2^1/2$ litre class did not attract any entries there was quite a gap down to the Porsches - two prototypes with eight-cylinder engines and five plastic bodied 904 GT coupes - which shared the two-litre class with the MGB of Andrew Hedges and Paddy Hopkirk. A Lotus Elan ran in the 1,600 cc prototype class while three Alfa Romeos of a similar capacity qualified as GT cars; in the 1,300 cc class, there was a Lotus Elite GT, a Deep Sanderson prototype and two Panhard engined C.D.s; their capacity was only 851 cc but they had been fitted with superchargers which under the current correction factor (1.4) took them up to a theoretical 1,191 cc. The smallest class was the 1,150 cc class; five Bonnets and four Alpine Renaults were kept company by a single Austin-Healey Sprite, and three Triumph Spitfires with special fastback coupe bodywork which formed the pattern for the later GT 6 model.

As it turned out, the new and untried Fords were worthy challengers of Ferrari's supremacy. The Ginther/Gregory car took the lead after the start but had to give way to the Surtees/Bandini Ferrari 330 P; while Phil Hill in another Ford set a new lap record at 131.375 mph. However, one of the Fords went off the road, and the Ginther/Gregory car retired with gearbox failure; the gearboxes apparently could not stand up to the sheer power of the engines. The only other Ferrari-challenger, the Maserati, which had been driven into third place, bowed out around midnight with electrical trouble. By then the remaining Ford GT 40, driven by Phil Hill and Bruce McLaren, was fifth after three Ferraris and an A.C. Cobra, until early Sunday morning when this Ford suffered gearbox failure as well. This left the Ferraris in control of the race.

The final result was a 1-2-3 Ferrari victory; the winning 3.3 litre 275 P model driven by Guichet and Vaccarella had covered 2,917.524 miles at an average of 121.563 mph. It was followed home by two four-litre 330 P models; in fourth place came the A.C. Cobra Daytona, entered by Carrol Shelby and driven by Dan Gurney and Bob Bondurant, and this car won the GT category as well as the five litre class. Ferrari took the four- and three-litre classes, while the Iso Rivolta won the unlimited (over five-litre) class; a Porsche 904/4 in seventh place was best among the two-litres, and the 1,600 cc class went to an Alfa Romeo TZ. The only British win came from a Lotus Elite in the 1,300 cc class, and the smallest class of 1,150 cc cars went to an Alpine Renault which also won the Index of Thermal Efficiency; whereas the Index of Performance went to the winning Ferrari. A total of 24 cars finished, including the MGB, one Triumph Spitfire and with the Austin-Healey Sprite hindmost, but neither the Aston Martin nor the Jaguars stood the distance.

FERRARI—the most likely winner. Graham Hill at Sebring with the Maranello car.

victory. The wheel has turned full circle again, and not for many years have there been so many big-car entries. These comprise Ferrari, Ford, A.C. Cobra, Sunbeam, Maserati, A.T.S., Jaguar, Aston Martin and Iso-Rivolta. Ferrari supremacy in prototype racing still remains to be shaken, but at Sebring the A.C. Cobras overcame the normally invincible GTOs, and Carroll Shelby firmly believes that his G.T. coupé has more than an outside chance of defeating the Maranello prototypes, a belief that is also shared by Ford of America and Maserati of France.

Some say that Enzo Ferrari is not in the least worried concerning this year's challengers, and that the Commendatore has every confidence in his latest proto-

LES VINGT-QUATRE HEURES DU MANS

Ford could offer challenge to Ferrari

By GREGOR GRANT

AT precisely 4 p.m. on Saturday, 20th June, the tricolour of France will fall, 55 drivers will sprint across the track to their waiting cars, and the classic 24 Hours Race of Le Mans for the *Grand Prix d'Endurance* will be on. Until the maroon is fired at 4 p.m. on Sunday, there will be ceaseless activity, and a grim struggle on a circuit which inevitably takes its toll in men and machines.

Many people decry *Les Vingt-Quatre Heures,* but the fact remains that it is one of the most widely publicized and important races in the calendar. It is more than a race: it is a carnival, drawing thousands of people from all over Europe, and from overseas, to enjoy the spectacle of day-and-night racing, with the world's fastest road-equipped machines. Le Mans is undoubtedly hazardous, not only in the immense speed differential between small-capacity and large-capacity vehicles, but for the disparity in ability amongst the contestants. This is perhaps understandable, for 55 cars require a minimum of 110 drivers, of which only a relatively small proportion can be considered in the top flight.

With the speed of the fastest cars approaching 200 m.p.h. on the Mulsanne straight, the limitation of engine capacity, the banning of sports-racing cars, insistence on more or less production-based cars after the dreadful disaster of 1955 all seem pretty pointless now. The idea was to limit the maximum speed of the competing cars, but the 1964 machines are, if anything, even quicker than the most powerful sports-racers of a decade ago. Such is progress, that the record distance for the race was set up last year by Scarfiotti/Bandini in a 3-litre Ferrari prototype, which covered 4,561.710 kilometres, to average 190.070 k.p.h. The lap record, also with a 3-litre Ferrari, stands to the credit of John Surtees with 3 mins. 53.3 secs., 207.714 k.p.h.

The Le Mans entry is divided into two categories, namely G.T. prototypes and G.T. cars. The former are defined as prototypes of cars which will eventually go into series-production, but even with the limitations imposed by body, weight, fuel tank capacity and dimensions regulations, they are, in many cases, as near as whatsit sports-racing machines. Quite apart from the *Grand Prix d'Endurance,* there are races within the race for both the Index of Performance and

the Index of Energy, worked out on a formula basis. Broadly speaking, the former goes to the car which, irrespective of capacity, improves on its minimum qualifying distance by the largest percentage, while the latter is mainly concerned with engine capacity, allied to speed and fuel consumption. It was this Index on which the Rover-B.R.M. entrants had to set their sights, and it is indeed a great pity that the gas-turbine car had to be withdrawn.

While there will always be a certain amount of interest in categories, and also in the classes which a few years ago existed only in the minds of motoring journalists, but are now officially recognized by the A.C.O., nothing can take the place of the battle for outright

types recording yet another victory for the Prancing Horse. However, his technicians do not under-rate the Ford G.T., backed by the immense resources of Ford of America. This car showed great promise at Nürburging, and could be even quicker than any of the Ferraris if the handling permits its undoubtedly high maximum speed to be used, together with more efficient and powerful braking. Problems which arose at the Le Mans practice days seem to be being sorted out, and John Wyer believes that the cars could quite feasibly pull it off!

Probably the fastest car on the circuit will be Col. Johnny Simone's 5-litre Maserati, to be driven by André Simon and Maurice Trintignant (Lucky Casner may deputize for the former, who re-

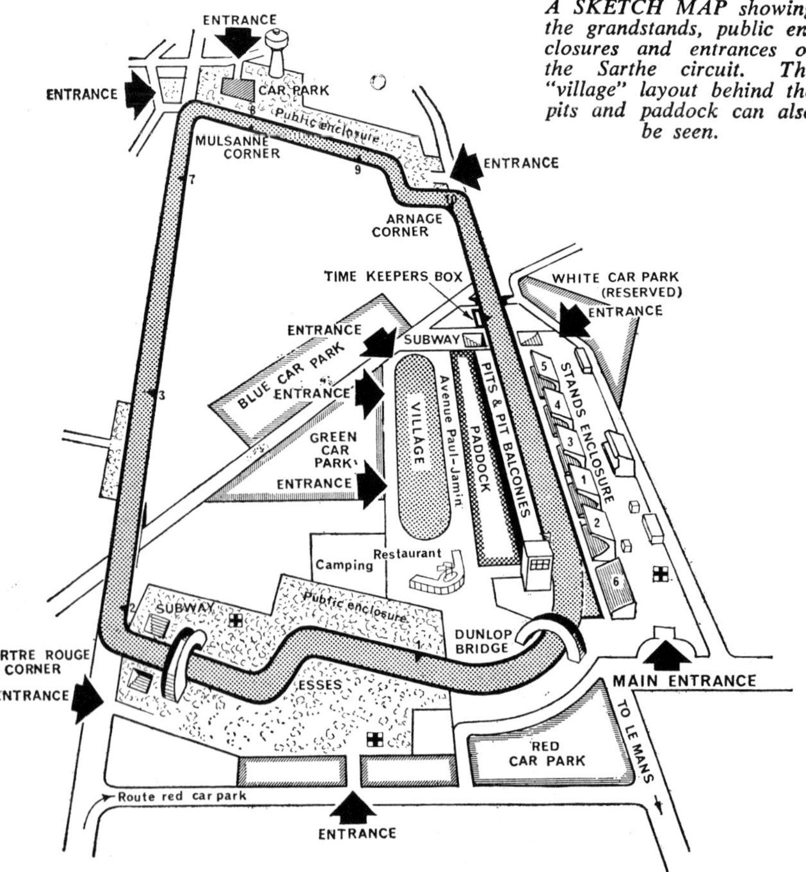

A SKETCH MAP showing the grandstands, public enclosures and entrances of the Sarthe circuit. The "village" layout behind the pits and paddock can also be seen.

THE RECORDS

Class	Make	c.c.	Drivers	Distance kiloms.	Speed k.p.h.	Date
14	A.C. Cobra	4,727	Bolton/Sanderson	4,171.180	173.798	1963
13	Ferrari	3,967	Gendebien/P. Hill	4,451.255	185.469	1962
12	**Ferrari**	**2,953**	**Scarfiotti/Vaccarella**	**4,561.710**	**190.070**	**1963**
10	Porsche	1,968	Gregory/Holbert	4,154.460	173.103	1961
9	Porsche	1,588	Behra/Herrmann	3,909.647	162.902	1958
8	Lotus Elite	1,216	Hobbs/Gardner	3,847.066	160.295	1962
7	Lotus-Climax	1,098	Chamberlain/Mackay-Frazer	3,826.099	159.458	1957
6	René Bonnet	966	Consten/Rosinski	3,421.551	142.565	1962
5	Fiat-Abarth	847	Hulme/Hyslop	3,531.974	147.166	1961

Lap Record: John Surtees (2,953 Ferrari), 3 m. 53.3 s., 207.714 k.p.h. 1963.

ceived slight injuries testing the car at Monza recently). This squat coupé, constructed in Italy for Maserati of France, could quite well set the pace. However, Maserati is not synonymous with reliability—at Le Mans especially—and it is a singleton entry. Shelby's coupé A.C. Cobra is another machine which could be amongst the pace-setters, but here again its reliability is not known.

The opening stages at Le Mans invariably develop into a sort of Grand Prix, and it is this contest which does grip the spectators. Team managers can talk about tactics and race strategy till the cows come home, but the "G.P." is almost inevitable. No one could afford to let the pace-setters establish too big a lead, and with very fast cars being driven by World Championship Formula 1 class drivers, the fight for the lead can dictate the result of the race at the end of the 24 hours. Ferrari can, better than others, adopt a race strategy based on the plan to wear down the opposition which is trying to force the pace. With such a powerful entry, and extremely skilful conductors, the red cars of Maranello will be extremely difficult to dislodge from the leading positions. Also, there is inter-Ferrari rivalry between the works drivers and entries from Equipe Nationale Belge, N.A.R.T. and Maranello Concessionaires which comprise machines more or less identical to the factory cars.

It would, of course, be quite possible to work out with a computer a reasonably accurate estimation of the average speed required to win the race. However, a hundred and one things could disturb even the most meticulous forecast, and consequently team-managers are understandably concerned that their charges do not fall back too far, should the unexpected occur.

Almost anything can, and invariably does, happen at Le Mans. An unscheduled pit stop for a minor adjustment can easily cost the race, and even when a car has had upwards of a couple of laps' lead over its nearest rival, few team managers would take the chance of slowing the drivers down to the point where pursuers are actually gaining on the road.

Not since 1949 has a car of so small a capacity as 2 litres won the *G.P. d'Endurance* (Chinetti/Selsdon's Ferrari). Yet this year, Porsche's 8-cylinder prototype must be considered as offering a real challenge to the bigger machines. Given a no-trouble run, this G.P.-based car might well be among the leaders at the end of the 24 hours. One must not overlook the fact that a 4-cylinder 904 G.T. car was third overall at Nürburgring—and the "eight" is a great deal quicker.

The British-entered A.C. Cobra ought to give a good account of itself, and it will be interesting to see how it fares as compared to the Shelby cars. Sunbeam's Alpine V8 is an intriguing experiment in that it is a racing version of the recently announced Tiger. The privately owned E-type Jaguars and Aston Martin could, with luck, work themselves into fairly high places at the end, but only a super-optimist would forecast outright victory.

The big Corvettes have never done much in full-scale international racing, and it is not surprising to see that they have once again been withdrawn. The Iso-Rivolta "Grifo", one imagines, will please its sponsors if it manages to finish the race.

The others are concerned with classes and indexes, and for the Index of Performance there is not much to choose between the very fast 1.6-litre Alfa Romeos and the smaller capacity Alpines with Renault-based 2-o.h.c. engines. The Triumph Spitfires are interesting, and their sponsors are placing their confidence in general reliability. It is a pity that the Marcos-Volvo and Jacobs M.G. Midgets are absentees, and that the 2-litre Abarth-Simcas have been withdrawn.

However, with such a concentration of big hairy motor-cars the 1964 Le Mans race should provide plenty of excitement for spectators. Ford have the toughest job of all, for the eyes of the world will be on their attempt to break the Ferrari stranglehold on prototype racing, not to mention their engines being used in the A.C. Cobra attack on Ferrari's G.T. laurels, and in the Sunbeam offensive.

The defection of Rover-B.R.M. permitted Graham Hill and Richie Ginther to accept other drives—in Ferrari and Ford respectively. Jim Clark and Jack Brabham will not be competing at Le Mans, but there will be an extremely strong turn-out of Grand Prix conductors, including Graham Hill, Richie Ginther, Dan Gurney, John Surtees, Lorenzo Bandini, Jo Bonnier, Innes Ireland, Bruce McLaren, Tony Maggs, Maurice Trintignant, Carel Godin de Beaufort, Jo Siffert, Phil Hill and Giancarlo Baghetti.

LISTE DES CONCURRENTS

No.	Car	c.c.	Entrant	Drivers
1	Iso-Rivolta	5,359	Société Sonauto	Pierre Noblet/X
2	Maserati Tipo 152	4,941	Maserati-France	André Simon/Maurice Trintignant
3	A.C. Cobra-Ford	4,727	A.C. Cars, Ltd.	Peter Bolton/Jack Sears
4	A.C. Cobra-Ford	4,727	Shelby-American, Inc.	Ken Miles/Bob Holbert
5	A.C. Cobra-Ford	4,727	Shelby-American, Inc.	X/X
6	A.C. Cobra-Ford	4,727	Briggs Cunningham	Briggs Cunningham/X
7	A.C. Cobra-Ford	4,727	Ed Hugus	Ed Hugus/X
8	Sunbeam Tiger	4,261	Rootes Group	Claude Dubois/Keith Ballisat
9	Sunbeam Tiger	4,261	Rootes Group	Peter Procter/Jimmy Blumer
10	Ford G.T.	4,168	Ford Motor Co., U.S.A.	Bruce McLaren/Phil Hill
11	Ford G.T.	4,168	Ford Motor Co., U.S.A.	Masten Gregory/Ritchie Ginther
12	Ford G.T.	4,168	Ford Motor Co., U.S.A.	Richard Attwood/Jo Schlesser
14	Ferrari 330P	3,967	Maranello Concessionaires	Graham Hill/Jo Bonnier
15	Ferrari 330P	3,967	North American Racing Team	Pedro Rodriguez/A. J. Foyt
16	Jaguar E	3,871	Peter Lindner	Peter Lindner/Peter Nöcker
17	Jaguar E	3,871	Peter Sargent	Peter Lumsden/Peter Sargent
18	Aston Martin DB4GT	3,751	Michael Salmon	Mike Salmon/Peter Sutcliffe
19	Ferrari 330P	3,967	SEFAC Ferrari	John Surtees/Lorenzo Bandini
20	Ferrari 275P	3,286	SEFAC Ferrari	Jean Guichet/Nino Vaccarella
21	Ferrari 275P	3,286	SEFAC Ferrari	Lodovico Scarfiotti/Mike Parkes
22	Ferrari 275P	3,286	SEFAC Ferrari	Umberto Maglioli/Giancarlo Baghetti
23	Ferrari 275P	3,286	Equipe Nationale Belge	"Beurlys"/Lucien Bianchi
24	Ferrari GTO	2,953	Equipe Nationale Belge	Georges Berger/Gerald Langlois van Ophem
25	Ferrari GTO	2,953	Maranello Concessionaires	Innes Ireland/Tony Maggs
26	Ferrari GTO	2,953	North American Racing Team	John Fulp, Jr./X
27	Ferrari GTO	2,953	Fernand Tavano	Fernand Tavano/X
28	A.T.S.	2,467	Automobili Turismo Sport	Theodore Zeccoli/X
29	Porsche "8"	1,981	Porsche System Engineering	Edgar Barth/Herbert Linge
30	Porsche "8"	1,981	Porsche System Engineering	X/X
31	Porsche 904	1,967	Porsche System Engineering	X/X
32	Porsche 904	1,967	"Franc"	"Franc"/Jean Kerguen
33	Porsche 904	1,967	Racing Team Holland	Ben Pon/Henk van Zalinge
34	Porsche 904	1,967	Auguste Veuillet	Robert Buchet/Guy Ligier
35	Porsche 904	1,967	Scuderia Filipinetti	Herbert Müller/X
36	Porsche 904	1,967	J. C. Mosnier	A. de Cortanze/J. C. Mosnier
37	M.G.B	1,801	British Motor Corporation	Andrew Hedges/Paddy Hopkirk
38	Lotus Elan	1,594	Royal Elysées	Bernard Consten/Pierre Gelé
40	Alfa Romeo Giulia TZ	1,570	Scuderia Sant Ambroeus	Giampiero Biscaldi/Roberto Bussinello
41	Alfa Romeo Giulia TZ	1,570	Scuderia Sant Ambroeus	Jean Rolland/X
42	Deep Sanderson	1,293	LawrenceTune Engines	Hugh Braithwaite/Chris Lawrence
43	Lotus Elite	1,216	Team Elite '62	Clive Hunt/John Wagstaff
44	C.D.	1,191	S.E.C.A. C.D.	Alain Bertaut/André Guilhaudin
45	C.D.	1,191	S.E.C.A. C.D.	Guy Verrier/X
46	Alpine	1,149	Société Alpine	Mauro Bianchi/X
47	Alpine	1,149	Société Alpine	José Rosinski/Roger de Lageneste
48	René Bonnet	1,149	Automobiles René Bonnet	Gerard Laureau/Jean-Pierre Beltoise
49	Triumph Spitfire	1,147	Standard-Triumph	Mike Rothschild/Bob Tullius
50	Triumph Spitfire	1,147	Standard-Triumph	David Hobbs/Rob Slotemaker
51	Alpine	1,108	Société Alpine	Jacques Féret/Pierre Orsini
52	René Bonnet	1,108	Automobiles René Bonnet	Robert Bouharde/Giorgio Basini
53	Austin-Healey Sprite	1,101	Donald Healey Motor Co.	Clive Baker/Bill Bradley
54	Alpine	1,002	Société Alpine	Jean Vinatier/Roger Masson
55	René Bonnet	1,002	Automobiles René Bonnet	Pierre Monneret/Roland Charrière
56	René Bonnet	1,002	Automobiles René Bonnet	Jean-Claude Rudaz/Michel de Bourbon Parma
57	Alfa Romeo Giulia TZ	1,570	Scuderia Sant Ambroeus	Gianni Bulgari/F. Masoero

RESERVES

No.	Car	c.c.	Entrant	Drivers
58	Ferrari GTO	2,953	North American Racing Team	X/X
59	Alpine	1,002	Société Alpine	Philippe Vidal/X
60	René Bonnet	1,002	Automobiles René Bonnet	Farjon/Pierre Lelong
61	Austin-Healey Sprite	1,101	Donald Healey Motor Co.	X/X
62	Porsche 904	1,967	Racing Team Holland	Carel Godin de Beaufort/Gerhard Mitter
63	A.C. Cobra-Ford	4,727	A. Chardonnet	Lucky Casner/J. M. Vincent
64	A.C. Cobra-Ford	4,727	A. Chardonnet	Régis Fraissinet/J. de Mortemart
65	Triumph Spitfire	1,147	Standard-Triumph	Jean-Francois Piot/Jean-Louis Marnat
66	Deep Sanderson	1,293	LawrenceTune Engines	Chris Spender/Gordon Spice
67	Elva Courier	1,798	R. J. Lutz	R. J. Lutz/R. G. Osteen

FIVE TIMES

ITALY TRIUMPHS IN FERRARI-FORD BATTLE : WINNER 3.5 m.p.h. FASTER THAN LAST YEAR'S RECORD

ONCE again Ferraris have dominated Le Mans, the winners being Jean Guichet and Nino Vaccarella in a 275P mid-engined GT prototype. These cars have now been victors five times in a row, the only marque ever to achieve this distinction, but perhaps the writing is on the wall. In the Grand Touring category Dan Gurney and Bob Bondurant's A.C.-Cobra coupé vanquished the GTOs at last, setting a new race distance record in the process. In the early laps Ritchie Ginther's Ford GT prototype set a spanking pace, which none of the Ferraris cared to match, and in the three hours that he was at the wheel he built up a lead of almost one lap. Unfortunately this car, like its team-mate driven by Phil Hill and Bruce McLaren, was eliminated with gearbox trouble.

In general, transmissions were scarcely coping with the increased power of the 1964 cars and the winning Ferrari was the only one of the prototypes of that make which did not suffer from clutch trouble at some time during the race. It is hardly a pointer to the trend of passenger car design, but nevertheless worthy of record, that the cars with engines behind the driver outnumbered those with the power unit in front of him to the tune of 31 to 28. New records were set up on all sides; the winners' speed of 121·62 m.p.h. is the best yet, 3·52 m.p.h. faster than last year's record. Ginther's first 15 laps were completed within the hour and his speed measured on the Mulsanne straight was 191·4 m.p.h. As so often, the Index of Thermal Efficiency went to a French car, this time the Gordini-Renault-engined Alpine.

The Main Runners

Ferrari: Four works cars in the GT Prototype class, one 330P (3,972c.c.) for Surtees and Bandini, three 275Ps (3,299,

PHOTOGRAPHS :
RON EASTON and MIKE BARNES

From the start Piper's Ferrari, followed by Salmon's Aston Martin and Barney's Iso Rivolta, sweeps under the Dunlop bridge in the wake of Rodriguez and Graham Hill, who have already passed

Above: The Index-winning Alpine of De Langeneste and Morrogh passes early morning spectators at Indianapolis.   Below: Vaccarella in the winning Ferrari leads Ireland's Ferrari through Arnage on Sunday morning

LE MANS . . .

3,294 and 3,290 c.c.) for Vaccarella-Guichet, Parkes-Scarfiotti and Maglioli-Baghetti respectively. These cars—mid-engined open—are little changed from last year; they have tubular semi-space frames and tubular double wishbone front and rear suspension, with co-axial coil springs and Koni dampers; it was noticed at scrutineering that the screwed spring collars on the dampers, which control the height of the car, were at the top limit and the team manager was warned not to lower them. Since Nürburgring, when a cracked tank caused Ireland to stop on the circuit with fuel shortage, the long sill tanks, running the whole length of the car between the wheels, have been reconstructed using thicker gauge light alloy, with re-arranged baffles and local glass fibre reinforcement.

Just before dusk, in the last practice period, Surtees lapped in 3min 42sec in the 4-litre, a speed of 218·29 k.p.h. (135·63 m.p.h.). Fastest in the 3·3 litre cars was Parkes, with a 3min 49sec lap during first practice. Maranello Concessionaires and North American Racing Team had 330P works-maintained private entries, drivers Graham Hill-Bonnier and Rodriguez-Skip Hudson, best practice times 3min 47·2sec and 3min 45·5sec respectively. Works-assisted 250GT private entries were those of Bianchi-Buerlys, Ireland-Maggs and Tavano-Crossman. Mid-engined 275LM coupés were driven by Piper and Rindt and Pierre Dumay with Gerard Langlois; practice times, 3min 53·9sec and 3min 59·4sec.

Ford: GT Prototypes based on the sensational Lola-Ford, which Attwood and Hobbs drove here last year, with Eric Broadley's basic layout. The alloy, 95.5×72.9mm V-8, push-rod engines were developed for the 1963 Indianapolis race and produce a genuine 340 b.h.p. Since practice in April, a tail lip has been added to eliminate rear-end lift at high speed, but there remains a tendency for the nose to lift. Drivers were Phil Hill-Bruce McLaren, Ritchie Ginther-Masten Gregory and Dick Attwood-Jo Schlesser.

The Hill-McLaren car is the first-

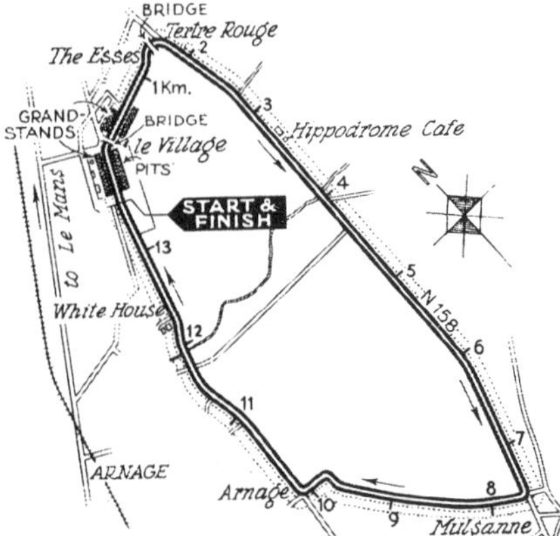

Highest placed Porsche, Koch and Schiller's works car, was unable to improve its Index of Performance placing even after Colin Davis's car retired with clutch trouble

First lap group in the Esses; Piper's Ferrari (No 58) is already laying a smoke screen and a trail of oil from a burst oil-filter, while Ginther's Ford (No. 11) jockeys to pass Bianchi's Ferrari and Lindner's Jaguar

built and heaviest car, 50lb more than the others. At scrutineering the fuel tanks were found to hold more than the 140 litre maximum and the excess capacity was taken up with displacement blocks. Ginther was fastest in practice with 3min 45·3sec (2nd session); Hill-McLaren, 3min 52·3sec; Attwood-Schlesser, 3min 55·4sec.

Porsche: Two eight-cylinder and one four-cylinder mid-engined 904GTS with drivers Barth and Linge in one eight-cylinder and Colin Davis-Gerhard Mitter in the other. Schiller and Koch had the four-cylinder car. Bonnier and Hill, their usual number one drivers, this year were in the Maranello Concessionaires

Ferrari 275P. Best times in practice: Barth-Linge 4min 4·6sec; Davis-Mitter, 4min 5·7sec.

A.C. Cobra: Of four entries, Carrol Shelby only managed to produce two coupés, due to chassis being held up in Italian customs. One was the Sebring-Daytona Brock car, the other a replica built in Modena. There was also the solitary Thames Ditton entry. Engines are Shelby-tuned 101·8 × 72·9mm (4,727 c.c.) iron block Ford V-8 with four speed Ford gearboxes. Carburation is by four, two-choke 48mm Webers. With fuel the cars weigh about 20lb more than the lightweight Ferrari GTOs. Both Shelby cars have final

drive oil-coolers. With the Aston-Martin they are the only GT cars to better the 4-min lap. Times: Gurney, 3min 56·1sec; Sears, 3min 59·9sec. Gurney drove with Bob Bondurant, while Chris Amon and Johannes Neerpach shared the other Shelby car, entered by Briggs Cunningham, who acted as reserve driver. Jack Sears and Peter Bolton were drivers of the Thames Ditton Cobra.

Sunbeam: Two works-entered, special Tiger coupés running as GT prototypes. The 4,181 c.c. Shelby-tuned V-8 engines produce 280 b.h.p. net, using the standard four-barrel Ford-Carter carburettors. Suspension modifications by

Fulfilment of an ambition for Carrol Shelby; Bob Bondurant speeds to GT class victory over the Ferrari GTOs in the A.C. Cobra he shared with Dan Gurney

Dynamic and aerodynamic, the Schlesse-Attwood Ford GT seems glued to the white line through the Esses

LE MANS . . .

Brian Lister include extra rear radius arms to take location loads off the springs. The cars were exceeding 140 m.p.h. on the Mulsanne straight, but the best lap time recorded was 4min 26sec by Peter Procter. Team policy was to keep lap times down to a realistic, race lap time, bearing in mind that the average lap time of last year's winner was about 4min 18sec. Ballisat's car ran a big end in the first practice and most of the second practice period was spent running-in a new engine.

Maserati: The five litre car which appeared in April has been modified to the extent of having a new two-plane rear window, let into the upper edge of the tail which doubles as a luggage locker lid. Drivers were André Simon and Maurice Trintignant, experienced but rather old for such a lusty piece of machinery. However, Maurice Trintignant lapped in 3min 59·5sec. This big, tough car has a 4,911 c.c. vee-8 engine, cylinder dimensions 94 × 89mm, with double o.h.c. and Lucas fuel injection into the manifolds. The Maserati five-speed gearbox is combined with the final drive, rear suspension being De Dion tube, located laterally by a sliding block with

The Race

BENEATH a five-tier wall of people stretching from end to end of the pits, 55 cars stood glistening in the sunshine by midday; by then most of the stands and enclosures, too, were packed with spectators anxious not to miss a thing, and content to study each other until the battle began. An old 2-litre Lagonda motored past quickly by its own standards, though very slowly by ours, under the Dunlop bridge and away on a lap. With discordant, anæmic sounds a band of the Boys' Brigade, or its French equivalent, marched through the pit area drowning the commentary, which happened to be in English at the time. And for some reason, a blonde, doing a lap on foot, headed up through the bridge to cheers, whistles and cat-calls. It was Le Mans as ever, bril-

Bill Bradley in the Austin-Healey Sprite coupé pulls out to pass the ill-fated Triumph Spitfire of Rothschild and Tullius going over the hill into the Esses

guides on the chassis, and longitudinally by trailing radius rods. Front suspension is by unequal length wishbones, the springing medium front and rear being co-axial spring and damper units.

liantly coloured under the blue sky, packed with people; and beneath the holiday atmosphere, tense with expectation. The vast Esso scoreboard, on which so many changes of fortune were to be recorded during the next 24 hours,

Left: Inscrutable signal from the Deep Sanderson signalling pit at Arnage could refer to the cloud of steam which this car gave off before it retired with overheating. Right: Tavano, brief leader of the GT category when the Cobra stopped for a split oil radiator to be by-passed, has a private, hectic moment at Indianapolis

Hopkirk's MGB, running like a train, passes two contenders for Index of Performance honours, Ferre's Bonnet and the Grandsire Vidal Alpine. All were finishers

stood ready and waiting—a row of 0s.

The minutes ticked past until—first in French, then in English—" All drivers opposite your cars," and the drivers taking the first shift wandered across the road to their starting positions opposite the waiting cars. Then the hush that always precedes the start and the unforgettable moment as 55 drivers scamper across the road at the drop of the flag. The race is on. Though several cars were on the move at about the same time, Pedro Rodriguez' Ferrari, with a terrific amount of snaking and sliding, shot off in the lead, followed by Graham Hill and David Piper; three red Ferraris away first, perhaps to set the expected pattern of the race.

As the red cars came over the White House horizon, their first lap completed, an official rushed out into the middle of

the road and started waving an oil flag violently. Then out went the yellow flags, and one started checking the numbers through, until 54 cars had gone past and by a process of elimination one could establish that it was the extremely fast Maglioli-Baghetti GTO Ferrari that was missing; it had spun at the Esses.

Phil Hill's Ford GT had been last off the start, some 70sec after the flag, but Ginther's sister car took over the lead from Surtees' Ferrari during the second lap. Quickly it began to pull out a commanding lead, lapping the tailenders by lap 3, only 25 miles after the start; lap 3 was completed in 3min 55·4sec, a speed of 127·9 m.p.h. Already the pit stops began. First Phil Hill came in, twice, the second stop being for a long time while misfiring was traced to a blocked jet; the Piper-Rindt

GTO Ferrari, which had shown such great promise, came in and was pushed to the dead car park with a split oil filter. Parkes' Ferrari was also in to have a distributor replaced—so early for these disappointments after such lengthy preparation and training. By 5 p.m. Ginther had a 40sec lead over Surtees' Ferrari, Rodriguez' Ferrari and Graham Hill's Ferrari; and Phil Hill took the Ford GT back into the race from the pits for the fifth time! Baghetti appeared at the pits in the Ferrari that had gone missing on lap 1, about which there had been so much needless flag waving.

Also visiting the pits at this early stage of the race were Verrier's CD, Zeccoli's Alpine, Grandsire's Alpine, Koch's Porsche and Richard's French-entered Elan, which was soon to retire with a

Mike Rothschild crashes his Spitfire right in front of the Rodriguez-Skip Hudson Ferrari. Hudson succeeded in avoiding the spinning car with difficulty

Left: Typical pit stop; Surtees leaps out of this Ferrari, while a mechanic already has fuel flowing into the tank.   A plombier stands by to seal the filler cap, while Vic Barlow of Dunlop checks rear tyre temperatures.   Right: The Hunt-Wagstaff Lotus Elite scored its second, class win

car was wrecked and bounced backwards into the middle of the road. Miraculously Rodriguez' Ferrari, now driven by Hudson, scraped through the wreckage and narrowly missed a stray wheel, though it, too, nearly went out of control. Fortunately, nobody hit the Triumph as it was being manhandled to the side, though there were officials all over the road and the race speed at this point on the course was perhaps 110 m.p.h.

Fastest along the measured kilometre on the Mulsanne straight by this stage was the Briggs Cunningham Cobra, at 183 m.p.h., with 180 m.p.h. fairly general among the faster Ferrari "spiders." Barth's Porsche eight-cylinder Prototype was credited with a lap in 3min 59sec, a speed of 202·76 k.p.h. (125·5 m.p.h.) and the first time a 2-litre car has beaten 200 k.p.h. As the sunshine began to grow a bit thin, and the Sarthe circuit distinctly chilly, the second round of pit stops began at 7 p.m., the race now having endured for rather longer than a modern Grand Prix. Surtees came in, refuelled, and the Ferrari rejoined the race with Bandini behind the wheel. Parkes brought his Ferrari in and stayed at the pit for a very long time. The 5-litre Maserati,

holed radiator after going off the track. By 5.15 the Ferraris hounding round at the Ford's heels began to close up, Surtees making up 7sec at this time. Le Mans was already producing its changes of fortune, but these were early moments in a very long journey. At 5.20 Baghetti rejoined the race, his Ferrari having done one lap to the leaders' 20.

By 5.35 the routine pit stops for driver changes and fuel were beginning, Surtees, Graham Hill and Tavano bringing their Ferraris in simultaneously, which seemed an unnecessary strain on the pits' resources. At 5.42 the leading Ford driven by Ginther came in (to be handed over to Masten Gregory), as did Rolland's Alfa, Dumay's Ferrari, Sears' Cobra and Barth's Porsche (in eighth place). When these stops were over Surtees, still driving, was in the lead 40sec ahead of Gregory, now in Ginther's Ford GT; in third, fourth and fifth places came Guichet, Bonnier and Skip Hudson in Ferraris, the last two having taken over from Graham Hill and Rodriguez respectively.

At almost exactly 6 p.m. came one of those incidents that occur all too often on the very fast curve beneath the Dunlop bridge. Rothschild's Triumph Spitfire, works entered, went out of control and hit the outside bank very hard; the

Above: Alfa Romeo hopes of a team prize were dashed when Masoero spun off coming out of Indianapolis.   The best car of this Giulia team, the Businello-Deserti car, was placed 13th.   Below: Sweeping-up the track after a spin can be tricky, too.   This photograph was taken immediately after Masoero's spin.   Lindner's Jaguar, with a leaking cylinder head gasket, motors slowly by

As dusk falls Bianchi's Ferrari GTO prepares to pass the Marnat-Piot Triumph, which later came to grief when Marnat was overcome by fumes

Trintignant at the wheel, was timed at 192 m.p.h. along the measured kilometre. Keith Ballisat's Sunbeam Tiger burst its engine in a cloud of oil smoke at the Esses and he retired. Paddy Hopkirk came in to change the left-side front wheel. Ben Pon, in the Dutch Racing Team's Porsche, hurtled down to Mulsanne corner, couldn't get round, and took to the escape road undamaged.

Positions at 4 hours

General Classification	Laps	Index of Performance	Index
1 Ferrari (Surtees-Bandini) (126·01 m.p.h.)	60	1 Porsche Barth-Linge	1·307
2 Ford Ginther-Gregory	59	2 Porsche Davis-Mittet	1·306
3 Ferrari G. Hill-Bonnier	59	3 Ferrari Guicher-Vaccarella	1·296
4 Ferrari Guichet-Vaccarella	59	4 Ferrari Surtees-Bandini	1·294
5 Ferrari Rodriguez-Hudson	58	5 Ford GT Ginther-Gregory	1·279
6 Ford Attwood-Schlesser	58	6 Ferrari Rodriguez-Hudson	1·263

With only 4¼ hours gone, No. 15 Ferrari (Rodriguez and Hudson) came into the pits . . . to be wheeled away to the dead car park with a burst oil radiator. No. 11, the Ford GT which had led the race for so long and by such a handsome margin, stood at the pits as the leaders went by a great many times. The Ford challenge, it seemed, was spent somewhat earlier than had been expected, for No. 12, driven by Schlesser, had caught fire on the Mulsanne straight, a tell-tale column of smoke rising into the evening sky. So as the sun went down, Bandini assumed a secure lead, with Guichet's Ferrari second, the 5-litre Maserati (Trintignant up) third, Graham Hill's Ferrari fourth,

Dumay, in the Ecurie National Belge 275LM Ferrari, spent part of the race in contact with the scenery.   Early on he embedded the car in the sand, later he hit something more solid

Neerspach's Cobra fifth (and smoking a litte ominously), Barth's Porsche sixth, Colin Davis's Porsche seventh and then Dumay's Ferrari, after losing ground in the sand at Mulsanne. The very purposeful-looking Lindner-Nocker Jaguar began to sound off colour, due to a blowing head gasket; the car had to be driven round very quietly to complete the 25 laps before the cylinder head could be lifted and a new gasket fitted.

Adding to the incessant clamour of the commentators came the noisy blare of the fairground at the Esses, and the music from the multitude of sideshows. As the light failed, drivers turned on their identification lamps, some of the Ferraris looking like high-speed Christmas trees. Grossman and Tavano sported red and green lamps, the Lindner E-type a single Z-car blue one, while the C.D.s and the Alpines confused each

FIVE TIMES FERRARI...

The Victor: Vaccarella and Guichet (centre) look modest, Graham Hill and Jo Bonnier look puzzled and the Index of Thermal Efficiency winners, Lageneste and Morrogh, look proud—they drove the only French award-winning car.

other by all having green lamps. To us, looking down from the Press stands, the cars' headlamps looked painfully inadequate for the high speeds.

At 9.45 p.m., the multi-tubular B.P. "totem pole" flashed out the news that the Ginther-Gregory Ford GT had retired with gearbox failure, leaving just the Phil Hill-McLaren car to carry the Dearborn hopes. At 10.15 another of Dearborn's links with the Vingt-Quatre Heures was severed when Bolton's A.C. Cobra and Baghetti's Ferrari were involved in an accident between Arnage and the approach to the notorious White House corner, Peter Bolton being taken off to hospital with a cut face and a suspected cracked rib. Unhappily, three spectators who had wandered from the official enclosure lost their lives in this accident. Five minutes later the leading Ferrari was in for another routine stop, Surtees taking the car back into the race after some 2min. By now, 18 of the original field of 55 cars had retired for one reason or another. At around 11 p.m. the Lumsden-Sargent E-type, dark-green sister car to Lindner's aluminium bodied one, went out with gearbox trouble. Just before this, Parkes' and Scarfiotti's Ferrari was out with a suspected broken piston.

The air was bitterly cold, despite the fact that it was midsummer's night, and a steady flow of spectators' cars left the track for the night. Parts of the circuit began to grow misty as the headlamps chased each other round at over 120 m.p.h. Phil Hill and Surtees put in laps in 3min 57sec soon after midnight, nearly 127 m.p.h. in the darkness, and Graham Hill went round in 3min 55sec.

The Maserati came in for brake adjustment, Bertaut brought the CD in for a wheel change. Neerpach brought in the Cobra, well up in fifth place, made a lengthy stop to have the generator repaired and dropped several places . . . and the Maserati, when lying well down in 15th place, retired with gearbox trouble.

Positions at 8 hours

General Classification	Laps	Index of Performance	Index
1 **Ferrari** Surtees-Bandini (124·96 m.p.h.)	119	1 **Porsche** Barth-Linge	1·294
2 **Ferrari** Guichet-Vaccarella	118	2 **Ferrari** Guichet-Vaccarella	1·288
3 **Ferrari** G. Hill-Bonnier	116	3 **Porsche** Davis-Mitter	1·286
4 **Cobra** Gurney-Bondurant	114	4 **Ferrari** Surtees-Bandini	1·282
5 **Ford** Barth-Linge	113	5 **Ferrari** G. Hill-Bonnier	1·252
6 **Ford** P. Hill-McLaren	113	6 **Porsche** Bucher-Ligier	1·237

Hugus' Ferrari, entered by the North American Racing Team, went out when the drive disintegrated as the car sped past the pits, the nose of the final drive denting Lindner's E-type, standing in its own pit. It would have meant at least a broken leg had it hit anyone. For a while, after the next batch of routine pit stops, Vaccarella took the lead in his Ferrari from Surtees, but by 2 a.m. Surtees was back in front again, with the Vaccarella-Guichet car second, Hill (G.) (Maranello Concessionaries' Ferrari) third, Hill now making up quickly for a pit stop of 8min to have a new condenser fitted. Gurney, in the Cobra had very nearly caught Hill's Ferrari and was on the same lap, leading the GT category by a good margin. Next came

the last surviving Ford GT, driven by Hill (P.) and McLaren, then Colin Davis's Porsche and the Grossman-Tavano Ferrari, lying second in the GT category.

Chardonnet's very standard-looking A.C.-Ford (drivers, Mange-de Mortemart), which had been going round steadily and unobtrusively, started to go round even more unobtrusively by about 3.30 a.m., since it was on only sidelamps. At around 4.30, as the sky lightened from the earliest yellow-green to pink, the Piot-Marnat Triumph Spitfire approached the pits area as if to make a pit stop, then veered inexplicably to the left, striking the wall opposite a hard, glancing blow. The car veered over towards the crowded pit counters, at no more than 50 m.p.h., and, losing speed, rammed the bank by the Dunlop bridge head-on, close to the remains of Rothschild's crashed Spitfire. As the officials removed the driver from the wreckage, firemen gave the car a precautionary squirt with the extinguishers as it was smoking threateningly. Piot had hit the bank earlier at Tertre Rouge and had holed the tail; exhaust fumes had got into the car and in hospital he was seriously ill with carbon monoxide poisoning. Only the Hobbs-Slotemaker Spitfire remained of the three cars entered.

Round came the routine stops again, the Bandini-Surtees Ferrari coming in and letting the Guichet-Vaccarella car into the lead, then vice versa, so close were these two after over 12 hours of racing. Lindner's Jaguar circulated in company with one of the two remaining Alfa Romeo Giulia TZ coupés, the third of which had left the road at Indianapolis earlier on. The Barth-Linge Porsche retired out on the circuit with clutch trouble after a fine performance. Almost unnoticed in its reliability, the Salmon-Sutcliffe Aston Martin had moved up to 12th place.

Positions at 12 hours

General Classification	Laps	Index of Performance	Index
1 **Ferrari** Guichet-Vaccarella (123·31 m.p.h.)	177	1 **Ferrari** Guichet-Vaccarella	1·280
2 **Ferrari** Surtees-Bandini	176	2 **Porsche** Davis-Mitter	1·278
3 **Ferrari** G. Hill-Bonnier	173	3 **Ferrari** Surtees-Bandini	1·261
4 **Cobra** Gurney-Bondurant	171	4 **Ferrari** G. Hill-Bonnier	1·236
5 **Ford** P. Hill-McLaren	170	5 **Porsche** Bucher-Ligier	1·235
6 **Porsche** Davis-Mitter	168	6 **Porsche** Pon-Van Zalinge	1·220

Last of the three Ford GTs, the Phil Hill-McLaren car came into the pits when lying fifth at around 5.30 a.m. and, after a lengthy stop, was wheeled away with gearbox troubles. For another hour the order settled down—Ferrari (Guichet and Vaccarella), Ferrari (Surtees and Bandini), Cobra (Gurney and Bondurant), Ferrari (G. Hill and Bonnier)—until suddenly drama struck again and the Surtees-Bandini car (Bandini up) ran out of fuel (due to a split pipe) near Mulsanne, struggled round to the pits and made a lengthy stop. At the same time, the Cobra was also in to have axle oil added. When eventually the two cars rejoined the race, the Cobra first, then the Ferrari, they still lay second

FIVE TIMES FERRARI...

and third, but separated by only one lap instead of four, and the Guichet-Vaccarella Ferrari held an eight-lap lead. Shortly, the Cobra was in again for another lengthy spell.

At 6.53 a.m., the Lindner-Nocker Jaguar E-type came in with clouds of steam blowing from the radiator. The pit crew made a quick survey and decided that, with more than 10 laps to go before they could refill the radiator, the car would never last, so it was driven into the dead car park. The Davis-Mitter Porsche, which had been lying eighth overall and second in the Index of Performance, came in at 6.17 a.m. In one hour the mechanics dropped the gearbox, tightened the flywheel bolts, replaced the clutch and had the car back on the road.

The Cobra was in dire need of engine oil and had three laps to do before completing the requisite 25 laps between refills, so it plodded round slowly. Graham Hill made an unscheduled pit stop at 7.15 a.m., with the left rear wheel collapsing, but was soon away again. After the cold night, Sunday's bright, warm sunshine was more than welcome, and the crowds began to trickle back to the circuit after their night's rest—either that or they roused their stiff joints after sleeping in such dismal places as the tunnels beneath the road. Though the public enclosures were an untidy litter of waste paper, the restaurant and sideshow proprietors had busied themselves overnight, tidying up for the day's trade.

Positions at 16 hours

General Classification	Laps	Index of Performance	Index
1 Ferrari Guichet-Vaccarella (123·5 m.p.h.)	235	1 Ferrari Guichet-Vaccarella	1·278
2 Ferrari Hill-Bonnier	228	2 Ferrari Hill-Bonnier	1·225
3 Ferrari Surtees-Bandini	227	3 Porsche Bucher-Ligier	1·222
4 Ferrari Tavano-Grossman	222	4 Ferrari Surtees-Bandini	1·220
5 Cobra Gurney-Bondurant	221	5 Ferrari Tavano-Grossman	1·217
6 Ferrari Bianchi-Beurlys	220	6 Porsche Koch-Schiller	1·209

By 9 a.m. Sunday, 28 cars remained of the original 55 starters, and the leading four on distance were Ferraris, with a Cobra fifth, then a couple more Ferraris. There didn't seem a great deal of doubt, even at this stage, of the outcome, though it was some slight comfort to the British crowds to see the B.M.C.-entered MGB and Austin-Healey Sprite, single representatives of their marques, still in the race. So was the lone Aston Martin which, at the time, was running under something of a cloud since the organizers claimed that it had replenished the oil in fewer than the stipulated 25 laps and was due to be disqualified.

After a lot of discussion, and an application to the R.A.C. delegate for help, the Aston was indeed disqualified, at 9.51 a.m., when lying 11th. Though it was scarcely the occasion for any excesses of national pride, one did observe that Britain was leading the 1,151 to 1,300 GT class, the only car in it being the Wagstaff-Hunt Lotus Elite, lying 27th out of 28 cars. The disc-jockey in charge of the deafening uproar that pervaded the circuit unearthed from his collection a gem entitled *Les Vingt-Quatre Heures du Mans*, set his machine at "Repeat" and went home. No. 27 Ferrari in the GT category, after climbing to fourth on distance and on Index, began to circulate rather slowly on fewer than its normal 12 cylinders.

The cars that had survived this far, 2,500-odd miles by noon, seemed, as they always do at this stage, to have reached a stage of infinite reliability. The cripples had gone; only the fittest remained and they could go on virtually for ever. The retirement rate had dropped, 25 cars now remaining of the original 55, and the two leaders—Guichet's and Hill's Ferraris—were separated by only six laps, or 50-odd miles in a total of 2,500. The Surtees-Bandini Ferrari in third place was 11 laps behind Hill's car; the Cobra, running with the oil radiator by-passed, led the GT class in fourth, with the Belgian Ferrari fifth and catching up quickly only two laps behind. The two survivors of the original three Giulia TZ Alfas—one of which had crashed—were running like very noisy clockwork with no unscheduled stops and leading their class.

The Colin Davis-Mitter Porsche, once so well placed, retired without a clutch.

Positions at 20 hours

General Classification	Laps	Index of Performance	Index
1 Ferrari Guichet-Vaccarella (123·4 m.p.h.)	292	1 Ferrari Guicher-Vaccarella	1·269
2 Ferrari Hill-Bonnier	286	2 Ferrari Hill-Bonnier	1·229
3 Ferrari Surtees-Bandini	280	3 Porsche Bucher-Ligier	1·227
4 Cobra Gurney-Bondurant	278	4 Porsche Koch-Schiller	1·216
5 Ferrari Tavano-Grossman	276	5 Porsche Pon-Van Zalinge	1·215
6 Ferrari Bianchi-Beurlys	273	6 Ferrari Bianchi-Beurlys	1·210

Routine pit stops continued. Each time the Hill-Bonnier Ferrari, lying second, pulled away again the commentator prophesied that the car would be in trouble. Yet, each time, its lack of power at low revs seemed not to matter as soon as the engine reached its useful range, and the car shot away from under the Dunlop bridge. For some time the Austin-Healey Sprite had been sounding off-tune with a brocken rocker, banging away up the hill from the pits on three cylinders for lap after lap. At 2.30 p.m., with 330 laps completed and 1½ hours still to go, Guichet and Vaccarella seemed set not only to win the race comfortably but to beat the existing all-time distance record for the 24 hours, which stood at 338 laps—only eight more than they had completed. Henry Morrogh, whose Alpine was leading the Index of Thermal Efficiency—and had been doing so for most of the race—is the man in charge of the French end of the Jim Russell Racing Drivers' School at Magnycourt.

By 3.15 p.m. the leading Ferrari had beaten the previous distance-covered record with 45 minutes to spare. Of the 25 cars now left in the race, seven were Ferraris, of a total of 12 Ferrari starters. Even better was the Porsche survival record, with five cars still racing from seven starters.

With 10 minutes to go, the pits area suddenly sorted itself out. A thin blue line of gendarmes formed up alongside the pit counters to keep the crowds at bay, while the 25 cars, with nothing more at stake than to maintain their positions, motored round as if to finish a treasure hunt by teatime. Once again victory went to Enzo Ferrari, and there was some satisfaction, at any rate, in the thought that the second and sixth-placed Ferraris had been entered by the British firm of Maranello Concessionaires.

Le Mans was over for another year, with the Ferrari-Ford-Cobra battle as open as ever.

CLASSIFICATION ON DISTANCE COVERED
(Lap distance: 8·86 miles)

	Car	Type	c.c.	Drivers	Miles	m.p.h.
1	Ferrari	P	3,299	J. Guichet and N. Vaccarella	2,917·7	121·55
2	Ferrari	P	3,977	G. Hill and J. Bonnier	2,872·5	
3	Ferrari	P	3,972	J. Surtees and L. Bandini	2,815.0	
4	Cobra	GT	4,727	D. Gurney and R. Bondurant	2,791·4	
5	Ferrari	GT	2,953	Beurlys and L. Bianchi	2,778·5	
6	Ferrari	P	2,953	I. Ireland and T. Maggs	2,736·4	
7	Porsche	GT	1,967	R. Bucher and G. Ligier	2,699·7	
8	Porsche	GT	1,967	B. Pon and Van Zalinge	2,660·4	
9	Ferrari	GT	2,953	R. Grossmann and L. Tavano	2,633·6	
10	Porsche	P	1,968	G. Koch and H. Schiller	2,627·3	
11	Porsche	GT	1,968	H. Müller and C. Sage	2,582·4	
12	Porsche	GT	1,966	Franc and R. Kerguen	2,574·3	

CLASSIFICATION ON INDEX OF PERFORMANCE

	Car	c.c.	Drivers	Index
1	Ferrari	3,299	Guichet and Vaccarella	1·262
2	Ferrari	3,977	Hill and Bonnier	1.277
3	Porsche	1,967	Bucher and Ligier	1·225
4	Ferrari	2,953	Buerlys and Bianchi	1·212
5	Alpine	1,001	Zeccoli and Masson	1·207
6	Porsche	1,967	Pon and Van Zalinge	1·207

INDEX OF THERMAL EFFICIENCY

	Car	c.c.	Drivers	Index
1	Alpine	1,149	Lageneste and Morrogh	1.48
2	Alpine	1,001	Zeccoli and Masson	1.31
3	Ferrari	3,299	Guichet and Vaccarella	1.28
4	Porsche	1,968	Muller and Sage	1.17
5	Porsche	1,967	Pon and Van Zalinge	1.16
6	Ferrari	2,953	Beurlys and Bianchi	1.15

General Classification: 1,000 to 1,350 c.c.: Alpine (Lageneste and Morrogh); **1,150 to 1,300 c.c.:** Lotus (Wagstaff and Hunt); **1,300 to 1,600 c.c.:** Alfa Romeo (Bussinello and Deserti); **1,600 to 2,000 c.c.:** Porsche (Bucher and Ligier); **2,500 to 3,000 c.c.:** Ferrari (Beurlys and Bianchi); **Over 4,000 c.c.:** Cobra (Bondurant and Gurney).

Fastest Lap (new record): P. Hill (Ford GT), 3 min 49·2 sec, 131·29 m.p.h. **General Classification on Distance:** Over 3,000 c.c.: Ferrari (Guichet and Vaccerella); Under 3,000 c.c.: Porsche (Kerguen and Franc). **G.T.:** Over 2,000 c.c.: Cobra (Bondurant and Gurney); 1,300 to 2,000 c.c.: Porsche (Bucher and Ligier).

BY HENRY N. MANNEY   PHOTOS BY MANNEY AND GEOFF GODDARD

ONCE UPON A TIME there was a great big monster named Fazzazz. He lived in a cave down in Italy hung with old *lambrusco* bottles, hunting trophies, *tagliatelle* presses, athletic supporters that he had faked people out of, money and the skeletons (picked clean) of former friends.

He was quite well off for a monster. Every once in a while he would come out from his cave and beat everybody about the ears with a red club before retiring with yet more money. Sometimes he didn't even have to come out, as the mere mention of his name was enough to give other monsters the pip. Better yet, rulers of neighboring forests would allow him to do pretty much what he wanted for fear that he, with his magical powers, would turn them into hoptoads like Toto Roche. Fazzazz wasn't absolutely infallible, as a Teutonic monster had swiped his prey once or twice, but that was generally because the Fazzazz had dropped his club in the weeds.

Now there appeared on the scene another monster, a very much bigger one from across the sea, who loved to hear his name mentioned in print even more than Fazzazz. Being very crafty, he saw that beating people over the head was the way to do it. So first he beat some local monsters but then he felt that getting his own name mentioned in Fazzazz' territory would be nice, too. Summoning up his best smile, (and holding his blue and white club behind his back) he approached the Fazzazz with many gifts and a proposal that the Fazzazz should rest (as he was very old) and that he (called Fawd) should do the beating for him. All he got was a splitting headache and a distinct feeling that he had narrowly escaped being jobbed.

So he went back to his own country and, getting Louisville Slugger to design him a new club, set out to battle. After a couple of false tries because he didn't really know how to hold it properly, he met up with Fazzazz in some godawful place named Luh Mahnz for the big ball of wax. There was a beautiful maiden as prize, just dripping with money. Now Fawd had brought some light and scientific clubs, worked out by computer, but Fazzazz had lots of the old heavy red ones. Whish, whish, whish they went at it with clubs breaking right and left, and it looked as if Fawd was going to win for a while as he was faster and the red clubs kept breaking. But when you bash light ones against heavy ones and you only have three light ones with weak handles, what happens? That's right, Virginia, Fazzazz now has more money, the bint, and a Fawd-skin rug on the wall. With a checkered flag sticking out the back.

This year's Le Mans looked, on paper, like a pretty good race. At least for the first four hours, which is just about as long as the real hurrying lasts for. Ferrari, of course, was highly favored to win, as the 12-cyl racing machinery (sorry, GT prototypes) is very highly developed by this time, being both reliable and fast. Showing that the competition worried him, though, Ferrari brought no less than three 4-liter roadsters (Jo Bonnier/Graham Hill, John Surtees/Lorenzo Bandini and the NART Pedro Rodriguez/Skip Hudson) plus three 3.3s of the same shape and configuration (Jean Guichet/Nino Vaccarella, Mike Parkes/Ludovico Scarfiotti, Giancarlo Baghetti/Umberto Maglioli) to do battle for the outright win. Backing these up were a couple of mid-engined 275 LM coupes (Léon Dumay/Pierre Langlois, David Piper/Jochen Rindt) and several GTOs entered under various handles ("Beurlys"/Lucien Bianchi, Innes Ireland/Tony Maggs, Ed Hugus/Jose Rosinski, Bob Grossman/Fernando Tavano) in case all the big bangers fell by the wayside. This makes a gross of busy liddle cylinders, which is a pretty fearsome thought if you are running in the same race.

Ranged against *Il Mago di Marnaello* were the brutal 5-liter Maserati coupe (Maurice Trintignant/Andre Simon), rebodied and re-chassised since last year, a pretty 5.3 Chevy-engined Iso coupe ("Ficho" Berney/Pierre Noblet), two Ford-engined Sunbeam Tigers (4260 cc) under the benevolent hand of Marcus Chambers for Keith Ballisat/Pierre Dubois and Peter Procter/Jimmy Blumer, and three Lola-based Ford coupes (4181-cc pushrod engines) driven by Richie Ginther/Masten Gregory, Dick Atwood/Jo Schlesser, and Phil Hill/Bruce McLaren, similar to that run in the 1000 km but with detail mods here and there. Very purposeful they were, all nicely finished in blue and white, and Ferrari engineer Forghieri was heard to remark that he would love to have something neat like that to play with. Wot's that about the grass being greener?

There was trouble a-brewing in the GT category as well for the invincible GTOs as Carroll Shelby appeared with two *tipo* Daytona 4727-cc coupes for Bob Bondurant/Dan Gurney and Chris Amon/Jochen Neerpasch, the latter being entered by the evergreen Briggs Cunningham complete with sideman Signor Alfred Momo. Amon's car was the original coupe, with aerodynamic wheel skirts on the back, while Gurney's was a new one. AC itself, not to be outdone, brought its own coupe of slightly different shape (Jack Sears/Peter Bolton), which looked even fiercer. Added to these as outsiders were Mike Salmon/

Ferrari, Ferrari, Ferrari, Cobra, Ferrari, Ferrari, Porsche, Porsche,

Peter Sutcliffe's light green Aston coupe, two light alloy E types (Peter Sargent/Peter Lumsden, Peter Lindner/Peter Nocker) and a stock-bodied AC Cobra for J. C. Magne and J. de Mortemart. Among the lesser capacities, there were two 8-cyl Porsche coupes in 904 skins (Edgar Barth/Herbert Linge, Colin Davis/Gerhard Mitter) plus a herd of 904s in GT, three bellowing Alfa Giulia *tubolares*, Paddy Hopkirk/Andrew Hedges' MG-B, one each of Elan and Elite, a Min-based Deep Sanderson, two blown Panhard CDs with tail fins on, three highly modded Spitfires for Mike Rothschild/Bob Tullius, David Hobbs/Rob Slotemaker and Marnat/Piot, a GTO bodied Healey Sprite (Bradley/Baker), and shoals of Renault-engined Alpines and René Bonnets to make up the 55 starters. Not making it to the starting line, thus letting in two of the reserves, were the ATS, which was held up in customs, an Alpine 904 and a Deep Sanderson that shunted, and Lutz/Osteen's 1800-cc Elva.

Le Mans is a high-speed course and nothing more clearly illustrates it than the list of practice times, by which the order of the Le Mans start was determined this year. Surtees was at the head of the line with a 3 min 42 sec (135.636 mph), an appreciable improvement on Scarfiotti's hot mark in the April trials of 3:43.8, but Ginther's Ford GT was next up with 3:45.3 ahead of Rodriguez' 4-liter Ferrari, Feel Heel's Ford, Bonnier's 4-liter, Parkes' 3.3, Guichet's 3.3, Piper's 275 LM, Attwood's Ford and Gurney's Cobra, fastest of the GTs with 3:56.1. It wasn't till you got eight cars further along, past all the big bores including the Iso, when the first 8-cyl Porsche appeared. Another 15, and Biscaldi's Alfa that took third overall in the Targa Florio. Slowest of all was Lelong's highly streamlined CD at 5:20.8, which illustrates one reason why most thinking drivers dislike Le Mans so . . . it is no fun to close on something, racing itself, while doing anything up to 100 mph quicker in the dark. Be that as it may, there is apparently one Dick Tracy born every minute, as the 55 drivers lined up in their little circles showed every indication to get on with the race. No rain, although the usual clouds were hanging about, an unseasonal cool temperature after the tropical Spa, and, well, not all the drivers were in their circles for at the last moment one of the busybody officials ran across the road and commenced a pushing match with Innes Ireland. It seems that Innes, having a right-hand drive Ferrari, was slightly to one side of his appointed place. Bloody clockwork gestapos.

Patter, patter, patter as all the little feet, led by someone from Ireland's approximate position, rushed across the road and leapt feverishly (they hoped) into the proper car. That pregnant moment of silence, and then a swelling crescendo of engines bursting into life, gears clashing, and tires squealing as Rodriguez' white-nosed Ferrari roadster broadsided out into the fairway and headed for the Dunlop bridge. Followed by what seemed an unceasing sea of red, he shot under it, and up over the rise to the Esses, the rest of the column half obscured by dust kicked up from the road surface. The enormous Maserati was late getting away, blubbering furiously, but by far the last was the unfortunate Phil Hill, Le Mans specialist, whose Detroit iron had refused to come to life on command.

Barely had he departed, leaving the excited buzz of Froggies commanding each other to sit down, when there was a 12-cyl humming noise down the straight from White House. Before Rodriguez could appear once more, several officials appeared on the track in front of the pits and commenced an extraordinary leaping about with red flags. Our first thought was that there had been an enormous shunt somewhere blocking the track or failing that, they were stopping the race because of the somewhat premature start! Closer inspection showed, as the startled drivers slowed to avoid collecting the foolhardly officials, that the flags were yellow-and-red ones—Piper's 275 LM had burst its oil filter on takeoff and had laid a gooey trail down the track through the Esses before expiring at Tertre Rouge. Baghetti was also missing in one of the 3.3 Ferrari roadsters, but his malady was that the clutch had stuck open.

Well, we figured, there was the motor race with the Ferraris out front, but it was not over just yet; the first car to heave into view leading the second lap was none other than R. Ginther, Esq. in the quickest of the Fords. Profiting from the getuttle, he had hauled himself up on the peloton of Ferraris and using their not inconsiderable drafts as stepping-stones down the Mulsanne straight, had flitted past them into the lead. By the end of the straight, he had glanced at his rev counter and had been slightly shaken to see it reading 7200 or approximately 210 mph. The engines, although pushrod, had been tested up to 7700 but 6500 was supposed to be the race limit in the interests of reliability. Once in front, though, there was no point in doing an after-you-Claude so he carried on, followed closely by a stern-faced Graham Hill, Surtees and Rodriguez, Parkes at two second or so more, Guichet towing Sears' AC coupe, Gurney's Cobra staving off Tavano's GTO, Salmon's noisy Aston, Attwood's Ford leading Barth's Porsche, Lindner's

The start—and Rodriguez leads the pack, if only briefly.

The winning Ferrari, trying to straighten out the Esses.

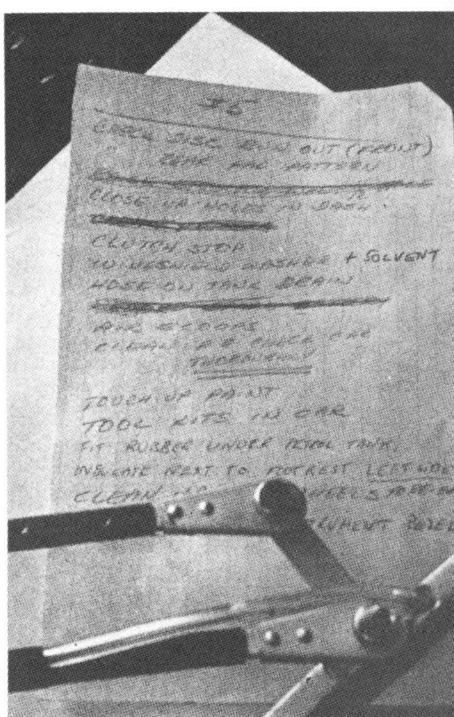

Job list for Cobra mechanics.

Jag, Ireland's GTO and Davis' other 8-cyl Porsche, and then bunches of Beurlys' GTO, Sargent's Jag, Pon's Porsche, Koch's Ditto, Procter's Sunbeam, Muller and Buchet's 904s, Amon's Cobra, and then a big gap before P. Hill's stammering Ford, Dewez' 904, Hugus' GTO, Dumay's 275 LM (which had spun), Richard's Elan, Ballisat's Sunbeam, Bussinello's Alfa, Magne's AC, Biscaldi's Alfa and the first of the Alpines with Mauro Bianchi at the wheel, followed by a mixed heap of Spitfires, Alpines and assorted BMC machinery.

We half expected to see the Ferraris put on a little steam in their traditional fashion, but on the next time around Ginther was even further in front, the blue and white coupe cornering like a rocket under the Dunlop bridge, and he continued to work on a lead which lengthened out to some 41 sec at the end of the first hour. Regardless of this provocation, the Ferraris of Surtees, Rodriguez and G. Hill were traveling in tight formation waiting for something to happen, backed up a few seconds behind by Guichet's 3.3, which was taking an extremely tight line through the Dunlop corner. Gurney, surprisingly enough, was next up in the rumbling Cobra and thus was the first of the GTs while Attwood had made up for an indifferent start by holding down seventh about 2:30 behind Ginther's sister car. Poor Phil Hill, beset with a foul-running machine, had made about a stop a lap before the trouble was diagnosed as a blocked carburetor jet and cured. His engine had gone sour in the last practice and had been changed, all except the carburetors, of course, the day before! Ferrari was paying a bit of a price, though, for Baghetti had struggled around to the

pits and then lost about 20 laps getting his clutch repaired while the tremendously quick Parkes had one of his distributor shafts seize and made several stops trying to sort it out. Misfiring from this cause eventually cracked a few pistons. The other grizzly, the big Maserati, came in to repair a broken accelerator pedal on the first lap and was somewhat delayed. At least it was still running, which was more than you could say for Richards' Elan (core plug), Piper and the Deep Sanderson which lost all its water. At least half of the Alpines seemed to have stopped out on the course for running repairs which makes one think about race preparation, doesn't it?

About 5:24 P.M. Rodriguez came in for fuel and a change to Skip Hudson, followed shortly afterwards by Surtees, Graham Hill and Grossman all in a bunch. In spite of the usual comic Italian pit stop, enough time was saved so that when Ginther came in 15 min later to refuel, on going out he had lost the lead to Fearless John Surtees in No. 19 Ferrari, and the others of Guichet, Bonnier and Rodriguez were following the Ford well within striking distance. Gurney had dropped to seventh, just behind Salmon's Aston as the result of a slow pit stop, and Barth's Porsche, Attwood's Ford and the big Maserati were next up with Trintignant busily making up time. Phil Hill, in the other Lola-Ford, had finally cleared the carburetor trouble with the aid of Ford's illustrious panel of engineers and was throbbing along at a fine rate.

About this time of day it is very interesting to rest against a pine tree in the Esses and watch the action. There are still lots of cars running, and they come whooping in bunches over the top of the hill, wheels barely touching as they crest the top, and commence shouldering each other aside with much blipping and shrilling of brakes before they line up to enter the Esses proper. Surprisingly enough, many of the bigger fish seem to have shorter braking distances than the smaller ones, or perhaps it is the drivers, and the Alpines and so forth are always getting their light cut off as some enormous rumbleguts like Gurney's Cobra moves into the queue. The little ones generally make way, perhaps because they know that Gurney would take it anyway, and then scuttle like crazy to get a tow down to Tertre Rouge in the draft. For the life of me, I don't see how 100 people a race aren't squashed in the Esses, as it is black-shiney with oil or rubber and they come in at a helluva rate. Gurney was boom-

Winner of the 1600–2000 class, the Buchet/Ligier Porsche.

Bondurant, and the Koch/Schiller Porsche at Mulsanne.

AC Cars entry—the Sears/Bolton Cobra coupe.

ing in practically under the lip of the protecting bank, hanging it out one way and then the other, while Surtees and Ginther were very fast but neat. Scarfiotti, whom I have always regarded as fast but unspectacular, was in a tearing hurry with Parkes' car to make up for its lack of speed and gave us some anxious moments going chippa chippa under braking and then horsing the back end around. We had already seen one shunt and didn't want another. Rothschild's Triumph had been looking more and more peculiar under the Dunlop bridge, cornering in a sawtooth fashion, but then it broke loose completely (rumor had it that the diff or a wishbone came off) and backed into the bank. In the Esses, there was considerably less room to avoid something like that and so we viewed with alarm Noblet's lurching tail-slides in the big Iso, the Maserati's little bursts of throttle, which resulted in sizeable sidewise jumps, and Paddy Hopkirk losing sales for BMC by his lurid cornering of the MG-B with first one rear wheel in the air and then the other. The great fun, though, was when Ballisat's Sunbeam crept in with a holed piston causing great clouds of smoke. He stopped right around the corner but, with true obstinacy, when shut off it continued to run on and brought visibility down to zero until something inside got just a little bit too hot to continue.

As night started to fall, the second set of pit stops began to come up, but even so some times were interesting. Surtees had been lapping about 3:53, averaging 125 mph, but Bandini, taking over, dropped to 4:01 and Bonnier 4:03 while Ginther was turning 3:52s. The quickest of all was P. Hill, who was doing 3:50, but then he was back in 32nd position somewhere. Hudson took over the Rodriguez NART roadster and was cornering quickly, if a trifle untidily, when it suddenly disappeared with what was variously described as head gasket (sealing ring) and/or gearbox and then Attwood found little flickering lights in his rear view mirror following him down the Muldoon straight. He bailed out just after the signaling pits, ever mindful of the many gallons of fuel aboard, just before the whole Ford went up with a whoosh. Scarcely had this news been assimilated when Parkes' big Ferrari went out with cracked pistons and then Masten Gregory, after 10 enjoyable laps in Ginther's Ford, found that he could only get first and second on the Colotti gearbox. The fault was unrepairable and to the imaginary sound of clubs whishing through the air, the

score on the mourner's bench stood at Ferrari 2, Ford 2. Shortly afterwards, the generator and brakes packed up simultaneously on the spectacular Maserati, which had pulled itself up to third, and so at the commencement of the sixth hour, at 10 P.M., the leader board was occupied by Ferrari-Ferrari-Ferrari (Surtees, Guichet, G. Hill), Cobra-Cobra (Neerpasch, Gurney), Porsche-Porsche (Barth, Davis), Ferrari-Ferrari-Ferrari (Ireland, Grossman, Bianchi, all GTOs) and then the Aston and Iso before P. Hill's Ford in 13th. All very normal for Le Mans except for the Cobras.

The dead of night at Le Mans is the only proper time to be there as most of the daily paper and *Paris Match* idlers are gone and one can watch the inevitable dramas in relative peace and quiet. Mechanics drowse around or sort hammers, the team manager is busy taking bulletins from the signaling pits at Mulsanne, and if nothing else is doing one can watch some of the long-range repairing jobs which take three or four days in the average garage. The Jags were in dead trouble as Sargent's had broken its gearbox and Lindner's was having its head gasket changed (unsuccessfully as it turned out), suffering a further indignity when Hugus in the Ferrari GTO had its diff blow up when passing the pits and the nosepiece caught the Jaguar in the sternsheets. Baghetti walked in from White House with a depressed expression on his already somber face as he had taken to the bushes to avoid Bolton's tumbling Cobra coupe and bent the Ferrari too seriously to continue. What Giancarlo didn't know at the time was that three young men had crept under cover of darkness into the shrubbery

Reliable, but not fast enough, was the Berney/Noblet Iso.

Ford-Ferrari-Ford sandwich (Attwood-Parkes-Hill) at Mulsanne.

The homely, but purposeful, Ford GT.

LE MANS

bordering the track and had been killed instantly as the Ferrari ran over them. Shortly afterwards, Procter strolled in from the other direction after a bit of the crank fell off (anyone know anything about 275 Fords? asked Marcus Chambers) and the Neerpasch/Amon Cobra, after a stop to repair the generator, was disqualified for putting fire into the flat battery with a fresh one.

As the night drew on, it slowly became clear that all was not too well in the Ferrari camp in spite of the absence of the usual inter-family strife. Both of the big 4-liters of Surtees and G. Hill were suffering from substantial water leaks probably caused by blowing sealing rings. In addition, Surtees' was dropping fuel and later stopped on the course when a petrol pipe broke off inside the tank, while Hill's changed one or more condensers, had a dodgy clutch, and possibly low gear gone as it motored away from the pits very gently indeed, blubbering as it went. There was a fine old punch-up at one of No. 19's pit stops as Bandini had just been in, forgotten to add water, and came in again to find the rad. cap seal gone. There was much hollering and team manager Dragoni pushing Bandini around (who went off pouting) so he could invent a fresh batch of excuses and then in the middle of all this Briggs Cunningham started a real row by inquiring why more than two mechanics were working on the car. Now there was some bad blood in this as a Ferrari spy had been the one who narked on the disqualified Cobra to the commissaires. Briggs knew which one because he used to have Ferraris. The not unsurprising result was that Cunningham got chased back to his pits while Bandini got let off the hook, largely because Ferrari occupies a very favored position at Le Mans. Besides the fact that many less people would come if Ferrari wasn't there (it is rumored that it is the only team to get starting money), one or two of the high ACO officials have connections with the Maranello firm in a business sense and are often seen on the stand at the motor shows. Of course it would be too much to expect the French, let alone the Italians, to stick to the rules, but it would be nice to feel that they applied the same for everyone. Salmon's Aston Martin, running in 11th place, later got disqualified because it had allegedly refilled with oil at the wrong time.

The only really healthy Ferrari was the remaining 3.3 of Guichet/Vaccarella, which was making its routine pit stops and whistling by rapidly in the dark. As a result of time lost by the other two, he was well in the lead but the 4-liters managed to hold onto the next two positions ahead of Gurney/Bondurant (who had stopped to bypass a leaky oil rad.) and P. Hill/McLaren's Ford at half distance—that is to say at 4 ayem on a frosty morning. Barth's Porsche 8 was out with clutch trouble while Davis' occupied sixth (but would retire from the same thing later), and the GTOs of Grossman and Ireland were suffering from various ailments of the clutch and gearbox which would seriously slow them later on. The Iso was having its rear suspension taken apart to change the brake pads, no less than three Alpines were in the pits at once being attended to, two of the shockingly noisy Alfas were running like trains after Rolland's had shunted at Indianapolis, five of the 904 Porsches were still motoring with Buchet's in 11th, the MG was going again after having its radiator filler neck

wrenched off by an enthusiastic *plombeur*, the Elite made yet another stop to repair its generator, and 22 of the 55 starters were out.

Twelve hours to go as dawn started to lighten the sky; 12 hours as Bonnier made a pit stop to change the brake pads and the Cobra and Ford passed into third and fourth places. Just then we got the shock of our lives as Marnat's Triumph, easing into the pit lane, slowly veered outward and bounced off the wall opposite the pits, trickled slowly down with faster machinery blasting past on both sides, bounced off the advertising hoarding just past the Alpine pit where two cars were being worked on, and cut back across the track to crash against the point where the road to Le Mans leaves the track. He had, a few laps previously, broken the exhaust system by backing into something solid and the resulting fracture had gassed him with carbon monoxide. Yellow lights went on as the fire laddies went into action and the unfortunate driver was removed to the hospital; it is a mercy that the Alpines weren't collected or that Phil Hill, rocketing through into third, managed to miss this wandering object.

Phil Hill, knowing Le Mans like the back of his hand, was really motoring in the half-light and justifying all the trust that Ford put in the car. On the 187th lap he set up a new record of 3:49.4 (131.375 mph), but shortly afterward drew in with despairing signs to team manager John Wyer. After some consultation, the mechanics set to work on the gearbox in a curiously lethargic fashion, but soon the car was pushed away. Perhaps there was something in the little bird's voice that whispered "oil pressure." In any case, even as the Ferraris snarled by to pick up the first three places again, it was an admirable performance for a maiden time at Le Mans. The Fords have proven their speed; now for some endurance.

Continued on page 148

Ferrari Wins, Ford Fizzles

FOR the fifth year in succession Enzo Ferrari showed everyone how to win the Le Mans 24-hour race when his cars outlasted—but did not entirely outpace—the Ford challenge. The 1964 cleansweep gave Ferrari his eighth Le Mans triumph since the war.

Ferraris also took second, third, fifth, sixth and ninth places, won at record speed, won the Index of Performance, and had seven finishers out of 12 starters.

But although Ferraris again proved their stamina—assisted in no small measure by weight of numbers—the Dearborn challenge showed itself to be a very real one.

A Ford GT led the race for the first 20 laps, even after a bad start, and another driven by 1958/61/62-winner Phil Hill turned in a new course record at 131.67 m.p.h. All three Fords were out of the race by 5.30 a.m. on the second day, but the impact had been felt, and there is no doubt that Maranello is now well aware of the presence of Ford.

The other Anglo-Americans, the AC-Cobras (out of Shelby), split the Ferrari ranks by winning the GT class and finishing fourth overall — with conducting by the redoubtable and great all-rounder Dan Gurney, with co-driver Bondurant who is American in spite of his Gallic-sounding name. Unfortunately the 7-litre Galaxie-engined o.h.c. AC-Cobra prototype was not really ready in time for the race, but wisecracking Carroll Shelby had no cause for complaint with his GT win, for that, is the category which he set out to dominate. Ford thus played a large part in the vanquishing of the marque Ferrari in the GT class, and quite definitely frightened the Italian equipe in the prototype deal.

The British-entered AC-Cobra was not so lucky. Dragged into a series of British newspaper stories a few days before the race when it was tested on the M1 motorway at speeds of around 190 m.p.h. (see London Letter), it was involved in a just-before-midnight crash with Baghetti's 3.3-litre Ferrari prototype and three spectators were killed. Cobra driver

Peter Bolton was hospitalised, but is progressing well, and Baghetti was unhurt. The three unfortunate spectators were sitting in a completely unauthorised and fearfully dangerous position near White House, and their bodies weren't found until nearly half-an-hour after the crash; Baghetti had not even known he had mown them down.

Driver injury rate was low this year. The Rothschild/Tullius Triumph Spitfire crashed spectacularly under Dunlop Bridge before the third hour, the car hitting the left bank after the pit area, bouncing off into the centre of the road where it narrowly missed the Rodriguez/Hudson Ferrari, ran along the grass and finally came to a stop without hitting anything else. The driver, Mike Rothschild, looked in poor shape and was taken away unconscious, but in fact he was not badly injured.

Strangely, after 12½ hours of racing, it was one of the other works Spitfires which crashed, but Jean-Louis Marnat suffered only minor injuries when his car hit the bank opposite the

GRAHAM HILL heads main pack away from start, but Rodriguez in sister Ferrari is already out of view.

pit area and also crashed into the bank near the Dunlop Bridge at about 100 m.p.h. He had made a pit-call some four laps earlier after damaging the car in a spin, and it was later found that the exhaust system had split and the fumes had overcome him just before the final crash. The third works Spitfire went on to 21st place overall, and 16th in the Index of Performance.

Another unfortunate accident to spectators occurred when a Martini sign on which they were perched collapsed just before the start at 4 p.m. Two of them broke their spines and eight others were seriously injured.

At exactly 4 p.m. on the Saturday Prince Metternich brought down the flag and after the customary patter of large and tiny feet, Rodriguez was away, and, in fact, led the mob through Mulsanne. He was followed by Graham Hill in the British-entered Ferrari, and behind him was David Piper (sixth last year) in the GTO Ferrari, Mike Salmon in the ex-works 212 Aston, Noblet in the amazing Iso Rivolta and Surtees in the four-litre works Ferrari. Ginther had had a poor start but was really eating his way through the field. His team-mate Phil Hill had fared even worse for his

FORD-POWERED trio in action — but none of them finished the race. Sunbeam Tigers (8 and 9) about to be lapped again by ill-fated Ford GT.

HEADLIGHTS blazing in the dusk, a horde of GTs swing into the oil- and rubber-coated Arnage Hairpin.

LE MANS 24 HOURS

GT-CLASS-winning AC-Cobra of Gurney and Bondurant takes un-successful E-type under braking.

BELOW: Cobra's Carroll Shelby looks on while Gurney adjusts Bon-durant's helmet at first pit stop.

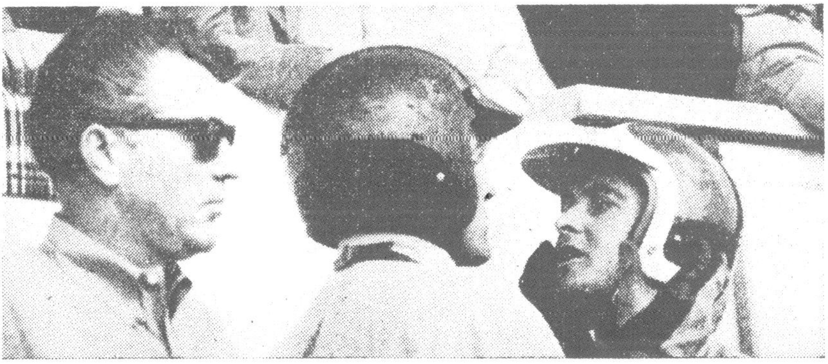

Ford GT was a reluctant starter and he was last away.

Ford's Early Lead

Dumay, in the Belgian 3.3-litre Ferrari prototype, managed to spin at Tertre Rouge on the first lap and the resulting mix-up caused things to slow a little; Baghetti stopped halfway round with clutch trouble, but Ginther was forcing his way relentlessly through. With only one lap gone Ginther took his blue and white Ford past the three scarlet Ferraris, but it was more than obvious that all drivers of the Italian cars had been instructed to play it cool and rely on stamina. The big and ugly Simon/Trintignant Maserati V8 made a sluggish start, but a pit-stop revealed a chunk of sponge in one of the fuel air-intakes.

After only 15 minutes' racing Piper retired his Ferrari with a spit oil-filter housing. Meanwhile Ginther and the Ford continued to pull away and after 25 minutes' racing was 20 minutes ahead of the next Ferrari (Graham Hill) in second place.

Ginther was lapping consistently at around 127 m.p.h. Phil Hill started a succession of pit-stops for misfiring troubles during which time a car-burettor vent was tightened, and the plugs were changed. Baghetti, mean-while, got back into the race. Ginther was setting the pace, John Wyer's strategy seeming to be to set a hare to break the opposition — but the opposition, with their weight of num-bers, weren't having any! Ginther was 32sec. ahead of Surtees after 40 minutes. Parkes made his second pit-stop for plugs; Richard's Lotus Elan ran out of water and was retired,

and Phil Hill came in yet again with a misfiring engine. This time the mechanics found a lump of rubbish blocking an air-intake pipe, and the car at last went away on eight healthy cylinders. After 50 minutes Ginther led the Ferraris by more than 40sec., and the British-entered AC-Cobra led the Shelby-entered Cobra. With typical zest Rodriguez shot past Hill, set his sights on Surtees and broke the lap record at 3min. 50.9sec. in the process.

At 5 p.m. the positions were: Gin-ther; Surtees; Rodriguez; Hill; Gui-chet; Gurney. The last-named Cobra driver had passed the British-entered car. The incredibly fast (and noisy) Alfa Romeo Giulia TZ led the 1.6-litre cars, and the peculiar blown twin-cylinder Rene Bonnet of Bourbon Parma was ahead of the small car brigade. Both Sunbeam Tiger V8s were circulating, but their bid was to be short-lived.

Rodriguez was first to come in for fuel. Surtees and Graham Hill were next, and both rejoined the race with-out changing drivers. Rodriguez change over with Hudson, and Frenchman Guichet handed over to Sicilian Vaccarella.

The refuelling put Ginther two minutes ahead of the field and he stuck it out until almost 6 p.m. before he brought the Ford in, but when the blue and white car rejoined the race Surtees was 36sec. ahead of the field —a lead which he commenced to in-crease. At 6 p.m. the leaders were: S u r tees/Bandini; Ginther/Gregory; Guichet/Vaccarella; Hill (G)/Bon-nier; Rodriguez/Hudson; Salmon/Sut-cliffe (Aston Martin); Gurney/Bon-

durant; Barth/Linge (8-cyl. Porsche); Attwood/Schlesser (Ford GT); Trin-tignant/Simon (Ford GT).

The Sunbeam Tigers held 24th and 26th places respectively but did not impress. The Deep Sanderson retired after losing all its water, the Roths-child Spitfire crashed under Dunlop Bridge, and Masoero crashed in one of the Alfa TZs, receiving only slight injuries.

Exit the Fords

At this stage the two works eight-cylinder prototype 2-litre Porsches led the Index of Performance and were very fast.

After four hours the first of the Ford GTs was out of the race when Schlesser's car caught fire after leav-ing Mulsanne Corner. Schlesser is very good at getting out of Ford GTs in a hurry (he completely wrote one off in the April Le Mans trials), and he got clear away from the car be-fore the flames grew. A fuel pipe had fractured at the rear-end of the car and the petrol had dripped on to the exhaust system.

And then two more were out. To keep it in the Ford family the Ballisat/ Dubois Sunbeam Tiger blew up in the biggest possible way at Tertre Rouge. Although the engine flew to pieces Dubois couldn't get it to stop and for some time it pumped a pall of oily brown smoke over the circuit. Rodriguez, already worried by an alarming oil consumption, had his problems solved when the Ferrari broke a half-shaft.

Around 10 o'clock the main thrust of the Ford challenge came to an end when the Ginther/Gregory GT broke its Colotti-Francis gearbox. The biggest threat to the Ferraris now was the Maserati of Trintignant/Simon, the AC-Cobras and the remaining Ford GT, although few expected it to last the rest of the long, long night.

The Surtees/Bandini car howled on through the darkness, followed by the Hill/Bonnier car, with the big Mas-erati in third place (it had been ex-ceeding 190 m.p.h. on Mulsanne straight). Gurney had moved into fifth place with the blustering Cobra coupe, but he was one place down on the sister car of Neerpach and Chris Amon. The works Porsches

(Continued on page 148)

LE MANS

Continued

were seventh and eighth overall, followed by the British-entered Ireland/Maggs Ferrari GTO which was experiencing clutch slip.

At 10 p.m. the Bolton Cobra and the Baghetti Ferrari were involved in the unfortunate crash which killed three spectators, and around the same time Rosinski's three-litre Ferrari GTO burst its differential as it passed the pits; pieces flew over the track and hit a stationary Jaguar and its mechanic.

At the witching hour the big Maserati retired with a flat battery—a quite definite change from its more usual mechanical failures. The remaining Ford GT was going well in seventh place. Graham Hill had a rear wheel partially collapse on the four-litre Ferrari, but by catching it in time he was able to take the car carefully to the pit and have the wheel changed.

Cobra Heads GT Class

In the early hours of Sunday morning it was still Ferraris 1-2-3 with Gurney's Cobra fourth, the Hill/McLaren Ford GT fifth and the amazing two-litre Porsches sixth and seventh, still leading the Index. The remaining Sunbeam Tiger was retired with severe lack of oil pressure. The leading Ferrari had to pit-stop for braking troubles, and the 3.3-litre car of Guichet and Vaccarella passed into the lead.

It was a perfect night without the infamous morning mist on Mulsanne. Marnat crashed his Spitfire at about 4.30 a.m., but was lucky to get away with a broken bone in his hand. There were 32 survivors when the sun came up, and Vaccarella led the Surtees/Bandini car by one lap. Gurney's Cobra was third, six laps behind the leader. The surviving Ford GT had moved into fourth place. At this stage Ferrari had taken the lead in the Index of Performance.

One of the big surprises of the race was the performance of the sole Iso Rivolta—a Corvette-engined coupe and the heaviest car in the contest. For much of the night it held 12th place overall.

Ford's hopes were dashed when the Hill/McLaren car was retired just before 5 30 a.m. — another gearbox failure. Half an hour later there were 30 cars left, and the Iso Rivolta made a lengthy pit-stop which dropped it to 21st place. A great loss was the Barth/Linge Porsche, and with its going Ferrari got back the Index of Performance lead.

From then on it became a tour, with Guichet/Vaccarella holding their lead of seven laps over the Hill/Bonnier car. Surtees had been delayed with a broken oil pipe and the Tavano/Grossman Ferrari GTO had moved ahead of the Gurney/Bondurant Cobra into fourth place and took the GT-class lead. Gurney, however, was chasing the Ferrari.

Porsche's second eight-cylinder prototype had a new clutch fitted, but such was the vibration after the change that Colin Davis was forced to retire. Nevertheless the Type 904s were going great guns with the Buchet/Ligier car in eighth place.

With four hours to go there were 25 cars circulating in brilliant sunshine, and the Guichet/Vaccarella car was six laps ahead of the Hill/Bonnier machine. With the Surtees/Bandini car back in third place it was Ferrari 1-2-3, followed by the Gurney/Bondurant Cobra (again leading the GT class), then three more Ferraris, and three Porsche 904s.

And so it ran out, with the winning Ferrari getting an especially big cheer from the French crowd as local-boy Guichet shared in the victory. Ferrari had done it again, but Ford had left a new lap record, and one of their engines had won the GT category.

Only 10 British cars were in this year's race, and the highest-placed was the MGB of Paddy Hopkirk and Andrew Hedges which took 19th place overall and seventh place in the 1301-2000c.c. GT class. The MG was a very production-type car and its performance was impressive.

The Lotus Elite of Wagstaff and Hunt won the GT class up to 1300c.c. for the second year running.

RESULTS: 1, Guichet/Vaccarella (3.3 Ferrari P), 121.6 m.p.h., 2917.7 miles; 2, G. Hill/Bonnier (4.0 Ferrari P), 2872.5 miles; 3, Surtees/Bandini (4.0 Ferrari P), 2815 miles; 4, Gurney/Bondurant (4.7 AC-Cobra GT), 2791.4 miles; 5, Bianchi/Beurlys (3.0 Ferrari GT), 2778.5 miles; 6, Ireland/Maggs (3.0 Ferrari GT), 2736.4 miles; 7, Buchet/Ligier (2.0 Porsche GT), 2699.7 miles; 8, Pon/van Zalinge (2.0 Porsche GT), 2660.4 miles; 9, Tavano/Grossman (3.0 Ferrari GT), 2633.6 miles; 10, Koch/Schiller (2.0 Porsche GT), 2627 miles; 11, Muller/Sage (2.0 Porsche GT), 2582.4 miles; 12, Franc/Kerguen (2.0 Porsche GT), 2574.3 miles; 13, Bussinello/Deserti (1.6 Alfa Romeo GT), 2565.6 miles; 14, Noblet/Berney (5.3 Iso Rivolta P), 2560.3 miles; 15, Sala/Biscaldi (1.6 Alfa Romeo GT), 2549 miles; 16, Dumay/van Ophen (3.3 Ferrari P), 2491.5 miles; 17, de Lageneste/Morrogh (1.1 Alpine P), 2436.5 miles; 18, de Mortemart/Fressinet (4.7 AC-Cobra GT), 2415.6 miles; 19, Hopkirk/Hedges (1.8 MG-B GT), 2398.8 miles; 20, Zeccoli/Masson (1.0 Alpine P), 2373.6 miles; 21, Hobbs/Slotemaker (1.2 Triumph P), 2273.5 miles; 22, Hunt/Wagstaff (1.2 Lotus GT), 2222.8 miles; 23, Lelong/Fargon (1.1 Rene Bonnet P), 2172.9 miles; 24, Baker/Bradley (1.1 Austin-Healey P), 2149.5 miles.

CLASS WINNERS: 1000-1150c.c., de Lageneste/Morrogh (Alpine), 101.5 m.p.h.; 1151-1300c.c., Hunt/Wagstaff (Lotus), 92.6 m.p.h.; 1301-1600c.c., Bussinello/Deserti (Alfa Romeo), 106.9 m.p.h.; 1601-2000c.c., Buchet/Ligier (Porsche), 112.5 m.p.h.; 2500-3000c.c., Beurlys/Bianchi (Ferrari), 115.8 m.p.h.; 3001-4000c.c., Guichet/Vaccarella (Ferrari), 121.6 m.p.h.; 4001-5000c.c., Gurney/Bondurant (AC-Cobra), 116.3 m.p.h.; Over 5000c.c., Noblet/Berney (Iso), 106.7 m.p.h.

GT CLASSES: 1300-1600c.c., Bussinello/Deserti (Alfa); 1601-2000c.c., Buchet/Ligier (Porsche); 2001-3000c.c., Beurlys/Bianchi (Ferrari); Over 4000c.c., Gurney/Bondurant (AC-Cobra).

INDEX OF PERFORMANCE: 1, Guichet/Vaccarella (3.3 Ferrari), 1.262 pts.; 2, Hill/Bonnier (4.0 Ferrari), 1.227; 3, Buchet/Ligier (2.0 Porsche), 1.225.

INDEX OF THERMAL EFFICIENCY: 1, de Lageneste/Morrogh (Alpine), 1.48; 2, Zeccoli/Masson (Alpine), 1.31; 3, Guichet/Vaccarella (Ferrari), 1.28.

LE MANS

Continued on page 144

Thus the race was over just after dawn, as so often happens. The leaders tiptoed around hoping that nothing would happen, Gurney and Bondurant confounded general opinion by not only keeping the Cobra going but winning the GT category off the Ferraris and Porsches, while the hitherto invincible GTOs came to bits and went more and more slowly except for the charming Bianchi who pulled his up to fifth. A few walking wounded dropped out, making the list of finishers 25 although the last, Vinatier's Alpine, was too slow to be classified, and for most it was a terribly long 10-hour drag till the finish at 4 P.M., especially so for the 4-liter Ferraris, who kept adding water and Baker's Sprite with a broken rocker. Four o'clock. Millons of people and millions of coppers. On the last lap Guichet literally crept around before all his cheering countrymen as the French announcer went mad with joy. If it wasn't a French car at least it was a French driver. And I don't imagine that part-time pilot Guichet, let alone law professor Vaccarella, felt too badly either. Not bad for a couple of amateurs. With a big red club.

LE MANS 24-HR RACE		
Drivers	Car	Laps
1 Guichet/Vaccarella	3.3 Ferrari P	348
2 Bonnier/G. Hill	4.0 Ferrari P	343
3 Surtees/Bandini	4.0 Ferrari P	336
4 Gurney/Bondurant	4.7 AC Cobra	333
5 Beurlys/L. Bianchi	3.0 Ferrari GTO	331
6 Ireland/Maggs	3.0 Ferrari GTO	326
7 Buchet/Ligier	2.0 Porsche 904	322
8 Pon/van Zalinge	2.0 Porsche 904	317
9 Grossman/Tavano	3.0 Ferrari GTO	314
10 Koch/Schiller	2.0 Porsche 904	313

11. Muller/Sage, 2.0 Porsche 904; 12. Franc/Kerguen, 2.0 Porsche 904; 13. Bussinello/Deserti, 1.6 Alfa Romeo TZ; 14. Berney/Noblet, 5.4 Iso A3L; 15. Biscaldi/Sala, 1.6 Alfa Romeo TZ; 16. Dumay/van Ophem, 3.3 Ferrari P; 17. de Lageneste/Morrogh, 1.1 Alpine P; 18. Magne/de Mortemart, 4.7 AC Cobra; 19. Hedges/Hopkirk, 1.8 MGB; 20. Grandsire/Vidal, 1.1 Alpine P; 21. Hobbs/Slotemaker, 1.1 Spitfire P; 22. Hunt/Wagstaff, 1.3 Elite; 23. Farjon/Lelong, 1.0 Rene Bonnet; 24. Baker/Bradley, 1.1 Sprite P; 25. M. Bianchi/Vinatier, 1.1 Alpine P.

Note: P indicates Prototype class cars, all others were entered in GT classes.

Distance: 348 laps of 8.357-mi circuit, 2917.5 mi, new record (old record: 339 laps, 2834.6 mi, Bandini/Scarfiotti, 3.0 Ferrari P, 1963).

Av speed: 121.562 mph, new record (old record: 118.1 mph, Bandini/Scarfiotti, 3.0 Ferrari P, 1963).

Fastest lap: 3:49.2, 131.375 mph, Phil Hill, 4.2 Ford GT P, new record (old record: 3:53.3, 129.071 mph, John Surtees, 3.0 Ferrari P, 1963).

Index of Performance: 1. Guichet/Vaccarella, 3.3 Ferrari; 2. Bonnier/G. Hill, 4.0 Ferrari; 3. Buchet/Ligier, 2.0 Porsche 904.

Index of Thermal Efficiency: 1. De Lageneste/Morrogh, Alpine; 2. Zeccoli/Masson, Alpine; 3. Guichet/Vaccarella, Ferrari.

The last year for two seasoned Le Mans marques: Maserati and MG. And the year when Ford attempted to bulldoze Le Mans but at the end of the day had nothing to show for their pains, but the Rover B.R.M. returned and did much to uphold Britain's honours.

The number of cars was slightly down this year to 51; these were split into 31 prototype cars and 20 GTs. Ferrari put most of their efforts into the prototype class with ten cars of varying engine sizes 3.3, 4.0 and 4.4 litres - entered by the works but also by American and Belgian teams. In addition there was a single Ferrari 275 GTB, a new model with a 3.3 litre engine. The opposition. meaning Ford, had six prototype cars; four GT 40s with either 4.7 or 5.3 litre engines, but topping even these, a pair of Mk II models with monstrous seven-litre engines - among the biggest ever seen at Le Mans. Maserati had a single five-litre mid-engined car; but most punters probably gave the five Cobras (nee A.C.) more of a chance, considering their fourth place the previous year. They used the same Ford V 8 4.7 litre engines again. The last big car was a Chevrolet engined 5.3 litre Iso Grifo.

Unusually, there was not a single car between two- and three litres; a class which had so often in the past been the most important one at Le Mans, and the emerging split between 'big bangers' on the one hand, and on the other a group of small cars mainly chasing the Index, may have caused the organisers some concern. Leading the two-litre class was Porsche with seven entries. four and eight cylinder cars but also two 911 six-cylinder models. They were countered by a single Elva B.M.W. while the Rover B.R.M. was now classified as the equivalent of 1,992 cc and therefore ran in the same class. So did the MGB which had returned to the fray for the third time.

The 1 600 cc class was strictly Italian territory: four Alfa Romeo TZ IIs entered by the Scuderia Autodelta, and a Dino (a Ferrari by any other name) with a V 6 engine amidships. In the smaller classes, there was a notable absentee: the air cooled flat twin Panhard engine which had been present at every Le Mans since 1950, and often as not had won the Index of Performance and its class. But with a new one-litre minimum rule also applying to supercharged engines, even the ingenuity of Charles Deutsch failed to find a solution. In consequence there were no C. D. entries this year: and his erstwhile partner Rene Bonnet was also absent from Le Mans in 1965, but engaged on staging an eventual comeback in Matra's regie. In the absence of these two stalwarts, French hopes for Index wins centred on the Alpine Renaults; a single 1,108 cc GT, and five prototypes - two in the 1,300 cc class and three in the 1,150 cc class. British opposition came from two 1,293 cc Austin-Healey Sprites.

and four 1,147 cc Triumph Spitfires which now ran in the GT class.

Bearing the events of the 1964 race in mind the big question was whether the Fords were reliable enough to stand the distance. No one doubted that they had the power; Phil Hill had made the fastest practice lap in a seven-litre Mk II. and would indeed put in the fastest lap of the race - a new record of 138.443 mph. As it turned out, the Ford troubles were not over. Although the McLaren/Miles car took the lead soon after the start (whereas the Maserati left the road almost immediately) none of the Fords lasted very long; their retirements were due to either blown head gaskets or to recurring gearbox and clutch problems which put out both the seven-litre cars. Phil Hill and Chris Amon lasted longest but even they were out they before midnight.

The race then became another Ferrari procession; but with frequent changes in the leading positions it proved more interesting than some past Le Mans races. Surtees/Scarfiotti and Guichet/ Parkes took turns to lead in their works entered 330 P2 models, but eventually both were forced out of the race with mechanical trouble. This allowed the Belgian entered 275 LM into the lead but in the closing hours of the race on Sunday afternoon this had to give best to the N.A.R.T. (North American Racing Team) 275 LM driven by Masten Gregory and Jochen Rindt. They became the winners at an average of 121.092 mph and a total distance of 2,906.215 miles. The Belgian Ferrari was second, followed home by the GT category winner, the lone Ferrari 275 GTB. Fourth and fifth were two Porsches, a 904/6 prototype and a 904/4 GT which took the two-litre honours in their categories; the 904/6 also won the Index of Performance and the 904/4 the Index of Thermal Efficiency.

French hopes of Index wins came to nothing, nor were there any French class wins and not a single Alpine finished the race. The 1,300 cc class went to an Austin-Healey Sprite, and a Triumph Spitfire won the 1,150 cc class. However, the highest placed British car was the Rover-B.R.M. which finished tenth, although at an appreciably lower average than in 1963. It was followed home by the MGB in eleventh place, MG's highest position at Le Mans in the post-war period. There were only 14 finishers. With a total of nine wins, of which six were in a row, Ferrari had built up a unique record in the annals of Le Mans; but 1965 marked the end of Ferrari's dominance, and thus the end of an era. It was also effectively the end of the era when British cars were among the most numerous entries at Le Mans; from 13 British cars in 1965 it dropped to 3 in 1966, and it was to be a long time before there was again a British car with a chance of winning the 24-hour race.

Le Mans—twice round the

The Ford-Ferrari duel renewed with increased fur

ENZO Ferrari has remarked that if his cars won a Formula 1 championship Grand Prix, then he received just a few congratulatory messages, but when his cars won Le Mans, why then the cables and messages came pouring in from all over the world. The Maranello postman must have been kept pretty busy every June for the past five years, for ever since the Aston Martin victory in 1959 Ferrari has had an unbroken—and unprecedented—string of Le Mans wins. Last year, however, a new challenger appeared: Ford. The new pretenders to the throne led during the early stages of the 1964

race, set a new lap record, then retired to lick their wounds.

This year, Ford are back in force with no fewer than six of the sleek low GT cars. Spearhead of the attack will be two new seven-litre monsters which were built by Ford Advanced Vehicles at Slough then shipped to Dearborn where the seven-litre engines and gearboxes were installed and fins added to the rear of the car. This pair is entered by Shelby-American. The Swiss Scuderia Filipinetti and Rob Walker (in place of the unready Serenissimas) are both entering 5.3-litre coupés, Ford-France are the entrants of the 4.7-litre open car that ran in the

Targa Florio and Ford Advanced Vehicles are the entrants of a 4.7-litre coupé. Chief modifications for 1965 to the GT40s are the replacement of the light alloy 4.2 Indianapolis type Ford V-8 engine with 4.7- and 5.3-litre variants of the cast iron Ford Fairlane V-8 developed originally for the Cobras. The extra weight of the cast iron engines is more than offset by the fact that they employ wet sump lubrication and therefore do not require the large oil tank needed by the dry sump Indianapolis engines. Also, they have only one oil pump instead of three. Even more to the point, they develop far more power low

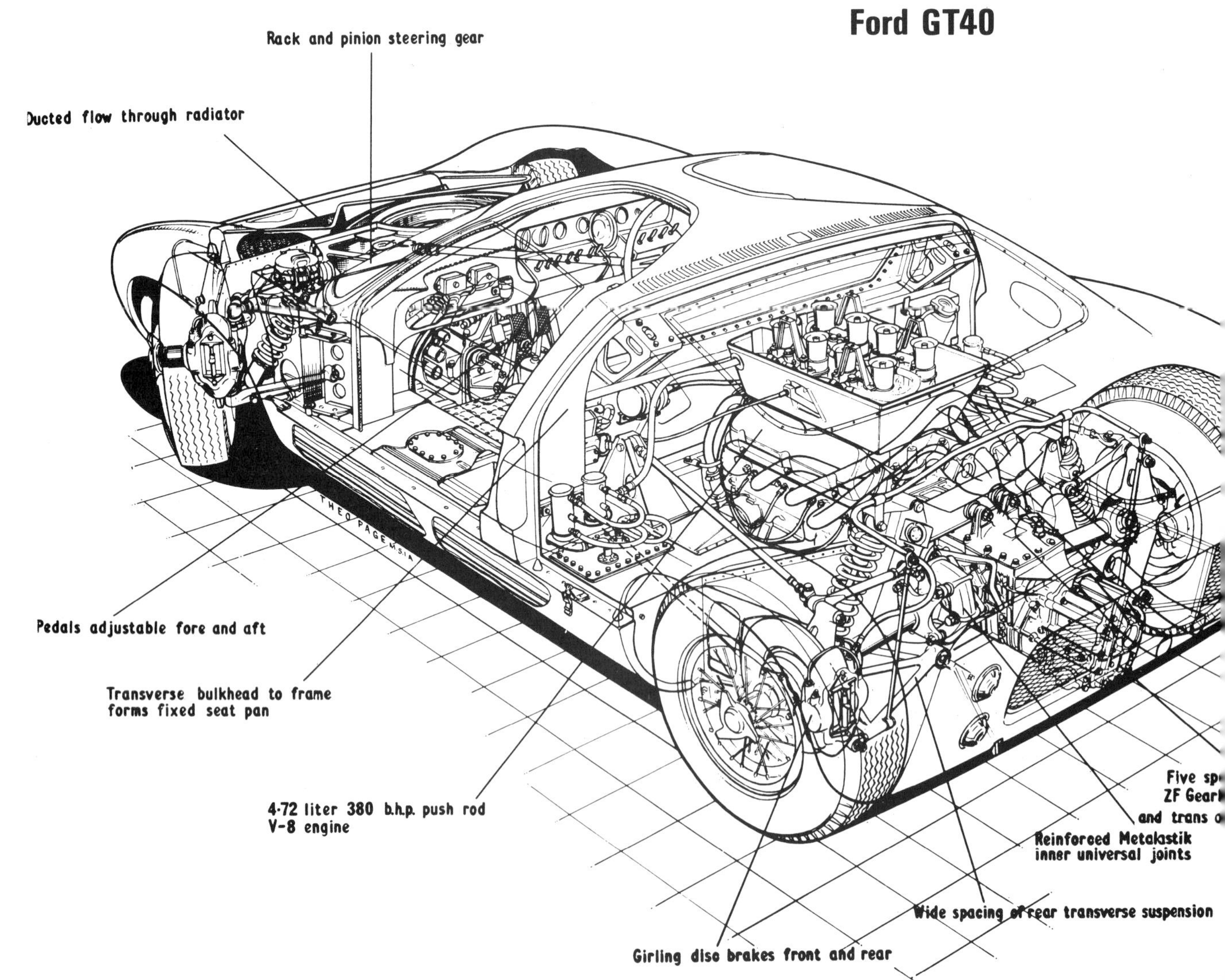

clock

The new Ferrari P2 GT prototype comes in two sizes, the 3.3-litre 275 and the four-litre 330 which knocked 14 seconds off the lap record at the Test Days last April.

down than the Indianapolis type engines. The 5.3-litre and 4.7-litre cars are fitted with a new ZF five-speed gearbox which is much lighter and more compact than the four-speed Colotti box it replaces.

After much wind tunnel research at M.I.R.A., a new nose has been developed for the cars which tidies up considerably that profusion of ducts, holes and vents the original nose had acquired in the course of a season's racing. The new nose is stated to reduce the overall drag by 14%, which is equivalent to a bonus of 55 extra b.h.p. at 200 m.p.h.

With what will Ferrari reply to this Anglo-American challenge from Ford? With a squadron of four works-entered P2s, the phenomenally fast new GT prototype with four overhead camshafts for its rear-mounted, V-12 engine and a new chassis embodying all the suspension lessons learnt from the current Formula 1 GP Ferraris. With the P2 in its four-litre 330 P2 form, John Surtees took no less than 14 seconds off the existing Le Mans lap record during the Test Days in April, and won the Nurburgring 1,000 kilometres race. And the 3.3 litre 275P2 version won the Targa Florio.

In addition to the works cars, there are many entries by the teams with works association such as the North American Racing Team, the Belgian Ecurie Francorchamps, the Swiss Scuderia Filipinetti and the British Maranello Concession-aires. The two British-entered Ferraris will consist of a 4.4-litre 365P2 and a 3.3 litre 250LM. Drivers will be Jo Bonnier, Innes Ireland, David Piper and Mike Salmon. Another Italian heavyweight competing will be the 5-litre Maserati V-8 of which a new rear-engined example has been rushed to completion to replace the front-engined car destroyed in the tragic Casner crash during the Test Days.

Competition in the class for 2-litre GT prototypes will be keen indeed this year. Favourites will be those rapid works Porsches with either flat-8 or flat-6 air-cooled engines, but in silent pursuit of them will be that most interesting British entry, the gas-turbine-

Le Mans Entries

Makes	Capacity	Category	Entrants	Drivers
A.C. Cobra Ford	7,010	P	Shelby-American Inc.	Gurney/Bucknam
A.C. Cobra-Ford	7,010	P	Shelby-American Inc.	Johnson/Payne
Ford GT	6,997	P	Shelby-American Inc.	Miles/McLaren
Ford GT	6,997	P	Shelby-American Inc.	P. Hill/Ginther
Iso Grifo	5,364	P	Iso Prototipi Bizzarini	Fraissiner/ de Mortemart
Iso Grifo	5,364	P	Iso Prototipi Bizzarini	Noblet/X
Iso Grifo	5,364	P	Iso Prototipi Bizzarini	X/X
Ford GT	5,300	P	R.R.C. Walker Racing Team	Amon/Bondurant
Ford GT	5,300	P	Scuderia Filipinetti	Ireland/Mueller
Maserati	5,044	P	J. H. Simone	X/X
A.C. Cobra-Ford	4,727	GT	A. C. Cars	Sears/Thompson
A.C. Cobra-Ford	4,727	GT	Ford-France	Schlesser/Grant
A.C. Cobra Ford	4,727	GT	John Willment Automobiles	Gardner/X
Ferrari 365P2	4,400	P	Maranello Concessionaires	Bonnier/Piper
Ferrari	4,400	P	North American Racing Team	P. Rodriguez/X
Ferrari	3,996	P	North American Racing Team	X/X
Ferrari 250LM	3,285	P	Ecurie Francorchamps	L. Bianchi/Langlois
Ferrari	4,000	P	S.E.F.A.C. Ferrari	Surtees/Parkes
Ferrari	4,000	P	S.E.F.A.C. Ferrari	Bandini/Scarfiotti
Ferrari	3,300	P	S.E.F.A.C. Ferrari	Guichet/Vaccarella
Ferrari	3,285	GT	Ecurie Francorchamps	Beurlys/Mairesse
Ferrari	3,285	P	P. Dumay	Dumay/Gosselin
Ferrari 250LM	3,300	P	Scuderia Filipinetti	C. Sage/A. Boller
Ferrari 250LM	3,300	P	Maranello Concessionaires	Salmon/X
Elva-B.M.W. GT	1,991	P	Anglian Racing Development	Wrottesley/Lanfranchi
Porsche	1,991	P	Porsche System Engineering	X/X
Porsche	1,991	P	Porsche System Engineering	X/X
Porsche	1,982	P	Porsche System Engineering	X/X
Porsche	1,982	P	Porsche System Engineering	X/X
Rover-B.R.M.	1,999	P	Owen Racing Organization	G. Hill/Stewart
Porsche 904GTS	1,966	GT	A. Veuillet	Buchet/X
Porsche 904GTS	1,966	GT	"Franc"	"Franc"/Kerguen
Porsche 904GTS	1,966	GT	Porsche System Engineering	X/X
M.G.B.	1,801	P	British Motor Corporation	Hopkirk/Hedges
Dino 166	1,600	P	Dino	Baghetti/Biscaldi
Alfa-Romeo GTZ	1,570	GT	Autodelta S.P.A.	Bussinello/Zeccoli
Alfa-Romeo GTZ	1,570	GT	Autodelta S.P.A.	J. Roland/Zuccoli
Alfa-Romeo GTZ	1,570	GT	Autodelta S.P.A.	Adamich/X
Alfa-Romeo	1,570	GT	Equipe Grand Ducale Luxembourgeoise	Hauser/Kobb
C.D.	1,568	P	Ste. des Auto C.D.	Bertaut/Guilhaudin
Alpine	1,296	P	Ste. des Auto Alpine	M. Bianchi/Vinatier
Alpine	1,296	P	Ste. des Auto Alpine	Gransire/de Lageneste
Austin-Healey	1,293	P	Donald Healey Motor Co.	Baker/Aaltonen
Austin-Healey	1,296	P	Donald Healey Motor Co.	Hawkins/Makinen
Alpine	1,149	P	Ste. des Auto Alpine	Masson/Morrogh
Alpine	1,149	P	Ste. des Auto Alpine	Verrier/Vidal
Triumph	1,147	GT	Standard-Triumph	Hobbs/Slotemaker
Triumph	1,147	GT	Standard-Triumph	Dubois/Piot
Triumph	1,147	GT	Standard-Triumph	Bradley/Bolton
Alpine	1,108	GT	Ste. des Auto Alpine	Cheinisse/Hanrioud
Abarth	1,001	P	Abarth France	Ballot Lena/Ruata
Ferrari	3,285	GTB	North American Racing Team	X/X
Ford Cobra	4,700	GT	Scuderia Filipinetti	X/X

Le Mans Preview

powered Rover-B.R.M. driven by Graham Hill and Jackie Stewart. The Le Mans regulations were issued before the new F.I.A. gas turbine formula was announced, otherwise the Rover-B.R.M. would be running in the up-to-1,600c.c. class, for this is its equivalent capacity under the new formula. The 1963 Rover-B.R.M. which made motoring history at Le Mans was a rather ugly open two seater, but the latest gas turbine car is a very sleek GT coupé. It also differs from the 1963 car in being equipped with two heat exchangers to improve its fuel consumption.

Also in the 2-litre prototype class are two other British entries, an Elva-B.M.W. and an M.G.B. which closely resembles the car which was the highest placed British finisher in 1964 and so won the *Motor* Trophy.

In the 1,600c.c. GT prototype class are the two Dino 166 cars, very small rear-engined coupés designed by Ferrari to be built in some numbers by Fiat and using the 1.6-litre V-6 engine that Ferrari will base his 1967 formula 2 single-seaters on.

In the small GT prototype class, two Austin-Healey Sprite prototypes with the latest sleek body styling developed by much wind tunnel testing will be matched against the fantasticly rapid Alpine GT coupés powered by twin overhead camshaft Renault-Gordini engines.

Le Mans is really two major races going on at once, for in addition to the fight for the outright lead by the GT prototypes, the homologated GT cars are competing for victory in the GT category and for GT class wins.

Second prong of the Ford attack is in the GT category. The A.C. Cobra Fords at present lead the Ferraris in the struggle for the International Championship of Makes—usually known as the Constructors' Championship—by 74.4 points to Ferrari's 43.9 points in Division 3 which is the big car section. There is, alas, no outright winner of the Constructors' Championship these days, but three separate champions for each of the divisions. Most of the A.C. Cobra Ford's points have been scored by one or other of the massive Daytona coupés of which only six have been built. All six are going to Le Mans. These six cars are all Mark 1 Cobras with transverse leaf springing at the front and 4.7-litre V-8 engines. An additional Mark 1 4.7-litre A.C. Cobra Ford has been entered by Willment Racing and will be driven by Frank Gardner and an as yet un-nominated pilot. The car is fitted with

The Rover-B.R.M. gas turbine car appears this year as a sleek GT coupé, and is fitted with two heat exchangers to moderate its thirst for paraffin.

Only British works team this year are three Triumph Spitfires, plus a fourth car in the reserve list.

Ferrari may be favourite for outright victory, but in the GT category the massive A.C. Cobra Fords may well repeat their 1964 triumph.

Willment's own coupé body which has been further modified since the car competed in the Tourist Trophy. A much smoother nose has been added for better penetration at high speed and the tail has been modified by the inclusion of a vertical rear window to improve the visibility. A spoiler has also been added to keep the tail down at speed.

In addition to the GT cars, at least one of the new 7-litre Cobras with coil spring suspension at front and rear will be entered as a GT prototype by Shelby American, Inc. Body for this Cobra III coupé was made in Britain by Harold Radford (Coachbuilders) Ltd.

With what will Ferrari defend his title, as reigning champion? With the new lightweight version of the 275GTB which has at last been homologated as a GT car. This is a front-engined V-12 of 3,286c.c. with a single overhead camshaft to each bank of cylinders. Two have been entered by the works and one by the Italian St. Ambroeus team.

Of course, should the big GT cars show the slightest sign of faltering, then those very reliable and fleet 2-litre Porsche 904GTs powered by flat-4 engines will be snapping at their heels. Already Porsche have an overwhelming lead in Division 2 of the Constructors' Championship. And not far behind the Porsches in the GT category will be the three new Alfa Romeo GTZ2s, the new, smaller, faster version of the GTZ, which made its first appearance at the Le Mans Test Days last April.

Finally, at the lower end of the GT scale will be the only British works team this year, three Triumph Spitfires. Last year, one of the Spitfires was lapping at over 100 m.p.h. and achieving 136 m.p.h. along the Mulsanne Straight. This year's cars are even faster, thanks to larger Weber carburetters and improved induction and exhaust systems which provide altogether 108 b.h.p. from the 1,147c.c. push-rod engines.

A merican enthusiasts can be thankful and proud that Luigi Chinetti decided to go to Le Mans with his North American Racing Team entry this year. Chinetti, a three-time winner at Le Mans himself, entered a factory-prepared, Goodyear-shod Ferrari 275/LM for Masten Gregory and Jochen Rindt, and a 365/P for Pedro Rodriguez and Nino Vaccarella. Gregory, an American living in Paris, and Rindt, a German living in Austria, upheld America's honor with a fine overall victory. Rodriguez and Vaccarella had enough trouble for five race cars, but they managed to finish in seventh place. Many of you will recall that there was another American team running at Le Mans, but they were less fortunate.

This other effort, a somewhat larger one, was sponsored by a group of enthusiasts in Dearborn, Michigan, known collectively as the Ford Motor Company. One way or another they were responsible for a mixed bag of eleven cars—some in America's colors, some French, some English, a couple of Swiss, but nothing from the Eastern bloc or the non-aligned nations of Africa and Asia. Of their eleven cars, one limped home to finish eighth—a Cobra Daytona coupe, driven by England's Jack Sears and Dr. Richard Thompson. Of the others, it's a long story…

24 heures du mans

BY DAVID E. DAVIS, JR.

CHRIS McCALL,

AL BOCHROCH

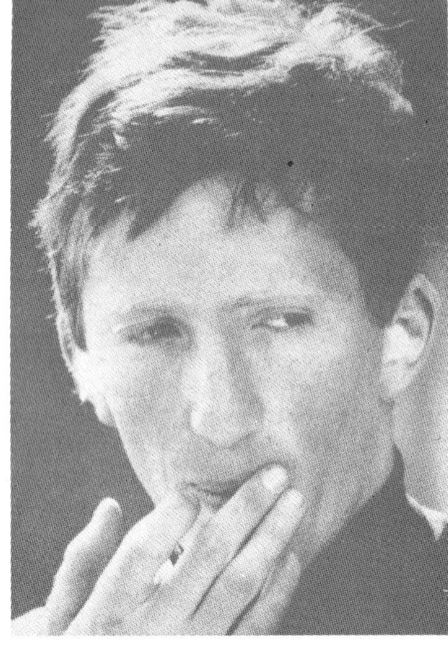

Phil Hill (left) watched the promising Ford challenge slip away, but managed to set a new lap record before his Ford GT expired. Jochen Rindt (top) and Masten Gregory (bottom) conserved their NART Ferrari 275/LM and took first overall as the faster entries fell by the wayside.

Masten Gregory and Jochen Rindt led three privately-entered Ferraris in a one-two-three sweep of the 1965 Twenty-Four Hours of Le Mans. It was the first time that a private entry had won the race since 1957, when it was captured by Ron Flockhart and Ivor Bueb in an Ecurie Ecosse D-Type Jaguar. A similar Ferrari 275/LM finished second, driven by the widely unknown Belgian team of Gustave Gosselin/Pierre Dumay, and Ferrari's newest GT car, the 275/GTB, was driven to third by thrill-driver Willy Mairesse and Jean Beurlys. Fourth and fifth places went to factory Porsches—the six-cylinder prototype Coupe of Linge/Nöcker, and the GT Coupe of Koch/Fischaber, in that order.

Gregory and Rindt drove the kind of pace that wins endurance races. They avoided the early, no-holds-barred sprint that always kills off so many of the front-runners, and never even approached the lead until after the race was half over. Phil Hill, acting as commentator for the ABC television broadcast, pointed out the sagacity of this approach right at the start, when he said, "I don't remember when a winning car has led this race from the beginning." At the time, he was expressing concern over the hot pace that his Ford teammates were setting in the first hour, but it really applied to everybody.

As it turns out, the imprudently high speeds of the seven-liter Ford GTs (designated the GT 40 Mk III) weren't important, because the bugs that retired them stemmed more from hasty preparation and inadequate testing than from over-enthusiasm. The big-engined Fords were unquestionably the fastest cars ever to run at Le Mans—setting fastest laps in both practice and the race, leading in one-two order for the first hour, and hitting something like 218 mph on the super-long Mulsanne straight—but the race lasts for twenty-four hours, and the Fords didn't.

They weren't alone. The only other real contender for top honors was the SEFAC Ferrari team, and they made out just as badly as the Fords—the difference being that Ferrari only had four cars to break, but they broke all four. The favorites were the 330/P2 (V-12, dohc engine) prototypes of Surtees/Scarfiotti and Parkes/Guichet. These were supported by the fantastic little Dino 166/P, to be driven by Baghetti/Casoni, and a new car designated 275/P2, for Bandini/Biscaldi. Surtees' and Bandini's cars suffered with brake problems. Parkes' car shared the same brake problems, but had electrical trouble as well. And Baghetti got the bit in his teeth on the first lap and wound the Dino's V-6 engine right off the scale—bringing it back to the pits to the clattering strains of valves meeting pistons—and that accounted for all four.

The SEFAC Ferrari team was supported by a host of private entries. The most promising were the two 4.4-liter 365/P2 (V-12, sohc engine) prototypes—one entered for Jo Bonnier and David Piper by Maranello Concessionaires Ltd. (England), and the other entered by Luigi Chinetti for Rodriguez and Vaccarella. After these came no less than five 275/LMs, and the Belgian-entered 275/GTB of Mairesse and Beurlys.

The important difference to note here is that the hot Fords went incredibly fast, in spite of insufficient experience, testing, and organization. The Ferraris couldn't go as fast and broke down anyway, in spite of a virtual stranglehold on Le Mans for almost ten years. It would seem that the past few years of uncontested

Upper left: Parkes (Ferrari 330/P2) leads Linge's fourth-place Porsche through the esses. Upper right: the third-place GTB before its nose was opened up for better cooling. Lower left: Hill's pace-setting Ford 427 GT covered with fins and whiskers. Lower right: the winning Ferrari 275/LM of smallish drivers Masten Gregory and Jochen Rindt.

superiority have slowed the Ferrari reflexes a bit. In Grand Prix racing, the red cars are obviously over-matched by the English, and now they're beginning to feel the same sort of pressure in the GT sphere of action.

The Ferrari-Ford combat is a classic example of the grizzled old bull trying to protect his herd from an aggressive young challenger. The old-timer has to pit experience and painfully-acquired skill against youthful enthusiasm, brute strength, and stamina. The veteran may withstand the first few charges, but the laws of nature give all the odds to the youngster. In this case, the youngster also has an unlimited bankroll, so we'll count the laws of economics on his side too.

But that's next year—maybe. This year the tough young challenger slipped and fell before he ever made contact with his aging adversary.

Ford's eleven-car task force was distributed among six different entrants-of-record because of the problems involved in getting entries for such a massive onslaught. The two seven-liter GTs and two Cobras were entered by Shelby American. Ford of France and the Swiss Scuderia Filipinetti each got one Cobra coupe and one GT, while Rob Walker and Ford Advanced Vehicles had a GT apiece, with one last Cobra entered by AC Cars Ltd. All the GTs, except the seven-liters, had been entered with 325-cu. in. Fairlane-based V-8 engines, while the Cobras were fitted with Ford's ubiquitous 289.

Although all of the cars were ostensibly under the control of the Shelby-American organization, the degree of control and cooperation varied greatly from team to team. For instance, the Ford Advanced Vehicles operation could only have been more hostile to its American allies if it had been running Chevrolets. All of the Cobras were prepared by the Alan Mann people, who've done a lot of this sort of thing for Ford in both racing and rallying. The new "superstock" GTs, with their mighty NASCAR engines, were built up by Roy Lunn in Detroit, but we really couldn't tell you who did what to which of the second-string GTs and their ill-starred 325 engines. We'll never know, for sure, but it's safe to guess that many of Ford's troubles stemmed directly from this "Tower of Babel" organization and the attendant breakdowns in communication. The CIA couldn't have done it better.

Practice was dominated by the seven-liter Fords—after some changes and adjustments were made, particularly to the aerodynamics. By race day the two big guns had grown "eyebrow" fins over the front wheel wells, a spoiler lip under the front air intake, and a pair of Flash Gordon tailfins on the rear deck. The new, longer nose section that these cars sported had come apart in early trials, and the drivers had complained of an eerie tendency for the cars to feel like they were climbing some kind of billowy, invisible mattress when they got past 200 mph. The fixes made the difference, and the four drivers were very enthusiastic about the modified cars by race time.

Ford practice times were about six seconds faster than the Ferraris, and Phil Hill was fastest of all. The first evening of practice was washed out by driving rain and gale-force winds. On the second night, Carroll Shelby approached Phil Hill and said, "Why don't you go out and set a new record?" "Set a record?" came the reply; "Would that be prudent?" "Yessir," said Ol' Shel, so Phil went out and shattered the record with an unbelievable 3:33 lap—an average speed of 142 mph, six-

Top to bottom: the battered Sears/Thompson Cobra, sole survivor of the 11-car Ford entry; the Belgians Dumay and Gosselin had the race in the bag when they hit something and blew a tire; the Rover-BRM, driven by G. Hill and Stewart to tenth overall.

SCHLEGELMILCH

33RD GRAND PRIX D'ENDURANCE 24 HEURES DU MANS
JUNE 19 & 20, 1965
4TH HOUR POSITIONS

1.	Surtees/Scarfiotti	4.0 Ferrari	Proto	62 laps
2.	Parkes/Guichet	4.0 Ferrari	Proto	62
3.	Bonnier/Piper	4.4 Ferrari	Proto	62
4.	Bandini/Biscaldi	3.3 Ferrari	Proto	61
5.	Gurney/Grant	4.7 Cobra	GT	60
6.	Bianchi/Salmon	3.3 Ferrari	Proto	59
7.	Rodriguez/Vaccarella	4.4 Ferrari	Proto	59
8.	Sears/Thompson	4.7 Cobra	GT	58
9.	Gosselin/Dumay	3.3 Ferrari	Proto	58
10.	Langlois/Elde	3.3 Ferrari	Proto	58

8TH HOUR POSITIONS

1.	Parkes/Guichet	4.0 Ferrari	Proto	122 laps
2.	Bandini/Biscaldi	3.3 Ferrari	Proto	121
3.	Rodriguez/Vaccarella	4.4 Ferrari	Proto	118
4.	Surtees/Scarfiotti	4.0 Ferrari	Proto	117
5.	Sears/Thompson	4.7 Cobra	GT	115
6.	Gosselin/Dumay	3.3 Ferrari	Proto	115
7.	Johnson/Payne	4.7 Cobra	GT	114
8.	Langlois/Elde	3.3 Ferrari	Proto	114
9.	Mairesse/Beurlys	3.3 Ferrari	GT	114
10.	Gurney/Grant	4.7 Cobra	GT	113

12TH HOUR POSITIONS

1.	Dumay/Gosselin	3.3 Ferrari	Proto	174 laps
2.	Gregory/Rindt	3.3 Ferrari	Proto	172
3.	Mairesse/Beurlys	3.3 Ferrari	GT	171
4.	Parkes/Guichet	4.0 Ferrari	Proto	169
5.	Klass/Glemser	2.0 Porsche	Proto	167
6.	Linge/Nocker	2.0 Porsche	Proto	167
7.	Surtees/Scarfiotti	4.0 Ferrari	Proto	167
8.	Buchet/Pon	2.0 Porsche	GT	166
9.	Boller/Spoerry	3.3 Ferrari	Proto	165
10.	Gurney/Grant	4.7 Cobra	GT	165

16TH HOUR POSITIONS

1.	Dumay/Gosselin	3.3 Ferrari	Proto	232 laps
2.	Parkes/Guichet	4.0 Ferrari	Proto	231
3.	Gregory/Rindt	3.3 Ferrari	Proto	231
4.	Mairesse/Beurlys	3.3 Ferrari	GT	228
5.	Linge/Nocker	2.0 Porsche	Proto	223
6.	Surtees/Scarfiotti	4.0 Ferrari	Proto	221
7.	Rodriguez/Vaccarella	4.4 Ferrari	Proto	220
8.	Koch/Fischaber	2.0 Porsche	GT	217
9.	Boller/Spoerry	3.3 Ferrari	Proto	217
10.	Buchet/Pon	2.0 Porsche	GT	217

20TH HOUR POSITIONS

1.	Gosselin/Dumay	3.3 Ferrari	Proto	293 laps
2.	Gregory/Rindt	3.3 Ferrari	Proto	292
3.	Mairesse/Beurlys	3.3 Ferrari	GT	285
4.	Parkes/Guichet	4.0 Ferrari	Proto	283
5.	Linge/Nocker	2.0 Porsche	Proto	279
6.	Koch/Fischaber	2.0 Porsche	GT	270
7.	Boller/Spoerry	3.3 Ferrari	Proto	268
8.	Rodriguez/Vaccarella	4.4 Ferrari	Proto	260
9.	Sears/Thompson	4.7 Cobra	GT	256
10.	deMortmart/Fraissenet	5.3 ISO Grifo	Proto	248

24TH HOUR FINISH

1.	Gregory/Rindt	3.3 Ferrari	Proto	348 laps
2.	Gosselin/Dumay	3.3 Ferrari	Proto	342
3.	Mairesse/Beurlys	3.3 Ferrari	GT	339
4.	Linge/Nocker	2.0 Porsche	Proto	335
5.	Koch/Fischaber	2.0 Porsche	GT	325
6.	Boller/Spoerry	3.3 Ferrari	Proto	324
7.	Rodriguez/Vaccarella	4.4 Ferrari	Proto	320
8.	Sears/Thompson	4.7 Cobra	GT	303
9.	deMortmart/Fraissenet	5.3 ISO Grifo	Proto	302
10.	Hill/Stewart	2.0 Rover-Turbine	Proto	284
11.	Hopkirk/Hedges	1.8 MGB	GT	282
12.	Hawkins/Rhodes	1.3 Austin-Healey	Proto	277
13.	Thuner/Lampinen	1.1 Spitfire	GT	273
14.	Piot/DuBois	1.1 Spitfire	GT	262

Race Distance: 2906.2 miles. Average Speed: 121.1 mph (new record)
Fastest Lap: Phil Hill (Ford GT) 3:37.5, 139.25 mph (new record)

teen seconds faster than the record lap of 3:49 he set in last year's race driving a 289 Ford GT.

When the Saturday of the race finally rolled around, there was a lot of speculation about the possibility of more rain, but the weather was sunny and hot, and it stayed that way. No official crowd figure was announced, but the usual drill with the ACO officials is to take whatever figure was announced at Indianapolis (almost 300,000 this year) and estimate something slightly higher (over 300,000 this year). It is possible that about ten percent of these were Ford team personnel.

The word was out that the second-string Ford GT's 325-cu. in. engines had been replaced with the "normal" 289-cu. in. units as used in the Cobras. The 325s had been overheating and some trouble had cropped up with crankshaft vibration dampers, so the old workhorse 289 was called once more into the breach. A bad omen. Ford spokesmen said that the months and months of transmission troubles that preceded this year's Le Mans had made it impossible to properly test the 325, but this seems a little incredible. And what's worse, it didn't change anything, as the results so grimly emphasized.

The start and the finish are perhaps the only times that the 24-hour grind gets the full attention of the crowd. They jammed the fences and barricades, and a substantial number of them were obviously and vocally Ford and/or Cobra partisans. Le Mans being the national institution that it is, the French would turn out to watch it even if the winner was announced in advance, but the added excitement of a real, worthy challenge to the Ferraris did catch their imaginations—heightening the drama for everybody concerned.

Meanwhile, back in the States, it was eleven o'clock in the morning and thousands of keen types were fuming and cursing in front of their television sets, waiting for the picture that never came. Phil Hill's co-driver, Chris Amon, was slated to start, and Phil was almost single-handedly delivering a description of the scene to the TV audience, handicapped by a West German relay station's technical problems and Jim McKay's trite observations about the blue of the sky and the mystique of motor racing. If America had not conferred hero-status upon Phil Hill before the morning of June 19, he earned it right there on their picture-less TV screens. His commentary during the start and the next day's coverage of the finish was excellent. He could wind up replacing Bert Parks on the Miss America Pageant.

Then, still unseen by the frustrated American TV audience, the flag fell. Fifty-one pairs of feet sprinted across the pavement, doors slammed, engines coughed and yowled, and tires chirped as the French announcer —as all French announcers must—babbled hysterically over the rising mechanical storm. The field plunged into the first corner, led by four GTs and Jo Siffert's ugly Maserati. It was Amon, McLaren, Bondurant, Siffert and Ireland, and it was one hairy start. The pack thundered away without Colin Davis, who sat at the pits, punching a reluctant starter. Two minutes later, however, he was tearing off, looking for the action.

Silence fell as the thousands craned to see Maison Blanche, where the leaders would appear. Into view popped two GTs, McLaren and Amon, then Surtees, then Guichet, Bondurant, Rindt, and *Gurney*, of all people, in a *Cobra*. An Alfa had looped into a sandbank on the first lap, and the attrition was on. Siffert spun and crept back to the pits with a crunched radiator, the over-revved Dino was retired with an unhappy engine, and Phil Hill worried in the broadcasting booth as the big GTs began pulling away from the field by about three seconds a lap. Hill wasn't optimistic, and he let America know it.

At the end of the first hour, McLaren and Amon were leading Surtees and Guichet, but when they all pitted for fuel, the lead changed hands several times. Amon had the first hint of future Ford woes when he spent 41 minutes in the pits with gear selector trouble. The McLaren/Miles 427 started losing gears, eventually abandoning when they were left with only fourth. The Hill/Amon 427 was back in the race, though ten laps behind, and Hill, in a desperate attempt to make headway, managed to set a new race lap record of 3:37.5. Then the clutch started to go and the Ford challenge faded.

At least there were the 289 GTs. Trintignant's had disappeared after an hour when he'd missed a shift and scrambled the gearbox, but there were three others—not as fast as the Ferraris, but running strong.

Actually, had Trintignant lasted a while longer, his GT would have in all probability have retired with an overheated engine. Every single one of the 289 engines, in both the GTs and the Cobras, was afflicted with this ailment. The problem was traced to a new—and apparently untested—head gasket material. The defective gaskets caused a water loss which cooked all the usually-infallible engines—except the Sears/Thompson Cobra, which trod gingerly for 23½ hours after an opening-laps shunt with an errant Renault Alpine; and Gurney's Cobra, which was going faster than anyone could believe.

Gurney thrust the big blue coupe up into third place in the middle of the night, and was gaining ten seconds a lap on the two leading (by then) Ferrari prototypes. Finally,

the tortured motor mounts started falling apart, setting up a feverish vibration of the engine and transmission. And when Gurney discovered he couldn't go fast anymore, he packed it in.

This left the field clear for the factory Ferraris, who were expected to cruise through the second half of the race with serenity and dignity. But they too were beset with grief from an untested part. SEFAC Ferrari, feeling the pressure from Ford, had gambled on vented discs. Vented discs are better than solid discs—at least they give faster lap times—but no one knew how long they'd last. By two in the morning, the Ferraris started making 30- and 40-minute pit stops to change discs, pads, calipers—everything. At one point, Parkes had a different disc-and-pad combination on each wheel, and that approach wasn't getting the job done. When he finally quit, though, the reason listed was "flat battery." Surtees' car suffered front suspension failure. One by one, the SEFAC Ferraris dropped back . . . or out . . . and the Belgian and American entries moved cautiously into the lead.

Dawn lightened into day, with Gosselin in first, followed by Rindt, Mairesse and Nöcker in the Porsche 906. The buzzing Alpines were all out, and only two Spitfires, a Healey and an MGB remained as traffic for the big guys.

On the Mulsanne Straight, Gosselin hit something and threw a tread right out through the bodywork. Rindt nipped into the lead as his opponent pitted, and Gregory soon took over to hold the NART entry in first place for the last two hours. The Dumay/Gosselin coupe rejoined the fray and moved into second. Everyone tiptoed around being careful not to break, until the flag fell on Greg-

ory, then Gosselin, then Mairesse. Linge and Koch brought Porsches in fourth and fifth, and the Year of the Private Entry at Le Mans was over.

The American TV audience did get to see the finish. First-time Le Mans-watchers marvelled at the crawling pace of the fourteen surviving machines, and took pleasure from the string of cars that was steadily piling in Gregory's wake—escorting him to the finish line. The joy in the NART pit was by now unrestrained, and the winning car had more people aboard than a float in the Rose Bowl Parade when it made its way to the winner's circle. Luigi Chinetti has never been a man to make much display of his emotions, but he glowed and smiled in the surrounding pandemonium, and his happiness was obvious. Gregory and Rindt were like school boys, laughing and waving to friends, not really hearing anything anybody yelled at them, exhausted, but buoyed up by the excitement that came with their unexpected victory.

Ford gathered all of their people together—away from the scenes of celebration—and talked about next year. "This is a victory meeting," the chairman began, but what it really was, was an attempt to reassure everybody—including himself—that they'd take the lessons learned at this year's Le Mans and come back next year . . . to win.

It's already been pointed out that it took them three years to win at Indianapolis, and next year will be their third at Le Mans. Superstition isn't the sort of thing that one relies upon for a major racing victory, but the short-lived performance of the seven-liter Fords should give them every reason to be optimistic. Ford's racing boss, Leo Beebe, has managed to straighten things out in the company's stock car racing and Indianapolis activities, with spectacular success. He'd already started to work on the GT program, but there simply wasn't time to do everything that needed doing.

The last thing the TV viewers heard was a windy treatise from ABC's number-two commentator, who'd never been to a race before. He explained what Ford had done wrong, and gave them a lot of valuable advice about what they should do next year. We're sure that Ford, and Carroll Shelby, and all the rest were very grateful, but we have a feeling that they *know* what they did wrong, and have every intention of doing it right next year.

But then, Enzo Ferrari probably feels exactly the same way. **C/D**

LE MANS—How the cars performed

RACE NO.	MAKE AND CATEGORY	DRIVERS	ENTRANT	Engine Position Front or Rear	Engine	Bore and stroke (mm)	Capacity (c.c.)	Induction System	Brakes (Disc or Drum)	Tyres	Body Type	Full Weight at Scrutineering (lb)	Tank Capacity Imp. gals.	Finishing position or reason for retirement	Laps Completed	Race average (mph)	Fastest Timed Speed along Mulsanne Straight (mph)	Estimated Distance in 24 Hours or Distance Covered (miles)	Fuel Consumption mpg
1	Ford (G.T.40) (P)	McLaren-Miles	Shelby American	M	Ford V-8	107·6×96	6,982	1×4C.H.	KH. Di. F. G. Di.R	G'dy'r	Cl	2,662	32·6	Gearbox failure	—	—	199	—	—
2	Ford (G.T.40) (P)	P. Hill-Amon	Shelby American	M	Ford V-8	107·6×96	6,982	1×4C.H.	KH. Di. F. G. Di.R	G'dy'r	Cl	2,645	35	Gearbox failure	—	—	188	—	—
3	Iso Grifo (P)	Fraissinet-de Mortemar	Iso Grifo	F	Chev. V-8	101·6×82·6	5,354	4DCW	C. Di.	Dun.	Cl	2,675	29·9	9th	302	105·2	186	2,525	—
6	Ford (P)	Ireland-Muller	Sc. Filipinetti	M	Ford V-8	101·8×72·9	4,727	4DCW	G. Di.	G'dy'r	Cl	2,446	35·2	Cyl. head studs	—	—	158	—	—
7	Ford (P)	Bondurant-Maglioli	R. R. C. Walker	M	Ford V-8	101·8×72·9	4,727	4DCW	G. Di.	G'dy'r	Cl	2,452	35	Cyl. head studs	—	—	161	—	—
8	Maserati (P)	Siffert-Neerspach	J. Simone	M	Mas. V-8	95·1×89	5,044	Inj. L	G. Di.	Dun.	Op	2,638	33·9	Cyl. head gasket	—	—	—	—	—
9	Cobra (G.T.)	Grant-Gurney	Shelby American	F	Ford V-8	101·8×72·9	4,727	4DCW	G. Di.	G'dy'r	Cl	2,468	29·9	Oil pressure failure	—	—	—	—	—
10	Cobra (G.T.)	Johnson-Payne	Shelby American	F	Ford V-8	101·8×72·9	4,727	4DCW	G. Di.	G'dy'r	Cl	2,495	29·3	Cyl. head studs	—	—	—	—	—
11	Cobra (G.T.)	Sears-Thompson	A.C. Cars Ltd.	F	Ford V-8	101·8×72·9	4,727	4DCW	G. Di.	G'dy'r	Cl	2,537	29·1	8th	303	105·5	—	2,533	8.5
12	Cobra (G.T.)	Schlesser-A. Grant	Ford-France	F	Ford V-8	101·8×72·9	4,727	4DCW	G. Di.	G'dy'r	Op	2,466	29·9	Crankshaft broken	—	—	—	—	—
14	Ford G.T.40 (G.T.)	Whitmore-Ireland	Ford Ad. Vehicles	M	Ford V-8	101·8×72·9	4,727	4DCW	G. Di.	Dun.	Cl	2,416	30·8	Cyl. head joint	—	—	180	—	—
15	Ford G.T.40 (G.T.)	Ligier-Trintignant	Ford-France	M	Ford V-8	101·8×72·9	4,727	4DCW	G. Di.	G'dy'r	Cl	2,350	29·9	Gearbox	—	—	168	—	—
17	Ferrari (P)	Bonnier-Piper	Maranello Con.	M	Ferr. V-12	81×71	4,390·4	6DCW	Dun. Di.	Dun.	Op	2,191	30·8	Exhaust manifold	—	—	174	—	—
18	Ferrari (P)	Rodriguez-Vacarella	N. Amer. Racing	M	Ferr. V-12	81×71	4,390·4	6DCW	Dun. Di.	Dun.	Op	2,246	31·2	7th	319	111·3	149	2,672	—
19	Ferrari (P)	Surtees-Scarfiotti	S.E.F.A.C.	M	Ferr. V-12	77·1×71	3,978	6DCW	Dun. Di.	Dun.	Op	2,229	31·0	Clutch bearing	—	—	171	—	—
20	Ferrari (P)	Parkes-Guichet	S.E.F.A.C.	M	Ferr. V-12	77·1×71	3,978	6DCW	Dun. Di.	Dun.	Op	2,092	30·8	Battery failure	—	—	177	—	—
21	Ferrari (P)	Gregory-Rindt	N. Amer. Racing	M	Ferr. V-12	77×58·8	3,285	6DCW	Dun. Di.	G'dy'r	Cl	2,233	30·4	1st	347	121·8	174	2,906	7·3
22	Ferrari (P)	Bandini-Biscaldi	S.E.F.A.C.	M	Ferr. V-12	77·1×58·8	3,289	6DCW	Dun. Di.	Dun.	Cl	2,233	31·0	Broken valve	—	—	177	—	—
23	Ferrari (P)	Bianchi-Salmon	Maranello Con.	M	Ferr. V-12	77×58·8	3,285	6DCW	Dun. Di.	Dun.	Cl	2,105	30·4	Burst gearbox	—	—	171	—	—
24	Ferrari (G.T.)	Beurlys-Maitesse	Ec. Francorchamps	F	Ferr. V-12	77×58·8	3,285	6DCW	Dun. Di.	Dun.	Cl	2,310	29·3	3rd	339	118·1	—	2,835	7·1
25	Ferrari (P)	Langlois-Elde	Ec. Francorchamps	M	Ferr. V-12	77×58·8	3,285	6DCW	Dun. Di.	Dun.	Cl	2,167	30·4	Clutch	—	—	—	—	—
26	Ferrari (P)	Dumay-Gosselin	P. Dumay	M	Ferr. V-12	77×58·8	3,285	6DCW	Dun. Di.	Dun.	Cl	2,119	30·1	2nd	342	119·2	—	2,860	8·4
27	Ferrari (P)	Bollep-Spoerry	Sc. Filipinetti	M	Ferr. V-12	77·15×58·8	3,293	6DCW	Dun. Di.	G'dy'r	Cl	2,125	29·7	6th	323	112·7	168	2,706	8·6
30	Elva-BMW	Wrottesley-Lanfranchi	Anglian Racing Deu	M	BMW 4L	89×80	1,991	2DCW	G. Di.	G'dy'r	Cl	1,681	20·7	Clutch & valve trouble	—	—	—	—	—
31	Rover-B.R.M. (P)	Hill-Stewart	Owen Racing Org.	M	2 Shft. Turb.		1,992	Inj. L.	Dun. Di.	Dun.	Cl	1,814	24·4	10th	283	98·8	—	2,371	13·5
32	Porsche (P)	Linge-Nocker	Porsche Eng.	M=	Por. H.O.6	80×66	1,991	2TCW	DA. Di.	Dun	Cl	1,700	23·5	4th	335	116·7	—	2,801	10·4
33	Porsche (P)	Davis-Mitter	Porsche Eng.	M=	Por. H.O.8	76×54	1,985	4DCW	DA. Di.	Dun.	Cl	1,667	24·6	Clutch	—	—	—	—	—
35	Porsche (P)	Klass-Glenser	Porsche Eng.	M=	Por. H.O.6	80×66	1,991	2TCW	DA. Di.	Dun.	Cl	1,631	23·5	Broken camshaft	—	—	—	—	—
36	Porsche (G.T.)	Koch-Fischaber	Porsche Eng.	M=	Por. H.O.4	92×74	1,968	2DCW	DA. Di.	Dun.	Cl	1,726	23·7	5th	324	113·1	155	2,713	12·0
37	Porsche (G.T.)	Buchet-Pon	A. Veuillet	M=	Por. H.O.4	92×74	1,968	2DCW	DA. Di.	Dun.	Cl	1,755	23·3	Oil pressure failure	—	—	158	—	—
38	Porsche (G.T.)	Franc-Kerguen	" Franc "	M=	Por. H.O.4	92×74	1,968	2DCW	DA. Di.	Dun.	Cl	1,795	22·9	—	—	—	149	—	—
39	MGB (P)	Hedges-Hopkirk	B.M.C.	F	BMC 4L	80·3×89	1,801	1DCW	Lo. Di. F:Dr. R.	Dun.	Cl	2,081	19·6	11th	282	98·2	—	2,358	13·3
40	Dino (P)	Baghetti-Casoni	S.E.F.A.C. Dino	M	Ferr. V-6	77×57	1,593	3DCW	Dun. Di.	Dun.	Cl	1,543	21·8	Broken valve	—	—	—	—	—
41	Alfa Romeo (G.T.)	Businello-Roland	Autodelta	F	A/R 4L	78×82	1,570	2DCW	Dun. Di.	Dun.	Cl	1,634	20·9	Bearings	—	—	124	—	—
42	Alfa Romeo (G.T.)	Geki-Zuccoli	Autodelta	F	A/R 4L	78×82	1,570	2DCW	Dun. Di.	Dun.	Cl	1,638	21·3	Broken oil pipe	—	—	137	—	—
43	Alfa Romeo (G.T.)	Zecolli-Rosinski	Autodelta	F	A/R 4L	78×82	1,570	2DCW	Dun. Di.	Dun.	Cl	1,691	21·3	Sandbank Mulsanne	—	—	—	—	—
44	Alfa Romeo (G.T.)	Koob-Finkel	Equipe Luxemb'rg	F	A/R 4L	78×82	1,570	2DCW	Dun. Di.	Dun.	Cl	1,664	19·6	Engine failure	—	—	143	—	—
46	Alpine (P)	Bianchi-Grandsire	Auto. Alpine	M	Ren. Gord 4L	75·7×72	1,296	2DCW	G. Di.	Dun.	Cl	1,475	17·4	Clutch	—	—	143	—	—
47	Alpine (P)	de Langeneste-Vinatier	Auto. Alpine	M	Ren. Gord 4L	75·7×72	1,296	2DCW	G. Di.	Dun.	Cl	1,431	17·2	Engine overheating	—	—	—	—	—
48	Austin-Healey (P)	Aaltonen-Baker	Healey Motor Co.	F	BMC 4L	71·1×81·2	1,293	1DCW	Lo. Di.	Dun.	Cl	1,543	17·4	Overheated, seized	—	—	—	—	—
49	Austin-Healey (P)	Hawkins-Rhodes	Healey Motor Co.	F	BMC 4L	71·1×81·2	1,293	1DCW	Lo. Di.	Dun.	Cl	1,543	18·0	12th	276	96·5	143	2,315	19·1
50	Alpine (P)	Vidal-Revson	Auto. Alpine	M	Ren. Gord 4L	71·3×72	1,150	2DCW	G. Di.	Dun.	Cl	1,464	17·8	Clutch	—	—	131	—	—
51	Alpine (P)	Masson-Verrier	Auto. Alpine	M	Ren. Gord. 4L	71·3×72	1,150	2DCW	G. Di.	Dun.	Cl	1,493	17·8	Clutch	—	—	137	—	—
52	Triumph (G.T.)	Hobbs-Slotemaker	St. Triumph	F	Triumph 4L	69·3×76	1,147	2DCW	G. Di. F.: Dr. R.	Dun.	Cl	1,521	16·1	Crashed	—	—	124	—	—
53	Triumph (G.T.)	Bolton-Bradley	St. Triumph	F	Triumph 4L	69·3×76	1,147	2DCW	G. Di. F: Dr. R.	Dun.	Cl	1,534	16·9	Split oil radiator	—	—	—	—	—
54	Triumph (G.T.)	Dubois-Piot	St. Triumph	F	Triumph 4L	69·3×76	1,147	2DCW	G. Di. F.: Dr. R.	Dun.	Cl	1,514	17·2	14th	262	91·3	—	2,191	—
55	Alpine (G.T.)	Chemisse-Boyer	Auto. Alpine	R	Ren. Gord. 4L	70×72	1,108	2DCW	Brd. Lo. Di.	Dun.	Cl	1,528	17·6	Clutch	—	—	131	—	—
59	Ford (G.T.)	Harper-Sutcliffe	Sc. Filipinetti	M	Ford V-8	101·7×72·9	4,727	4DCW	G. Di.	G'dy'r	Cl	2,535	28·6	Cylinder head studs	—	—	155	—	—
60	Triumph (G.T.)	Thuner-Lampinen	St. Triumph	F	Triumph 4L	69·3×76	1,147	2DCW	G. Di. F: Dr. R.	Dun.	Cl	1,510	17·4	13th	273	95·1	—	2,283	—
61	Alpine (P)	Monneret-Bouharde	Auto-Alpine	M	Ren. Gord. 4L	71·7×62	1,002	2DCW	G. Di.	Dun.	Cl	1,459	16·1	Clutch	—	—	—	—	—
62	Porsche (G.T.)	Poiret-Stommelin	Poirot	M*	Por. H.O.	92×74	1,966	2DCW	DA. Di.	Dun.	Cl	1,709	23·5	Clutch	—	—	—	—	—

CODE: —*Air-cooled. L., in-line. H.O., horizontally-opposed. Ren. Gord., Renault Gordini. Ferr., Ferrari. Por., Porsche. Cl., Closed. Op., open. Inj., L., Injection Lucas. C., Choke. D.C., Double-choke. T.C., Triple-choke. W., Weber. H., Holly. Tyres: Dun., Dunlop. G'dy'r, Goodyear. Brakes: G., Girling. C., Campagnola. Bnd., Bencix. Lo., Lockheed. DA., Dunlop-ATE. K.H., Kelsey Hayes. Di., Discs. Dr., Drums. Engine position: F., In front of driver. M., between driver and rear axle. R., behind rear axle.

FERRARI...
FERRARI...
FERRARI

Ford bid fails with fastest cars ever to be seen at Le Mans —Victory for Masten Gregory/ Jochen Rindt in N.A.R.T. 3.3-litre 250LM—Ferrari also leading G.T. car with Mairesse/ "Beurlys" (GTB)—Porsche again prominent

By GREGOR GRANT

Photography by GEORGE PHILLIPS

Ford's greatest onslaught at Le Mans ended in dismal failure when their 7-litre machines went out early on, after setting a cracking pace. With the disappearance of the McLaren/Miles and the Phil Hill/Amon cars, and the mechanical troubles of the smaller-engined G.T. Fords, Ferrari swept on to an undisputed victory. True, the Sefac machines had troubles, but the independent entries were there to score a 1-2-3 success, followed by a couple of the inevitable Porsches.

Highest-placed British entry was the Rover-B.R.M. turbine of Graham Hill/ Jackie Stewart, which finished in 10th place having covered 3,815.36 kms.—only 20.6 kms. more than the perfectly standard Stage 2 M.G.B driven by Paddy Hopkirk and Andrew Hedges.

Actually only 14 of the original 52 starters were classified, with the British cars filling the last five places. Sole American car to finish was the Cobra of Jack Sears/Dick Thompson in eighth place, just ahead of the Iso Grifo of de Mortemart/Fraissinet.

The winners did not set up a distance record, but Phil Hill (7-litre Ford G.T.) achieved a new Le Mans lap record with 3 mins. 37.5 secs. (138.44 m.p.h.) just 11.7 secs. quicker than his own 1964 record with the 4.7-litre Ford.

Class wins went to Triumph, Austin-

SPOT THE WINNERS. Gregory and Rindt are there somewhere.

Healey Sprite, Porsche, Ferrari and Iso Grifo. The Koch/Fischhaber Porsche, despite being pushed over the line, won the Index of Energy. To the Linge/Nöcker Porsche went the Index of Performance from the outright-winning Ferrari. After the withdrawal of the Alpines, the Austin-Healey Sprite of Aaltonen/Baker seemed a certainty for both Index awards, but a broken fan belt led to a seized engine. It was also another stage in the fierce tyre battle, for the Gregory/Rindt Ferrari was equipped with American Goodyears!

IT must have been a record crowd which assembled to watch the start of the 24-hours. In front of the tribunes it was a solid mass of people, and it had been like that for several hours. The airport was packed to capacity with private and charter aircraft and after a dullish, humid morning, out came the sun.

Withdrawals and so on had brought the field down to 52 cars, but never before has such a massive array of powerful machinery been on view, with Ford, Ferrari and Cobra dominating the line-up. Tension was everywhere as the usual preliminaries took place. There was the typical Le Mans light relief, as a couple of gendarmes chased a photographer who evidently didn't have the essential chain round his wrist.

As 4 p.m. approached, it seemed impossible that any more folk could jam themselves into the start area. The pits and balconies were a solid mass of humanity, as the drivers lined up against the wall to await the maroon. Gradually the noise abated, and almost dead silence fell on the circuit.

The start was tremendous. First away was Chris Amon (Ford) followed in quick succession by Bob Bondurant (Ford), Bruce McLaren (Ford), Jo Siffert (Maserati) and Innes Ireland (Ford). Left behind were Richard Wrottesley (Elva-B.M.W.) and Paddy Hopkirk (M.G.B), but last of all was Colin Davis in the eight-cylinder Porsche.

The announcer jabbered, almost incoherently through the PA. It was Ford, Ford at Mulsanne, but Surtees had brought his Ferrari up from about 15th place at the start to third.

Then everyone in the tribunes stood up —all eyes on Maison Blanche. Sure enough, it was Ford, Ford, Ferrari, Ferrari, and the big 7-litres thundered past the pits, and into the old Dunlop right-hander in the order: McLaren, Amon, Surtees, Guichet, Bondurant, Rindt, Gurney, Siffert and Ireland.

Zeccoli stuffed his Alfa into the sandbanks at Mulsanne. Dumay (Ferrari) stopped at his pit as did Bucknum (Ford), the latter with a door that would not close. Graham Hill was well down the field with the Rover-B.R.M., tailing the blue Alpines of Mauro Bianchi and de Lageneste.

The big Fords were certainly setting the pace, and McLaren bombed through with fellow-New Zealander Amon on his tail. Surtees was already 5 secs. behind the leader, and Bondurant had pulled well away from Rindt and Gurney.

The guy in the Cobra jacket said "Boy, we're gonna blow them red cars right off the circuit." Lap 3, and Bruce was already 11 secs. ahead of Guichet, for Surtees had done a minor gilhooley and had dropped to fifth spot behind Bondurant. Into the pits went Baghetti, to abandon the Dino with a deranged engine. "Franc" stopped with his Porsche.

CHRIS AMON (Ford G.T.) takes the lead (top) at the start from Bruce McLaren (Ford G.T.), Bob Bondurant (Ford G.T.), Jo Siffert (Maserati) and Innes Ireland (Ford G.T.). SEVEN LITRES at the Esses. Amon leads McLaren on the first lap (above). TWO JOS. Jo Schlesser (Cobra) leads Jo Bonnier's 4.4-litre Ferrari round Mulsanne (below).

FERRARI'S DINO—a fast but unreliable car—in front of the pits (above). Its practice lap was only a few seconds over the magic 4 mins.—incredible for 1.6 litres. WINNING FERRARI, the North American Racing Team entry of Masten Gregory/Jochen Rindt, seen passing the Mulsanne signalling pits, was a production 250LM (below). All you need is money.

Siffert spun the Maserati at Tertre Rouge; the car eventually crawled into the pits, but was withdrawn with damaged suspension and a split radiator. Trintignant was in the pits with misfiring on his Ford G.T.

McLaren had set a new lap record on lap 2 with 3 mins. 45.2 secs., and then brought this down to 3 mins. 41.2 secs. (136.13 m.p.h.) However, Chris Amon was credited with 3 mins. 37.7 secs. (138.32 m.p.h.) on lap 5, when he closed on his team-mate to be 20 secs. ahead of Guichet. Already the Fords were doubling the tail-enders.

Zeccoli, stripped to his underpants, dug frantically at Mulsanne in the blazing sunshine, but the Alfa remained embedded in the sand. Bondurant hared past Guichet in Rob Walker's Ford, but Surtees was noticeably closing up. Behind him the order was Rindt, Bonnier, Gurney, Ireland, Bianchi, Rodriguez, Schlesser and Sears, but by lap 7 Bonnier had moved up a couple of places and Guichet had retaken Bondurant.

The Fords were getting away from their rivals at around 5 secs. a lap and Gurney was easily leading the G.T. category in his Cobra. Eight laps and McLaren was 36 secs. ahead of the duelling Guichet and Bondurant, with Surtees always moving closer. Peter Bolton's Spitfire broke its engine and Masson's Alpine had a lengthy sojourn in the pits.

So rapid were the Fords, that when nine laps were signalled McLaren had doubled Langlois van Ophem (Ferrari) and only 16 cars were on the same lap. Surtees closed on Bondurant, but seemed quite content to sit behind the dark blue Ford. Dan Gurney was travelling at a tremendous rate of knots, actually outstripping Rodriguez in an N.A.R.T. Ferrari.

With 16 laps came the end of the first hour, and 48 cars still in the race. McLaren's average was 133.83 m.p.h. Leading British car was the Rover-B.R.M. in 32nd place, then the Austin-Healey Sprite of Paul Hawkins.

Then almost immediately McLaren went into the pits to refuel and the car dropped to ninth place. Amon now had 47.5 secs. over Surtees who had smartly whipped into second place. Into the pits came Amon, dropping to seventh place. Still the Ferraris marched on and now Fords were the pursuers. Bondurant pitted and fell to tenth spot and Bonnier refuelled and carried on without dropping a place, as Rodriguez also came in.

Surtees stopped to refuel on lap 18 and Guichet went into the lead, but next time round he was in too and Bandini led the race for just one hour till he also pitted. Back into the lead went the McLaren/Miles Ford 15 secs. ahead of Surtees, who was followed closely by Mike Parkes.

Phil Hill had taken over Ford No. 2 from Amon, but was way down the list. Rumour had it that all was not well in the gearbox department. Surtees sat behind Miles, with a gap of 16 secs. The Ferrari challenge was now pretty complete, with Guichet/Parkes, Bonnier/Piper and Bandini/Biscaldi threatened only by the well-driven Ford G.T. of Bondurant/Maglioli.

Speeds on the Mulsanne straight were going up and up, although not quite as quick as Phil Hill's 213 m.p.h. in practice. McLaren did 199 m.p.h. over the flying kilometre and the Iso Grifo was credited with 186 m.p.h. Paul Hawkins did 143 m.p.h. with the Sprite.

"Geki" abandoned his Alfa Romeo with transmission bothers and the Wrottesley/Lanfranchi Elva-B.M.W. came to an abrupt halt when the gearbox jammed itself in two ratios.

As two hours came up there were only four cars on the same lap. Bondurant's Ford was belching smoke and steam and Gurney's Cobra was the only G.T. machine up with the prototypes.

Race average was 131.61 m.p.h. and at 6 p.m. the McLaren/Miles Ford led the Surtees/Scarfiotti Ferrari by 22 secs. In third place was Ronnie Hoare's Ferrari (Bonnier/Piper), and Ferraris filled positions down to sixth place, followed by the Whitmore/Ireland Ford.

Bob Bondurant's fine drive came to an end with a blown cylinder head gasket, leaving 43 cars still in the contest. The Iso Grifo had dropped back with brake problems, but was now circulating at a respectable pace.

Our guy still maintained that the Ferraris would be blown off the circuit, but the advance of the red Maranello machines was relentless. The Zeccoli/Rosinski Alfa was left in the sandbanks, Zeccoli deciding to give up trying to dig himself out. The Rover-B.R.M. lost 12 mins. while mechanics checked the fuel system. Jackie Stewart took over, the car then being in 28th place, but obviously something was wrong for it was passed on the Mulsanne Straight by an Alpine and a Sprite!

The Ford onslaught was now very weak, with the McLaren/Miles car down to sixth place and the Phil Hill/Amon machine in the pits with gearbox problems. At 7 p.m. the leading car was the Parkes/Guichet Ferrari, followed by the Surtees/Scarfiotti machine. Ferrari 1-2-3-4-5—and our American friend swallowed a double coke and a couple of purple hearts.

Runners were down to 41, the official retirement list being: Müller/Bucknum (Ford), Bondurant/Maglioli (Ford), Siffert/Neerpasch (Maserati), Trintignant/Ligier (Ford), Baghetti/Casoni (Dino 166), "Geki"/Zuccoli (Alfa Romeo), Zecolli/Rosinski (Alfa Romeo), Wrottesley/Lanfranchi (Elva-B.M.W.), Bianchi/Grandsire (Alpine), Bolton/Bradley

(Triumph) and Poirot/Stommelen (Porsche).

The Monneret/Bouharde Alpine led the Index of Performance from the Ferrari of Bandini/Biscaldi.

A major blow to Ford was when the McLaren/Miles 7-litre was abandoned with a broken gearbox. The Davis/Mitter 8-cylinder Porsche was withdrawn with a burnt-out clutch. Paul Hawkins had his accelerator pedal repaired on his Sprite, as the Gregory/Rindt Ferrari came in with distributor problems.

It was a perfect evening, with just a hint of mist towards Mulsanne. Fords were more or less out of the running, with only the Gurney/Grant Cobra being anywhere near the leading Ferraris. Phil Hill, allegedly short of gears, had dropped to 26th place, but was lapping consistently under 3 mins. 40 secs. Highest placed British car was Donald Healey's little Sprite, driven by Aaltonen and Baker. The former scared himself and the signalling staff by doing a spectacular gilhooley at Mulsanne.

Stewart, in the turbine, was travelling in close company with the Monneret/Bouharde Alpine. Paddy Hopkirk was doing remarkable things with the M.G.B hard-top, in a duel with the Hobbs/Slotemaker Spitfire.

Apart from the Gurney/Grant, Johnson/Payne and Sutcliffe/Harper Cobras, the Ford empire machines were becoming very much out of breath. Phil Hill, notwithstanding gear selection problems, began motoring to such an effect that he turned in a new circuit record of 3 mins. 37.5 secs.

Meanwhile, both the Rover-B.R.M. and the Whitmore/Ireland Ford were showing signs of overheating, and down came lap times accordingly.

While others were circulating on less than the stipulated number of cylinders, the leading Ferraris were charging round on full song. Twelve cylinders seem to

be the proper wear for long distance dicing and at 8 p.m. the Surtees/Scarfiotti led the Index of Performance as well as the race.

At 8.48 p.m. the Hill/Amon Ford had almost a major overhaul, and off went Chris Amon to try to keep it going. Around 9 p.m. Whitmore set off in the *Weekend Telegraph* Ford G.T., but obviously did not care for the water temperature reading and handed over to Innes Ireland after a couple of laps.

Surtees/Scarfiotti led the four Ferraris and the Gurney/Grant Cobra was ahead of the Rodriguez/Vaccarella Ferrari. Moving up were the Ferraris of Salmon/Bianchi (250LM) and Dumay/Gosselin (250LM). The GTB of Mairesse/"Beurlys" was also very much in the picture, chasing the Cobra of Sears/Thompson.

Stewart handed over the turbine to Graham Hill after another check for fuel pump difficulties. Innes Ireland was now out of water, stopped at his pit but was signalled to carry on. The poor Ford motor stank of molten metal and the exhausts were cherry-red. One more tour and at 9.30 p.m. he came in with a "frying tonight" motor and abandoned.

Gurney's Cobra was suffering from low oil pressure, and it looked as though Shelby's quickest G.T. machine was going to have trouble in keeping going.

At 10 p.m. Surtees/Scarfiotti had covered 93 laps to average 130.49 m.p.h., one lap ahead of Parkes/Guichet. With Pedro Rodriguez pushing his car up into fifth place and Mike Salmon whistling the 250LM ahead of Jack Sears, Ferrari were 1-2-3-4-5-6.

Phil Hill was travelling very rapidly in the 7-litre Ford, but it was only a matter of time before the gearbox finally packed up. Thirty-seven cars were still circulating, but quite a few sounded decidedly secondhand. The Rover-B.R.M. was becoming slower and

slower and one had the idea that fuel supply problems were leading to higher fuel consumption.

It was a really wonderful night and as darkness approached Le Mans took on that unique atmosphere that others have tried to emulate but never quite succeeded in doing so. Patches of mist swirled on Mulsanne but visibility was otherwise excellent.

Now Ferrari began to have troubles as the Surtees/Scarfiotti machine pulled into the pits with broken front suspension.

Ferraris were still 1-2-3-4, led by the Parkes/Guichet 330P2. In second spot were Bandini and Biscaldi, followed by Surtees/Scarfiotti and Rodriguez/Vaccarella.

Spectators began to leave the circuit and a monumental traffic jam developed. Huge crowds still remained, but the failure of the Ford challenge obviously damped their ardour and they sought the diversions of side-shows and the many restaurants.

One or two of the Ferraris were being braked rather early for Arnage and the Surtees/Scarfiotti machine came in to find more powerful anchors. Just after 11 p.m. the Gurney/Grant Cobra stopped for a routine refuel, but started off sounding as if it was only on one bank. The Gregory/Rindt Ferrari had all of its wheels changed and brake pads replaced. John Rhodes took over from Paul Hawkins after brake pads were swopped.

Midnight and only the Sears/Thomp-

SOLE REMAINING *American representative was the sick Cobra of Dick Thompson/ Jack Sears, which bears a few battle scars (above).* BELGIAN-ENTERED FERRARI *of Langlois van Ophem/"Elde" takes Mulsanne wide (below). The abandoned Alfa of Zeccoli is seen in the foreground.* SIFFERT'S *ill-fated Maserati—a car built in a few weeks—leads a bunch through the Esses (bottom).*

son Cobra was anywhere near the quartet of Ferraris, led by Mike Parkes/ Jean Guichet at an average of 127.75 m.p.h. The Phil Hill/Amon Ford was confirmed as succumbing to gearbox maladies, so the Ford G.T. effort was *caput.* There were now 34 cars still circulating, the best-placed British entry being the Aaltonen/Baker Sprite in 27th place. The Rover-B.R.M. was no fewer than 29 laps behind the leading Ferrari.

Leading the Index of Performance was Vidal's Alpine, but so far no one had worked out who had the advantage in the Index of Energy.

The Salmon/Bianchi 250LM had to be withdrawn with transmission failure (the 4.4-litre Maranello car of Bonnier/ Piper had gone out earlier with the exhaust system adrift), and the Sears/ Thompson Cobra had a lengthy stop to have its radiator repaired. Andrew Hedges had the rear lights of the M.G.B fixed and the Schlesser/Grant Cobra had a half-shaft replaced. The "Franc"/Kerguen Porsche was in battery trouble.

The Gurney/Grant Cobra seemed to be cracking along again and was rapidly overhauling the similar car of Johnson/ Payne. Yet all the Ferraris, despite worsening brakes, were building up a formidable lead, with the Parkes/Guichet car nearly six laps ahead of Surtees/ Scarfiotti at 1 a.m. Into the reckoning was coming the well-driven Belgian Ferrari of Dumay/Gosselin and also the rare-sounding GTB of Mairesse/ "Beurlys".

One also noted the advance of the splendid Porsches, which were circulating like trains headed by Linge and Nöcker. The Sutcliffe/Harper Cobra put a rod through the side on Mulsanne and added to what was rapidly becoming Tombstone City—the vast Ford Cobra caravan site.

Jean Redélé's hopes lessened when Vidal blew up his Alpine. Surtees was in the pits for over 5 mins. as wheels were changed and brake pads replaced.

Mike Parkes came in with serious brake problems and 51 mins. elapsed before Jean Guichet re-entered the fray. The Cobra tale of woe continued when Johnson stopped with the temperature gauge needle off the clock.

The vicissitudes of Sefac Ferrari gave Dumay/Gosselin the lead in the Belgian entry, with another yellow car second, the Mairesse/"Beurlys" GTB. Gurney and Grant had worked the Cobra up to fifth place, some five laps behind the leader. Porsches were now closing on the Masson/Verrier Alpine in the Index of Performance.

The Surtees/Scarfiotti Ferrari dropped even farther back as 47 mins. were lost trying to find some brakes. The Sears/Thompson Cobra was suffering from falling oil pressure, while just after 3 a.m. the Langlois van Ophem/"Elde" Ferrari was abandoned with serious engine maladies.

Mike Parkes was delayed another few minutes with lamp bothers and Dan Gurney was in for over 20 mins. with various problems before Jerry Grant took over.

Half-distance and the false dawn came with 27 machines still being bashed around, led by Dumay/Gosselin and Gregory/Rindt. Average speed had fallen to 121.37 m.p.h. and the only cars near to the four leading Ferraris were a pair of Porsches.

Dawn approached and the circuit once again came to life. Weary mechanics kept their continuous vigil, partially envying those whose charges had been long carted to the dead car park.

Rob Slotemaker pranged his Spitfire at Maison Blanche but was fortunately uninjured.

It was only a matter of waiting to see which Ferrari would win, for the leading quartet sounded as if they could go on *ad infinitum!*

Higher rose the sun and still the oil-stained survivors bashed on. Cars were beginning to trickle back to the circuit, but somehow the bite had gone out of the race. Monneret/Bouharde had taken their Alpine to the head of the Index of Performance, but the Porsches were now a definite menace, with Buchet/Pon hard on the tail of Linge/Nöcker.

Gurney's Cobra was suffering from excessive vibration and a broken engine mounting was suspected. At 6 a.m. Dumay/Gosselin had covered 203 laps at 121.56 m.p.h., but were being chased by the N.A.R.T. car of Gregory/Rindt.

The de Lageneste / Vinatier Alpine went out with severe overheating problems and the Gregory/Rindt Ferrari lost time having brakes fixed. Porsches lost a car when the Klass/Glemser 914 dropped a valve, and the Index-leading Alpine dropped several minutes having the clutch adjusted.

TWO WINNERS. The Index of Performance-winning Porsche of Linge/Nöcker leads the first-place Ferrari 250LM of Gregory/Rindt (top). TWO SPRITES. Phenomenally quick considering their size were the two Donald Healey-entered Sprites, one of which unfortunately dropped out in the closing stages (above). FASTEST BRITISH CAR, the Elva-B.M.W. of Wrottesley/Lanfranchi, is chased through the Esses by Maurice Trintignant's Ford G.T. below.

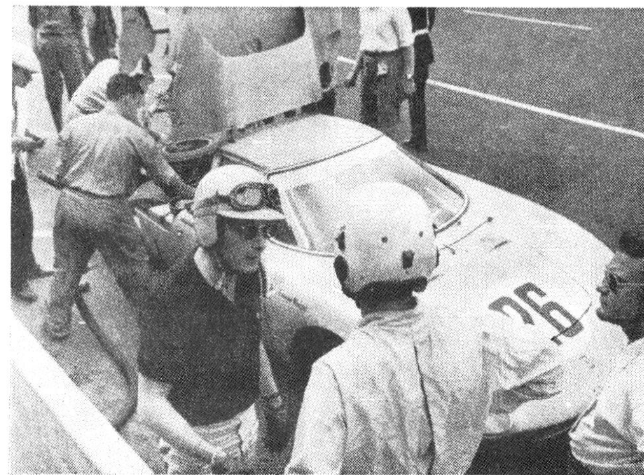

SHOCK AT MIDDAY came when the leading Ferrari 250LM of the Franco-Belgian crew Dumay/Gosselin stopped with a rear tyre blown to shreds. The Belgian-entered car lost time while the wheel was replaced, the bodywork straightened, and dropped to second place behind the American-entered 250LM of Masten Gregory/Jochen Rindt which went on to victory.

Graham Hill and Jackie Stewart were merely joy-riding the Rover-B.R.M. and had come up on to the same lap as the Iso Grifo. Paul Hawkins/John Rhodes easily led the British contingent with the Sprite; both surviving Cobras sounded a bit off-tune, the Sears/Thompson car being 22 laps behind the leading Ferrari.

Just after 7.30 a.m. the Gurney/Grant Cobra was buried in the dead car park with a broken crankshaft damper, adding to the multitude of unemployed Ford-Cobra mechanics. The Surtees/Scarfiotti Ferrari spent 1½ hours in the pits having a clutch plate replaced and the Parkes/Guichet car dropped many minutes also to have a clutch fixed.

Blue skies and bright sun brought thousands of onlookers back to the circuit, but the Esso scoreboard carried a distressing number of red crosses. Renault ran their much-appreciated shuttle service to Mulsanne, to give Pressman the opportunity of seeing drivers in action.

Yet what had been a somewhat boring procession was turning into quite a race. Dumay/Gosselin were being pursued relentlessly by Parkes/Guichet and by Gregory/Rindt, while the only non-Maranello machine in the first seven was the rapid Porsche of Linge/Nöcker, which had taken the lead in the Index.

At 9.30 a.m. Bussinello's Alfa Romeo broke and not long afterwards Koob's engine seized—so bang went Alfa hopes! The Rodriguez/Vaccarella Ferrari was in dire straits with clutch troubles and remained stationary for over an hour.

Surtees's troubles were not over and the Ferrari was wheeled away with a broken gearbox. To the delight of Donald Healey, Paul Hawkins/John Rhodes took the lead in the Index of Energy.

By 10 a.m. the runners were down to 18 and the Belgians had about half a lap on the N.A.R.T. machine. The Iso Grifo had come up into 10th place, four laps ahead of the turbine. The surviving Alpine was very secondhand and was obviously booked for retirement. Hawkins/Rhodes tightened their grip on the Energy and with the Parkes/Guichet car in again for brakes adjustment, Gregory/Rindt were in hot pursuit of the Belgian Ferrari. Willy Mairesse had taken the GTB up into third place.

Midday and four hours to go, and the Belgians were still holding off the N.A.R.T. car. Then came a complete reversal as Dumay burst a tyre after running over a chunk of flint on the Mulsanne straight. He came into the pits with a collapsed wheel and sadly bent bodywork. Officials objected to the state of the machine and it was "modified" by some judicious panel-bashing with a spade.

This put the Gregory/Rindt car into the lead, and the Belgians could do nothing other than hope that something might slow the N.A.R.T. machine.

Shortly after 2 p.m. the Aaltonen/Baker Sprite broke its fan belt and the engine seized solid, leaving 15 cars on the circuit.

By the time the Belgian pair rejoined the race Gregory/Rindt had piled on a five-lap lead, while Parkes/Guichet had dropped behind the Porsche of Linge/Nöcker.

It was now just a matter of seeing whether or not the survivors could hold out till the end. During the closing stages there was a bit of a panic when Koch stopped at his pit with his Porsche. He set off very slowly and was still out on the circuit when the flag dropped on the battered Belgian Ferrari—over five laps behind the N.A.R.T. car.

As Gregory/Rindt were acclaimed, Koch's Porsche was pushed over the line, the engine having conked a few yards from the finish.

It was yet another demonstration of the efficiency of Ferrari automobiles, whether in the hands of the works team or as independent entries.

Practice notes

For the first time in history, Le Mans practice was cancelled. A rainstorm of great intensity flooded the circuit and was accompanied by winds approaching gale force. Trees were blown down and it was so dangerous that after Jo Bonnier, on behalf of G.P.D.A. members, had made a couple of recce drives,

the A.C.O. agreed that it was impossible to continue.

On Saturday an extra session was arranged, and it was soon found that the big 7-litre Fords were the fastest machines ever to be presented at Le Mans. Phil Hill achieved the remarkable time of 3 mins. 33 secs. (141.37 m.p.h.) and was said to have obtained 213 m.p.h. on the Mulsanne straight.

This was no less than 5.9 secs. faster than the next best, Ken Miles in another 7-litre Ford G.T. Fastest Ferrari was the 4.4-litre of Vaccarella, with 3 mins. 41 secs., and then Müller's Ford G.T. with 3 mins. 41.1 secs.

RESULTS

1. Masten Gregory/Jochen Rindt (3.3 Ferrari 250LM), 4,677.11 kms. (2,906.23 miles), 121.09 m.p.h.
2. Pierre Dumay/Gustave Gosselin (3.3 Ferrari 250LM), 4,602.6 kms.
3. Willy Mairesse/"Beurlys" (3.3 Ferrari 275GTB*), 4,562 kms.
4. Herbert Linge/Peter Nöcker (2.0 Porsche "6"), 4,507.5 kms.
5. Gerhard Koch/Toni Fischhaber (2.0 Porsche 914GTS*), 4,366.66 kms.
6. Armand Boller/D. Spoerry (3.3 Ferrari 250LM), 4,354.16 kms.
7. Pedro Rodriguez/Nino Vaccarella (4.4 Ferrari 365P), 4,300.19 kms.
8. **Jack Sears**/Dick Thompson (4.7 Shelby American Cobra*), 4,076.12 kms.
9. Jean de Mortemart/Régis Fraissinet (5.4 Iso Grifo), 4,063.57 kms.
10. **Graham Hill/Jackie Stewart (2.0 Rover-B.R.M. gas turbine)**, 3,815.36 kms.
11. **Paddy Hopkirk/Andrew Hedges (1.8 M.G.B*)**, 3,794.75 kms.
12. **Paul Hawkins/John Rhodes (1.3 Austin-Healey Sprite)**, 3,726.43 kms.
13. Jean-Jacques Thuner/Simo Lampinen **(1.1 Triumph Spitfire*)**, 3,673.77 kms.
14. Jean-Francois Piot/Claude Dubois **(1.1 Triumph Spitfire*)**, 3,525.67 kms.

Fastest lap: Phil Hill (7.0 Ford G.T.) 3 m. 37.5 s., 138.44 m.p.h.

*Grand touring car.

Class Results

1,001-1,150 c.c.: 1, Thuner/Lampinen (Triumph); 2, Piot/Dubois (Triumph). **1,151-1,300 c.c.:** 1, Hawkins/Rhodes (Austin-Healey). **1,601-2,000 c.c.:** 1, Linge/Nöcker (Porsche); 2, Koch/Fischhaber (Porsche); 3, G. Hill/Stewart (Rover-B.R.M.); 4, Hopkirk/Hedges (M.G.). **3,001-4,000 c.c.:** 1, Gregory/Rindt (Ferrari); 2, Dumay/Gosselin (Ferrari); 3, Mairesse/"Beurlys" (Ferrari); 4, Boller/Spoerry (Ferrari). **4,001-5,000 c.c.:** 1, Rodriguez/Vaccarella (Ferrari); 2, Sears/Thompson (Cobra). **Over 5,000 c.c.:** 1, de Mortemart/Fraissinet (Iso Grifo).

Index of Performance

1, Linge/Nöcker (Porsche), 1.248 per cent; 2, Gregory/Rindt (Ferrari), 1.22; 3, Koch/Fischhaber (Porsche), 1.211; 4, Dumay/Gosselin (Ferrari), 1.201; 5, Mairesse/"Beurlys" (Ferrari), 1.19; 6, Boller/Spoerry (Ferrari), 1.136; 7, Hawkins/Rhodes (Austin-Healey), 1.12; 8, Rodriguez/Vaccarella (Ferrari), 1.096; 9, Hopkirk/Hedges M.G.), 1.068; 10, G. Hill/Stewart (Rover-B.R.M.), 1.056; 11, Sears/Thompson (Cobra), 1.0; 12, de Mortemart/Fraissinet (Iso Grifo), 1.0; 13, Piot/Dubois (Triumph), 1.0; 14, Thuner/Lampinen (Triumph), 1.0.

Index of Energy

1, Koch/Fischhaber (Porsche); 2, Dumay/Gosselin (Ferrari); 3, Hawkins/Rhodes (Austin-Healey); 4, Linge/Nöcker (Porsche); 5, Mairesse/"Beurlys" (Ferrari), Gregory/Rindt (Ferrari) and Hopkirk/Hedges (M.G.B).

LOOK-BACK AT LE MANS

Edward Eves Comments on the Successes and Failures

Rear spoiler extension and stabilizing fins for the 7-litre Ford GT which was said to exceed 200 m.p.h along the Mulsanne straight

ON the face of it, the Le Mans results seem to indicate complete annihilation of the Dearborn threat to Ferrari supremacy in G.T. and G.T. Prototype racing. Yet the hot pace set by the big 7-litre Ford GT prototypes in the opening hours of the race could well have weakened the works Ferraris, for although they had brake trouble, this was not the reason for their retirement.

If Ford had serious intentions of finishing with their 7-litre cars, it was unfortunate that they were put out by gearbox trouble. In the early part of the race they did not know the speed at which their porous element fuel tanks could accept fuel. After a few stops they found that they could take on 100 litres instead of 70 litres if the refuelling time were extended by 10 secs. This enabled them to stop every 23 laps instead of every 17 laps, considerably improving the overall average. Their Kar Kraft 4-speed gearboxes used gears of the proportions and sizes of those in the standard Galaxie gearbox. There appeared to be a weakness here, for one of the cars stripped its final-drive gears in practice when accelerating hard in first. In the race, an oil seal between the gearbox and clutch housing of Phil Hill's car failed, causing first of all clutch slip and then gear failure due to lack of lubricant. The other gearbox failed for reasons so far unrevealed.

A spate of cylinder head failures put most of the 4·7-litre Fords—GTs and Cobras—out of the race. There is no doubt that this was due to faulty head stud material, and will not be allowed to happen again. The two cars which did survive this trouble, Gurney's and Sears' Cobras, both had chronic oil pressure trouble. The former ran for six hours with no oil pressure at all, while the latter struggled along with the gauge showing only 5 p.s.i. in surges. The same kind of thing happened last year, so there is obviously something to be learned before engines as supplied to the mass American market can win at Le Mans.

Airflow Problems

There is also a lot to be learned about the aerodynamics of high-speed cars. Ford found that there was a tendency for the noses of their cars to lift in proportion to the size of the rear spoiler flap. They offset the deviationist tendency by fitting a transverse "fence" under the nose to reduce the air cushion effect under the car. Every alteration to these bodies had to be treated as a new problem; the extra long and aero-dynamically clean noses on the 7-litre cars created extra lift along the whole length of the car. This was neutralized by adding a 4in. extension to the existing rear spoilers, with the aforementioned under-nose fence. Fins and nose strakes were added for good measure, but could have been removed. Phil Hill told me that, from being absolutely frightening at speed, the 7-litre became completely docile and safe with the extra spoilers.

Higher speeds and low drag bodies mean more work for brakes. With the wide base rims and cast wheels favoured today, there is little air flow round brake discs. Dunlop developed radially-vented discs for the Ferraris, which have

LOOK-BACK AT LE MANS...

Attention to detail; streamlined fairings on the wishbones of the French Alpines

An under-nose fence and "dive vanes" were fitted to the 7-litre Fords to keep the nose stable

been used successfully all this year. However, the conditions of Le Mans, especially at night, where the long rush down the Mulsanne straight cools discs right off and the heavy braking at the corner raises them almost to white heat, eventually gave rise to surface fatigue cracks on all the Ferrari works cars. As an insurance these had to be changed, losing much time—it took almost an hour to strip and rebuild each pair of front hubs—but did not put any of the cars out of the race; other mechanical troubles saw to that. Incidentally, a notable American advance which went unannounced was the fitting of Kelsey-Hayes discs to the front wheels of the 7-litre Ford GT prototypes; unfortunately the cars did not run long enough for it to be discovered if they would suffer from the same trouble as the Ferraris.

Because of the retirement of the works Ferraris, Goodyear were able to chalk up their first major European win on the Sarthe circuit. Goodyear technicians are learning fast, and produced three different tread and rubber compound variations for the race, for dry, wet-dry and wet conditions. However, so far they have been unable to match Dunlop's general purpose "yellow spot" compound. Dunlop, too, have overcome the chunking trouble which affected the R7 tyres in earlier sports car races, which was due to the tread pattern being insufficiently self-supporting under the high cornering forces which the tyre construction permitted. At 9 a.m. on Sunday morning, after 17 hours racing, Dunlop had only changed six tyres in all, including the puncture on Paddy Hopkirk's MGB; two were put on the Iso Grifo and one each on the Surtees', Rodriguez' and Parks' Ferrari.

Maserati Frame

It was unfortunate that the new rear-engined vee-8 Maserati did not have a longer run to allow its designers to find out more about the handling problems, which undoubtedly exist. It was a wonderful effort on the part of Ing. Alfieri and the Maserati racing shop to design and build this car in the space of three months. One wonders, looking at the Maserati birdcage frame, whether the frame maker is given a general outline shape, 1,000ft of $\frac{3}{8}$in tube, and told to fill in the gaps. However, the engine

can be inserted and removed by unbolting just three tubes. The 5,044 c.c. vee-8 engine is a racing version of the power unit fitted to the de luxe Maserati GT cars. It differs in having bigger valves, revised timing and two plugs per cylinder.

Transmission and Suspension

A completely new transmission was designed for the car, with a 2-shaft, 5-speed gearbox. Drive from the 2-plate Borg and Beck diaphragm-spring clutch is taken to the back of the gearbox through a long torsion shaft, the drive being stepped up to the first motion shaft through quick-change gears. An extra gear drives the alternator, mounted on the gearbox rear cover. Suspension is of the now universal low roll-centre type at the back, with parallel wishbones at the front. An unusual addition is a short reaction arm running directly aft from the bottom end of the wheel carrier, parallel to the chassis centre line, which seems to conflict with the general front suspension geometry.

Rear suspension is by fore-and-aft torsion bars backed up by coil springs mounted co-axially with the telescopic dampers to give a double-rate effect. In common with the car in which Casner was killed in April, during the practice weekend, the front brake discs are inboard of the wheel carriers and driven by live stub axles. This arrangement permits the use of larger discs than would be possible if they had to be housed inside the wheel rims; those used are 15in. diameter. In practice, the engine overheated badly and extra nose slots were cut for the race.

Engine and transmission assembly of the French Alpine. An extremely worthy design which was put out by clutch trouble

For practice Ferrari produced this 275P2 Berlinetta. The cabin was subject to extreme pressurization. The streamlined window tended to blow out and a vertical one inside the roll-hoop was substituted for the race

Clutch trouble beset all the fast French Alpines. While they were going they headed the Index of Performance quite easily, and proved that the new Amedée Gordini twin-cam engine is producing all of the 135 b.h.p. which is claimed for it. Based on the 75·7 × 55·4mm Renault formula 2 engine, but with the stroke extended to 72mm, bringing the capacity to 1,296 c.c., it has a single chain drive to the camshafts, taken from a half-time gear driven off the nose of the crankshaft. Valve angle is believed to be 90deg., the valves being opened by fingers with roller cam followers. A skew-gear-driven vertical shaft at the front of the engine has stacked pressure and scavenge pumps at its lower end and the ignition distributor at the top.

The cars fitted with these engines—there were two of them—had Alpine formula 3 rear suspension and Hewland gearboxes, the engines being mounted ahead of the axles.

Rover Progress

Not enough has been made of the achievement of the Rover-B.R.M., which made history by being the first gas turbine car to take part in a motor race anywhere. That it was the first British car to finish was gratifying; and that it should complete the 24 hours at practically 100 m.p.h. with a fuel consumption of 13·5 m.p.g. says a great deal for the work of Noel Penny and his team. They, in turn, praise more than highly the work that Corning Glass have put into developing the glass ceramic discs which transfer exhaust heat back to the work cycle. Corning shipped over more than 50 discs during the nine months Le Mans car development period, and 25 transatlantic discussions were held. The result has been to advance the state of the heat exchanger art by at least two years, which is

the way of motor racing. The troubles experienced with the engine during the race were not concerned with the high ambient temperature during the day, which was 35deg C., since the unit had been tested at 30deg. C. Loss of the tip of a compressor vane and the bending of two others led to a very high jet-pipe temperature, and made it essential to govern down the compressor speed, with consequent loss of power. The cause is not yet known, but may have been a "foreign body" passing through the engine.

One can only admire the technical virtuosity of the Engines Branch of B.M.C. who have, over the years, developed the 28 b.h.p., 800 c.c. A-series engine into the 1,293 c.c. Cooper S and formula 3 units giving off 95 b.h.p. plus. To have done this without changing the cylinder centres is a technological achievement, not only for the foundry who cast the blocks, but also for Brico who make the pistons.

Retrograde?

It is in its tendency to encourage the building of mid-engined cars that Le Mans is drifting away most from its original terms of reference, which were the development and improvement of touring cars. When the race became a proving ground for disc brakes, that was a good thing and of benefit to all. But it would be hard to find a passenger-car designer who is prepared to defend the location of the power unit just ahead of the back wheels, where it uncompromisingly takes up two passenger spaces. He would place the engine ahead of, or on top of, the front axle or behind the rear axle. Any handling difficulties so created might well be sorted out in a race which had rules to encourage entries of such cars.

Joint effort, the chassis of the Rover-B.R.M. was a particularly exacting design task because of the need for faultless braking and high cornering power without help from the engine. Ventilated discs on the Kelsey-Hayes front brakes of the 7-litre Ford GT prototypes

RESULTS

The following tables are not a complete list of results but list the most important results of each race, as follows: first three cars finishing; all class and category wins; subsidiary awards, such as Biennial Cup and Index wins. The tables are in nine columns as follows:

Column 1:
Overall placing.
Colum 2:
Make and nationality of car; nationalities: B Belgium, CS Czechoslovakia, D Germany, F France, GB Great Britain, I Italy, US U.S.A.
Column 3:
Number of cylinders; where appropriate arrangement of engine if other than in-line as follows: F Flat (horizontally opposed), V V, t/s two-stroke.
Column 4:
Capacity of engine in cc.
Column 5:
Names of drivers; quotation marks indicate pseudonym.
Column 6:
Distance covered, in miles.
Column 7:
Average speed, in miles per hour.
Column 8:
Class-winners only: indicates which capacity class won. Note changes in capacity class structure in 1960. NB: Not listed from 1975 onwards.

Column 9:
Category wins – particularly important from 1975 onwards – and subsidiary awards. Abbreviations used: Bi-cup, Biennial Cup; Tri-cup, Triennial Cup; Ind. Perf, Index of Performance; Index T.E., Index of Thermal Efficiency. Categories: 1959: Sport-prototype and Grand Tourisme; 1960–61: Sports Cars and Grand Tourisme; 1962: Experimental Cars and Grand Tourisme (with subsidiary category for under-2,000 cc GT); 1963–65: as 1962 but Prototypes replace Experimental Cars; 1966: as 1963–65 but with added Sports Car category; 1967: as 1966 but under-2,000 cc GT deleted, and under-1,300 cc Sports Car category added; 1968–71: Sports Car, Sports Prototype and Grand Tourisme – last category is called GT Special 1970–71; 1972–74: Group 5 sports cars, Group 4 GT special, Group 2 special touring; 1975: Group 6 sports-prototypes (with subsidiary two-litre class), and GTX – experimental GT cars – in addition to 1972–74 categories; 1976–81: Group 6, Group 5 and Group 4 as in 1975, GTX now unhomologated production GT cars, new class for GTP – Le Mans prototypes, and categories for I.M.S.A and N.A.S.C.A.R cars. Group 2 category deleted. N.A.S.C.A.R category only in 1976. 1981: Group C cars first admitted.
Note: There have not been entrants, or finishers, in all categories and classes every year.

All results listed in the Appendix have as far as possible been checked against official Automobile Club de l'Ouest figures and have been converted from kilometres to miles using 1.60935 kilometres equals 1 mile.

1	2	3	4	5	6	7	8	9

26th race—1958, 21–22 June. Circuit: 8.364 miles.
55 cars starting, 20 cars finishing. Fastest lap: M. Hawthorn (Ferrari 250 TR), 121.416 mph

1	2	3	4	5	6	7	8	9
1	Ferrari 250 TR (I)	V-12	2,953 cc	O. Gendebien/P. Hill	2,548.813	106.200	3,000 cc	
2	Astron Martin DB3S (GB)	6 cyl	2,993 cc	P. Whitehead/G. Whitehead	2,448.749	102.031		
3	Porsche RS K (D)	F-4	1,587 cc	J. Behra/H. Herrmann	2,429.337	101.222	2,000 cc	
4	Porsche RS K (D)	F-4	1,498 cc	E. Barth/P. Frère	2,420.352	100.873	1,500 cc	
11	Osca (I)	4 cyl	749 cc	A. de Tomaso/C. Davis	2,103.815	87.815	750 cc	Ind. Perf.

27th race—1959, 20–21 June. Circuit: 8.364 miles.
53 cars starting, 13 cars finishing. Fastest lap: J. Behra (Ferrari 250 TR), 124.995 mph

1	2	3	4	5	6	7	8	9
1	Aston Martin DBR 1 (GB)	6 cyl	2,993 cc	R. Salvadori/C. Shelby	2,701.654	112.569	3,000 cc	Sport-proto.
2	Aston Martin DBR 1 (GB)	6 cyl	2,993 cc	M. Trintignant/P. Frère	2,695.229	112.313		
3	Ferrari 250 (I)	V-12	2,953 cc	J. Blaton ('Beurlys')/'Eldé'	2,486.474	103.602		GT
7	A.C. Bristol (GB)	6 cyl	1,971 cc	E. Whiteaway/J. Turner	2,289.647	95.375	2,000 cc	
8	Lotus Elite (GB)	4 cyl	1,216 cc	P. Lumsden/P. Riley	2,259.353	94.140	1,500 cc	
9	D.B. Panhard (F)	F-2	744 cc	L. Cornet/R. Cotton	2,165.752	90.239	750 cc	25th Bi-cup & Ind. Perf.
11	D.B. Panhard (F)	F-2	745 cc	B. Consten/P. Armagnac	2,073.730	86.405		Index T.E.

28th race—1960, 25–26 June. Circuit: 8.364 miles.
55 cars starting, 20 cars finishing. Fastest lap: M. Gregory (Maserati Tipo 61), 123.407 mph

1	2	3	4	5	6	7	8	9
1	Ferrari TR 60 (I)	V-12	2,958 cc	P. Frère/O. Gendebien	2,620.644	109.193	3,000 cc	Sport
2	Ferrari TR 60 (I)	V-12	2,958 cc	R. Rodriguez/A. Pilette	2,587.177	107.798		
3	Aston Martin DBR 1 (GB)	6 cyl	2,992 cc	R. Salvadori/J. Clark	2,558.620	106.609		
4	Ferrari 250 GT (I)	V-12	2,953 cc	F. Tavano/P. Loustel	2,520.231	105.009		GT
8	Chevrolet Corvette (US)	V-8	4,640 cc	J. Fitch/R. M. Grossman	2,350.025	97.917	5,000 cc	
10	Porsche 1600 GS (D)	F-4	1,588 cc	H. Linge/H. Walter	2,249.209	93.716	1,600 cc	
12	MGA Twin-Cam (GB)	4 cyl	1,762 cc	E. Lund/C. Escott	2,188.700	91.195	2,000 cc	
13	Lotus Elite (GB)	4 cyl	1,216 cc	C. Laurent/R. Masson	2,182.879	90.953	1,300 cc	
14	Lotus Elite (GB)	4 cyl	1,216 cc	J. B. Wagstaff/A. E. Marsh	2,146.772	89.448		Index T.E.
15	D.B. Panhard (F)	F-2	702 cc	G. Laureau/P. Armagnac	2,116.042	88.168	850 cc	26th Bi-cup & Ind. Perf.
16	Austin-Healey Sprite (GB)	4 cyl	996 cc	J. F. Dalton/J. K. Colgate	2,055.142	85.630	1,000 cc	

29th race—1961, 10–11 June. Circuit: 8.364 miles.
55 cars starting, 22 cars finishing. Fastest lap: R. Rodriguez (Ferrari TR 61), 125.020 mph

1	2	3	4	5	6	7	8	9
1	Ferrari 250 TR (I)	V-12	2,961 cc	O. Gendebien/P. Hill	2,781.612	115.902	3,000 cc	Sport
2	Ferrari 250 TR (I)	V-12	2,961 cc	W. Mairesse/M. J. Parkes	2,758.086	114.920		
3	Ferrari 250 GT (I)	V-12	2,953 cc	P. Noblet/J. Guichet	2,645.799	110.241		GT
5	Porsche RS (D)	F-4	1,967 cc	M. Gregory/R. Holbert	2,581.456	107.561	2,000 cc	
10	Porsche 695 GS (D)	F-4	1,588 cc	H. Linge/Ben Pon	2,372.811	98.867	1,600 cc	
12	Lotus Elite (GB)	4 cyl	1,216 cc	W. E. Allen/T. Taylor	2,234.916	93.121	1,300 cc	
14	Fiat Abarth (I)	4 cyl	847 cc	D. Hulme/A. Hyslop	2,194.662	91.444	850 cc	
16	Sunbeam Alpine (GB)	4 cyl	1,592 cc	P. Harper/P. Procter	2,182.070	90.919		Index T.E.
18	D.B. Panhard (F)	F-2	702 cc	G. Lauren/R. Bouharde	2,148.182	89.507		Ind. Perf.

30th race—1962, 23–24 June. Circuit: 8.364 miles.
55 cars starting, 18 cars finishing. Fastest lap: P. Hill (Ferrari 330 LM), 126.884 mph

1	2	3	4	5	6	7	8	9
1	Ferrari 330 LM (I)	V-12	3,967 cc	P. Hill/O. Gendebien	2,765.876	115.244	4,000 cc	Experimental
2	Ferrari GTO (I)	V-12	2,953 cc	J. Guichet/P. Noblet	2,724.169	113.507	3,000 cc	GT
3	Ferrari GTO (I)	V-12	2,953 cc	'Eldé'/J. Blaton ('Beurlys')	2,618.375	109.720		
7	Porsche 1600 GS (D)	F-4	1,588 cc	E. Barth/H. Herrmann	2,397.576	99.898	1,600 cc	GT to two-litre
8	Lotus Elite (GB)	4 cyl	1,216 cc	D. W. Hobbs/F. K. Gardner	2,390.451	99.602	1,300 cc	Index T.E.
13	Morgan Plus-Four (GB)	4 cyl	1,991 cc	C. Lawrence/R. Shepherd-Barron	2,255.130	93.963	2,000 cc	
16	Panhard C.D. (F)	F-2	702 cc	A. Guilhaudin/A. Bertaut	2,129.451	88.727	850 cc	Ind. Perf.
17	René Bonnet Djet (F)	4 cyl	996 cc	B. Consten/J. Rosinski	2,126.049	88.585	1,000 cc	

1	2	3	4	5	6	7	8	9

31st race—1963, 15–16 June. Circuit: 8.364 miles.
48+1 cars starting, 12+1 cars finishing. Fastest lap: J. Surtees (Ferrari 250 P), 129.067 mph

1	2	3	4	5	6	7	8	9
1	Ferrari 250 P (I)	V-12	2,953 cc	L. Scarfiotti/L. Bandini	2,834.509	118.104	3,000 cc	Prototype & Ind. Perf.
2	Ferrari GTO (I)	V-12	2,953 cc	J. Blaton ('Beurlys')/G. Langlois	2,700.672	112.528		GT
3	Ferrari 250 P (I)	V-12	2,953 cc	M. J. Parkes/U. Maglioli	2,700.598	112.525		
5	Ferrari 330 LMB (I)	V-12	3,967 cc	J. G. Sears/M. Salmon	2,621.926	109.246	4,000 cc	
7	A.C. Cobra (GB)	V-8	4,728 cc	P. Bolton/N. Sanderson	2,591.833	107.991	5,000 cc	
8	Porsche 718 (D)	F-8	1,962 cc	E. Barth/H. Linge	2,516.703	104.862	2,000 cc	
9	Jaguar E-type (GB)	6 cyl	3,781 cc	Richards/R. M. Grossman	2,372.446	98.851	4,000 cc	
10	Lotus Elite (GB)	4 cyl	1,216 cc	J. B. Wagstaff/Fergusson	2,256.933	94.049	1,300 cc	GT to two-litre
11	Rene Bonnet LM6 (F)	4 cyl	1,108 cc	J. P. Beltoise/C. Bobrowski	2,254.889	93.953	1,150 cc	Index T.E.
—	Rover-B.R.M. (GB)	gas turbine		G. Hill/R. Ginther	2,592.916	107.712		Special A.C.O. award

32nd race—1964, 20–21 June. Circuit: 8.364 miles.
55 cars starting, 25 cars finishing. Fastest lap: P. Hill (Ford GT 40), 131.375 mph

1	2	3	4	5	6	7	8	9
1	Ferrari 275 P (I)	V-12	3,299 cc	J. Guichet/N. Vaccarella	2,917.524	121.563	4,000 cc	Prototype & Ind. Perf.
2	Ferrari 330 P (I)	V-12	3,972 cc	J. Bonnier/G. Hill	2,872.369	119.682		
3	Ferrari 330 P (I)	V-12	3,972 cc	J. Surtees/L. Bandini	2,814.893	117.287		
4	Cobra Ford (GB/US)	V-8	4,727 cc	D. Gurney/B. Bondurant	2,791.243	116.301	5,000 cc	GT
5	Ferrari GTO (I)	V-12	2,953 cc	L. Bianchi/J. Blaton ('Beurlys')	2,778.393	115.766	3,000 cc	
7	Porsche 904 (D)	F-4	1,967 cc	R. Buchet/G. Ligier	2,699.597	112.483	2,000 cc	GT to two-litre
13	Alfa Romeo TZ (I)	4 cyl	1,570 cc	R. Businello/D. Deserti	2,565.152	106.881	1,600 cc	
14	Iso Rivolta (I)	V-8	5,354 cc	E. Berney/P. Noblet	2,560.137	106.672	unlimited	
17	Alpine Renault (F)	4 cyl	1,149 cc	H. Morrogh/R. Delageneste	2,436.379	101.515		Index T.E.
22	Lotus Elite (GB)	4 cyl	1,216 cc	C. Hunt/J. B. Wagstaff	2,222.696	92.612	1,300 cc	

33rd race—1965, 19–20 June. Circuit: 8.364 miles.
51 cars starting, 14 cars finishing. Fastest lap: P. Hill (Ford Mark 2), 138.443 mph

1	2	3	4	5	6	7	8	9
1	Ferrari 275 LM (I)	V-12	3,285 cc	M. Gregory/J. Rindt	2,906.215	121.092	4,000 cc	Prototype
2	Ferrari 275 LM (I)	V-12	3,285 cc	P. Dumay/T. Gosselin	2,859.917	119.163		
3	Ferrari 275 GTB (I)	V-12	3,286 cc	W. Mairesse/J. Blaton ('Beurlys')	2,834.721	118.113		GT
4	Porsche 904 (D)	F-6	1,991 cc	H. Linge/P. Nocker	2,800.825	116.701	2,000 cc	Ind. Perf.
5	Porsche 904 (D)	F-4	1,967 cc	G. Koch/T. Fischaber	2,713.311	113.054		GT to two-lire & Index T.E.
7	Ferrari 365 P.2 (I)	V-12	4,385 cc	P. Rodriguez/N. Vaccarella	2,672.009	111.333	5,000 cc	
9	Iso Grifo (I)	V-8	5,354 cc	R. Fraissinet/J. de Mortemart	2,524.980	105.207	unlimited	
12	Austin-Healey Sprite (GB)	4 cyl	1,293 cc	P. Hawkins/J. Rhodes	2,315.491	96.478	1,300 cc	
13	Triumph Spitfire (GB)	4 cyl	1,147 cc	J. Thuner/S. Lampinen	2,282.770	95.115	1,150 cc	